REFLECTIONS ON LAW AND HISTORY

Reflections on Law and History

Irish Legal History Society Discourses
and Other Papers, 2000–2005

N.M. DAWSON
EDITOR

FOUR COURTS PRESS

in association with

THE IRISH LEGAL HISTORY SOCIETY

Typeset in 10.5pt on 12.5pt EhrhardtMt by
Carrigboy Typesetting Services, County Cork for
FOUR COURTS PRESS LTD
7 Malpas Street, Dublin 8, Ireland
e-mail: info@four-courts-press.ie
and in North America for
FOUR COURTS PRESS
c/o ISBS, 920 N.E. 58th Avenue, Suite 300, Portland, OR 97213.

A catalogue record for this title is available
from the British Library.

ISBN (10–digit) 1–85182–937–7
ISBN (13–digit) 978–1–85182–937–8

Printed in England by MPG Books, Bodmin, Cornwall.

Contents

THE MAKING OF LAW

Irish Legal History Society publications

ALSO AVAILABLE

The Irish Legal History Society (1989)

* Volumes 1–7 are published by Irish Academic Press.

Editor's preface

PAPERS READ AT MEETINGS of the Irish Legal History Society are, by tradition, gathered together every four or five years and published in a volume of 'collected discourses'.[1] *Reflections on law and history* is the fourth such volume to be published since the inauguration of the Society in 1988, and comprises fourteen papers, ten of which were first read at our meetings, with four others, on the theme of criminal justice, submitted for publication by the Society. In bringing to a wider audience material that has enriched our meetings, we hope not only to further our constitutional aim of advancing the knowledge of the history of the law, especially Irish law, but also to increase interest in the Society's programme of activities and, more importantly, stimulate further research.

Spanning five centuries, from the 1600s to the present day, the papers in this collection provide rich and varied fare. They have been grouped together under three headings: personalities in the law; crime and punishment, and the making of law. Six papers focus on particular legal personalities as a means of providing insights of broader historical significance: the subjects are Christopher Wandesford (1592–1640); Sir Richard Nagle (c.1636–1699); Albert Venn Dicey (1835–1922); Timothy Healy (1855–1931); Matthias McDonnell Bodkin (1849–1933), and Lord Cooper of Culross (1892–1955).

The first of these, Christopher Wandesford, is the subject of a paper by *Nial Osborough*. Wandesford was an English MP who followed Wentworth into the service of Charles I in Ireland in the 1630s. Elected an Irish MP, he held judicial office and became lord deputy of Ireland for some months in 1640. In addition to the family's English estates, Wandesford secured an Irish estate, once owned by the Brennans, a native Irish sept. Wandesford's desire not only to make provision in his will for his widow and children, but also to make reparation to the Brennans, made the survival of his will of more than usual importance. Osborough's account of the extraordinary tale of the will's temporary disappearance but ultimate survival of the upheavals of the period, sheds light on events in the wider political arena, in Ireland and in England, from the 1640s to the end of the century. Although the careers of Wandesford and Sir Richard Nagle, the subject of James McGuire's paper, did not overlap – Nagle was born just four years before Wandesford's death

---

1 Earlier volumes in the series are W.N. Osborough (ed.), *The Irish Legal History Society: inaugural addresses* (Dublin, 1989), W.N. Osborough (ed.), *Explorations in law and history* (1995), and D.S. Greer and N.M. Dawson (eds.), *Mysteries and solutions in Irish legal history* (2001).

– the closing passages of Osborough's paper, dealing with the title to Wandesford's Irish estates in the 1680s, raise issues developed by McGuire.

Placing his study of Sir Richard Nagle in the context of growing evidence of the influence of lawyers in the politics of seventeenth-century Ireland, *James McGuire* brings into focus the career of this successful catholic barrister who entered politics in 1686, when tensions were running high between the 'protestant political nation' that had developed in the years following the Restoration, and dispossessed catholic landowners who saw the accession of James II as an opportunity for securing legislation modifying the restoration land acts. He examines Nagle's influence, as Tyrconnell's legal and political adviser, in promoting the revival of the catholic interest and in articulating the case for modification of the land settlement, and reconstructs and assesses his roles as attorney general in Tyrconnell's administration, as speaker of the house of commons in 1689, and in James II's service in exile at St Germain.

Nationalism – political, constitutional, and legal – is a strong undercurrent in the next four papers. In 'Dicey and the sovereignty of parliament: lessons from Irish legal history', *John McEldowney* traces the influences on the work and writings of this great constitutional lawyer of the late Victorian era – evangelical zeal, involvement in journalism, practice at the bar, an exposure to the US legal system, and an interest in legal education – and analyses his conception of parliamentary sovereignty. He considers how Dicey's understanding of what sovereignty meant in the context of a *United* Kingdom influenced his (changing) attitude to Irish home rule, and suggests that his writings on the home rule question in turn influenced the form in which he articulated his doctrine of sovereignty in his *Law of the constitution*, published in 1885. McEldowney assesses Dicey's legacy in the context of more recent challenges to parliamentary sovereignty – membership of the European Community, the advent of the Human Rights Act 1998, and devolution within the United Kingdom.

If Dicey could coolly mull over the Union and home rule within the groves of academe, the same could not be said of Timothy Healy. *Frank Callanan*, biographer of Healy, returns to his subject in his paper, 'T.M. Healy: the politics of advocacy', which addresses the *combination* of Healy's roles as advocate and constitutional nationalist. He explores Healy's contribution at Westminster in the period leading up to the Land Law (Ire.) Act 1881, and his efforts, largely ignored by historians, to use his role at the Irish bar to promote the development of the law as a brake on the power of the executive, with subtly important consequences for the political history of Ireland. Callanan contends that Healy's survival of the political upheavals of his times, culminating in his appointment in 1922 as the first governor-general of the Irish Free State, can only be fully understood by reference to his legal career.

One of Healy's contemporaries at the Irish bar was Matthias McDonnell Bodkin, the subject of a paper by *Felix Larkin*, entitled 'Judge Bodkin and the 1916 Rising: a letter from his son'. This, and the fact that Healy and Bodkin had similar political perspectives, explains numerous resonances between the two papers. Unlike Healy, however, perhaps Bodkin's greatest contribution to Irish public life was as a journalist, notably with the *Freeman's Journal*; he was also appointed, somewhat controversially, to the county court bench in 1907, and, as Larkin describes, was the author of a body of detective fiction. But what of the title of this paper? In this 90th anniversary year of the Easter Rising, Larkin's paper includes Judge Bodkin's vivid account of, and reaction to, the events of April and early May 1916, in the form of a letter to his son, published here for the first time.[2] Bringing both father and son to life in his paper, Larkin concludes with an analysis of the political significance of the letter – a contemporaneous assessment of the Rising, written by a 'stalwart' of the Irish party.

In an essay in the intellectual history of Scots 'legal nationalism', constructed around the career and writings of Lord Cooper of Culross, *Hector MacQueen* reflects on Cooper's conception of the 'historical mission' of Scots law. Cooper, an advocate, lord advocate, and lord president of the court of session, has been credited by other commentators as the co-author, with T.B. Smith, of the 'Cooper-Smith ideology' that sees Scots law, with its unique mix of common law and Roman law, as an aspect of 'nation' and something to be defended from outside, especially English, legal influences, but at the same time as having a role as a bridge between common law and civilian systems within Europe. Exploring published sources, including Cooper's own writings, MacQueen disputes this attribution of authorship of the ideology, both in terms of its chronological and substantive accuracy, pointing, for example, to a statement by Lord Cooper that Stair (the author of *The institutions of the law of Scotland*, 1681), had 'enslaved his country to an alien system', namely the Roman law system. In doing so, he provides a clearer understanding not only of Lord Cooper's actual views on Scots law, but also of the real origins of the so-called 'Cooper-Smith ideology'.

The first of five papers to take up the theme of crime and punishment is a study by *Brian Griffin* of the prevention and detection of crime in nineteenth-century Ireland through the agency of the Irish Constabulary, rationalised in the 1830s, and its urban counterpart, the Dublin Metropolitan Police, established in 1836. Drawing on press and other contemporary sources for (occasionally hilarious) illustration and for comparison with English police forces, he deals with matters such as police training in the law and in personal demeanour; the use of rewards; the obtaining of information;

---

2   As noted later in Larkin's paper, the letter is in the possession of the National Library of Ireland, and is published by kind permission of the board of the National Library.

the importance of local knowledge and an ability to recognise suspects from published descriptions, and the early use of forensic procedures and technological aids in the detection of crime. Griffin also addresses the relationship between the police and the community, highlighting, for example, the suspicions aroused not only among the public but also the magistracy by the activities of plain-clothes police.

That the police had an enormous body of criminal law to commit to memory is borne out by *Desmond McCabe* in his paper on the expansion of summary jurisdiction in Ireland from the 1820s to the end of the nineteenth century. (Although this paper has been included in this group of papers on the broad theme of 'crime and punishment', it should be noted that the courts of summary jurisdiction also had a significant *civil* case load, as the author describes.) McCabe's extensive survey of the monumental body of legislation relating to the exercise of summary jurisdiction captures its expansion by reference to some 17 headings, such as larceny, vagrancy, alcohol-related offences, assault, cruelty to animals, and so on. The day-to-day operation of the petty sessions is also explored, along with the character of the magistracy and other court personnel. The paper further provides statistical analysis of petty sessions usage according to the nature of the case; rates of prosecution by city and county in Ireland, and of sentences handed down by the magistrates. (Some of McCabe's account of the routine operation of the petty sessions is further illustrated in Desmond Greer's paper on the operation of the truck acts in Donegal.)

Lord Denman's argument (advanced in the 1840s) that a court of criminal appeal would provide 'security against illegality' in the execution of the criminal law prompts the title chosen by *Desmond Greer* for his paper on the reservation of crown cases in nineteenth-century Ireland. Victims of miscarriages of justice then had limited opportunities for redress; chief among these was the reservation of questions of law by the trial judge for the consideration of the twelve common law judges. The fact that in Ireland, unlike the position in England, the twelve judges assumed jurisdiction to hear some '*civil* cases reserved', including some of a highly political nature, generated a unique debate about the nature of the twelve judges as a 'court'. The paper explores all aspects of the exercise of this jurisdiction and highlights its weaknesses, not least the variations in judicial practice, which provided a compelling case for reform. Although the celebrated case of William Burke Kirwan's conviction in 1852 for the murder of his wife on Ireland's Eye island increased the pressure for statutory protection against miscarriages of justice, reform was slow in coming. Greer probes the reasons, legal and political, why this was so.

The use of criminal and judicial statistics, and related sources, as a basis for researching the social history of Ireland is the theme considered by *Mark*

Finnane in his paper, 'Irish crime without the outrage: the statistics of criminal justice in the later nineteenth century'. Based on the view that 'agrarian outrages' were not generally of major significance in the criminal justice system of this period, he advances the argument that statistics and other surviving sources relating to the various elements of the criminal justice system – arrest, prosecution and punishment – at once inform our general understanding of crime in Ireland and suggest a more nuanced research agenda for social historians, probing regional or local variations in patterns of arrest or punishment, for example, or gender differences. The need to explain an upwards trend in rates of arrest for assaults on women and children compared with the downwards trend shown by global rates of arrest for assault generally, is just one instance of further research suggested by published statistics. The paper concludes with an archival note, indicating a range of unpublished sources available in NAI and PRONI, which will facilitate detailed research on the use of petty and quarter sessions and the assizes.

Drawing extensively on Irish and English archival sources, *Gerard O'Brien* provides a detailed history of the use of the death penalty in Ireland, and of public discourse surrounding it, from the early years of the Irish Free State until the abolition of capital punishment in Ireland in 1964. Although one draft of the constitution of the Free State would have prevented the use of the death sentence in the new state, this clause was not included in the final text, and practice continued much as it had done under British administration, although executions became increasingly rare. In a paper which combines atmospheric accounts of individual cases and public reaction to them with detailed exposition of the Irish executive's practice in relation to the death penalty, O'Brien considers why, once the troubled post-civil war period was over, the abolitionist cause did not became a political issue in Ireland as it had done in 1950s Britain, and reflects on the reasons for the abolition of the death penalty in 1964 (subject to a number of exceptions, including the murder of a police officer), on the recommendation of the minister of justice of the time, Charles J. Haughey (whom the author interviewed on the subject of capital punishment).

The theme of law-making runs through the remaining three papers in the collection. *James Kelly* examines the political and constitutional relationship between the kingdom of Ireland and the English crown through the lens of Poynings' law, the act of 1494 that required legislative proposals for Ireland to be certified by the Irish privy council to the English privy council, which in turn had power to amend, veto, postpone or allow them. He explores the making of law for Ireland from the Restoration until the Union, beginning with the rise of the 'heads of bill' process which enabled the seventeenth-century Irish parliament to develop as a law-making body, albeit subject to English political control. By means of an audit (anticipating a larger study by the author) of the legislative achievements of the Irish parliament in various phases of the seventeenth and eighteenth centuries, and an account of the changing relationship between the parliament and the Irish and English privy councils, Kelly reveals the administrative, procedural and, finally, political accommodations that allowed the eighteenth-century Irish parliament to function as it did – by virtue of 'no ordinary dependent colonial relationship'.

In his paper on truck (payment of wages in kind) in Donegal in the 1890s, *Desmond Greer* demonstrates the futility of making law that is unenforceable in the prevailing economic and social conditions. O'Connell's view, expressed in the 1830s, that truck was a price worth paying for a job when jobs were scarce, militated against the enforcement of anti-truck legislation in Ireland, but this sense of the law's adverse economic consequences was lost on the home office in the late 1880s. This study deals with the case of a Burtonport shopkeeper who gave out 'home-work' in the form of sewing and knitting to local women in return for vouchers which could only be used in his shop. The paper depicts the strenuous but unsuccessful attempts of home office factory inspectors to enforce the truck acts against him, involving several forays in the petty sessions and the queen's bench division, and explores the impact of the litigation on the community and the consequences for those home-workers who dared to give evidence against the defendant. The author shows that, where the law was a dead letter, improving economic conditions gradually eliminated the power of local shopkeepers to reduce home-workers to a state of economic dependency.

In the concluding paper in the collection, *the Honourable Mr Justice Ronan Keane*, recently-retired chief justice of Ireland, reflects on the role and influence of the 'one judgment rule' in Irish constitutional law. The rule requires the supreme court to publish one judgment only in cases where the court is considering the validity, under the constitution, of a bill or act of the Oireachtas; it thus prohibits the publication of dissenting judgments or of more than one assenting judgment in such cases. Exploring the history and rationale of the rule, Judge Keane probes the difficulties that the rule causes for members of a court of final appeal, and highlights the apparent anomaly that the ban does not apply to cases where fundamental constitutional principles arise but the validity of no specific legislative measure is in issue. He considers the question whether this constraint on judicial influence and on the development of the law should, in a mature democracy, be consigned entirely to the realm of legal history.

My task as editor has been made easier by the enthusiastic co-operation of the various contributors. I have very much enjoyed working with them to prepare the results of their considerable scholarly researches for publication. I wish to express my thanks to them all for their help in bringing this volume to fruition. I am also grateful to Helen Kenny for secretarial assistance, and to Martin Fanning and his colleagues at Four Courts Press for their assistance at all stages of the production process. On behalf of the Society, I acknowledge our debt to those who allowed us to use their premises for our meetings, as indicated in the papers which follow.

Further information about the Society's activities, including our publishing programme, may be found on our website: http://www.irishlegalhistory.com

NORMA DAWSON
Queen's University, Belfast

List of contributors

FRANK CALLANAN is a lawyer and writer. He is the author of *The Parnell split* (1992) and of *T.M. Healy* (1996), and edited E. Byrne, *Parnell, a memoir* (1991) and *The Literary and Historical Society, 1955–2005* (2005). He was called to the Irish bar in 1979, and to the inner bar in 1998. He lives and practises in Dublin.

MARK FINNANE is Research Professor in the Centre for Public Culture and Ideas at Griffith University, Australia. His doctoral thesis on the history of lunatic asylums was published in 1981 as *Insanity and the insane in post-Famine Ireland*. His main research interests are the history of criminal justice and the social history of crime and violence. He is currently writing a biography of John Vincent Barry (1903–1969), Australian judge, historian and pioneer criminologist.

DESMOND GREER is professor emeritus of Queen's University, Belfast, where he was Professor of Common Law from 1973–2004. He has written a number of papers on nineteenth-century Irish legal history, and is co-author (with J.W. Nicolson) of *The factory acts in Ireland, 1802–1914* (Dublin, 2003). He was President of the Society from 1997–2000.

BRIAN GRIFFIN lectures in history and Irish studies at Bath Spa University, where he is coordinator of the Irish Studies Centre. He is the author of *The Bulkies: police and crime in Belfast, 1800–1865* (Dublin, 1997), and *Sources for the study of crime in Ireland, 1801–1921* (Dublin, 2005).

RONAN KEANE was appointed to the Irish high court in 1979, and to the supreme court in 1996. He was chief justice of Ireland from 2000 to 2004. A former patron of the Society, he is the author of books on the law of local government, company law, and equity and the law of trusts, and of numerous papers.

JAMES KELLY is head of the history department in St Patrick's College, Drumcondra, and the author of, among other books, *'That damn'd thing called honour': duelling in Ireland, 1570–1860* (1995); *Henry Flood: patriots and politics in eighteenth century Ireland* (1998); *Sir Edward Newenham: defender of the protestant constitution* (2004), and *The Liberty and Ormond Boys: factional riot in eighteenth-century Dublin* (2005). He is completing a major study on Poynings' law.

FELIX M. LARKIN studied history at University College, Dublin, and has been a public servant in Dublin for the past thirty years, most recently with the National Treasury Management Agency. He has a continuing research interest in the history of the press in the late nineteenth and early twentieth centuries in Ireland, especially the *Freeman's Journal*. He is an external contributor to the Royal Irish Academy's forthcoming *Dictionary of Irish biography*, and is honorary treasurer of the National Library of Ireland Society.

DESMOND McCABE was awarded a doctorate in history by University College Dublin in 1991. He has worked in the old Dublin County Council libraries, and as a tax specialist with Price Waterhouse in Dublin. He has lectured in the Centre for Urban History, University of Leicester, and worked as a researcher on the Famine Network Project (UCD and TCD) and for the *Dictionary of Irish biography*. He is currently working on a history of the Office of Public Works.

JOHN McELDOWNEY is Professor of Law at the University of Warwick. He has written in the fields of legal history and public law (including the environment). He was the Distinguished Visiting Fellow of the New Zealand Law Foundation in 2001. He is currently working on a new analysis of environmental law to be published in 2006 by Edward Elgar.

JAMES McGUIRE is a senior lecturer in history at University College Dublin. He is currently editing the Royal Irish Academy's *Dictionary of Irish biography* which will be published by Cambridge University Press in 2008. He has been chairman of the Irish Manuscripts Commission since 2003.

HECTOR L. MACQUEEN is Professor of Private Law at the University of Edinburgh. He completed his Ph.D. at Edinburgh, the subject being medieval Scots law, and he has published widely in this and other fields of legal history. He has been literary director of the Stair Society, the Scottish legal history society, since 1999.

GERARD O'BRIEN is Reader in History at the University of Ulster and has published in most areas of Irish history from the twelfth to the twentieth centuries. Dr O'Brien's most recent book, *Irish governments and the guardianship of historical records, 1922–1972*, was published by Four Courts Press in 2004.

W.N. OSBOROUGH is emeritus Professor of Jurisprudence and Legal History at University College Dublin. A former President of the Irish Legal History Society and first recipient of the Society's Gold Medal, he is the author of *Law and the emergence of modern Dublin* (1996) and *Studies in Irish legal history* (1999). His most recent publication is an edition of a 1739 judgment of the Irish king's bench.

List of illustrations

Illustrations appearing in black and white on the pages indicated
are asterisked if they also appear in the plates section after p. 42.

List of abbreviations

AC	Law Reports, Appeal Cases, 1891–
Alcock & Napier Rep	Alcock and Napier's reports, Kings Bench (Ire.), 1831–1833
BL	British Library
C./Cd./Cmd.	Command paper
Cal.treasury bks.	*Calendar of treasury books and papers preserved in the Public Record Office*
Cal.S.P.Dom.	*Calendar of state papers*, Domestic series
Cal.S.P.Ire.	*Calendar of state papers*, Ireland
Car & P	Carrington and Payne's reports, *nisi prius*, 1823–1841, in vols. 171–3, English Reports
Cl & Fin	Clark and Finnelly's reports, House of Lords, 1837–1846, in vols. 6–8, English Reports
Commons' jn. Ire.	*Journals of the house of commons of the kingdom of Ireland*, 1631–1791 (Dublin, 1753–1791), reprinted and continued, 1631–1800 (Dublin, 1796–1800)
Co Rep	Coke's reports, King's Bench, 1572–1616, in vols. 76–7, English Reports
Cox CC	Cox's Criminal Cases, 1843–1941
Cr & Dix	Crawford and Dix's Irish Circuit reports, 1839–1846
Dáil Deb.	Parliamentary debates in Dáil Eireann (Dublin, 1922–)
Denison CC	Denison's reports, Crown Cases, 1844–1852, in vol. 169, English Reports
DNB	*Dictionary of national biography*
Econ Hist Rev	*Economic History Review* (London, 1927–)
EHR	*English Historical Review* (London, 1886–)
El & Bl	Ellis and Blackburne's reports, Queen's Bench, 1851–1858, in vols. 118–120, English Reports
Eng Rep	English Reports, 1210–1865
Hansard's Parl.Deb.	*Hansard's parliamentary debates* (London, 1829–)
H.C.	House of Commons papers
H & C	Hurlstone and Coltman's reports, Exchequer, 1862–1866, in vols. 158–9, English Reports

HMC	Historical Manuscripts Commission
How St Tr	T.B. Howell, *A complete collection of state trials* (London, 1816–1828)
Hudson & Brooke Rep	Hudson and Brooke's reports, King's Bench (Ire.), 1827–1831
ICLR	Irish Common Law Reports, 1849–1866
IESH	*Irish Economic and Social History* (Dublin, 1974–)
IHS	*Irish Historical Studies* (Dublin, 1938–)
ILT & SJ	*Irish Law Times and Solicitors' Journal* (Dublin, 1867–)
ILTR	Irish Law Times Reports (in *ILT & SJ*)
IR	Irish Reports, 1894–
Ir Cir Rep	Irish Circuit Reports, 1841–1843
IRCL	Irish Reports, Common Law series, 1867–1878
Ir Jur	*Irish Jurist* (new series, Dublin, 1966–)
Ir Jur Rep	Irish Jurist reports (in *Ir Jur*)
Ir LR	Irish law reports, King's Bench, 1838–1850
Ir WLR	Irish Weekly Law Reports, 1895–1901
Jebb Rep	Jebb's reports, Crown Cases (Ire.), 1822–1840
JSSISI	*Journal of the Statistical and Social Inquiry Society of Ireland* (Dublin, 1868–)
KB	Law Reports, King's Bench Division
LQR	*Law Quarterly Review* (London, 1885–)
LR CCR	Law Reports, Crown Cases Reserved, 1865–1875
Leach	Leach's reports, Crown Cases, 1730–1815, in vol. 168, English Reports
Lewin	Lewin's reports, Crown Cases, 1822–1838, in vol. 168, English Reports
Liber mun. pub. Hib.	*Liber munerum publicorum Hiberniae* 1152–1827, ed. Rowley Lascelles (London, 1852)
LR Ir	Law Reports, Ireland, 1878–1893
Moo CC	Moody's Crown Cases, 1824–1844, in vols. 168–9, English Reports
NA	National Archive (UK) (formerly, PRO)
NAI	National Archive of Ireland
New Ir Rev	*New Ireland Review* (Dublin, 1894–1906)

NLI	National Library of Ireland
Oxford DNB	*Oxford dictionary of national biography*
PC	Privy Council
Pr	Price's reports, Exchequer, 1814–1824, in vols. 145–7, English Reports
PRO	Public Record Office (UK), now the National Archive (NA)
PRONI	Public Record Office of Northern Ireland
Proc RIA	*Proceedings of the Royal Irish Academy* (Dublin, 1890–)
QB/QBD	Law reports, Queen's Bench Division
Russ	Russell's reports, Chancery, 1823–1829, in vol. 38, English Reports
Russ & Ry	Russell and Ryan's reports, Crown Cases, 1799–1824, in vol. 168, English Reports
SC	Session Cases, Scotland, (Edinburgh, 1906–)
SLT	Scots Law Times (Edinburgh, 1959–)
Seanad Deb.	Parliamentary Debates in Seanad Eireann (Dublin, 1922–)
TCD	Trinity College Dublin
UCD	University College Dublin
UKHL	United Kingdom, House of Lords
Willes	Willes Reports, Common Pleas, 1737–1760, in vol. 125, English Reports

Wills that go missing: the quest for the last testament of Christopher Wandesford, lord deputy of Ireland, 1640

W.N. OSBOROUGH*

WILLS THAT GO MISSING HAVE proved a fertile source of inspiration for writers of fiction. Ezra Quaggin's will, described in a short story of 1949 by Nigel Kneale, is a case in point.[1] Drawn up by Ezra himself, though perhaps with some professional assistance, and written in the testator's own hand-writing on 'a long sky-blue paper', what was important about it was its principal provision – the bequeathing of Ezra's farm and farmhouse to his niece Sallie. This at the expense of bachelor Ezra's assorted male relations. Tom-Billy Teare, Sallie's husband and the leading actor in the drama that unfolds after Ezra's funeral, was made executor and told by Ezra, prior to the latter's demise, where the will meanwhile has been secreted: it had been put 'in a proper black box on top o' the kitchen dresser'. As Ezra lay dying in hospital during his final illness, Tom-Billy was unable to resist the temptation to take the box down from the dresser in Ezra's kitchen and peruse the will's contents. Riches beckoned, Tom-Billy soon learnt, as he rushed off to tell Sallie, his wife.

The day of the funeral, Tom-Billy and Sallie prepared a meal to which all members of the Quaggin family were invited. This Tom-Billy calculated would soften the blow when the will came to be read, and the alarming intelligence relayed that Ezra had left the farm, not to any of his male relatives, but to his niece Sallie. While the assembled throng continued to gorge themselves, Tom-Billy retreated to the kitchen to fetch down the black box. The 'old receipts' were still there, so too were 'the backless prayer-book'

* The text of a presidential address given to the Society in the Old Bar Library, Belfast, on 12 December 2003.

1 'The putting away of Uncle Quaggin', in N. Kneale, *Tomato Cain and other stories* (London, 1949). The story is included in D. Hudson, *Classic English short stories, 1930–1955* (Oxford, 1972), the paperback reprint of a volume previously entitled *Modern English short stories: second series* (Oxford, 1956).

and 'letters dealing with an unsatisfactory grubber' – all things Tom-Billy had seen before. But of Ezra's will itself written on its distinctive sky-blue paper there was no trace at all. If it could not be found, Tom-Billy swiftly concluded, the prospect of an intestacy loomed, presaging an outcome he was personally loath to contemplate, that 'the farm would be divided amongst the whole brood'. Tom-Billy soon deduced what must have happened. A late arrival at the funeral lunch – who had missed both the church service and the burial – aroused Tom-Billy's immediate suspicions: a member of the despised brood of male relations, known within the inner circle as 'Lawyer Quaggin'. Lawyer Quaggin had scarcely enjoyed an altogether respectable career: first an advocate's clerk, then 'a signwriter or something'. It was also bruited abroad that Lawyer Quaggin 'had tried to live by raising ferrets'.

Persuaded that Lawyer Quaggin had entered the farmhouse while everyone was at Uncle Ezra's funeral, located the will on top of the kitchen dresser and then purloined it, Tom-Billy conceives a strategy on how to outsmart the culprit, bring about the restoration of the will to its proper place, and thereby secure the inheritance for his wife Sallie. As the company settles down, post-prandially, for the reading of the will, a fire, clandestinely lit by Tom-Billy in the adjacent kitchen, breaks out and the mourners are forced to evacuate the farmhouse. In the confusion, Tom-Billy announces that the will is in the black box which he retrieves and then hurls across to Lawyer Quaggin, taking care that everyone should witness his action. 'Watch it close and no monkey business', Tom-Billy admonishes Lawyer Quaggin in everyone's hearing.

The fire is rapidly extinguished, the company reassembles. Lawyer Quaggin sheepishly returns. When Tom-Billy opens the black box this time, Uncle Ezra's will has miraculously been returned. Tom-Billy draws out the long, sky-blue paper. Kneale then brings his account of this family saga to a halt:

> 'This aforesaid document', Tom-Billy starts to read shakily,
> 'is the only will whatsoever of me, Ezra John Quaggin, pig, general, dairy and poultry farmer –'
> His head sang with relief as he looked round the grimy, eager faces.
> 'Go on! Go on, Tom-Billy,' they cried.
> He found the place, cleared his throat, and read again. Soon, he knew, the real fun would begin.

Another will that goes missing is the final testament of Squire Indefer Jones of Llanfeare in Carmarthenshire, the document that provokes the violent *dénouement* in Anthony Trollope's 1879 novel, *Cousin Henry*. Squire Indefer is unable to make up his mind as between the two claimants on his largesse – his nephew Henry Jones or his niece Isabel Brodrick. He dislikes his cringing nephew but admires his niece. A way out of his dilemma was to propose the marriage of the two cousins – that way the family name of Jones at least would be preserved. Isabel, for her own very good reasons, is not enamoured of the plan at all. Furious at this rebuff and to express his displeasure, Indefer makes yet another will – one in a long sequence, for Indefer vacillated over the entire question of the succession for many months – and this was in favour of Henry. But this was not the final expression of the squire's testamentary intentions, for in Indefer's last days he repents of his loss of temper, and draws up and has witnessed another will in which he leaves Llanfeare to his niece. It is this final will and testament which cannot be found after Indefer's death.

Henry who now takes up residence in Llanfeare does, however, find the will – hidden in a volume of Bishop Jeremy Taylor's sermons on a shelf in the library. He is naturally dismayed to discover that this last will of his Uncle Indefer deprived him of what he had come to view as his rightful inheritance. In the same fashion in which Indefer had vacillated over his course of conduct, so likewise now does Cousin Henry: would he disclose the existence of the will? Would he perhaps destroy it? For Henry, the dilemma is protracted and it is this which is splendidly evoked by Trollope: in fact, it lies at the heart of the novel.[2] We learn that Henry, though greatly tempted, 'lacks the courage to burn the will and so commit a criminal act rather than a sin of omission'.[3] In fact, he does nothing.

Meanwhile, suspicions are aroused in the neighbourhood. There are the two people who witnessed the will that has seemingly disappeared. Apjohn, Indefer's attorney, becomes equally convinced that it exists somewhere in the house at Llanfeare. When Henry takes to sitting in the library at Llanfeare staring blankly at a shelf of books on the far wall, Apjohn concludes, not altogether unreasonably, that it is somewhere in this particular room that the will must have been secreted and that Henry had indeed found it. Apjohn and Isabel's father, another attorney, confront Henry in the library. Apjohn suddenly recalls that he had noticed a volume of Jeremy Taylor's sermons on Squire Indefer's reading table some months before. Judging – correctly as it turns out – that the 10-volume set of Jeremy Taylor's works would be the place to commence the search he and his colleague were now determined to carry out, Apjohn announces his intentions. Henry predictably protests: 'You shall not touch a book without a regular order'.[4] Discovery of the missing will soon follows.

> Mr Apjohn fixed the man's eye for a moment. He was the smaller man of the two, and much the elder; but he was wiry, well set, and strong.

2 'The psychological reactions of Henry when he finds this other will in the library are beautifully explored': J. Pope Hennessy, *Anthony Trollope* (London, 1971), ch. 27.

3 Ibid.

4 *Cousin Henry*, ch. 21.

The other was soft, and unused to much bodily exercise. There could be no doubt as to which would have the best of it in a personal struggle. Very quickly he turned round and got his hand on one of the set, but not on the right one. Cousin Henry dashed at him, and in the struggle the book fell to the ground. Then the attorney seized him by the throat, and dragged him forcibly back to the table. 'Take them all out one by one, and shake them', he said to the other attorney, – 'that set like the one on the floor. I'll hold him while you do it'.

Mr Brodrick did as he was told, and, one by one, beginning from the last volume, he shook them all till he came to volume 4. Out of that fell the document.

The claim that fact is stranger than fiction is certainly borne out by the curious tale of one will that actually went missing in the Ireland of the 1640s only to be rediscovered in unusual circumstances in Dublin in 1653. The will in question was that of Christopher Wandesford who filled the office of Irish lord deputy for eight months from April to December 1640.

Wandesford, of Yorkshire stock, was born near Beverley in 1592.[5] Feudal dues payable on the occasion of five successive wardships had impoverished the family, and these continued to cast a shadow over the family's finances as Christopher grew up. H.B. McCall, in his history of the family, asserts that Christopher's grandfather was obliged to pay £900 to the crown to release Christopher from the obligation to marry whomever the king might choose.[6] Christopher's own father did little to improve the family's wealth. He proved no businessman and the rents he charged were much too low: property had been 'leased out to old servants and retainers for mere quitrents and nominal acknowledgments'. Christopher set out to alter the situation and appears very largely to have succeeded.[7]

But this is to anticipate. The young Christopher attended the free school at Well near Kirklington where lay the Wandesfords' principal estate. Kirklington lies a little to the north of Ripon, off the A1. In 1607, at the age of 15 he was sent to Clare College, Cambridge.[8] Thomas Wentworth, a distant kinsman and an exact contemporary, was up at Cambridge at the same time, albeit at a different college, St John's. They were to become close friends. At the age of 20 Christopher entered Gray's Inn,[9] but there is no certain evidence that he was ever called to the bar. It appears rather that at this early

5 H.B. McCall, *Story of the family of Wandesforde of Kirklington and Castlecomer* (London, 1904), p. 65.
6 Ibid., pp. 65–6.
7 T.D. Whitaker, *An history of Richmondshire in the north riding of the county of York*, 2 vols (London, 1823), ii, pp. 149–51.
8 McCall, *Family of Wandesforde*, p. 65.
9 Ibid., p. 67.

Christopher Wandesforde. Watercolour attributed to George Perfect Harding, early 19th century, after an unknown artist of a portrait of the same, *c.*1630, National Portrait Gallery, London.

stage, though he soon found public duties to perform, he largely devoted himself to farming the family's lands in Yorkshire, managing in the process to secure that improvement in the family's wealth previously mentioned. As his father's heir, Christopher had little alternative. Annuities were chargeable on the estate; there were three brothers and a sister to provide for, and his father had left innumerable creditors.[10] Firth, in his entry on Wandesford in the *Dictionary of national biography*, summarises his achievement in the following words: '[b]y strict economy, the skilful management of his lands, and the judicious employment of his wife's marriage portion, he paid off all these encumbrances'.[11]

Wandesford had married at Staveley in Yorkshire in 1614 Alice, the daughter of Sir Hewet Osborne of Kiveton, also in Yorkshire.[12] They had seven children, five of whom survived into adulthood: three sons – George, Christopher and John – and two daughters – Catherine and Alice.[13] Alice Wandesford, the mother, outlived her husband by nearly twenty years, dying in 1659.[14] Two of her children predeceased her. The older daughter Catherine died in childbed of her sixteenth child at the age of 30 in 1645.[15] George, the oldest boy, drowned in the River Swale in Yorkshire in March 1651.[16] This second family tragedy has a particular bearing on the story to be recounted. The second daughter, another Alice, married a William Thornton of East Newton in Yorkshire in 1651, and survived into the next century, dying in 1707.[17] Alice Thornton composed an autobiography which remains the exclusive source of enlightenment on the searches family members were to undertake for Lord Deputy Christopher Wandesford's will after his death in 1640.[18]

Wandesford entered parliament in England in 1621, successively representing Aldborough, Richmond and Thirsk. He strongly supported Wentworth in the latter's electoral campaign in Yorkshire in 1621, from which point their

---

10 Whitaker, *History of Richmondshire*, ii, p. 149.

11 *DNB*, s.v. Wandesford, Christopher.

12 McCall, *Family of Wandesforde*, pp. 68–9; Whitaker, *History of Richmondshire*, ii, p. 150.

13 *The autobiography of Mrs Alice Thornton of East Newton, Co. York*, ed. C. Jackson, Surtees Society, lxii (1875), p. 97.

14 *Autobiography of Alice Thornton*, p. 106.

15 *Autobiography of Alice Thornton*, p. 49; A. Fraser, *The weaker vessel: woman's lot in seventeenth-century England* (London, 1984), p. 75.

16 *Autobiography of Alice Thornton*, p. 61. John, the youngest brother, dies in 1666: ibid., p. 159; Christopher, the sole surviving brother thereafter, in 1686: B. Burke, *A genealogical and heraldic history of the landed gentry of Ireland* (London, 1912), s.v. Wandesford, pp. 744–5.

17 *Autobiography of Alice Thornton*, pp. 61, vii.

18 There is a great deal of interesting other material in this long autobiography which comes to an end in 1669. Apart from information on narrow family matters such as accidents and deaths, there are accounts of a childhood in Dublin, of the perils of the Irish Sea crossing, of the flight from Ireland in the wake of the rising of 1641 and of the difficulties encountered by a Yorkshire family of royalist inclinations in an England wracked by civil war. On Alice and her autobiography, see, too, Fraser, *The weaker vessel*, pp. 75–6.

close association can be dated. Originally part of the political opposition that orchestrated the impeachment of Buckingham and that forced Charles I to concede the Petition of Right, Wandesford followed Wentworth into the king's service in 1629.[19] Wentworth, in the wake of his nomination by Charles to move to Ireland as lord deputy in 1632, experienced little apparent difficulty in persuading Wandesford to accompany him to Ireland 'in order to reduce that savage and intractable people to law and order'.[20] In his *Instructions to his son*, Wandesford explained his decision: '[m]y affection to the person of my lord deputy, purposing to attend upon his lordship as near as I could in all fortunes, carried me along with him whithersoever he went, and no premeditated thoughts of ambition.'[21]

In July 1633 Wandesford travelled to Ireland in the company of Wentworth to assume his office as master of the rolls, thus filling an office that had become vacant on the death of Francis Aungier.[22] The next year he was elected an MP in the Irish parliament, for Kildare. By that year's end his immediate family had joined him, they all appearing at this date to have resided in Dame Street in Dublin. Wandesford had already set about a number of administrative reforms in the Rolls office. A table of fees was posted up; and a clerk, 'a young man of good family in Yorkshire', found to have been guilty of extortion, was both fined and dismissed.[23] Wandesford had already determined to acquire substantial property in Ireland. His preference was lands in Co. Kildare, but when Wentworth, as lord deputy, expressed his interest in these lands at Jigginstown, near Naas, Wandesford who had previously bought them from the earl of Kildare agreed to surrender the property to his patron. An alternative investment was quickly found. An inquisition held at Kilkenny in May 1635 established the title to the territory of Idough or Edough in the county of the same name to rest in the crown. The earl of Ormond and Sir Robert Ridgeway claimed rights in the territory under a grant of James I, but those actually in possession were a tribe or sept of 'the mere Irish', the O'Brennans who held the lands in question 'by strong hand', 'a title', J.P. Prendergast was later to write, 'they had probably held it by from before the birth of Christ'.[24] Representations, previously planned it would seem, were then made by Wandesford to secure as a country residence for himself and as an investment the lands we

19 *DNB*.
20 Whitaker, *History of Richmondshire*, ii, p. 157.
21 Quoted, McCall, *Family of Wandesforde*, p. 71.
22 *Liber mun. pub. Hib.*, i, pt. 2, p. 19.
23 Whitaker, *History of Richmondshire*, ii, p. 159.
24 J.P. Prendergast, *Ireland from the Restoration to the Revolution 1660–1690* (London, 1887), p. 129. Prendergast adds that the red-brick edifice that Wentworth started to build at Jigginstown was to survive as a monument of the latter's 'disappointed ambition, for before it was finished Strafford's head was taken off, and it remained a ruin ever after': ibid.

recognise as those of Castlecomer in Co. Kilkenny, comprising a castle and an estate of 20,000 acres. Eventually, in 1637, Wandesford, having bought out Ormond and Ridgeway for £2,000, and advanced further moneys, secured what he probably came to regard, judged by Irish standards at the time, as an indefeasible title.[25] Intriguingly, however, the plight of the O'Brennans or Brennans was to prick Wandesford's conscience and would continue to do so. In the mid-1630s members of the sept had repulsed solicitations from Wandesford designed to secure their acquiescence in the new state of affairs with regard to ownership of Idough. For Wandesford, however, it seemed right even so that some reparation should be attempted. So, by deed executed in September 1640, only a few months before his death, he conveyed the territory of Idough to four trustees for a term of 41 years to answer the trust in his will, executed on the ensuing 2 October, in favour of the Brennans. The relevant section of the will was to read as follows:

> Whereas, also, the natives of Idough, called Brennans, who have for many years possessed the same, have several times refused such proffers of benefit as I thought good out of my own private charity and conscience to tender unto them – not that I ever believed, either by law or equity, I could be compelled to give them any consideration at all for their pretended interest – my will is that the trustees shall, out of the said rents, pay unto so many of them (the said Brennans) or their children, as by a commission out of Chancery shall be found to have been the reputed possessors and ter-tenants of the lands at the time of the finding of the office of Idough for His Majesty, dated the 21st May, 1635, so much money severally as a lease for 21 years of the moiety of those lands so in their possession respectively, shall be by the said commissioners valued to have been worth unto the said possessors at the time of finding the said office after the common course of bargaining.[26]

As we shall see, this attempt on the part of Wandesford to play fair by the sept of the Brennans created difficulties for his family after his death, as they struggled to adjust to a downturn in the family's fortunes, quite apart from the quarrel that broke out amongst them, which made it essential in the end to find Wandesford's original will – the will of 2 October 1640 – which in the interim was to go missing.

Wandesford himself had come to play an important role in the government of Ireland. In 1636, he served as lord justice in tandem with Loftus, the lord chancellor, and in 1639 he served in the same capacity again,

---

25 McCall, *Family of Wandesforde*, pp. 275–81; Prendergast, *Ireland from the Restoration*, pp. 129–30; A. Clarke, *The Old English in Ireland 1625–42* (London, 1966), p. 108.
26 Prendergast, *Ireland from the Restoration*, pp. 133–4; McCall, *Family of Wandesforde*, p. 283.

in tandem with Lord Dillon. Wentworth's recall to England in 1640 to assist Charles I in manoeuvring against his political foes – that led first to the abortive impeachment proceedings and then the attainder and execution of 1641 – created a vacancy in the post of lord deputy, which Wandesford was advanced to fill in April 1640. Wandesford inherited no easy job, though he was to be spared having to contend with the constitutional breakdown of the early months of 1641, the ensuing impeachments and the rebellion of the last months of that year. As lord deputy, Wandesford was obliged to face down a revolt over taxes in the Irish commons. A remonstrance against Wentworth's administration was presented on 7 November. On 12 November, parliament was prorogued. And a week later, Wandesford, acting on instructions, sent for the journals of the commons and tore out the contentious resolutions on taxes.[27]

Less than a week after that, on 24 November, Wandesford felt unwell at church. He retired to his bed. In a fruitless attempt at assuaging the fever from which the lord deputy was plainly suffering, split pigeons were ordered to be applied to the soles of his feet. This did no good at all. On 1 December, the family and others gathered round his bedside to hear the reading of his last testament of 2 October. Two days later Christopher Wandesford was dead.[28] He was buried a week later in Christ Church cathedral in Dublin. The king ordered the expenses of his funeral to be borne by the treasury – this sum, apparently, was of the order of £1,300; he also sanctioned a remission on the wardship of his heirs – a feudal burden with which, as we have had occasion to note, the Wandesford family was only too familiar. The lord deputy's daughter, however, was to insist that the family never received the financial benefit of these concessions: Charles's opponents in parliament saw to that.[29]

Further difficulties for the family soon emerged. The rising of the catholics at the end of 1641 forced the widow and her family to seek shelter first in Dublin and then, during a lull in what remained a tense security situation, to take ship for England. At Castlecomer the Brennans, it was later claimed, possessed themselves of the estate, seizing all the stock and destroying buildings, in an occupation that was to last over ten years. Christopher, the second son, escaped the siege at the family's principal residence there 'in an Irish disguise', and with important 'writings' 'secure in his trousers'. Various adventures awaited the family as they made their way from Dublin first to Chester, then on through Warrington, Wigan and Snape Castle,

---

27 *Commons' jn. Ire.*, I, pt. 1, pp. 162–66; Clarke, *The Old English in Ireland*, pp. 134–5.

28 *Autobiography of Alice Thornton*, pp. 21–4; William Wandesford to Sir Rowland Wandesford, 12 December 1640: C.H. Firth (ed.), 'Letters of William Wandesford to Sir Rowland Wandesford', *EHR*, ix (1894), 551–2. Another view was that 'upon the first word' Wandesford heard of Wentworth's accusation and imprisonment – at the end of November – the former 'swooned, and died within a very few days after': HMC, *Cowper MSS*, ii, 267.

29 *Autobiography of Alice Thornton*, pp. 26–7.

before arriving back in Kirklington, where the family made one last move, again in Yorkshire, to Hipswell.[30]

Rental income from the lord deputy's investment in Irish land was now set to dry up. The financial prospects in England, ravaged by civil war, looked little better. Troops, both Scots and parliamentary, were quartered on the family's estates in Yorkshire and these did not shrink from extorting money payments.[31] Sequestration of the land owned in the county by George, the eldest son and the lord deputy's heir, ensued in 1645 when the family was identified as allying its fortunes too closely with those of the king. His sister Alice is scathing in her condemnation of this damaging development. The sequestration of George's property had been pushed through, she was to write, 'under the pretence of godlinesse and religion, because he did not joyne in such practices of rebellion against the church of God and our lawfull King, whom God had commanded to be obeied.'[32] As it happened, the specific sequestration was to be set aside following a successful traverse, in 1653, undoubtedly achieved through resort to political influence. For the young Alice Wandesford, however, a price seems to have been demanded: her marriage to William Thornton, a nephew of the family's volunteer go-between.[33]

Christopher Wandesford's will was drawn up and signed by him in the presence of witnesses, as we have already heard, on 2 October 1640; and this will was admitted to probate in the Irish court of the prerogative on a date in 1641 – one source says 1 April, the other 23 September.[34] There were five witnesses: John Burniston, George Strahernes, James Wallis, James Foxcroft and Ezra Woolston. Burniston and Wallis were to feature in the aftermath, as indeed was the principal executor, a cousin of Christopher, who, confusingly, like the latter's own half-brother, was called William Wandesford. The will, in a number of respects, was unremarkable. It made financial provision for his wife Alice, by means of an annuity. Specific financial provision was made for his three sons, George, Christopher and John; George, as the heir at law was, of course, especially favoured. Portions were to be raised for the benefit of his daughter Alice, then still unmarried. Catherine, his eldest child, was already married and no provision seems to have been made for her. As

---

30 *Autobiography of Alice Thornton*, pp. 27–32. Prendergast, *Ireland from the Restoration*, p. 135; *Cal. treasury bks.*, x, pt. 2 (1693–96), pp. 993–4.

31 *Autobiography of Alice Thornton*, p. 43. Mrs Thornton adds she was lucky to escape a forced marriage with a Scots officer, a Captain Innis.

32 Mrs Thornton explains that the sequestration was resolved upon because George, in exercising his right of presentation to the parish of Kirklington, had ignored the claims of a cleric of the Presbyterian faction: *Autobiography of Alice Thornton*, pp. 57–8. It probably did not help that the family's motto was '*Tout pour l'église*'.

33 *Autobiography of Alice Thornton*, p. 61.

34 Ibid., pp. 184–5.

previously mentioned, she was to die in 1645. One unusual feature of the will, of course, was the instruction to the trustees under the deed of September 1640 to compensate the sept of the Brennans. A codicil drawn up and signed on the same day as the will obliged his executors to honour a commitment in respect of a tobacco farm in Ireland, in which Wandesford had taken an eighth share.[35]

The main provisions of this document were known to Wandesford's immediate family who had heard the will read in the lord deputy's presence on 29 November 1640.[36] And custody of the document remained with the family prior to probate in 1641, during which period, according to Alice Thornton, she read and reread it frequently.[37] The family, however, do not appear to have secured an actual copy of it before their withdrawal from Ireland following the rising at the end of 1641. It is possible that in the confusion that then obtained the failure to do so was the least of the family's concerns at the time. As the months passed, the lack of intelligence on the precise entitlements of each member of the family became much harder to bear and also on how best the debts falling on the estate might most equitably be discharged. In 1646 steps were finally taken to rectify the situation. George, the eldest son, travelled to Ireland in an attempt to obtain an authentic copy of his father's will. At this point, there is no suggestion that members of the family itself were disputing their various entitlements. Alice Thornton, in her account of George's expedition in 1646, repeats that a main purpose of the mission was to arrive at a consensus as to how the estate could pay Wandesford's various creditors – a task that had up till then largely fallen to William Wandesford, the lord deputy's cousin and executor in Ireland, to carry out.[38]

George's expedition to Ireland in 1646 was met with success. He located the will and arranged for a certified copy to be made and, armed with this copy, he returned to Yorkshire. A crucial detail is that he was permitted to travel back with this certified copy even though he lacked the £5 or £6 to pay the fee demanded by the relevant clerk as the charge for the making of the copy. This had an important consequence, for it led the clerk in question to remove the original will from the file where up until George's visit it had been kept, and secure it elsewhere, against the day when the £5 or £6 which was outstanding had been paid, as George had promised that it would be.[39]

---

35 McCall, *Family of Wandesforde*, p. 282.

36 *Autobiography of Alice Thornton*, p. 22.

37 Ibid., p. 186.

38 On the confusion of the two William Wandesfords, one the cousin and executor, living originally in Ireland, and the other, the half-brother living in England, see McCall, *Family of Wandesforde*, pp. 90–1. Alice Thornton, it is worthy of note, had disputes with both these relatives and does not mince words in her criticisms of them.

39 *Autobiography of Alice Thornton*, p. 184.

Following George's return, his mother and other members of the family sought to procure their own copy of the document brought back by George, the so-called authentic copy as certified in Dublin by Sir William Rives. George himself commenced the exercise which was apparently completed in turn by his brother Christopher and his sister Alice.[40] This second copy was not, of course, a certified copy itself, and this defect, along with the apparent disappearance of the original will itself, survived to plague members of the family in a few years' time. George's certified copy came into the hands of his uncle William, the lord deputy's half-brother, and, after the death of George in 1651, appears to have been transferred by him to the new heir, the second son Christopher, who according to Alice, had assisted in the making of the second, uncertified copy.[41]

With George's drowning in the River Swale between Richmond and Catterick on 31 March 1651, Christopher junior now stepped into another pair of his brother's shoes: he married Eleanor, the daughter of Sir John Lowther of Lowther Castle in Westmorland, to whom George had earlier been betrothed. Alice Thornton makes it plain in her account of subsequent events that the Lowthers persuaded Christopher to adopt a stance over the Wandesford inheritance that was destined to make life miserable both for their widowed mother and for herself. Though rental income was to start flowing again from Castlecomer in Ireland around 1654, Christopher opposed the payment out of that income of sums due both his mother and his sister under the terms of the lord deputy's will. Alice also claimed that tenants on the lands at Kirklington had been duped into making no payments to her of her entitlement to a proportion of the rental income there.[42] The inference from this that we are invited to draw is that Christopher junior, if not the Lowthers, had put the salient pressure on the tenants. It was Christopher's general stance that made it all the more imperative that a fresh authentic copy of Wandesford's will be obtained. George, as we have seen, had finally managed to procure a copy of the vital instrument in 1646, but at some later stage – so Alice Thornton was to aver – this had been lost by her brother, Christopher junior.

Egged on by his father-in-law, Alice infers, Christopher junior, after his marriage, now brazenly argued that his father had left no will at all, and talk of the supposed financial arrangements benefiting both his mother and his sister was nothing more than hot air.[43] With this family crisis intensifying, the proposal of a further mission to Ireland to locate Lord Deputy Wandesford's will was made. Though William Wandesford, the lord deputy's half-brother,

---

40 *Autobiography of Alice Thornton*, p. 193. McCall states that this second copy was in 13 folios, the first three of which were in George's handwriting: *Family of Wandesforde*, pp. 285–6.
41 Ibid.
42 Ibid., pp. 183, 195.   43 Ibid., pp. 183, 184.

since he was also being harassed by Christopher junior, could be counted on to offer assistance, Alice Thornton was far from convinced that the initiative would prosper. In Alice's view, as she phrased it herself, it was more probable that by 1651 such a will would have been 'burned by the rebells, or the Protector's [Cromwell's] soldiers, who had don soe to all the wills which was [sic] found then on the file'.[44] Thornton, Alice's husband, was reluctant to admit defeat, and he commissioned a lawyer, one William Mettcalfe – a 'servant' to Alice's uncle, William Wandesford – to travel to Dublin to undertake a fresh search. Mettcalfe's initial report, forwarded to Yorkshire, must have confirmed Alice's worst fears. All wills on file in the Rolls office had been destroyed under the regime of Charles Fleetwood, who had been made commander in chief in Ireland in 1652: they were 'gon, or cutt in peeces for tailors' measures, or any idle use', to repeat Alice's eloquent précis of Mettcalfe's first report.[45]

But Mettcalfe's persistence was ultimately rewarded in 1653. The full story that emerged had links with what George Wandesford had managed to accomplish in 1646. George had returned to England with his copy of the will, a copy based on the original that had been admitted to probate on the initiative of cousin William Wandesford and as attested by Sir William Rives. George, '… not having mony to discharge it, the said will was laid by in a chest by the clerk who had writt it out, and ther was secured for severall years of the warre after my brother George died, and non knew what became of it.'[46] This clerk, who remains anonymous, had thus of his own volition removed the original will from the file where it almost certainly would have met the same fate as wills that were retained there. The clerk also had an eye to the future in regard to the administrative confusion that was soon to engulf court offices in Dublin. For he put to one side in this chest not only Christopher Wandesford's will and accompanying probate certificate lodged by the lord deputy's cousin and executor, but also other 'writings' of 'persons of quality' – plainly a form of investment since, when things started to settle down, many other individuals would follow in George Wandesford's footsteps and seek out, and pay for, copies of their ancestors' wills.[47]

The story Alice Thornton tells is that our clerk fell ill and died. He resided in a house kept by a Mr Kerny in Dublin, and knowing on the eve of his death that he still owed his landlord money for his keep – his 'table' – he assured Kerny that the latter would not be out of pocket. Giving into Kerny's charge an iron-bound chest with its key, the clerk pointed out, doubtless to his landlord's surprise, the form of investment that the contents

44 Ibid., p. 183.
45 Ibid., p. 199.
46 Ibid., p. 184 n.
47 Ibid., p. 200.
48 They would be 'of soe great valew that the parties would pay well for them, and that he could not lose by them': ibid.

of the chest represented.[48] On the clerk's death, matters gathered momentum. Kerny inserted the key, opened the chest and found at the bottom 'a large stately writing in five sheets of parchment'. This was soon identified as Lord Deputy Wandesford's missing will. Kerny, to convince himself that this was the genuine article, showed the five sheets to Richard Wallis, one of the witnesses to the will of 1640, to confirm the latter's signature. Wallis reported the find to a second witness, also still living, John Burniston. Burniston informed William Wandesford, the lord deputy's half-brother, and Mettcalfe, who had also been put in the picture, conveyed to Alice's husband William Thornton the 'sircumstances of the strange preservation' of her father's will.[49]

This was not quite the end of the story. Christopher junior, possibly continuing to be pressed by his father-in-law, refused to accept the will found in Ireland as genuine. The consequences were dire, as Alice was to recount:

> The adversarys to it, beeing unwilling to alow soe great a blow to there designe as to enter uppon my father's estate without satisfaction of all dues out of it, therefore was raised in court objectives against us of forgerye and fallshood, with designe to cheat the heire of his estate and right; which suites and charges and objections lasted for severall yeares against my uncle William Wandesford and my deare husband, to the great loss and damage of us all.[50]

One such lawsuit came to the boil in 1658, when in November of that year both Alice Thornton and her mother swore informations in Yorkshire before a master in chancery, a Benjamin Norcliff, regarding the claim to validity of the lord deputy's will of 1640. Attached to these informations in the family muniments consulted by McCall there was found the copy of the will made, following George's return in 1646, in the handwriting successively of George, Christopher and Alice.[51]

Within the Wandesford family a compromise was in fact finally worked out, in 1664, by which time the lord deputy's widow was dead, Christopher junior had been made a baronet, and 'indevours of friends' as Alice Thornton put it, had moved the heart of her brother 'to be inclinable to an end'. The settlement was drawn up by Baron Thorpe (1595–1665), who had served as a baron of the English exchequer under the Commonwealth but had been removed from office in 1660. The settlement was reflected in three deeds briefly described by Alice Thornton in her autobiography.[52]

49 *Autobiography of Alice Thornton*, pp. 201–2.   50 Ibid., p. 202.
51 McCall, *Family of Wandesforde*, pp. 285–6; *Autobiography of Alice Thornton*, p. 184. The lawsuit in question had been initiated by one Nettleton, a creditor of the lord deputy's. The informations were dated 3 Nov. 1658, five years after the rediscovery of the original will in Dublin and 18 years after the lord deputy's death.
52 *Autobiography of Alice Thornton*, p. 203.

To complete one leg of the story, Alice avers that her father's original will was 'againe putt on the file', doubtless back where it belonged, with, she adds, 'all the essential serimoneys belonging to it'.[53] In 1875 it still survived, the single Irish prerogative will from the years 1640 to 1650 to have managed to do so.[54] Alice's verdict on the significance of the ultimate locating of her father's will could not perhaps be bettered: '[h]ad it not bin lost, we had bin lost; and had it not bin found againe, we had bin lost.'[55]

The sept of the Brennans were in no way involved in the dispute within the Wandesford family over the genuineness of Lord Deputy Wandesford's will and testament. Nor did they, in the short term at least, reap any legal advantage from the lord deputy's clearly expressed wish that they should receive compensation for their eviction from the territory of Idough. On the occasion of the rising in the autumn of 1641, however, members of the sept were not slow to act. It was then that they took forcible possession of the lands at Castlecomer, a move that signalled the loss to the Wandesford family for over ten years of the rental income from these lands that they would otherwise have enjoyed. The move thus, naturally, exacerbated the family's financial problems at the time.[56]

The treatment accorded the Brennans in the mid-1630s, understandably, will have rankled. That the lord deputy planned some degree of reparation became known to them, however, and many years later, towards the end of the reign of Charles II, an attempt was made to secure payment of the lord deputy's legacies. In 1679, twenty-two members of the sept filed a bill in chancery against Christopher junior, now Sir Christopher Wandesford, seeking their payment. A Charles Brennan led what was a concerted campaign. Sir Christopher died in March 1686, shortly before the lawsuit was determined. Alice Thornton, now reconciled to her brother's widow, wrote to her about the suit, explaining her father's planned munificence in regard to the Brennans, despite the fact, as she asserted, that the latter had 'no right title'.[57] This can have been little consolation when a few months later, in June 1686, the then Irish lord chancellor, Sir Charles Porter, pronounced in favour of the Brennans. A master in chancery was then appointed to investigate the inheritance, and to determine how the lord chancellor's decree was to be implemented. The matter dragged on, and had not been finally resolved

---

53 Ibid., p. 202.

54 Ibid., p. 202n; the note is by Charles Jackson, who edited the *Autobiography* for the Surtees Society. And see, too, the inclusion of Wandesford's will in Vicars's list: A. Vicars, *Index to the prerogative wills of Ireland, 1536–1810* (Dublin, 1897), p. 475.

55 *Autobiography of Alice Thornton*, p. 204.

56 *Cal. treasury bks.*, x, pt. 2 (1693–96), p. 993; Prendergast, *Ireland from the Restoration to the Revolution*, p. 134.

57 Alice Thornton to Lady Wandesford, her sister-in-law, 21 April 1686: McCall, *Family of Wandesforde*, p. 94.

when, under the regime of Tyrconnell, Sir Christopher's Irish lands were pronounced forfeited. The affair did not end there, however, for when war broke out between James II and William III, the Brennans identified with the losing side. And in 1694 Sir Christopher's heir, yet another Christopher by name, and the lord deputy's grandson, moved successively to have Porter's decree of 1686 set aside, outlawries against the Brennans upheld, and the legacies annulled. What then transpired was that the interests of all the Brennans were held to have been found forfeit by an inquisition held at Kilkenny in May 1694 before the king's escheator and the commissioners of inspection into forfeitures in Ireland. Following which, on 17 April 1695, the lords justices in Ireland were directed to grant the new Sir Christopher crown title to all the lands declared forfeited by the Brennans.[58]

The background to this last controversy over the lord deputy's inheritance is strangely redolent of a short story of Honoré de Balzac. In '*L'interdiction*'[59] the marquise d'Espard seeks to have her husband, the marquis, adjudged a lunatic, incapable of looking after his own and his family's affairs. The precise allegation was that 'the moral and intellectual powers' of the marquis had 'undergone so serious a change, that at the present day they have reached the state of dementia and idiotcy provided for by Article 448 of the Civil Code', and thus required 'the application of the remedies set forth by that article, for the security of his fortune and his person, and to guard the interest of his children whom he keeps to live with him.'[60] The marquise d'Espard had learnt, to her very considerable consternation, that her husband had secretly been paying over the rental income from his property to a Madame Jeanrenaud and her son.[61]

The examining magistrate instructed to carry out inquiries, a Monsieur Popinot, does as he has been bid. He learns that the marquise's allegations are true: these moneys had indeed been paid over to the Jeanrenauds. But there was an explanation which he gathers from the marquis's own lips. And this was nothing to do with a mistress or with being insane. The marquis had learnt of a blot on the family's escutcheon, 'an unconfessed and horrible stain of blood and disgrace'[62] which he was now intent to make it his business to wipe out. The wealth of the d'Espard family was one blighted consequence of the revocation of the edict of Nantes. The circumstances involved actions of singular injustice. 'It is enough to say', the marquis tells Popinot:

---

58 Prendergast, *Ireland from the Restoration to the Revolution*, p. 134; McCall, *Family of Wandesforde*, p. 99; *Cal. treasury bks.*, x, pt. 2 (1693–96), pp. 993–4. The finality of denial of relief to the Brennans was confirmed by s. 57 of the Act of Resumption of 1699, 11 Will III, c.2 (Eng.).

59 The story is called in English 'The commission in lunacy': in *The atheist's mass and other stories* (the Everyman library volume in its series of works by Honoré de Balzac).

60 'The commission in lunacy' in *The atheist's mass*, p. 207.

61 In English fiction, Surtees's creation, Jorrocks, the fox-hunting grocer, was to be proceeded against in similar vein and on similar grounds.

62 'The commission in lunacy', p. 254.

... that the lands of Nègrepelisse, comprising twenty-two churches and rights over the town ... were at [the time of the Revocation] in the hands of a Protestant family. My grandfather recovered them by gift from Louis XIV. This gift was effected by documents hall-marked by atrocious iniquity ... This unfortunate family were named Jeanrenaud.[63]

Popinot had thus got to the bottom of the business, but if this entailed the marquis's escape from his wife's manoeuvres, one would be mistaken. The marquise had friends in high places. Popinot was removed from the investigation but recommended at the same time for the award of the cross of the Legion of Honour. Unlike the Brennans, however, the descendants of this Huguenot family in Balzac's story perhaps faced no spoliation. Before the marquise initiated proceedings, the marquis had already forwarded to the Jeanrenauds a sum which represented the value at the time of what had been taken from them in the reign of Louis XIV: a sum of 1,100,000 francs.[64]

63 Ibid., p. 255.   64 Ibid., p. 257.

A lawyer in politics: the career of
Sir Richard Nagle, *c*.1636–1699

JAMES McGUIRE*

IF THE SEVENTEENTH-CENTURY HOUSE of commons was overwhelmingly representative of the landed elite, it was the lawyers in the house of commons who could articulate the concerns and grievances of rustic gentlemen. It was the lawyers in particular who offered plausible legal or constitutional solutions and gave form and content to the aspirations and demands of parliament. Not all parliamentarians appreciated this role and after the failure of the 1692 parliament, Bishop William King of Derry could blame the members of the house of commons for 'minding the harangues of lawyers too much who could not forget their being for clients and so colouring the sense of their party'.[1] It has only recently become possible to quantify the extent to which members of the Irish parliament in the seventeenth and eighteenth centuries were either practising lawyers or at least the recipients of a legal education.[2] But it has long been clear that lawyers played a significant, often leading, role in parliament in the seventeenth century. Each of the seventeenth-century speakers of the Irish house of commons was a lawyer, at a time when the holder of that office enjoyed a political significance

---

* The edited text of an address given to the Society in Archbishop Marsh's Library, Dublin, on 3 November 2000. The paper was first published in J. Devlin and H.B. Clarke (eds), *European encounters: essays in memory of Albert Lovett* (Dublin, 2003), and is reprinted here by kind permission of UCD Press.

1 Trinity College Dublin (hereafter TCD), Lyons MSS 264 A.
2 For further information on lawyers in parliament and politics in the seventeenth century, see D.F. Cregan, 'Irish recusant lawyers in politics in the reign of James I' in *Ir Jur*, v (1970), 306–20; J. Ohlmeyer, 'Irish recusant lawyers during the reign of Charles I' and B. McGrath, 'Parliament men and the confederate association', both in M. Ó Siochrú, *Kingdoms in crisis* (Dublin, 2001). For invaluable biographical information on MPs and lawyers, *inter alia*, see B. McGrath, 'The membership of the Irish house of commons, 1613–15' (unpublished, M.Litt. thesis, University of Dublin, 1986) and 'A biographical dictionary of the membership of the House of Commons, 1640–41' (unpublished, Ph.D. thesis, University of Dublin, 1997); A. Clark, *Prelude to Restoration in Ireland* (Cambridge, 1999), ch. 6 of which contains a biographical account of all members of the 1660 convention, many of whom went on to sit in the 1661–6 parliament. For lawyer MPs from the 1690s (some of whom sat in the 1661–66 parliament), see the magisterial E.M. Johnston-Liik (ed.), *History of the Irish parliament*, 6 vols (Belfast, 2002).

perhaps comparable, however anachronistically, with a modern speaker of the United States house of representatives.[3] Three of these seventeenth-century speakers were serjeants at law: Sir Nathaniel Catelyn in 1634, Sir Maurice Eustace in 1640 and Sir Audley Mervyn in 1661. Sir Richard Levinge in 1692 was solicitor general. Three were attorneys general: Sir John Davies in 1613, Sir Richard Nagle in 1689 and Robert Rochfort in 1695.[4] Of these lawyers in politics, Nagle is one of the less well known, his obscurity perhaps having more to do with the extent to which success determines posthumous fame, than with the relative importance of the role he actually played. This paper seeks to reconstruct Richard Nagle's career to the extent that the sources allow and attempts an evaluation of its significance for later seventeenth-century Ireland.

Richard Nagle was born *c*.1636 into a prominent Co. Cork family, whose surname is sometimes given as Nangle and occasionally Neagle. The Nagles were an Old English catholic family, whose forebears had lived in the Blackwater valley in north Co. Cork since the early fourteenth century. Richard was the second of at least five sons of James Nagle of Clenor and his wife Honora, one of the Nugents of Aghanagh, also in Co. Cork.[5] By the time Richard was born, Old English families such as the Nagles had, to their great resentment, lost to the protestant New English those places of 'honour, profit and trust'[6] which they regarded as their birthright. They were still in the 1630s substantial landowners, though that too was soon to change in the aftermath of the confederate wars. James Nagle, Richard's father, forfeited his estate under the Commonwealth, though after the Restoration he was again living in Co. Cork, this time at Annakissy.

A second son, Richard, grew to adulthood at an unpropitious time for the catholic gentry. He was said to have been educated by the Jesuits, and may have been intended for the priesthood,[7] but there are no career details for the 1650s. Three years after the restoration of the monarchy, he turned to the law, seemingly the first member of his family to do so in the seventeenth century, and in 1663, at the comparatively late age of twenty-seven, he was

---

3 In England the situation was largely similar: twenty of the speakers who served from the beginning of the seventeenth century to the 1689 convention were lawyers by profession, another had attended at the Middle Temple, and only two appear to have had no legal education. See D.L. Smith, *The Stuart parliaments, 1603–1689* (London, 1999), pp. 243–4.

4 For a list of speakers of the Irish house of commons, see T.W. Moody et al. (eds), *A new history of Ireland, vol. ix: maps, genealogies, lists* (1984), p. 537.

5 B. O'Connell, 'The Nagles of Garnavilla' in *Irish Genealogist*, iii:1 (1956), 17–24; 'The Nagles of Mount Nagle' in *Irish Genealogist*, ii:12 (1955), 377–89; 'The Nagles of Annakissy' in *Irish Genealogist*, ii:11 (1954), 337–48.

6 D.F. Cregan, 'The confederate catholics of Ireland: the personnel of the confederation, 1642–9' in *IHS*, xxix (1994–5), 508.

7 [William King], *The state of the protestants of Ireland under the late King James's government* (London, 1691), p. 83.

admitted to Gray's Inn which, before the upheavals of the 1640s and the 1650s, had traditionally attracted Irish and recusant applicants.[8] Five years later he was called by King's Inns to the Irish bar.[9] In 1669 he married Joan Kearney of Fethard, Co. Tipperary, whose sister would later marry his elder brother Pierce.[10] They lived at Carrigacunna, a Nagle property in Co. Cork, and from 1684 in Dublin. As a barrister he appeared for both protestant and catholic clients, and clearly built up a reputation which later hostile pamphleteers willingly conceded: 'a cunning Irish lawyer ... he was a man of great parts, educated among the Jesuits and therefore very inveterate'.[11] Bishop William King would later write that Nagle studied law to 'a good perfection' and appeared for many protestants 'so that he knew the weak part of their titles'.[12] Sporadic glimpses of his legal practice can be seen in contemporary correspondence.[13] As it expanded he acquired more land in north Cork and Waterford and the extent of his earned wealth is evident from substantial loans which he had the funds to make, in 1683 (£1,800) and 1686 (£2,000), and which are recorded in the Dublin statute staple.[14] In 1686 he could tell the lord lieutenant that no chief justice's place 'would equal his present gains which he must consider because of his great charge of children', which now amounted to seven sons and six daughters.[15]

Nagle's involvement in politics began in 1686, a year after James II's accession. Initially he appeared as a reluctant participant. At least that was how it seemed to the hapless viceroy, the second earl of Clarendon, whose correspondence during 1686 provides the most frequent references to Nagle's growing involvement in public affairs, an involvement which invariably rests on his role as legal advisor for dispossessed catholic landowners. After their first meeting in February, when Nagle had brought him a petition for reversal of outlawries from Lord Gormanston and other catholic petitioners, Clarendon wrote of him with comparative warmth: 'a Roman Catholic, and a man of the best repute for learning as well as honesty

---

8 *The register of admissions to Gray's Inn, 1521–1889* (London, 1889); D.F. Cregan, 'Irish Catholic admissions to the English inns of court 1558–1625' in *Ir Jur*, v (1970), 95–114.

9 E. Keane et al. (eds), *King's Inns admission papers* (Dublin, 1982), p. 360.

10 O'Connell, 'Nagles of Annakissy' , p. 348.

11 *A full and impartial account of all the secret consults, negotiations, stratagems, and intriegues* (sic) *of the Romish party in Ireland, from 1660, to this present year 1689, for the settlement of popery in that kingdom* (2nd ed., London, 1690), p. 55.

12 [King], *State of the Protestants*, p. 83.

13 BL, Add. MSS 46958, ff. 17–20: correspondence between Richard Nagle, 'counsellor at law' and Sir J. Perceval of Co. Cork, 1681; NLI, Orrery papers on microfilm: Richard Nagle's opinion on the will of the late earl of Orrery.

14 J. Ohlmeyer and É. Ó Ciardha (eds), *The Irish statute staple books, 1596–1687* (Dublin, 1998), p. 127.

15 *Cal. S. P. Dom., 1686–7*, p. 153; O'Connell, 'Nagles of Annakissy', p. 337.

Sir Richard Nagle (1635/6–1699), portrait by an unknown artist. Photograph courtesy of the
National Gallery of Ireland.

amongst that people'.[16] That initial impression remained for some months, and was not even shaken by Nagle's nomination at Whitehall to the Irish privy council along with ten other, mostly catholic names, whose appointment required dispensation from taking the oath of supremacy.[17]

More telling perhaps, though Clarendon does not seem to have averted to it in his correspondence, was the fact that Nagle's nomination can only have come from advice tendered by Richard Talbot, earl of Tyrconnell, and that his nomination suggested that Nagle was to be part of Tyrconnell's emerging plans to replace protestants with catholics in positions of both civil and military significance. Clarendon, however, found more professional reasons for disapproval, which he expressed to the earl of Sunderland, the secretary of state at Whitehall:

> ... he is a very learned and honest man, but I beg leave to observe to your lordship that he is a practising lawyer and I doubt will think it hard to quit his profession for that which brings no advantage, though it will be a great honour, for it will not look well that a man who has the honour to be of the King's privy council should be crowding at the bar of the chief justice bare-headed and his bag in his hand ... but I will speak with Mr Nagle tomorrow and let him know the king's gracious intentions towards him.[18]

To Clarendon's manifest approval Nagle turned down the offer of a seat on the privy council, making it clear that it was not a position for which he had lobbied. As Clarendon reported to Sunderland: 'he [Nagle] was extremely surprised and wonders his friends will move in his behalf without first consulting himself; he tells me to leave his practice will be his ruin, and to appear at the bar after he is a councillor will be very indecent, even for the king's service'.[19] He asked, however, that he might keep the formal letter of appointment 'as a mark of the king's grace and favour'.[20]

Nagle's refusal of a seat on the privy council came just days before Tyrconnell's arrival in early June with a commission to be commander-in-chief of the army in Ireland (a humiliating snub for Clarendon, who was being deprived of one of the traditional viceregal functions). And soon Nagle's growing political engagement with Tyrconnell became apparent even to the trusting and beleaguered Clarendon. If Tyrconnell's formal commission was

---

16 Clarendon to earl of Rochester, 27 Feb. 1686, in S.W. Singer (ed.), *The correspondence of Henry Hyde, earl of Clarendon, and his brother, Laurence Hyde, earl of Rochester, with the diary of Lord Clarendon from 1687 to 1690*, 2 vols (London, 1828), i, p. 273; (hereafter cited as *Clarendon correspondence*).

17 *Cal. S. P. Dom., 1686–7*, pp. 117–18; HMC, *Ormonde MSS*, new series, vii, 423.

18 *Cal. S. P. Dom., 1686–7*, p. 147.

19 Ibid., p. 153.   20 *Clarendon correspondence*, i, p. 445.

to reform the army (which meant purging protestants and appointing catholics), he was quick to raise the cause of the dispossessed catholic proprietors, with which he had been associated since the 1660s. Both Sunderland at Whitehall and Clarendon in Dublin Castle had recognised that, with a catholic king on the throne and Tyrconnell's political power in the ascendant, catholic expectations would inevitably focus on a significant modification of the restoration land acts, with all the consequences that would entail for the protestant political nation which had emerged over the preceding thirty years. To head off the inevitable catholic demands for amending legislation in a new Irish parliament, they sought instead a commission of grace under which catholic proprietors, or ex-proprietors, who had fared badly under the 1660s settlement would be financially compensated from a fund to which protestant proprietors would contribute in return for confirmation of their land titles.[21] Tyrconnell was clearly determined to thwart this stratagem. He saw it as imperative to preserve his freedom of action so that, on his return to Whitehall in the autumn, he might press for the summoning of an Irish parliament to pass amending legislation. The disadvantaged catholic proprietors wanted land, not monetary compensation.

As the summer advanced, Nagle's role as Tyrconnell's adviser became increasingly apparent. In late July it was noted in Dublin Castle that he had been present at a three-hour meeting between Tyrconnell and the catholic primate, Archbishop Dominic Maguire.[22] When Tyrconnell went to see Clarendon to arrange a consultation on what Clarendon called 'our great affair', he asked that Nagle should be present, along with Major-General Justin MacCarthy, Lord Chief Justice Keating and the solicitor general.[23] Soon after, Clarendon invited both Nagle and Lord Chancellor Porter to dinner, after which Nagle, somewhat disingenuously, told Clarendon that Tyrconnell had told him 'something' of Clarendon's plans for a commission of grace, and had asked him to prepare something on it in writing. But in the conversation which followed, Nagle left the viceroy in no doubt about what his opinion would be:

> ... he could not believe a commission would be useful, or that it would bring in any money considerable; that whatever should be thought fit to be done, either for confirming the present settlements, or for the relief of such of the old proprietors as ought to be relieved, would be done best by parliament; but that he thought it was yet too soon to think of calling a parliament; that many things were necessary first to be done, and even the acts ought first to be prepared and agreed on;

21 R. Bagwell, *Ireland under the Stuarts*, 3 vols (London, 1909–16), iii, pp. 169–70.
22 Clarendon to Rochester, 31 July 1686: *Clarendon correspondence*, i, p. 514.
23 Ibid.

which he owned would take up very much time, for the several interests
ought to be first felt [?] and discoursed with, that is, some of the most
considerable of them; and till he had done that and fully weighed
things (for there were many difficulties in the way) he could not put
anything into writing tho' my Lord Tyrconnell was in great haste.[24]

This passage has been quoted at length as it shows the extent to which Nagle,
the well-briefed catholic barrister, had become not only a legal adviser but a
political strategist for Tyrconnell and the catholic interest. The strategy he
unfolded was the strategy that Tyrconnell and he would follow over the
coming twelve months. Any doubts about Nagle's political commitment that
Clarendon may have had before this after-dinner conversation were now
unsustainable. In the light of what he had just heard, he told his brother
Rochester that the forthcoming conference with Tyrconnell would allow him
to see 'what these people drive at', though he could hardly have been in much
doubt. He added rather lamely: 'I will keep them to the point; that is, that Mr
Nagle and his people shall set down what they would have, and what they
would think fit for the king to do'.[25]

The weakness of Clarendon's position was made humiliatingly clear a
week later on 7 August, the day arranged for the conference on the land
question. It was to have started at 10.00 a.m., but only the lord chancellor, Sir
Charles Porter, and the solicitor general, Sir John Temple, showed up.
Tyrconnell arrived three hours late and full of excuses, but without Nagle.
When asked where he was, he replied: '[f]aith, my lord, it is very late: we
cannot talk much now. Mr Nangle, I believe, is not so ready as he will be a
few days hence'. Asked by Clarendon to propose a day when Nagle would be
ready, Tyrconnell suggested the following Friday.[26] When the plenary
meeting eventually took place, Nagle admitted that he had drawn up nothing,
and that 'many things were to be considered of before matters could be put
into writing'. But he did tell them that both he and Chief Baron Rice were of
the opinion that a commission would do nothing, bring in a very small sum
of money, if any, and confirm those estates which ought not to be confirmed.
At this point both Tyrconnell and MacCarthy 'closed with that [Nagle's]
opinion with much vehemence'.[27] Looking back at these events a month later,
Clarendon chose to represent Nagle's reluctance to engage with contrary
opinions as a sign of weakness: 'with all his learning and skill he could not
confute the reasons of those who differed with him, by any other arguments,
than the single saying he was of another opinion'.[28] But clearly Nagle and

---

24 Ibid., pp. 515–16.   25 Ibid., p. 516.
26 Clarendon to Rochester, 7 Aug. 1686: *Clarendon correspondence*, i, pp. 524–6.
27 Clarendon to Sunderland, 14 Aug. 1686: *Clarendon correspondence*, i, pp. 537–9.
28 HMC, *Ormonde MSS*, vii, 461: Clarendon to the duke of Ormond.

Tyrconnell were keeping their arguments for Whitehall, where ultimate power lay. There was no advantage to be gained by revealing their position to an increasingly enfeebled Dublin Castle administration which they hoped soon to replace.

Nagle's commitment to the Tyrconnell enterprise, and the centrality of his role in it, were underlined soon after the Dublin Castle conference when he accompanied Tyrconnell on his return to Whitehall. Before setting out he told Clarendon, whose political talents he could not be accused of over-estimating, that he was going to England purely for health reasons.[29] Ineffective Clarendon may have been, but he had no doubt about Nagle's purpose. He was quick to warn those with an interest in Irish land of the news that Nagle would be accompanying Tyrconnell to court and of its likely import. As he told his brother Rochester: he 'is a very able man and therefore more to be watched'.[30] Nagle's increasingly pivotal role heightened the already anxious political atmosphere among the protestant interest in Ireland. Lord Longford told the duke of Ormond: '[t]he English are much alarmed at my Lord Tyrconnell's carrying over Mr Nagle with him, which they conjecture, and will not be persuaded out of it, his lordship has done with a design to prevail upon his Majesty to call a parliament here in order to the breaking of the Acts of Settlement and Explanation'.[31] And why, Sir Robert Southwell asked rhetorically of Sir William Petty, was 'Mr Nagle, the great surveyor of Ireland' in London?[32]

But opinion at Whitehall was not so easily convinced that it was either possible or desirable to modify the land settlement by means of a new act of parliament. And there was open scepticism about Tyrconnell's unconcealed ambition to be viceroy in place of Clarendon. In this climate Nagle seems at first to have been cold-shouldered and, if an admittedly hostile pamphleteer is to be believed, had to wait 'some time e'er [he] could gain admittance to kiss the king's hand', spending the meantime with Fr Petre and 'the rest of that furious cabal'.[33] The prevailing view at Whitehall, argued by Sunderland, the secretary of state, was that a declaration confirming the acts of settlement and explanation would be needed should Tyrconnell prevail on the King to appoint him viceroy. This of course would tie Tyrconnell's hands.[34] The means devised by Tyrconnell and Nagle to thwart Sunderland's plan was the Coventry letter.

---

29 Ibid., 449: Clarendon to the duke of Ormond, 28 Aug. 1686.
30 *Clarendon correspondence*, i, p. 555.
31 HMC, *Ormonde MSS*, vii, 449–50.
32 Marquis of Lansdowne (ed.), *Petty-Southwell correspondence* (reprint ed., New York, 1967), p. 233.
33 *A full and impartial account of all the secret consults*, p. 54.
34 J.G. Simms, *Jacobite Ireland 1685–91* (London, 1969), p. 31.

The Coventry letter was in effect a manuscript pamphlet written by Nagle in which he argued robustly, though anonymously, against any royal declaration confirming the existing settlement.[35] What was needed, ran the argument, was a new Irish land act, which would restore many 'innocent' catholics whose cases had not been heard by the court of claims in the 1660s. For catholics in Ireland the unique opportunity offered by a co-religionist on the throne must not be lost. Nothing could support the catholic religion in that kingdom, but to make catholics there considerable in their fortunes, which was an argument clearly designed to prick the conscience of the pious James II.

Ostensibly written by Nagle on 26 October, during an insomniac night in Coventry on his return journey to Ireland, the letter had all the appearances of having been carefully drafted while Nagle was still in London. Indeed it is likely that its origins lay in Nagle's undisclosed ruminations in the summer, though the device of a letter from Coventry may have been suggested by the political situation Tyrconnell and Nagle found at Whitehall. Among protestants, as word got out about its contents and manuscript copies were gradually passed around, it became notorious and added to that sense of uncertainty which the beneficiaries of the restoration settlement increasingly felt. Indeed Sir William Petty immediately wrote a ten-page reply, which was never published. In the short term the Coventry letter achieved its immediate objective and put paid to Sunderland's plans for a royal declaration to accompany the announcement of Tyrconnell's appointment as viceroy. But despite this significant, if limited success, Nagle found it politic to disown authorship, letting it be known on his return to Dublin that 'he would arrest any man in an action of ten thousand pound, who should father it on him', a threat which very likely explains Petty's sardonic comment to Southwell: '[h]ere is an answer of 10 sheets to the "Coventry letter" – we must not say Mr Nagle's'.[36]

With Tyrconnell's formal appointment as lord deputy in January 1687, Nagle moved from being an influential strategist for the catholic interest to being part of the new viceroy's administration. Two days after being sworn in, Tyrconnell appointed him attorney general in succession to Sir William Domville, who had held the post since 1661.[37] In becoming attorney general, Nagle was taking a position which, in the latter half of the seventeenth century, had superseded in importance, if not in precedence, the post of prime serjeant. Besides giving legal advice the attorney general by the 1680s was responsible for instituting and pursuing proceedings on behalf of the

35 HMC, *Ormonde MSS*, vii, 464–7; J.T. Gilbert (ed.), *A Jacobite narrative of the war in Ireland*, (Dublin, 1892), appendix, pp. 193–201.

36 *A full and impartial account of all the secret consults*, p. 55; Lansdowne, *Petty–Southwell correspondence*, p. 271.

37 J.L. Hughes (ed.), *Patentee officers in Ireland, 1173–1826* (Dublin, 1960), p. 95; Nagle's patent was dated 15 Feb. 1687.

crown.[38] The implications for protestant Ireland of Nagle's being attorney general were anticipated with anxiety and glee, the latter most triumphantly in Dáibhidh Ó Bruadair's 'Caithréim an dara Séamuis' ('The triumph of King James').[39]

From the beginning of the new viceroyalty Nagle was a member of what Thomas Sheridan, Tyrconnell's somewhat semi-detached chief secretary, called the lord deputy's 'cabinet'.[40] Given a knighthood on his appointment as attorney general, he lost no time in implementing the strategy outlined to Clarendon the previous summer.[41] On 12 February, the day Tyrconnell was sworn in, he lodged an information against the City of Dublin concerning their claims to certain liberties and franchises.[42] It was an early indication of what would occupy his attention in the coming months, reforming borough charters. The *quo warranto* challenges, which Nagle as attorney general orchestrated throughout Ireland, where necessary taking recalcitrant boroughs to court, were designed to restore local government to the previously ousted catholic elite while at the same time ensuring that borough representation in the anticipated parliament would be predominantly catholic.[43] Closely linked with these proceedings was the appointment of catholic sheriffs, which Nagle, along with Thomas Nugent and Stephen Rice, both recent appointees to the bench, strongly urged and with success.[44]

The main purpose of the anticipated parliament, the substantial modification of the restoration land acts, was never in doubt. Policy and its implementation in the first six months of Tyrconnell's government were clearly the means to that end, though the lord deputy could not openly announce his intentions. While the catholicisation of the army, the boroughs, the judiciary and other civil offices was perfected, the land question as such remained off the agenda, at least until Tyrconnell travelled to Chester in August 1687 to meet the king. Nagle accompanied him to what was apparently intended as a meeting to discuss the state of the Irish revenue and its administration. What emerged was far more significant: the sidelining of Thomas Sheridan, Tyrconnell's secretary and first commissioner of the

---

38 A.R. Hart, *History of the king's serjeants at law in Ireland* (Dublin, 2000), pp. 51–2.

39 J.C. Mac Erlean (ed.), *Duanaire Dáibhidh Uí Bhruadair: the poems of David Ó Bruadair*, pt. III (London, 1917), pp. 88–9; see É. Ó Ciardha, *Ireland and the Jacobite cause, 1685–1766: a fatal attachment* (Dublin, 2002), p. 77.

40 HMC, *Stuart papers*, vi, 18.

41 HMC, *Ormonde MSS*, viii, 349.

42 *Calendar of the Clarendon state papers*, 5 vols (Oxford, 1970), v, 672.

43 *A full and impartial account of all the secret consults*, pp. 79, 85; *Clarendon state papers*, v, 678; J. Hill, *From patriots to unionists: Dublin civic politics and Irish protestant patriotism, 1660–1840* (Oxford, 1997), pp. 59–60; Simms, *Jacobite Ireland*, pp. 35–6; Hart, *History of king's serjeants*, p. 52.

44 HMC, *Stuart papers*, vi, 18.

revenue, in which Nagle had some role, and secondly, and more fundamentally, permission to consider and recommend substantial amendments to the restoration land settlement.[45] Tyrconnell and Nagle returned to Dublin with James's permission to have alternative bills prepared to modify the restoration land acts.

The extent of Nagle's involvement in the subsequent drafting of these bills can be inferred from the office he now held and the role he had played in 1686 in providing the intellectual justification for new legislation. But it is important to stress that the far-reaching repeal legislation, enacted in very changed circumstances in the Jacobite parliament two years later, bore little resemblance to the bills drafted in Dublin over the winter of 1687–8. One of these drafts provided for claims of innocence not heard by the original court of claims to be reopened, with monetary compensation for any Cromwellian settlers who lost out in the process. The other draft, apparently favoured by Tyrconnell, provided that all estates in contention should be divided equally between old and new proprietors, with the latter allowed to retain all improvements made since the 1650s.[46] Either of these bills, if enacted, would have met the expectations of the old proprietors while leaving intact a substantial amount of land in protestant ownership.

When the draft bills were taken to London in March 1688, Nagle did not travel with them. That was left to Sir Stephen Rice and Chief Justice Nugent, though both Nagle and Rice were alleged to have advised against the unimpressive Nugent's appointment as emissary. According to the well-informed anonymous author of *The secret consults of the Romish party in Ireland*, either Nagle or Rice told the author that Nugent was 'good for nothing but to spoil a business'.[47] Whatever fears there may have been about Nugent's suitability for the task, the delegation seems to have convinced Whitehall by May that a bill should be prepared on the lines of the compromise enshrined in the Tyrconnell draft.

The whole enterprise came to a sudden halt in the summer of 1688 with the crisis of James's monarchy. After the king had gone into exile, Nagle was alleged to have been involved in 'a Jesuitical stratagem' to have a delegation sent to the exiled court seeking James II's permission for terms to be made with Prince William of Orange.[48] Certainly there were brief contacts but they may have had no more significance than a desire by Tyrconnell to play for time sufficient to assess the prospects for a Jacobite stand in Dublin.

45 Ibid., 28, 36; Bagwell, *Ireland under the Stuarts*, iii, p. 172; J. Miller, 'Thomas Sheridan (1646–1712), and his "Narrative" ' in *IHS*, xx (1976), 105 at pp. 120–1; J. Miller, 'The earl of Tyrconnell and James II's Irish policy, 1685–1688' in *Historical Journal*, xx (1977), 803–23.
46 Simms, *Jacobite Ireland*, pp. 40–1.
47 *A full and impartial account of all the secret consults*, p. 115.
48 Ibid., p. 146.

When James II came to Ireland the following spring, Nagle was at the height of his power and influence. He was continued in office as attorney general.[49] The parliament which met in May was returned on the basis of Nagle's handiwork in remodelling the borough charters, and Nagle was himself returned for Co. Cork (of which his brother Pierce was sheriff); at the same time his younger brother David became a member for Mallow.[50] Another brother, James, was appointed sergeant-at-arms to the commons (and later clerk and engrosser of chancery writs).[51] On 7 May, the day parliament assembled, Richard was elected to the speakership, effectively a government appointment if seventeenth-century precedents in both England and Ireland are taken into account.[52]

Nagle's role as speaker is difficult to reconstruct. The 1689 parliamentary journals were burned by the common hangman in 1695 and the accounts of the parliament that survive deal mostly with proceedings in the house of lords. Glimpses of the proceedings can be gleaned from other sources, such as the reports of the French ambassador, comte d'Avaux. One of his despatches described how Nagle successfully headed off an attempt by MPs to have the house send its thanks to Louis XIV for his military support, arguing that this was a matter for James II, not the commons.[53] Williamite accounts quite reasonably blamed Nagle for legislation which, in repealing the restoration land acts and attainting over 2,000 substantial protestants, went much further than anything Nagle had actually planned or envisaged in 1687–8. He was after all both chief law officer of the crown (even if the prime serjeant technically took precedence) and the author of the Coventry letter. The proviso in the act of attainder putting it 'out of the king's power' to pardon protestants was apparently attributed to Nagle's 'malice and jesuitical principles', though Conor Cruise O'Brien has quite ingeniously seen it as evidence of the conditional character of catholic loyalty to the crown, suggesting that in 1689 the catholic MPs were the 'true whigs'.[54]

With the prorogation of parliament in July, Nagle's role in the Jacobite administration became increasingly significant. In August, when the earl of Melfort was effectively forced to resign as secretary for war, the French

49 HMC, *Stuart papers*, i, 40.
50 A list of members returned to the house of commons is printed in *An exact list of the lords spiritual and temporal who sat in the pretended parliament at Dublin* (London, 1689); see J.G. Simms, *The Jacobite parliament of 1689* (Dundalk, 1966), appendix.
51 HMC, *Stuart papers*, i, 42, 45.
52 Smith, *The Stuart parliaments*, p. 79. The exception to the rule in Ireland was the election of Sir Audley Mervyn in 1661, when Dublin Castle had made known its preference for Sir William Domville, the attorney general.
53 Bagwell, *Ireland under the Stuarts*, iii, 224.
54 C. Cruise O'Brien, *The great melody: a thematic biography of Edmund Burke* (London, 1992), pp. 16–17.

James McGuire

ambassador, D'Avaux, was astonished that Melfort should be replaced by the militarily inexperienced Nagle, '*un habile homme pour les affaires de droit, mais qui est si neuf dans celle de la guerre qu'il n'en a pas les premiers éléments*'.[55] The king weekly defended himself to the ambassador on the grounds that he could not withstand the continual importuning of the Irish.[56] As might be expected the clever and adaptable Nagle threw himself with enthusiasm into his new duties, preparing army lists and equipping the Jacobite forces for now imminent war.[57] And even the sceptical D'Avaux seems to have been won around, writing to Louis XIV the following February of '*une grande union entre le duc de Tirconnel, le chevalier Negle et moy*'.[58]

Despite defeat at the Boyne and James II's hasty departure for France, the war was not yet over, as William III's subsequent failure at the first siege of Limerick showed. In September 1690, when Tyrconnell travelled to France for consultations with both James and the French government, Nagle either accompanied him or followed on soon after. They returned to Ireland together in January 1691, landing at Galway, and with a meagre £8,000 from Louis XIV travelled on to Limerick.[59] Nagle resumed his duties as secretary of state for war and attorney general, but little is discernible of his role or influence over the succeeding months when Jacobite politics in Ireland was deeply divided, over seeking peace or continuing the war, between the followers of Patrick Sarsfield and Tyrconnell. As the unsympathetic Charles O'Kelly put it in his allegorical account of the war, Tyrconnell had 'returned to Ireland better prepared to manage a treaty than to continue the war; for the chief Cyprian [Irish] gownmen [lawyers] who fled into Syria [France] after the battle of Lapithus [the Boyne] were now returned with their patron'.[60] On Tyrconnell's death in August 1691, which Nagle described as 'a fatal stroke to this poor country in this nick of time', a sealed commission from James II came into effect, appointing Nagle, Alexander Fitton, the Jacobite lord chancellor, and Francis Plowden, commissioner of the revenue, as lords justices.[61] They seem, however, to have had no significant part in the treaty negotiations of late September and early October. The senior law officer on the Jacobite side was in fact James II's solicitor general for Ireland,

55 J. Hogan (ed.), *Négociations de M. le comte d'Avaux en Irlande, 1689–90* (Dublin, 1934), p. 445.
56 Ibid., pp. 429–30.
57 J. D'Alton, *Illustrations, historical and genealogical, of King James's army list (1689)* (Limerick and Kansas, 1997), pp. 893–4; Simms, *Jacobite Ireland*, p. 133.
58 *Négociations de M. le comte d'Avaux*, p. 623.
59 T. Crofton Croker (ed.), *Narratives illustrative of the contests in Ireland in 1641 and 1690* (London, 1841), p. 132.
60 C. O'Kelly, 'Macariae excidium or the destruction of Cyprus' in Croker, *Narratives illustrative of the contests in Ireland*, p. 74.
61 P.W. Sergeant, *Little Jennings and fighting Dick Talbot: a life of the duke and duchess of Tyrconnell*, 2 vols (London, 1913), i, 561; Simms, *Jacobite Ireland*, p. 242.

Sir Theobald (Toby) Butler. By November Nagle was on his way into permanent exile in France. Outlawed since October 1689 by the court of king's bench in London, Nagle forfeited his estate when Co. Cork was taken by the Williamite army and it was subsequently granted to Viscount Sydney, William III's lord lieutenant of Ireland.[62]

Throughout the 1690s, Nagle remained in James II's service at St Germain. He is referred to in court correspondence as secretary for war and attorney general for Ireland up to his death in 1699, though it is clear from the Stuart papers that his duties were not confined to Irish business.[63] He was inevitably drawn into disputes at the exiled court, in particular with Thomas Sheridan, over the strategy to be adopted for a Jacobite restoration.[64] He continued, nonetheless, to enjoy the king's confidence to the extent that James appointed him a commissioner of the royal household in 1698 and nominated him in his will as a member of a council to advise the queen on the guardianship of the prince of Wales.[65] In fact Nagle predeceased the king by two years, dying at St Germain-en-Laye on 4 April 1699.[66]

Nagle's is one of those careers that faded into obscurity at an early stage. Indeed it was only in the 1930s that his death date was discovered by Richard Hayes, his entry in the *Dictionary of National Biography* assigning him only *floruit* dates. Yet, in his day, his role was of central importance to the revival of the catholic interest. Without its revival, made possible through the accident of a catholic monarch, he might have lived out his days as an able and increasingly wealthy counsel at the Irish bar. But he could not resist the allure of politics. In that respect he resembles and is comparable with another seventeenth-century lawyer, Sir Audley Mervyn, the eloquent defender of the protestant interest.[67] Both were senior law officers of the crown, one as prime serjeant under Charles II, the other as attorney general under James. Both were speakers of the house of commons. For his part Nagle may have had more practical experience as a practising counsel than had Mervyn, but both of them used their positions under the crown to serve the interest out of which they came. Both their careers ended in relative obscurity, though Mervyn at least enjoyed his estates.[68]

62 J.G. Simms, *The Williamite confiscation in Ireland, 1690–1703* (London, 1956), pp. 32–3; *Cal. S. P. Dom., 1693*, pp. 2–3.

63 HMC, *Stuart papers*, i, 68, 109, 110, 127–8; ii, 88.

64 V. Geoghegan, 'Thomas Sheridan: toleration and royalism' in D. George Boyce et al. (eds), *Political discourse in seventeenth and eighteenth-century Ireland* (Basingstoke and New York, 2001), p. 46.

65 HMC, *Stuart papers*, i, 127–8.

66 R. Hayes, 'Biographical dictionary of Irishmen in France' in *Studies*, xxxiv (1945), 109.

67 A.R. Hart, 'Audley Mervyn: lawyer or politician' in W.N. Osborough (ed.), *Explorations in law and history* (Dublin, 1995), pp. 83–105.

68 I am very grateful to Professor Jane Ohlmeyer for her helpful advice in the preparation of this paper.

Dicey and the sovereignty of parliament: lessons from Irish legal history

JOHN McELDOWNEY*

Summary

DICEY'S ANALYSIS OF LEGAL SOVEREIGNTY remains an invaluable source for our understanding of an important doctrine of British constitutional law. Dicey developed his thinking through an analysis of John Austin and an obsessional interest in protecting the Act of Union with Ireland. Dicey's belief in the Union became a political passion in his writing, and through a study of his analysis of the Irish question it is possible to have a clearer understanding of his attitudes to sovereignty.

INTRODUCTION

Professor Dicey's lectures, later to form the basis of his influential *Law of the constitution*, provided the first substantial legal analysis of the constitution of the United Kingdom in 1885.[1] The focus of this paper is Dicey's analysis of sovereignty and the influences that gave rise to his analysis. The two major biographies of Dicey, published around the time of the centenary of his major work on the constitution, provide a useful insight into his under-standing of the constitution. Dicey's papers in the Bodleian Library, Oxford, are also useful. Taken together with his extensive publications on the Irish question, they help to reveal how Dicey's ideas were shaped and how he was influenced by his early education and training at Oxford. Dicey's concerns about Irish nationalism led him to fear the break-up of the Union and although this may have been exaggerated in the various polemical texts published at the time, polemical arguments entered into his consciousness and held sway. Despite the claim that his *Law of the constitution* was a

---

*   This is a revised version of an address given to the Society in the judges' assembly rooms, Royal Courts of Justice, Belfast, on 6 May 2005.

1   A.V. Dicey, *Lectures introductory to the study of the law of the constitution* (London, 1885). See J.F. McEldowney, 'Dicey in historical perspective – a review essay' in P. McAuslan and J.F. McEldowney (eds), *Law, legitimacy and the constitution* (London, 1985), pp. 39–61.

Albert Venn Dicey. Portrait in oils by Désiré-François Laugée, 1872. Photograph reproduced by kind permission of the Master and Fellows of Trinity College, Oxford.

'scientific' study of the British constitution,[2] the study was greatly influenced by Dicey's own personal beliefs and opinions, held with a strong evangelical conviction and defended with remarkable determination and zeal.

THEMES AND IDEAS

Dicey's recognition, over one hundred years ago in *Law of the constitution*, of the sovereignty of parliament, the rule of law and conventions as the three pillars of the constitution, has endured. Since the seventeenth century there had been a traditional belief that the sovereignty of parliament was one of the fundamental doctrines of constitutional law in the United Kingdom. Dicey's influence ensured that the doctrine of parliamentary sovereignty survived as a legal principle, enforceable by the courts, and through his remarkable influence it entered into the constitutional, legal and political life of the nation. The acceptance of the sovereignty of parliament by the judges inhibited them from having a major constitutional role and ensured a general deference to parliament and its electoral mandate representing the people. This paper considers Dicey's understanding of sovereignty and particularly how his attitude to Ireland and the Act of Union 1800, and his belief that nationhood was defined by legal as well as political sovereignty, influenced his analysis of the constitution. His motivation was that any weakening of sovereignty might imperil the authority of the state itself.

It is clear that Dicey's understanding of legal sovereignty defined the United Kingdom as a state and established its legality in international law. It also underpins the political process, and as an institution parliament's forum for political debate and accountability defines government itself. Parliamentary sovereignty may appear at times to threaten judicial independence. This requires a degree of judicial self-restraint that avoids conflict between the judiciary and the executive. This may ultimately protect judicial power by defining the political process whereby laws and legislation are passed in a political framework, rather than through any reliance on judicial legislation. Dicey's attitudes to sovereignty were shaped by many events in Ireland and his concerns about the fragmentation of the United Kingdom. His visit with James Bryce to the United States and his attitudes to Gladstone's plans for home rule shaped his concern that the Irish question held the key to preventing the disintegration of the United Kingdom.

It is timely to consider Dicey's analysis today as the nature of sovereignty has been adjusted with membership of the European Union. It has been difficult to reconcile this adjustment with the time-honoured assertion that

---

2   Bryce to William Gladstone, 31 Oct. 1884: Bryce papers, Bodleian Library, Oxford. See
    R.A. Cosgrove, *The rule of law: Albert Venn Dicey, Victorian jurist* (London, 1980), p. 69.

parliament may not bind its successors or create limitations on its own power and authority. The courts in terms of community law must disapply an act of the United Kingdom parliament to the extent that it may conflict with community laws. While the Human Rights Act 1998 reserves the form of parliamentary authority, it allows the courts to declare that legislation is incompatible with the European Convention on Human Rights. However, it remains an important doctrine to reconcile historical continuity with the changing nature of the constitution. The flexibility of the United Kingdom's constitution may ultimately have to address the question of defining sovereignty in modern times – this may require a written constitution for the United Kingdom. As the executive and the judiciary struggle over the limitations on their respective powers, parliament may have to be open to a gradual dilution of sovereignty to a shared notion of legitimacy whereby the courts, in common with a supreme court under a written constitution, assert their role in defining the boundaries of political and legal power. Dicey's legacy that flows from his legal and political understanding of the constitution may be considered in another form to face the needs of contemporary society that countenances gradual change.

DICEY, THE MAN AND HIS TIMES

Albert Venn Dicey[3] was born on 4 February 1835, at Claybrook Hall, near Lutterworth in Northamptonshire, one of four brothers. From birth he suffered from muscular weakness, a problem that arose because he was premature and due to some medical errors at his birth. This was to affect him in later life. Dicey was physically tall and his angular figure suffered from muscular spasms which were difficult to control. His early life was dominated by poor health and his physical weakness. Under the influence of his mother he was educated at home until the age of 17. His strict evangelical background taught him self-discipline and dedication to scholastic endeavour. His family background brought him into contact with two of the great families of the Victorian era – the Venns and notably the evangelical leader, John Venn,[4] and the Stephens, notably James Stephen[5] – leading in turn to contact with the Clapham sect. Thus evangelical attitudes and liberalism were combined. Dicey's father and family were closely associated with newspaper

---

3 (1835–1922). Details of Dicey's life and times may be found in *Oxford DNB*. There are two leading biographies: T.H. Ford, *Albert Venn Dicey* (Chichester, 1995), and Cosgrove, *Rule of law*, see note 2 above. There are also sources in the Bodleian Library, Oxford.

4 John Venn (1758–97), born in Clapham, evangelical and prominent member of the Clapham sect.

5 Notable members of the family included Sir James Stephen (1829–94), first Baron Stephen and judge of the high court, 1879–91.

publishing, in particular the *Mercury*. His father believed in reform through evolution and, under his influence, Dicey had a passion for fairness, believed in legal due process and possessed an evangelical belief that injustices should be remedied. Bigotry or extreme views were subjected to intense intellectual rigour and debate and demonstrated to be untenable. Religious belief was subject to the same intensity of scrutiny and intellectual questioning as any other subject that came within Dicey's notice. Intellectual self-questioning soon became a methodology of analysis that filled any gaps in Dicey's religious dogma which defined his beliefs or convictions. From his earliest upbringing Dicey engaged in developing an analytical method to probe the truthfulness of any cause or belief. Committed to hard work, Dicey was intensely self-critical and deprecating of his own achievements because they fell far short of what he expected. At the same time once he had made up his mind through a tortuous method of self-doubt and interrogation, he firmly held to his belief, even if that meant later defending his belief against others. This socratic element to Dicey's convictions, measured by evangelical enthusiasm for hard work and commitment to the truth, ensured that his analytical style of reasoning and thought provided him with a powerful intellect.

At 17, Dicey left home and was educated at King's College School in London. In 1854 he matriculated at Balliol College, Oxford. His education at King's in the classics strengthened his dedication to supreme reasoning and intellectual rigour. These qualities he took into the study of classics at Oxford, under the instruction of the remarkable Benjamin Jowett.[6] This was a break with family tradition where mathematics had been the pursuit of early generations. Dicey's university career was overshadowed by his physical weakness and concerns that the stress of university life would be too much. Jowett's kindness as a tutor was well-known; his exacting style of analysis and argument further strengthened the tone of Dicey's own predilection for an analytical style. Individualist in focus and evangelical in zeal, Dicey came under the influence of the writings of John Stuart Mill[7] and de Tocqueville.[8] Dicey was naturally drawn to historical works including the remarkable J.A. Froude's *History of England*[9] covering the rise in protestantism. He joined the Old Mortality society in 1856, read papers at the society's meetings and

6   Benjamin Jowett (1817–93), born in Camberwell and educated at Oxford University; master of Balliol College, Oxford, in 1870. His essays on moral philosophy were influential.
7   John Stuart Mill (1806–73), English philosopher and writer. He contributed to the *Westminster Review*. His work, *Principles of political economy*, 2 vols (London, 1848), was very influential.
8   Alexis de Tocqueville (1805–59), French historian and philosopher. His book, *L'ancien régime et la révolution* (Paris, 1856), was influential.
9   J.A. Froude, *History of England from the fall of Wolsey to the defeat of the Spanish Armada*, 12 vols (London, 1856–70). James Anthony Froude (1816–1894) was a well-known historian and fellow of Exeter College, Oxford.

published a paper on Plato's *Republic* and the Christian religion. The society provided an intellectual forum for the exchange of ideas that spanned literature, religion, morality, and history. Its membership numbered James Bryce, Thomas Hill Green[10] and T. Erskine Holland.[11] A record of its activities may be found in the Bodleian Library, along with minute books and published papers. Dicey fell under a number of other influences such as the utilitarianism of many of the members and this was combined with his pre-existing predilection for evangelicalism. His family's links with publishing drew Dicey towards journalism and from journalistic ambitions he took over and ran *Undergraduate Papers*, a small circulation student paper, for three years. Through this combination of religious study, historical analysis and evangelical philosophy, Dicey's ideas, beliefs and prejudices were formed. It proved to be the perfect foundation for Dicey's future career in the law. Dicey's analytical style, religious belief and self-critical stance became the hallmarks of his investigative approach to the constitution. It is understandable that in format and tone Dicey's underlying beliefs add a biblical quality to his work and a preacher-like quality in his methods and in the art of persuasion and debate.

Dicey graduated from Oxford in 1858. His father died at this time resulting in a considerable loss of family income. Although he applied for various fellowships, he was at first unsuccessful but eventually obtained a fellowship at Trinity College, Oxford, in 1860. He also wrote a prize essay on the privy council in 1860 although this was a less significant achievement than that of his rival Bryce[12] who had secured the prestigious Arnold prize for an essay on the Holy Roman Empire. In 1861, Dicey left Oxford and set himself the aim of reading for the bar at the Inner Temple. At this time he was greatly attracted to the writings of John Austin especially on the links between law and politics. Austin's work on jurisprudence published in 1832 had become a major analytical set piece that had not been fully appreciated in England until the death of the author. As a young barrister with a fixation on persuasion and analysis, this attracted the attention of Dicey who believed that problem-solving was a matter of superior reasoning. Austin's methodology had three elements that attracted Dicey's interest and found relevance when he embarked on his *Law of the constitution*. First, there was the pre-eminence given to command and authority through defining sovereignty.

10 Thomas Hill Green (1836–82), philosopher born in Birkin rectory, Yorkshire, later professor of philosophy at Oxford.
11 T. Erskine Holland (1835–1926), English jurist; Chichele professor of international law and diplomacy, 1874–1910. His *Elements of jurisprudence* (Oxford, 1880) was a standard work of reference.
12 James Bryce, first Viscount Bryce (1838–1922), British jurist and statesman, born in Belfast, Regius professor of civil law at Oxford University, 1870–93. His work, *The American commonwealth*, 2 vols (London and New York, 1888), became well-known.

Second, duty and obedience, rationality, and good and evil could be distinguished by the idea of public duty and responsibility. Penalties for wrongdoing accompanied sovereign law and this required the citizen to obey a duty of responsibility to the sovereign as well as allegiance. Finally, Austin believed that law might be contained in a relatively few propositions that might be distilled into elementary concepts. This last point appealed to Dicey, who devoted himself to Austinian jurisprudence.

Dicey's life as a barrister involved him directly in applying the logic of synthesising difficult problems into a few valuable and defensible propositions. The analysis of cases lent itself to this approach, as did the idea that law might be reduced to scientific and therefore provable concepts. One motivation in practising at the bar was that the cases he might take had the potential to end up as political causes. The link between politics and the bar attracted Dicey. Even the possibility of high office through legal preferment offered him career possibilities that made the bar attractive. Dicey's sensitivity to politics is best understood from his interest in journalism; the use of pamphlets to propagate religious and political causes left Dicey in no doubt as to the need to link legal issues with the political life and times of society. It is striking how such a serious intellect as Dicey's was prepared to adopt popular forms of communication to engage in political beliefs and causes. The influence of religious tracts, so carefully studied by Dicey, may have inspired the publications of political pamphlets later in his life. However, his success at the bar was limited and he achieved more by writing articles for the *Mercury* and engaging in political discussion. He obtained an inland revenue position in 1876 as junior counsel to the commissioners of inland revenue, which provided much needed income. His legal career did not give rise to a political career, the career to which Dicey aspired perhaps more than any other.

Dicey's career as a lecturer did not begin in an auspicious way. He taught logic at the Working Men's College in London in 1866. Political events were moving rapidly towards universal franchise and this gradually motivated Dicey in a more radical pursuit of change rather than the defence of the *status quo*. Procedural and practical, Dicey's publications were directed to the bar, pleading and practice: *A treatise on the rules for the selection of parties to an action* was published in 1870.[13] Soon after Dicey and Bryce visited the United States and, significantly, studied the United States constitution, the impact of their visit began to shape their thinking. In the case of Bryce, the visit led to the publication of his monumental *The American commonwealth*,[14] one of the most influential works of the time. In Dicey's case, his interest in the legal profession and legal education in the role of law schools and the education of

13 London, 1870.
14 See note 12.

practitioner lawyers came from his study of the American legal system. The American visit also helped Dicey when he came to understand the foundations of the British constitution while working on *Law of the constitution*.

Dicey's American visit did much to add value to his knowledge about legal systems in general. It also showed the benefit of studying different constitutions and the need to make comparative studies. Particularly significant was Dicey's friendship with Charles William Eliot,[15] the then newly-elected president of Harvard University, and Oliver Wendell Holmes.[16] Equally significant for Dicey was the nature of American politics – the rise of the Democratic party, with a large number of Irish emigrants a dominant influence. Indeed Irish politics, on which Dicey had strong views, seemed to inform him of American issues; the strength of organised party politics alarmed both Bryce and Dicey. Party political discipline seemed to threaten the individual responsibility of any political representative – fears that Dicey later raised in relation to the rise of political factions and parties in the United Kingdom. Dicey returned from his eight-week stay in the United States refreshed and enlivened. He set to work to understand in greater detail how law and legal education might be reformed in England; how law schools at universities might afford a better foundation and training than legal practice, and how democratic institutions might grow and provide opportunities for all citizens.

In 1872, Dicey married Elinor Bonham-Carter, daughter of John Bonham-Carter MP. She was well-connected into English intellectual life and this provided an attractive connection given Dicey's intellectual curiosity. Elinor, however, suffered constant ill-health which made it difficult for Dicey to travel or engage in much social interaction at home.

Dicey's career still largely depended on his writing – book reviews, tracts and papers engaging in major social issues of the period. His work as junior counsel for the inland revenue brought him into the appeal courts defending and applying legal issues often for the first time in test cases. There followed the publication of his *Law of domicil* in 1879,[17] again a practitioner guide following strict Austinian logic and reducing complexity to a simplified series of defensible propositions. His greatest work, and probably technically his best book, was the *Conflict of laws* published in 1896.[18] This was an authori-

15 Charles William Eliot (1834–1926), American educationalist and mathematician, who became president of Harvard University, 1869–1909.

16 Oliver Wendell Holmes, junior (1841–1935), American jurist born in Boston and educated at Harvard. His book, *The common law* (Boston, 1881), was influential; he became associate justice of the US supreme court, 1902–32.

17 A.V. Dicey, *Law of domicil as a branch of the law of England, stated in the form of rules* (London, 1879).

18 A.V. Dicey, *A digest of the law of England with reference to the conflict of laws* (London and Boston, 1896).

tative digest that defined the subject and became one of the best known works of the period.

Dicey's interest in lecturing and in legal education brought him to teach at London. Along with Bryce he had helped to found law schools at Manchester and Liverpool, through the development of Owens College for working men. In 1880, the death of John Kenyon[19] provided Dicey with his greatest opportunity to date, a return to Oxford to the Vinerian chair at All Souls College; founded in 1758, it is the oldest chair in English law. Dicey was fortunate to be appointed against stiff competition from his rivals including Sir William Anson[20] and Sir Frederick Pollock.[21] Dicey's acceptance of this prestigious appointment shifted his career from practice at the bar with the potential of a judicial appointment, to that of an academic. It also signalled the end of his political ambitions, though it did not inhibit Dicey from fully engaging in the matters of concern of the time. Ireland was a major issue in English politics and Dicey engaged in the debate about how Ireland might be ruled.

DEFINING SOVEREIGNTY: DICEY'S CONTRIBUTION AND INFLUENCE

Dicey's acceptance of the Vinerian chair and his inaugural lecture allowed him to explore one of his recurring ideas: whether law could be taught at the universities?[22] This set his career in an academic direction, but it did not inhibit his publications as a pamphleteer and propagandist of just causes. In 1885 his monumental *Law of the constitution* was published in which Dicey enunciated the three legal pillars of the constitution.[23] His work drew inspiration from several writers. On sovereignty he was influenced by the work of John Austin.[24] Although he read in minute detail the writings of Burke[25] and Bagehot,[26] it was Austin who convinced him of the need for a pre-eminence to be located under parliamentary authority. Dicey followed

---

19 John Kenyon, d. 1880, previous holder of the Vinerian chair of law at Oxford.
20 William Anson (1843–1914), warden of All Souls from 1881. His *Law and custom of the constitution*, 2 vols (Oxford, 1886) was a standard work of reference.
21 Frederick Pollock (1815–88), English jurist, master of the court of exchequer.
22 A.V. Dicey, *Can English law be taught at the universities?* (London, 1883).
23 See note 1 above.
24 John Austin (1790–1859), English jurist, born Suffolk; in 1826, appointed professor of jurisprudence, University of London; author of *Lectures on jurisprudence* (London, 1863).
25 Edmund Burke (1729–97), Irish statesman and philosopher, author of *Observations on the present state of the nation* (London, 1769).
26 William Bagehot (1826–77), mathematician and lawyer. His *Treatise on the English constitution* (London, 1867) was very influential.

Austin's analytical approach and revealed through exhaustive dissection of the problem its basic and rudimentary elements.[27] This scientific approach to find the truth and determine the boundaries of the law allowed evidence to be adduced that supported the postulations that Dicey went on to defend. In that way he was adept at merging political data into the formulation of legal rules. The empirical nature of the inquiry should not be underestimated as part of how problems might be conceptualised, understood and then solved. Law, as defined by Dicey, was one that could be enforced by the courts, and he looked to the courts and their historical role to provide the benchmark to apply the sovereignty of parliament. In aid of Dicey's analysis was a miscellany of acts of parliament including the Acts of Union, and the Septennial Act 1716. The fact that historical precedent up to 1885 was used to support his analysis encouraged him to believe that sovereignty was 'the keystone of the law of the constitution'. His analysis was formulated in terms of a set of simple postulations, often recast and later reiterated at length in his writings:

> Under the English Constitution, the right to make or unmake any law whatever, and, further, that no person or body is recognised by the law as having a right to override or set aside the legislation of Parliament.[28]

Having decided on a legal definition of sovereignty, Dicey reflected on how there might be limitations to that sovereignty, not in any legal sense, but outside the boundaries of the formal law. This was defined in terms of the popular idiom of the day and the politics of choice that reflected some of the aspirations of the people. Although Dicey was no populist, he was a clever propagandist of his own beliefs. His writings fall between two mediums of communication: first, the intellectual and academic that established his reputation as a constitutional lawyer and adviser, and second, the journalistic or polemical that espoused his beliefs and causes, strongly held and argued with strong evangelical zeal. Only occasionally have evaluations of Dicey considered how both provide the real clues to understanding Dicey and his ideas. His *Lectures on the relation between law and public opinion in England*,[29] published in 1905 and 1914, often overlooked, contains an analysis setting the boundaries of law and politics.

---

27 A. V. Dicey, '*Droit administratif* in modern French law' in *LQR*, 17 (1901), 302–18.
28 Dicey, *Law of the constitution*, pp. 39–40.
29 Published under that title (London, 1905), and as *Lectures on the relation between law and public opinion in England during the nineteenth century* (London, 1914).

DICEY AND IRELAND: INTERPRETING THE CONSTITUTION

In strict constitutional theory, Ireland under the Act of Union 1800 provided a demonstrative definition of legal sovereignty. We have already seen how in Dicey's mind sovereignty was also defined by the realities of politics. Political tracts about Ireland provided a salutary lesson that challenged his enthusiasm for symmetrical rules and predictable order. Dicey's greatest dilemma was how to reconcile a growing tide of popular political opinion with the traditions of an unchanging constitution. The former was represented in parliament through the reform of the franchise and its determination to utilise parliamentary power to advance political causes. The latter was articulated by the unelected house of lords, reluctant to agree changes that altered the *status quo*. The Irish question brought the issues of reconciling different interests to the fore. At first Dicey assumed that some form of home rule might be achieved through delegated self-governance. This necessitated no change in the constitutional status of Ireland, in particular the Act of Union. Conceding some form of self-governance was not the same as conceding the constitutional status of home rule, which Dicey reasoned required a weakening of the Act of Union. On this he was not prepared to compromise.

His attitudes to Ireland were complex and at times appear contradictory. There are two distinct periods which mark Dicey's attitudes and an eventual change of emphasis. The first period coincided with the publication of his *Law of the constitution* in 1885 when Dicey was broadly sympathetic to Irish home rule, if not as a legal entity certainly in political aspiration. This was a period marked by his whig principles and a general sympathy to Irish distress caused by English wrongs. It also marked the high water mark of Gladstone's ambitions to pacify Ireland and Dicey's pleas for a more tolerant attitude to catholics in Ireland.[30] Disillusionment with Gladstone's passion to see Ireland under self-rule, a passion that Dicey believed had gone too far, gave him grounds for shifting his attitudes. As a result, during the 1880s a general tolerance to Irish home rule gave way to a fundamental rejection of any constitutional change in relations with Ireland. The dominant concern was to protect the entity of the United Kingdom from any dramatic change in its unity. Consequently Dicey's shift of emphasis to unionism aimed to preserve the entity of the United Kingdom while maintaining the sovereignty of parliament based on ordinary principles of law. The latter became the main brake on any use of parliamentary power. Irish grievances could and should be remedied by strict application of the ordinary law. It was almost that he feared that should a parliamentary majority exist for home rule, it might be confronted by objections based on an appeal to the rule of law.

---

30 William Ewart Gladstone (1809–98), born in Liverpool, educated at Eton and Christ Church, Oxford, prime minister and leading Liberal statesman.

Christopher Wandesforde. Watercolour attributed to George Perfect Harding, early 19th century, after an unknown artist of a portrait of the same, *c.*1630, National Portrait Gallery, London.

Albert Venn Dicey. Portrait in oils by Désiré-François Laugée, 1872. Photograph reproduced by kind permission of the Master and Fellows of Trinity College, Oxford.

Timothy Healy. Portrait in oils by Sir John Lavery, exhibited 1923. By courtesy of Felix Rosenstiel's Widow and Son Ltd, London, on behalf of the Estate of Sir John Lavery. Photograph reproduced by kind permission of the Dublin City Gallery The Hugh Lane.

Baron Cooper of Culross. Portrait in oils, by W.O. Hutchison, 1956. Reproduced by kind permission of Mr R.E. Hutchison. Photograph reproduced by kind permission of the Faculty of Advocates, Edinburgh.

Dicey's writings on Ireland move from the analytical to the polemical with increasing fervour. A number of pamphlets deserve particular mention as examples of his craft of the political pamphlet, *England's case against home rule* (1886);[31] *A leap in the dark: an examination of the leading principles of the Home Rule Bill of 1893*,[32] and *Letters on unionist delusions* (1887).[33] These were in addition to numerous articles in *The Nation* and *The Contemporary Review*. These reflected his gradual conversion to unionism and his objections to ruling Ireland through some form of arbitrary government. It is clear that from 1881 to 1884, Ireland dominated Dicey's thinking: at the same time, from 1883 to 1884, he laid the basis of his manuscript for *Law of the constitution*.

What was the impact of Ireland on Dicey's analysis of sovereignty? There are three aspects to this question that deserve examination. First, the Irish question convinced Dicey of the failures that came from non-observance of the rule of law. In enunciating sovereignty Dicey's symmetrical constitution had to preserve order and maintain respect for the law. Sovereignty could not be confused with authoritarianism – an aspect that Dicey was only too aware might occur either under a tyrannical government or through organised party political power acting as a counter weight to individual responsibility. Second, Dicey saw the unions with Scotland and Wales as instructive of the strength of a unitary constitution. Ireland's problems arose because of the way in which England implemented the Union and Ireland's solution lay in upholding the rule of law and preserving the Union. Ireland must not be ruled as a separate case but on a par with the prevailing order in England. Third, Dicey adopted the stance that is best described as English nationalism preferring the moral high ground and representing the unity of the United Kingdom as based on the link with the English nation. As Gladstone drifted towards the inevitability of home rule in 1885, Dicey reacted in the opposite direction, driving him inevitably to a trenchant stance in opposition to the government's policy. He regarded Gladstone as a threat to the Union which Dicey defined as the basis of the United Kingdom's success as an economic power and a dominant influence in the world. Paradoxically the ardent English nationalist in Dicey failed to recognise the same character trait of nationalism in writers from Ireland or Scotland. Dicey resolutely stuck to his views, notwithstanding his difference of opinion with Bryce, with whom he remained friends, and the prime minister, Gladstone, from whom he distanced himself.

Dicey's analysis of Ireland is a revealing and engaging part of how his approach to sovereignty should be interpreted. His polemical approach in

31 London, 1886.
32 *A leap in the dark, or Our new constitution [An examination of the leading principles of the Home Rule Bill of 1893]* (London, 1893).
33 *Letters on unionist delusions, republished from 'The Spectator'* (London and New York, 1887).

terms of espousing political causes followed the fashion familiar in Austinian jurisprudence and one that characterised his analytical method. Evidence-based and forensically dissected, Dicey's approach subjected complex legal and political problems to the same treatment. He provided a series of postulations which he defended with great passion and attempted to synthesise problems into abstract principles that might inform future opinion.

In fact Dicey's analysis on Ireland was that it made out the case in favour of the Union, thus securing the maintenance of the United Kingdom as a whole, and that through the supremacy of the law, it would provide for every citizen's rights and liberties. This was despite the political reality that Ireland demonstrated how fragile the rule of law was against a determined effort to overthrow the state. Nevertheless, Dicey was a determined protagonist, at one time in favour of home rule and later in favour of unionism, keen to advance the legal justification for the sovereignty of parliament despite the absence of any feasible method of enforcing the ordinary law. Historical analysis might have helped Dicey to understand the clear miscalculation in his thinking. In reality the argument about the sovereignty of parliament could be used to support the arguments for home rule as easily as those for the Union. Dicey could not accept that the political and historical legacy provided evidence of this.

SOVEREIGNTY AND DICEY'S ANALYTICAL METHOD

Dicey's analytical method suffered from a number of obvious shortcomings when exposed to criticism. He was not an historian and his knowledge of history was rather patchy and often unsystematic. He had a selective memory for case law, remembering only those cases that helped him apply some general principles. His attitude to cases might well have assisted the writing of a legal opinion rather than providing an analysis of a fundamental character. He lacked a grasp of statute law and often ignored the voluminous quantity of statute law and regulation that had stemmed from parliament's new ambition to address social problems, from health and education to the poor law and labour relations. Only later in life were these matters addressed in his *Law and public opinion* treatise. Perhaps most surprising of all is the fact that Dicey was concerned with polemical argument and party politics as much as law. Although he attempted to separate law from politics, this proved an artificial separation and one that clouded his judgment. One clue to interpreting Dicey's style and analysis in *Law of the constitution* is his belief in the rule of law and in the role of constitutional conventions. His analysis rested on the assumption that the force of law was sufficient to secure obedience to the law. This proved controversial and was later shown to be unreliable as the power of party politics far exceeded the influence of the rule of law.

Dicey also exhibited too narrow an understanding of administrative law. He emphasised delegated legislation and the role of remedies, rather than powers and discretion. He lacked knowledge of the essentials of administrative decision-making and had a simplistic notion of administration or institutions. Perhaps his greatest error and one for which many generations of students were to suffer was the narrowness of his perception of administrative law, and his objections to *droit administratif* or French administrative law. Dicey mistakenly believed that the sole purpose of this system was to render officials immune from the ordinary law ultimately giving them too much autonomy and removing them from the process of the courts. The reality was the opposite of his analysis. In fact, later in his life and as subsequent editions of *Law of the constitution* were to show, Dicey retreated from his original stance. Indeed in 1915, he was to retract his objections to *droit administratif*, but the damage was done.[34] Dicey helped to foster the belief that administrative law did not exist in England and if it did it was a thoroughly bad thing. Ironically it was the *Report on ministers' powers* in 1932,[35] a decade after Dicey's death that asked what safeguards were desirable or necessary to secure the constitutional principles of the sovereignty of parliament and the rule of law. Had Dicey asked this question he would have found that it was the judges who were most likely to provide the answer. Ironically, the French judicial system had looked at the role of the courts in medieval times to consider how best to prevent administrative abuse. Dicey was at his most determined when confronted with any evidence counter to his own views. This characteristic made him appear strong-minded while in reality he held differing views on the same subject at the same time. His adversarial style left little room for compromise or reconciliation.

An additional dimension to Dicey's analysis is the Austinian perspective of defining constitutional law as 'all rules which directly or indirectly affect the distribution or the exercise of the sovereign power in the state'. His adaptation of Austin's thinking focused on the role of the courts in setting the parameters on the generality of Austin's analysis. The courts could only enforce laws and thus Dicey focused on the sovereignty of parliament, whereas conventions of the constitution, while recognised by the courts, could not be enforced.

It is important to understand Dicey's analytical method and philosophy before interpreting what he wrote. There are a number of significant points that underpin an understanding of his approach:

34 A.V. Dicey, 'The development of administrative law in England' in *LQR*, 31 (1915), 148–53.
35 *Report of the committee on ministers' powers* (Cmd. 4060, 1932), known as the Donoughmore committee.

i.   His analysis changed and shifted as each edition of the *Law of the constitution* was considered.

ii. His understanding of the constitution was more descriptive than prescriptive. The fact that many, including his critics, adopted his observations as prescriptive was misleading and has helped to add confusion to how Dicey's work should be interpreted.

iii. His basic principles such as his observations on administrative law are no longer valid.

iv. Dicey's analysis of the Irish question and eventual conversion to unionism led him to attribute a political legitimacy to his ideas on legal sovereignty that failed to take fully into account the role of the judiciary in accepting and applying his version of sovereignty.

v.   Dicey's idea of unlimited sovereignty was fundamentally flawed as there were many exceptions to this. Parliament had effectively curtailed its own powers under the Colonial Laws Validity Act 1865 and in cases where the sovereignty of parliament conflicted with the rule of law, such as indemnity acts or acts of parliament in general. This was despite Dicey's belief that the rule of law could hold sovereignty within proper boundaries.

vi. Indeed even the Act of Union had undergone considerable alteration after 1800 with changes to the franchise, the disestablishment of the Church of Ireland and alterations in religious tests for admission to Scottish universities.

vii. Representative government was likely to become proactive in the use of legislation and executive power might encroach on parliamentary power. This was recognised by Dicey but not taken account of in his analysis.

Despite these limitations, Dicey's *Law of the constitution* became accepted orthodoxy. It was, as A.W.B. Simpson observed, 'an oracle';[36] by lawyers of the period, the book was read as if it was an uncodified statute of the constitution. In fact, it was a description of the constitution with little historical analysis and was intended to support a legal view of what the courts might or might not do when confronted with problems that were at the heart of the relationship between parliament and the executive. Further, it set the boundaries on the relationship between parliament and the courts. It is this legacy that remains today. Lawyers welcomed the focus of Dicey's analysis and the assumption that the constitution could be defined in terms of legal principles. His analysis offered a legal analysis that helped set limits on political and legal debate. This elevated constitutional debate into the arena of legal analysis.

---

36 A.W.B. Simpson, 'The common law and legal theory' in idem (ed.), *Oxford essays in jurisprudence*, second series (Oxford, 1973), pp. 77–99.

THE PARLIAMENT ACT 1911

One of Dicey's enduring legacies is his understanding of how sovereignty might be defined in terms of its legal and political implications. His views have to be considered in the context of his fears for the future of sovereignty in light of his opposition to Irish home rule.[37] Such matters came to the fore when the Parliament Act 1911 was passed. In the past there had been considerable concern that the house of lords might reject a money bill, the main basis of the government's ability to govern. This power while formally preserved had *de facto* fallen into abeyance on the threat that, were the lords to reject such a bill, then the government might create new peers to have the bill accepted. The lords adopted a self-limiting fetter on their own as a preferable option to legislation. This had been adopted in 1860 after a resolution of the house of commons warned the lords of what might happen were they to continue to obstruct government money bills. However, the relations between commons and lords remained under strain. Earlier there had been conflict over the Reform Bill in 1832, with the lords eventually giving way. Further conflict arose over the Irish Church Disestablishment Bill in 1869, the Irish Land Bill in 1870 and a series of measures reforming the electoral system in the Representation of the People Bill 1884. The Finance Bill 1909 faced severe opposition and, following a general election in 1910, the government though weakened in electoral support was able to command a majority through the assistance of Labour and Irish nationalist MPs. Various proposals for home rule for Ireland also encountered opposition. The result was the Parliament Bill with its far-reaching proposals to limit the house of lords' legal and constitutional powers. Simultaneous to the introduction of the Parliament Bill, the government threatened to create 400 new peers to ensure that the bill would be passed. The Parliament Bill in effect abolished the power of the house of lords to reject a money bill and preserved only a delaying power for the lords. This was subject to a time limit of two years spread over three sessions, which was later amended to one year under the Parliament Act 1949, and with the exception of a bill to prolong the lifetime of parliament.

Dicey was opposed to the passage of the Parliament Act 1911 because of his fear that it undermined the authority of parliament by diminishing the house of lords, thus destroying one of the protections against arbitrary elected government.[38] His opposition was political rather than legal, as Dicey fully accepted the legality of the legislation. The political nature of his

---

37 See A.V. Dicey, 'The Parliament Act 1911 and the destruction of all constitutional safeguards' in Sir William R. Anson et al., *Rights of citizenship: a survey of safeguards for the people* (London, 1912), pp. 81–107.

38 Dicey's opposition is detailed in Cosgrove, *Rule of law*, pp. 214–15, 221–2.

concerns centred on the union and his fear that parliament might then pass some form of Irish home rule bill. Dicey warned of the consequences of the Parliament Act, saying 'these are dark days before us'.[39] Cosgrove notes:[40]

> By the Revolutionary device of the Parliament Act, he [Dicey] wrote, the Asquith government had destroyed the last constitutional check on the power of the House of Commons. Any coalition could legislate in the name of the nation. And of course the act allowed the opportunity for Home Rule to succeed without an appeal to the country. Amid the turmoil of 1912–14, these arguments never attracted the public attention he hoped.

Dicey's opposition to the Parliament Act 1911 resulted in a turning-point in his attitude to law and opposition. His passion for protecting the Union led him to despair of the future which he saw as an inevitable road to some form of home rule for Ireland. This, however, should not obscure Dicey's legacy.

In contemporary times, Dicey's influence is well illustrated in *Jackson v. Attorney General*,[41] a case involving a challenge to the Hunting Act 2004 under the Parliament Act 1911. Lord Nicholls explained how Dicey's analysis of the question of sovereignty was relevant to the case today. In upholding the legality of the Hunting Act 2004, Lord Nicholls explained:

> Not surprisingly, AV Dicey, our greatest constitutional lawyer, writing a few years after the events which led to enactment (of the) Parliament Act 1911 stated that the House of Lords 'cannot prevent the House of Commons from, in effect, passing under the Parliament Act 1911 any change of the constitution provided always that the requirements of the Parliament Act 1911 are complied with ...' I would respectfully follow Dicey on this point.[42]

Lord Hope also accepted the significance of Dicey's views, but conceded that '[s]tep by step, gradually but surely, the English principle of the absolute legislative sovereignty of Parliament which Dicey derived from Coke and Blackstone is being qualified.'[43]

---

39 Ibid., p. 210; Dicey in his letter to Eliot, 28 March 1912, Charles William Eliot papers, Harvard University Archives, Cambridge, MA.

40 Cosgrove, *Rule of law*, p. 216.

41 [2005] UKHL 56

42 [2005] UKHL para. 95, pp. 43–4.

43 [2005] UKHL para 104, p. 48. See O. Dixon, 'The law and constitution' in *LQR*, 51 (1935), 590, at p. 596.

CONCLUSIONS

Dicey's concept of sovereignty has evolved in response to changes, unforeseen and unpredicted by Dicey, such as membership of the European Union and the constitutional settlements with independent countries previously ruled by England. His opposition to the Parliament Act 1911 pushed Dicey further away from advocating constitutional change to outright political opposition. Just as his approach to sovereignty has been influential in our understanding of the law, equally compelling in the minds of many members of the judiciary is the idea that there is emerging, in the words of Lord Bridge, 'two sovereignties',[44] or as Sedley LJ believes a 'bi-polar sovereignty'. The rule of law supports the sovereignty of the judiciary, while parliamentary sovereignty supports the authority of parliament. The concern that one may be eroded by the other was trenchantly expressed by Sedley LJ: '[b]ut the domination of the legislature by a party-controlled executive has, if anything, been consolidated.'[45]

There are different views on how this challenge to the balance between executive and judicial power might be addressed. Writing in 1995, both Sir John Laws[46] and Lord Woolf[47] believed that as the courts defined the scope of parliamentary and judicial power, it is important to strengthen the independence of judicial power through the creation of fundamental freedoms and rights. The emerging jurisprudence under the Human Rights Act 1998 has, if anything, not answered the fundamental question of how to strike a balance between executive and judicial powers, but it has underlined the need for an answer.[48]

Sir Stephen Sedley, as he then was, bravely attempted to answer the question, just as Dicey had done, by considering how sovereignty was defined. He examined how the judiciary had the pivotal role in setting the boundaries of debate and analysis. He pointed to a decision that had attracted Dicey's attention, that of the United States supreme court in *Marbury v. Madison*,[49] where the court defined its own powers and set its authority on judicial review. This was reasoned from the fact that the United States

---

44 Quoted in A.W. Bradley, 'The sovereignty of parliament' in J. Jowell and D. Oliver (eds), *The changing constitution* (Oxford, 2004), p. 28; see *X. v. Morgan-Grampian (Publishers) Ltd* [1991] 1 AC 1, at p. 148, and S. Sedley, 'Human rights: a twenty-first century agenda' in *Public Law* [1995], 386, at p. 389.

45 S. Sedley, 'The constitution in the twenty-first century' in Lord Nolan and Sir Stephen Sedley, *The making and remaking of the British constitution* (London, 1997), p. 85.

46 Sir John Laws, 'Law and democracy' in *Public Law* [1995], 72.

47 Lord Woolf, '*Droit public* – English style' in *Public Law* [1995], 57.

48 See the Inquiries Act 2005 and the Supreme Court Act 2005 as examples of unresolved issues setting the boundaries of judicial and legislative powers.

49 (1805) 5 US (1 Cranch) 137.

constitution contained a bill of rights that forbade congress to legislate to particular ends. The courts on their own initiative developed judicial review as an instrument of enforcing or commanding the checks and balances of the constitution. Similar examples may be found in Australia in the 1990s, and also in the supreme court of Canada. A similar attitude shaped the development of the role of the New Zealand court of appeal under the presidency of Sir Robin Cooke. Remedies built upon rights could give rise to an enhanced role for the courts.

There is a contemporary relevance to this question, in terms of moving forward the debate about constitutional checks and balances. It emerges that despite the fact that the constitution has undergone considerable changes since Dicey's *Law of the constitution*, there is remarkable validity in his understanding of the United Kingdom's constitution. Parliament is at the apex of the constitution. It underpins the legal system and in its central role provides the main mechanism for government accountability as well as defining executive powers.

Dicey advanced the notion that the sovereignty of parliament was a legal entity. In recent times, the traditional orthodoxy of parliamentary sovereignty has become more fragile than ever before in its long history. The European Communities Act 1972 allows courts the broadest extension of judicial power to decide whether an act of parliament complies with community law and, if it does not, in appropriate circumstances to disapply the act of parliament. Potentially, narrowly defined parliamentary sovereignty is ebbing away. The Scotland Act 1998 creates the potential for further powers to be devolved to a subordinate parliament, powers that are unlikely to be reclaimed by the United Kingdom parliament. The Human Rights Act 1998 provides for a shared responsibility between the courts and parliament, first, to decide if there is incompatibility, and second, to have the final say in what to do. The proposed European constitution (to be ratified) marks a further shift towards a European and therefore civil law focus to the constitution, and away from the historical legacy of a domestic common law constitution. These changes underline the inherent mistake in adopting Dicey's analysis too prescriptively – unlimited sovereignty in parliament may today mean unlimited executive power, while in reality even a strong democratic government is ultimately subject to the electorate.

T.M. Healy: the politics of advocacy

FRANK CALLANAN*

[Professor MacHugh] turned towards Myles Crawford and said:

- You know Gerald Fitzgibbon. Then you can imagine the style of his discourse.
- He is sitting with Tim Healy, J.J. O'Molloy said, rumour has it, on the Trinity college estates commission.
- He is sitting with a sweet thing, Myles Crawford said, in a child's frock. Go on. Well?

(James Joyce, Ulysses)[1]

IN T.M. HEALY THE ROLES OF politician and barrister seemed inextricably fused. Francis Cruise O'Brien wrote in 1910 that Healy had 'the mind, nay the soul, of a barrister. Special pleading is his religion'.[2] Cruise O'Brien was not alone in thinking that Healy was in some way existentially a barrister. In the course of the Parnell split, 1890–1, the attack on Healy as a perfidious barrister was a dominant motif, culminating in a gross (and for Healy extremely lucrative) libel in the *Freeman's Journal* relating to Healy's role as a defence counsel in the trials at Maryborough in October 1889 arising out of the murder of an RIC district inspector in Gweedore.[3] Healy was routinely depicted in Parnellite caricature in wig and gown. Parnell made a number of thinly veiled references to Healy identifying him only as a lawyer, refusing to dignify him by the use of his name. Thus in his inflammatory manifesto at the outset of the split, Parnell asserted that John Morley had in their discussions on home rule 'put before me the desirability of filling one of the law offices of the crown in Ireland by a legal member of my party'.[4] Likewise

---

* The edited text of an address given to the Society at the Royal Irish Academy, Dublin, on 1 November 2002.
1 James Joyce, *Ulysses*, ed. H.W. Gabler (London 1986), p. 116. This exchange occurs in the Aeolus chapter, set chiefly in the offices of the *Freeman's Journal*.
2 *Leader*, 9 Apr. 1910, quoted F. Callanan, *T.M. Healy* (Cork, 1996), p. 442.
3 Callanan, *T.M. Healy*, pp. 218–9.
4 F.S.L. Lyons, *The fall of Parnell* (London, 1960) p. 324.

51

when Parnell made reference to 'a certain budding Lord Chancellor or Chief Justice', he was immediately understood to mean Healy.[5]

The Irish leader's comments on the post-Union Irish bar had Healy as their principal target:

> ... the bar of Ireland was at one time a patriotic body, but it unhappily ceased to be a patriotic body when we lost our Parliament, and it will never again become a patriotic body until a self-governing nation shows these gentlemen that the only way to preferment is through the hearts of their fellow countrymen.[6]

That Healy did not do a great deal to enhance the political popularity of the Irish bar does not mean that his combination of roles was wholly unconstructive through the length of his career. A consideration of his career in its legal aspect conduces to a slight but significant shift in the understanding of the interrelationship of law and politics in modern Irish history.

If it is in significant respects true that all of Parnell's lieutenants and coadjutors made their most creative contributions to Irish politics in the late 1870s and in the 1880s, this was most demonstrably so in Healy's case. While his career as the most vehement publicist of Parnellism in the 1880s has received its due, his extraordinary role at the intersection of law and politics merits further attention.

In the redirection of the politics of the land question of the 1870s into the channels of enlarged tenants' rights, and towards proprietorship, Healy was the most ideologically astute and driven of Parnell's lieutenants. If this direction was set by Parnell, Healy was the most relentless adversary not only of those who, like Davitt, espoused somewhat vague ideas of agrarian socialism, but – of greater political significance – of those who feared that the establishment of a framework for peasant proprietorship would deprive the movement for home rule of its agrarian impetus. Healy's lifelong loathing of John Dillon was not merely a matter of rivalry and temperament, but arose from a fundamental disagreement over the interrelationship of the land question and home rule. Healy was the chief nationalist advocate of a solution by land purchase. His extraordinary rhetorical adroitness enabled him to descant into the pursuit of land purchase all the immemorial grievances and emotions of catholic nationalism, in a rhetoric of such calculated aggressiveness towards the Irish landlord class as to squeeze the left and centre of the Irish party. He maximised the advantage created by the fact that the divisions on the issue were not openly fought out during the decade of Parnell's hegemony.

---

5 Callanan, *T.M. Healy*, p. 308.
6 F. Callanan, *The Parnell split* (Cork, 1992), p. 234.

Timothy Healy. Portrait in oils by Sir John Lavery, exhibited 1923. By courtesy of Felix Rosenstiel's Widow and Son Ltd, London, on behalf of the Estate of Sir John Lavery. Photograph reproduced by kind permission of the Dublin City Gallery The Hugh Lane.

Healy, 'of 15 Doughty St., London, journalist, second son of Maurice Healy, of Bantry in the county of Cork, gentleman', was admitted to Gray's Inn on 7 June 1880 at the age of twenty-five, four months before his election to parliament as a member for Wexford.[7] Under the regime in force until 1885, Healy was obliged to keep terms in London as a preliminary to his admission to the degree of barrister-at-law of the King's Inns in Dublin.[8] He was admitted as a student of the King's Inns in the Trinity term of 1881, and was called to the Irish bar on 10 November 1884.[9]

While Healy rapidly established a diverse and substantial practice, what was of immediate political significance was his work as a counsel appearing on behalf of Irish tenant farmers. Healy the advocate from the outset merged indistinguishably into Healy the politician and parliamentarian. The Land Law Act 1881 provided the arena for Healy's first brilliantly assured combination of the roles of agitator, legislator and law student. The origins of Healy's high standing as a parliamentarian at Westminster lie in the debates on the bill. Healy's younger brother Maurice, then a solicitor's apprentice and probably the better lawyer, by his notes and correspondence contributed much to Healy's acclaimed mastery of the bill's provisions. Even though the prize of what became known as the Healy clause (which provided that no increase in judicial rent could be allowed in respect of improvements effected by the tenant) was drastically curtailed judicially, its symbolic impact was immense.[10] Healy's publication of a highly successful *Tenants' key to the Land Law Act, 1881*, which the chief secretary W.E. Forster advised the prime minister would 'tempt the tenants into court', scandalised the agrarian radicals.[11] This expertise also set the trajectory of his future practice. Plunket Barton later wrote that his strongest point as a lawyer was 'an unrivalled familiarity with the Irish Statute law of his own time'.[12]

Healy's political advocacy had a second dimension of greater significance in terms of his contribution to Irish law, in the sense of the judge-made body of legal precedent. It was in relation to, if not the revolution, the quickened

7   Gray's Inn, Records of admissions and calls; T.M. Healy, *Letters and leaders of my day*, 2 vols (London, 1928), i, p. 94. It seems likely that the £100 which Healy was required to deposit with Gray's Inn came in whole or in part from the sum of £140 he received from the Land League. His bond was at his request cancelled on 5 July 1884, and his name withdrawn. As a preliminary to his greatly delayed call to the English bar, the resolution of 5 July 1884 was rescinded on a further petition from Healy on 24 April 1903 and it was resolved that 'Mr Healy be allowed to count the eight terms which he kept between the years 1881 and 1884 for the purpose of being called to the English Bar': Gray's Inn, *Book of Orders*, xvii, xx.
8   D. Hogan, *The legal profession in Ireland, 1789–1922* (Dublin, 1986), pp. 34–5.
9   Memorial of T.M. Healy to be admitted as a barrister-at-law, Michaelmas term 1884, and related documents, King's Inns; Callanan, *T.M. Healy*, p. 102.
10 Callanan, *T.M. Healy*, pp. 56–7.   11 Ibid., p. 59.
12 Sir Dunbar Plunket Barton, *Timothy Healy, memories and anecdotes* (Dublin, Cork, London, 1933), p. 84.

evolution of *habeas corpus* and judicial review in Ireland in the 1880s that Healy's role as an agitating nationalist parliamentarian and advocate were most happily married. Healy's purpose was to bring a sense of nationalist power to bear on the magistracy across Ireland, which he saw as the spine of Anglo-Irish legal hegemony and English power.

Healy was not unique in the ranks of the Irish party – the practising barristers included T.C. Harrington and J.J. Clancy – but he was easily the most forensically able. He gleefully coupled the roles of *farceur* before the magistrate and the jurist of *hauteur* in the high court. With the defeat of the first home rule bill, and the commencement of the chief secretaryship of Arthur Balfour, whose crude and archly provocative reversion to a policy of coercion masked the inception of the Conservatives' sustained and highly sophisticated spoiling strategy directed against home rule, the tempo increased.

Healy invented a Parnellite variation of the folkloric Irish patriot lawyer. In advance of the prosecution of William O'Brien at Mitchelstown in 1887, he declared that his client was 'to go before this brace of gibbeting Castle hacks, who would settle everything beforehand'. Defending O'Brien the same year in Loughrea, Healy and Matthias McDonnell Bodkin in the course of an elaborately filibustering defence had a bet as to which of them could cross-examine the crown witnesses at greater length, their watches open in front of them as the coin passed back and forth.[13] This of course depended upon enlightened members of the judiciary. As lord chief baron of the court of exchequer in Ireland from 1874, whose role was enlarged with the Judicature (Ire.) Act 1877, Palles played a crucial role[14] but was not altogether alone. The author, under the pseudonym 'Rhadamanthus', of the extraordinary *Our judges* which was among other things a kind of political form book on the Irish judiciary, observed that:

> The Exchequer has of late years been a sort of permanent court of jail delivery. The searching mind of Palles will detect a flaw in proceedings the most regular, and before the tribunal where he presides a clever lawyer, if so minded, with the Habeas Corpus Act in his hand, could empty all the prisons in Ireland. Baron Dowse knows this well, and lives in constant dread of the attempt being made. Mr. Justice Andrews,

---

13 Callanan, *T.M. Healy*, p. 217.
14 V.T.H. Delany, *Christopher Palles* (Dublin, 1960), pp. 97–106. Barry O'Brien wrote, musing on the chief baron's 'splendid Dublin brogue' and 'extraordinary intellect': 'lamentable it is that he is not in touch with the national sentiment of his country; for, in any case, Ireland must be proud of him': R.B. O'Brien, *Dublin Castle and the Irish people* (2nd ed., London, 1912), p. 141. More generally, O'Brien denounced the partnership of judicial appointments in Ireland, made effectively by the chief secretary for Ireland on the basis of party allegiance: 'in England when an advocate reaches the Bench he ceases to be a politician. In Ireland he is always a politician': ibid., p. 146.

on the contrary, looks as if nothing would give him keener pleasure than to throw open every prison gate in the country – just to see how the thing could be done in law.[15]

Healy did not concede there was any change, and continued to hammer away through the 1880s at the Irish judicial system, on occasion in the commons inveighing against individual judges. Later he was more ready to concede a progression over time. Writing to his brother after losing a legal challenge on behalf of an alien in England during the Great War, he wrote 'the English judges just now are of course like what the Irish judges used to be in the days of Balfour, but with more justification'.[16] Such enlightened receptiveness was not by any means universal among the higher judiciary, but the Irish legal order displayed a greater resilience in accommodating itself to the shifting balance of social power in the country than might have been anticipated, or Healy's unremitting fierce attacks on the Irish judiciary might have seemed to suggest.

For the great endeavour of Parnellism, the Irish courts afforded an important subordinate theatre to that of Westminster. Its significance as a second front in constitutional nationalist politics has rarely been acknowledged. Nationalist political and social power, if not quite brought to bear, was seen to count for something within the juristic bastion of the Union. That the Irish bench – while largely unionist in political orientation and protestant in religious allegiance – was prepared in some degree to hold the ring, and to constrain the powers of the Irish executive and the magistracy, was to have far-reaching significance in institutionalising – to however imperfect a degree – the shifting configuration of power in Ireland when it ultimately occurred in a quite different manner to that which had been for long anticipated.

II

A sense of the quasi-political milieu of the Four Courts in the last three decades of the Union is necessary for an understanding of the less highly lit hemisphere of Healy's career as a barrister-parliamentarian. The Parnellite obloquy which Healy's profession as a barrister attracted in the course of the split was succeeded by the dark and not wholly unfounded suspicions, of

15 'Rhadamanthus', *Our judges* (Dublin, 1890), p. 23. Dowse was amusing, humanely cynical, and famously outspoken. He once observed from the bench that 'the resident magistrates could no more state a case than they could write a Greek ode'. Quoted in the commons by J.G. Swift MacNeill, this was rendered by his parliamentary reporter as 'the resident magistrates could no more state a case than they could ride a Greek goat'. M. MacDonagh, *Parliament: its romance, its comedy, its pathos* (London, 1902), p. 373.
16 Healy to Maurice Healy, 12 Sept. 1915, typescripts of letters of T.M. Healy to Maurice Healy 1892–1918, Healy–Sullivan papers, UCD, P6/E/2 (hereafter 'Healy typescripts').

John Dillon in particular, that Healy was incessantly intriguing in the Four Courts against the Irish party. That Healy had a secure professional base in Dublin where he spent most of his time, away from Westminster where the Irish party leadership was confined for the duration of the parliamentary sessions, served to exacerbate Dillon's morose unease.

Healy's familiar professional relations with influential unionist colleagues at the Irish bar were not innocent of political consequence. For his unionist brethren, Healy had a number of attributes to commend him. He was from very early on a considerable parliamentary celebrity, and possessed of a wit that anarchically outran his partisanship as a nationalist. As a nationalist politician he was commendably refractory, falling out with every leader of the Irish party from Isaac Butt onwards. He was a proponent of a settlement by land purchase, and was after the deaths of Parnell and Gladstone increasingly drawn away from the Liberal-Nationalist alliance into a loosely Tory orbit: at Westminster he came to enjoy what were for an Irish nationalist uniquely cordial, if superficial, relations with leading Conservative figures. He was also capable of immense geniality towards anyone not a supporter of the Irish party leadership. C.P. Curran, reviewing Healy's memoirs in 1929, shrewdly noted: 'towards his English adversaries Mr. Healy shows himself uniformly, studiously benign; towards his Irish one-time colleagues he turns the unblunted cutting edge of memory. As it was in the beginning it is now'.[17]

Among the previously inconceivable collaborations brought about by the unfolding of land purchase in Ireland was that of Healy and Gerald Fitzgibbon on the Trinity College Estates Commission, which attracted the reference in *Ulysses* which provides the epigraph to this piece. It would be hard to imagine an Irishman of more different background and political temperament to Healy than Fitzgibbon: Trinity scholar, high unionist, friend of Randolph Churchill, former Tory solicitor general for Ireland and from 1878 lord justice of appeal in Ireland. Healy reported to his brother in August 1904:

> I think we shall make some hand of this Trinity College Commission, so far as helping sales goes. I found Fitzgibbon a very unassuming and hard-working and resourceful colleague. In fact we have been more like two working barristers than anything else; and I have, and intend to let him do all the work, and indeed he is a glutton for work. I never met a more insatiable man for grubbing up facts.

The prime example of Healy's politically deviant legal relationships was that with James Campbell. James Henry Mussen Campbell, barrister and unionist parliamentarian, came to be loathed by the Irish party, in the home rule crisis, as a southern unionist without northern connections other than that he had

17 *Irish Statesman*, 23 Feb. 1929.

been a leading member of the north-eastern circuit, who was prepared to advocate armed resistance to home rule in Ulster. Healy in the home rule crisis sought to turn to political advantage his relations with Campbell. He believed that the concession of an Ulster council with a veto on legislation affecting Ulster would permit the enactment of home rule, and harboured the naïve belief that he could detach Campbell from Carson. Healy completely underestimated Campbell's readiness to countenance extreme measures.[18] It might be surmised that Healy's faith in the personal relations of politicians of opposing parties (the depth and warmth of which he was especially prone to overestimate in his dealings with Conservative politicians), one of his besetting deficiencies as a politician, owed something to a false analogy between the achieving of high political compromise and the barrister's art of the settlement.

On 19 May 1915 the British party leaders announced the formation of a coalition government and the new cabinet met on 27 May (Asquith retained the premiership until December 1916). To the fury of the leaders of the Irish party it was proposed to replace Ignatius O'Brien as lord chancellor for Ireland by Campbell in what would have marked a sharp further diminution in the influence of the Irish party. In a characteristic letter to his brother, Healy attributed the proposed substitution of Campbell to his own influence:

> I have had my revenge on Ignatius. Yesterday he was firmly in the saddle under the contract with Redmond that the Irish offices are to be left intact. Today, thanks to my efforts, James Campbell is Chancellor. The Ministry has to be constructed with such travail and anger that in my opinion it could not last an hour with the jealousies created, only for the war. Carson has done with Ulster, and will never again take or get the salute from the Orange Volunteers!! Birrell was not at the Cabinet today, having been sent to Dublin to break the dreadful news of his defeat to Redmond and Dillon. They will be furious but, as one of the Government said to me, "He may defeat us, but we shall not resign"!![19]

Healy's exultant self-congratulation was premature. Pressure from the Irish party averted the appointment at that time. Healy wrote two weeks later:

> It looks today as if it would be Pim [Jonathan Pim, the attorney general for Ireland] who would be sacrificed instead of my uncle Ig.!! Campbell has evidently weakened, or been made aware that his friends would not create a crisis against the Party administration. They threatened, I hear, to raise Ireland against the Government and throw the country into turmoil. I expect it is all Dillon's work.[20]

18 Callanan, *T.M. Healy*, pp. 493–7.
19 Healy to Maurice Healy, 28 May 1915, Healy typescripts.
20 Healy to Maurice Healy, 10 June 1915, Healy typescripts.

Campbell was however appointed attorney general. Dillon considered this 'a very great outrage'.[21] Campbell was ultimately appointed lord chancellor for Ireland in June 1918, from which position he was induced to retire in 1921, when he was created Lord Glenavy.[22] It was in some respects fitting that the two barristers (fellow benchers of the King's Inns and of Gray's Inn) and wits, allies in intrigue against the Irish party, were to emerge as the twin pillars of continuity in the independent Irish state, as governor-general and chairman of the senate of the Irish Free State. (They were also to die within four days of each other in March 1931.)

III

Healy was given silk in April 1899, invited by the lord chancellor for Ireland, Lord Ashbourne, through the medium of James Campbell. He solicited the views of his brother Maurice:

> I don't know if I told you that some months ago Ennis, Walker's [lord chancellor for Ireland, 1892–5] late secretary, asked me would I take silk; and that I gave an evasive reply. On Friday James Campbell came to me, evidently acting on instructions, and told me that silks were to be made, and that I should apply. I said I would never ask for silk, but that it might be another matter if it were offered. His reply was that the Chancellor would never expose himself to a rebuff or a refusal but that, if I wished to take it, I should have this fact conveyed; but that probably none would be made until before the Circuits were going out; but that Ashbourne did things suddenly, that there were about thirty applicants, but only three or four would be created. I heard through Brereton Barry that the likely men were Wakely, Fetherston, Bates and myself.
>
> I confess I don't like the idea of becoming a Queen's Counsel, but that otherwise it would suit me very well. I don't think I should make anything less by the change, while the work would be more congenial, as I hate pleadings. Of course there is not very much in it one way or the other, but I should like to know your opinion.[23]

---

21 F.S.L. Lyons, *John Dillon* (London, 1968), p. 367; see also p. 375.

22 Healy's treatment of this subject in *Letters and leaders*, ii, pp. 552–3, omits reference to any role of his own, and gets the political sequence of the ultimate appointment of Campbell wrong. Curiously, Healy attributes the opposition to Campbell to the concern of the Irish party not to forfeit 'the power of making magistrates': ibid. This I think rather reflects a longstanding preoccupation of Healy's, vented on the hapless John Morley as chief secretary in 1892: Callanan, *T.M. Healy*, p. 419.

23 Healy to Maurice Healy, 21 April 1899. I have taken the text of the letter from the Healy typescripts, and the date of 21 April 1899 from the proofs of *Letters and leaders* carried over

Healy wrote to his father on the eve of his taking silk after nearly fifteen years a junior:

> The Lord Chancellor sent for me on Wednesday, and altho' I had not responded to several indirect proposals previously, as 5 of the new Q.C.s would be much my juniors if I remained at the outer bar, this would have many inconveniences in practice ... On political grounds I would prefer being as I am, but as the matter is a purely professional step, I don't see any valid objection to it, & this is Maurice's view also. Whether I shall lose or gain in practice remains to be seen, but in view of my relative position towards other Barristers I had not much option to remain as I was, unless I was to be outstripped in practice. I fancy I shall earn about as much as before, but in a different groove ... Lord Ashbourne made the proffer in very courteous and complimentary terms, but as there are over a dozen others admitted, it places me under no personal obligation & indeed the Chancellor himself pointed out, that the matter was only a recognition of professional status. Neither directly nor indirectly did I ask for me. Everyone at the bar is very kind and friendly to me.[24]

The first reference in Healy's correspondence to the possibility of his being made a bencher of the King's Inns, something of which he should strictly not have been aware, came in a letter he wrote to Maurice from the house of commons on 18 May 1904:

> Dodd [William Houston Dodd, serjeant at law and Liberal politician], who was over in the boat with me, told me that Denis Sullivan would be made a Bencher as a certainty in June, and he added the extraordinary fact, which I was quite ignorant of, that Palles proposed me as a Bencher last time, and said he would renew the proposal next time. It is very decent of the Chief Baron; and of course I never would have had any intimation of his courtesy only that I was accidentally travelling with Dodd.[25]

into the published version of the letter (Healy, *Letters and leaders*, ii, p. 434) which omits the material referring to his call to the inner bar. The typist who transcribed the letter in the typescripts could not make out the words 'did things' which I have taken from the proofs. Curiously E.H. Ennis in his days as a journalist on the *Freeman's Journal* during the split had been the author of the paper's libellous campaign against Healy in relation to the Maryborough trials: *Letters and leaders*, ii, pp. 360, 385; Callanan, *T.M. Healy*, pp. 218–9.

24 To Maurice Healy senior, 22 Apr. 1899. Healy-Sullivan papers, UCD P6/A/34, quoted in part in Healy, *Letters and leaders*, ii, p. 434.

25 Healy to Maurice Healy, 18 May 1904, Healy typescripts.

26 Book of the benchers of the King's Inns, 1901–17, p. 97.

It was almost a year before Healy was elected a bencher, on 15 April 1905.[26]

The *Freeman's Journal* carried a mild disparagement of his election in terms that convey the suspicion in which the benchers were held even by moderate nationalists a hundred years ago, at the time in which *Ulysses* is set:

> The election of Mr. T.M. Healy KC ... by the Benchers of the Honorable Society of the King's Inns, to be one of their number is a somewhat significant indication that Mr. Healy is no longer regarded by the Judges and Crown Prosecutors, and actual and potential Castle place-men, who mostly constitute that body, as a formidable opponent of the 'friends of the Union'. That the position of Bencher of the King's Inns is not conferred as a mere professional distinction is demonstrated by the fact that lawyers of little if any prominence, but of sociable qualities and no dangerous political faith, have been elected to 'the Bench', whereas lawyers of the greatest eminence but Nationalist politics have never been Benchers. Daniel O'Connell, who had a patent of prece-dence entitling him to rank at the Bar immediately after the Law Officers of the Crown, on whose acceptance the Mastership of the Rolls was unsuccessfully pressed, who was for more than a generation not merely the foremost Irishman of his day, but the acknowledged Leader of the Irish Bar, was never a Bencher of the King's Inns. His views on Repeal did not commend him to the coterie. Mr. Isaac Butt, whose eminence at the Bar was unquestioned, was never a Bencher.[27]

According to Healy, who was very well-informed on such matters, this was written by J.G. Swift MacNeill, who had been professor of constitutional and criminal law at the King's Inns until his election as a nationalist for South Donegal in 1887, a seat he was to hold until the 1918 election. Healy wrote to his brother:

27 *Freeman's Journal*, 18 Feb. 1905, carried also by its evening sister paper the *Evening Telegraph*, 18 Feb. 1905. The *Freeman's Journal*'s account of the opening of the law term which carried the news of Healy's election as a bencher at the meeting which followed was itself capable of raising the hackles of nationalists: 'at eleven o'clock the Lord Chancellor (Lord Ashbourne) held a levee of members of the Bar at his residence, Merrion Square, which was very largely attended. This over, his lordship drove to the Four Courts and entered by the grand entrance from the quay. A large crowd, a number of ladies gathered to witness the procession. The Lord Chancellor wore the usual state robe of black and gold, with the full bottomed wig, and stood on the steps under the clock to receive the other members of the judicial Bench as they arrived. His lordship was attended by Mr H.C. Colles, purse-bearer; Mr George Pilkington, train-bearer; the Hon. Edward Gibson, private secretary; and Mr N.W. Orr, mace-bearer. The other judges came in the following order ... All the judges were attired in state robes. The ceremony of reception over, their lordships proceeded to the Benchers' Chamber': *Freeman's Journal*, 17 April 1905. This account did not convey the characteristic editorial tenor of the *Freeman's Journal*, but of its 'legal intelligence'. It does have some of the lofty grandiloquence of the high Dublin journalistic style of the era which Joyce exquisitely played upon and to which he rendered satiric homage in *Ulysses*.

> My election as Bencher, I see from tonight's *Telegraph* – copied, I
> presume from the *Freeman* – does not please Pongo, on the ground that
> O'Connell and Butt (my great predecessors, of course!!) never got it.
> There was great want of taste in those olden days about their great
> men. *Nous avons changé tout cela.*[28]

Healy wrote to his father on 26 April 1905 immediately after his benching at
the King's Inns:

> I know it will give you pleasure to hear of the big muster of the Bar,
> that came to do me honour on my first dining as a Bencher at the
> King's Inns tonight. So I thought, I would write & tell you, as I hope I
> have not been given to noising little triumphs, & that you would appre-
> ciate it more on that account. These men being all my competitors and
> 'rivals' made me feel it all the more, and indeed the Chief Baron &
> T. O'Shaughnessy used the selfsame words, that it was a 'splendid demon-
> stration in my favour'. Nearly every man on the Munster Circuit, and I
> think every Munsterman in Dublin attended – the Protestants and
> Tories making it a point to be there. Many leading men from the other
> Circuits also came & there was not a vacant place in the Hall. I have
> received nothing but kindness and courtesy at this Profession, from
> gentle and simple for 20 years, & it is not for my own satisfaction but
> yours, because I know it will make you glad, that I say this. I could see
> the incident was very acceptable not only to the Chief Baron but to L.J.
> Holmes & Fitzgibbon who secured my Election, and came especially to
> dine with us. I asked no-one to propose or vote for me as Bencher. I
> didn't even know I was to be elected, but by a majority of 2 to 1 (which
> never occurred before) I was elected, being proposed by Lord Justice
> Holmes who pushed me in every way, altho' I never spoke a civil word
> to him in my life, attacked him in Parliament when he was Attorney
> Genl., & was often rough on him in the Ct. of Appeal! … Still, 'woe to
> you when all men speak well of you', but I am far from that situation,
> & it is only as a reaction & reproof to the rancour of the political
> campaign against me, that as you have seen so much abuse of me, &
> tonight's demonstration can never reach the public eye, I thought I wd.
> make you aware that I have plenty of friends as well as enemies.[29]

28 Healy to Maurice Healy, 18 April 1905, Healy typescripts. The letter appears in slightly
   altered form in Healy, *Letters and leaders*, ii, p. 473, with the insertion as the penultimate
   sentence of the words: 'he does not disclose that the constitution of the Benchers was then
   wholly different'. The letter is to his brother rather than his father. The edited version
   published identifies 'Pongo' as Swift MacNeill: the origins of the soubriquet are unknown.
29 T.M. Healy to Maurice Healy senior, 26 April 1905, *Healy-Sullivan papers*, UCD,
   P6/A/44; part quoted, in edited form, in Healy, *Letters and leaders*, ii, p. 474.

The letter conveys much of Healy's sense of political embattlement and the highly emotional deference he owed his father. It reflects Healy's conception of the Law Library as something of a sanctuary from the asperities of politics, and something of the gradual abatement within the Irish bar of political and sectarian animosities: a little of the letter's force is lost in the published version which refers only to 'the Tories' making it a point to be there, and omitting the reference to 'the protestants'.

IV

Healy was called to the English bar in 1903, as Sir Charles Russell had urged him years before. He had discussed his intentions in the letter to his father on taking silk in Ireland four years previously: 'I think I will avail of the new Rule in England to claim admission to the English bar, for which I have more than kept sufficient terms in 1880–3. Alex [Sullivan] & Jim Murphy have already gone to London but like myself I suppose only to have a "second string" to the bow, in case it ever comes in handy.'[30] While Healy's professional career in England could not be regarded as a failure, it was markedly less successful than his Irish career. The practice he won was not proportionate either to his professional prominence in Ireland or to his larger celebrity. He was given silk in England in November 1910,[31] chiefly as a reflection of his parliamentary standing. In his memoirs he gave an account of the circumstances of his appointment:

> I got 'silk' in England under the Chancellorship of Lord Loreburn. Meeting me in the Commons corridor after his appointment, he said, 'Healy, can I do anything for you?' 'Well', I laughed, 'are there any vacant bishoprics?' 'No', he murmured wonderingly. 'Then', said I, 'since you can't give me lawn you might give me silk'. He smiled, for, as Bob Reid, he, too, often urged me to come to the English Bar. So I became a King's Counsel in England as well as Ireland.[32]

---

30 Healy to Maurice Healy senior, 22 April 1899. In an interview in January 1929 for *Graya*, a Gray's Inn magazine, Healy proffered an explanation for the 'long interval' between his joining the Inn in 1880, and his call in 1903: 'I had gone to the Irish bar in 1881, and could not well afford to pay the fees and stamp duty on the Calls in both Islands, so I did not complete my barristerial connection with Gray's Inn, until 1903, being sufficiently engaged in practice in Dublin': 'Some recollections of Gray's Inn, by the treasurer [Master Timothy M. Healy KC]' in *Graya*, iv (Easter 1929), 10. Healy was admitted in 1881 to the King's Inns rather than to the Irish bar.

31 Healy, *Letters and leaders*, ii, p. 502; Callanan, *T.M. Healy*, p. 475.

32 Healy, *Letters and leaders*, i, p. 225.

Healy having lodged his patent of precedence as king's counsel was elected a bencher of Gray's Inn.[33] He put the episodic nature of his practice in England down to national and religious prejudice. Writing in October 1920 from the National Liberal Club to his brother on this subject, he referred first to his kinsman Serjeant Sullivan with whom he had a fractious relationship. A.M. Sullivan had been fearlessly outspoken in his opposition to the recourse to violence by republicans in Ireland, and there had been an attempt on his life in Tralee in January 1920. He was to settle in England after the foundation of the Irish state and have a successful career at the English bar. Healy's letter to Maurice continued:

> Although I am supposed to regard Alex like Dillon, this is not so; and I don't like to say he is making a mistake in thinking he will be a big draw in London; but I told Maurice [*fils*], who agreed, that there is not the least fear about him in Ireland. He should return to Dublin, I think. My own idea of the English is that they will not have an Irishman if he is a Catholic or a Nationalist in big business unless they are compelled. I settled a case today with Purchase of the Dunlop Co. on appeal from Ireland to the House of Lords, about a libel by picture on old Dunlop like Johnny Walker and, although the case was signed in Dublin by two Irish counsel who were Protestants, both were omitted; and no Irish counsel except myself stood on the record.[34]

Healy's satisfaction that he had continued to be retained while the other Irish counsel were not rather undercut his assertion that the prejudice he claimed to discern was religious as well as ethnic in nature.

Sir James O'Connor inserted in his *History of Ireland* a snide and patronising disparagement of Healy as an advocate:

> A lawyer most unquestionably he is not; nor, I think, does he profess to be. I sometimes fancied he had rather a contempt for the science of law … When Mr. Healy came to London, his fame as a politician brought him into several important cases, but, in spite of this, legal business never really came his way. In Ireland, the clients rather than the attorneys chose him; he said such good things that they thought all things which he said should be good. Ireland too, is full of people who would rather lose a law case gaily – with the salt rubbed into the sore spots of the opponent's carcass – than win it soberly and sombrely.[35]

---

33 Gray's Inn, *Book of orders*, xxii, 9, 17, 20 Nov. 1906. On 18 January 1911 it was ordered that Healy 'do have a voice and vote in Pension and do take his place according to the order of his call to the bench': *Book of orders*, xxiii.

34 Healy to Maurice Healy, 14 Oct. 1920, Healy typescripts.

35 Sir James O'Connor, *History of Ireland*, 2 vols (London, 1925), ii, p. 80. Healy's daughter

O'Connor was archly invoking Healy's rhetoric against Parnell in 1890–1:[36] deprecations of Healy's attacks on Parnell by those who had not taken Parnell's side were not always free from cant. However malignly disposed to Healy O'Connor was, there was some basis for his casting of Healy's professional profile as that of an implacable forensic mercenary.[37] Healy was certainly possessed of the idea of litigation as a somewhat primitive form of moral retribution by ordeal. His conception of the advocate's role comprised that of a hired scourge. If this had assumed grotesque form in his pseudo-forensic attacks on Parnell in the split,[38] it was not in purely professional terms a wholly indefensible position.

In January 1922, at the start of his last year of practice, Healy despatched to his brother one of his periodic remonstrations on the frugality of his fees:

> I return proofs; and I don't think you will suppose it is loss of fees that compels me to say the fee is absurd. This is a rich English client accustomed to business on the English scale. The recovery of money is not his impelling motive, but the punishment of a trickster. Whether or no, I don't know any solicitor who would send three guineas with bunch of papers on which the postage is tenpence ... The case is one of fraud, and not of a bona fide mercantile dispute. I think clients who neglect the most ordinary business precautions should pay for their legal revenge. There is no solicitor I think alive except yourself who would mark such a brief with a three guinea fee!![39]

V

Looking at Healy's career in the round, one is tempted to conclude that his vocation as an advocate provided him with an aqueous medium more fitted to his peculiar genius than the rigidly bounded *terra firma* of politics. His profession bestowed on Healy a final dividend in helping to bring about the remarkable rapprochement with Arthur Griffith and Michael Collins which,

---

Maev Sullivan wrote in the draft of the unpublished sequel to her *No man's man* that Healy had declined a request from O'Connor to exercise his political influence in his favour: Callanan, *T.M. Healy*, pp. 701–2, n. 25.

36 See Callanan, *T.M. Healy*, pp. 292–3.

37 Ibid., *T.M. Healy*, pp. 442–3.

38 Callanan, *Parnell split*, pp. 121–4; Callanan, *T.M. Healy*, passim.

39 Healy to Maurice Healy, 10 Jan. 1922, Healy typescripts. Years before Tim Healy had tendered his brother beautifully judged advice on whether Maurice's son and namesake should qualify as a solicitor or go to the bar, as he ultimately did: Healy to Maurice Healy, 13 Aug. 1904, 15 Oct. 1905, 31 Jan. 1906, Healy typescripts; Callanan, *T.M. Healy*, p. 442, p. 701, n. 22.

however guarded on their part, brought about their acquiescence in his appointment as governor-general of the Irish Free State. The professional services which Healy rendered as counsel for Sinn Féin activists or in Sinn Féin causes, of which his appearance at the inquest of the death of Thomas Ashe was the most significant, did much to permit him to emerge buoyant from the general wreck of parliamentary nationalism.[40] Healy had also attorned to the new order through a limited number of appearances in the Sinn Féin, or Dáil, courts. In the extraordinary correspondence he maintained with his brother tracking the rise of Sinn Féin, to which Maurice was unreconciled, Healy wrote on 15 July 1922:

> I am glad to have your certificate that the republican courts in Cork are behaving so impartially. Praise from Sir Charles [?]!! The closing down of the republican courts here must be a surprise for the judges, and I don't know what led to it. I was before them three or four times; and in every case justice triumphed!! I took quite a liking to them, in spite of the inconvenience, as they were devoid of all "side" and struggled to be fair. I never was before [Cahir] Davitt, but I heard he made an excellent judge, but I once reversed him in a Limerick seduction case. A new trial was ordered there, and I suppose the parties will now have to begin again in the High Court! The judges of course were inexperienced, but their zeal made up for this, I thought. There was, I gathered, a leaning towards Protestants!![41]

The bar council had in June 1920 determined that it was professional misconduct to appear in Sinn Féin courts. At a general meeting of members of the Law Library in November, Healy argued that the bar council was acting *ultra vires* and had usurped the prerogatives of the benchers of the King's Inns. The adjournment of the meeting ensured that the issue remained in abeyance until such time as it no longer mattered.[42]

Healy, despite his protests, was held by the government of W.T. Cosgrave to a five-year term as governor-general, which ended on 31 January 1928. In 1929 he served as treasurer of Gray's Inn. He is believed to be the only barrister who had appeared in a Sinn Féin court to have held that office.

40 Callanan, *T.M. Healy*, pp. 328–9.
41 Healy to Maurice Healy, 15 July 1922, Healy typescripts. Regrettably only Tim Healy's side of the correspondence survives.
42 M. Kotsonouris, *Retreat from revolution: the Dáil courts, 1920–4* (Dublin, 1994), pp. 32–3.

Judge Bodkin and the 1916 Rising: a letter to his son

FELIX M. LARKIN[*]

THE MAIN FOCUS OF THIS DISCOURSE is a letter written by Judge Matthias McDonnell Bodkin KC to his younger son, also Matthias McDonnell Bodkin, shortly after the 1916 Easter Rising. It is dated 8 May 1916. The Rising had begun on 24 April, the rebels surrendered on 29 and 30 April, and by 8 May twelve of the leaders had been executed by firing squad. The letter is among some 300 items relating to Judge Bodkin in the F.S. Bourke Collection in the National Library of Ireland,[1] and has not been published before. It is the property of the Board of the National Library of Ireland, and has been reproduced here with their kind permission:

> 52 Upper Mount Street, Dublin.
> May 8th, 1916.
>
> My darling boy [he was nearly 20 years old!],
> I hasten to answer your loving letter as soon as possible. All at home are first class. Your mother bore the ordeal.[2] Tom [Judge Bodkin's elder

* The edited text of a discourse delivered to the Society at the Royal Courts of Justice, Belfast, on 12 December 2003. I acknowledge the assistance of my late brother, Fr Arthur Larkin, in relation to some of the research for this discourse. My thanks are due to the following who also assisted me in various ways: Dr Ian d'Alton, Mr Philip Hamell, Mr Seán P. Cromien, Professor L. Perry Curtis jr (formerly of Brown University, Providence, RI), Dr Anne Kelly, Mr Peter Lacy, Ms Stephanie Larkin, Mr Terence A. Larkin, Dr Síghle Bhreathnach-Lynch, Mr Gerard Lyne and Mr Gerard Long (both of the National Library of Ireland), Professor Lucy McDiarmid (of Villanova University, Philadelphia, Penn.), Mr Paul McElroy, Mr James McGuire and Mr Richard Hawkins (both of the Royal Irish Academy's *Dictionary of Irish biography*), Dr Deirdre McMahon, Revd Robert Marshall, Mr Gregory O'Connor (of the National Archives of Ireland), Fr Stephen Redmond SJ and Ms Sara Smyth (of the National Photographic Archive). I am also grateful to those who contributed to the discussion that followed my discourse: The Honourable Mr Justice Hugh Geoghegan, Mr Anthony P. Quinn, Mr John Pinkerton (President of the Law Society of Northern Ireland) and His Honour Judge John Martin QC.

1 NLI, MS 10702; Bodkin's letter to his son is to be found in folio 19. The National Library of Ireland also holds Bodkin's surviving literary manuscripts: NLI, MSS 14252–64. The National Archives of Ireland has further relevant material, mainly Bodkin family correspondence: NAI, private accession no. 1155; hereafter cited as 'Bodkin family correspondence'.
2 Fierce fighting had taken place at Northumberland Road and Mount Street Bridge (close to

son][3] did splendid work as [a] volunteer Red Cross bearer at the Castle bringing in the wounded.[4]

The insurrection or revolt was very insignificant so far as the number of insurgents was concerned. A high government official told me that it was calculated that no more than two thousand all told took part in the disturbance in Dublin.[5] They behaved with desperate courage, but they did their best to put a stop to looting and there was no instance of wanton pillage or destruction of property on their part.

It was, of course, a mad attempt on their part. Some of the leaders were no doubt influenced by German gold,[6] but the majority were mere wild missionaries and the rank and file were duped into [the] grotesque belief that they were fighting for Ireland instead of against the best interests of the country.

There has been enormous destruction of property. More than half of Sackville Street is gone, a good part of Henry Street and Eden Quay and many places in the outlying district. These injuries arose mainly from accidental fires kindled by the looting of a comparatively small number of drunken men and women while the city was unprotected by the police.

---

the Bodkin family home, at 52 Upper Mount Street) on Wednesday, 26 April 1916. Moreover, there had been an incident in Northumberland Road on Easter Monday, 24 April (i.e. the first day of the Rising): an unarmed group of the Georgius Rex Volunteer Training Corps who, unaware of the Rising, had gone out on a routine practice march came under fire from rebels when returning to Beggars Bush barracks, and five were killed and seven wounded: see *The cruel clouds of war, a book of the sixty-eight former pupils and teachers of Belvedere College who lost their lives in the military conflicts of the 20th century* (Dublin, 2003), pp. 3, 4 and 81.

3 Thomas Patrick Bodkin (1887–1961), director of the National Gallery of Ireland, 1927–35. See p. 77 below. See also A. Kelly, 'Perfect ambition: Thomas Bodkin, a life (with particular reference to his influence on the early development of Irish cultural policy)', 2 vols (unpublished, Ph.D. thesis, Trinity College, Dublin, 2001). There is a collection of Thomas Bodkin's papers in the library of Trinity College, Dublin: TCD, MSS 6910–7079; hereafter cited as the 'Thomas Bodkin papers'. I am grateful to the Board of Trinity College, Dublin for access to this collection.

4 A note in the Thomas Bodkin papers, possibly written by Judge Bodkin's youngest daughter, Emma, records that 'Tom came home early [on Friday, 28 April 1916]. He had a terrible time out all night with the ambulance. The Sinn Féin[er]s fired on them even when they had Sinn Féin wounded': TCD, MS 7013/11. The Thomas Bodkin papers also contain rough drafts of a memoir of Easter week 1916 by Thomas Bodkin, mostly personal impressions: TCD, MS 7013/6–10.

5 In fact, it seems that fewer than 1,600 persons participated in the Rising. See F.S.L. Lyons, *Ireland since the Famine* (London, 1971), p. 366.

6 The proclamation issued by the rebels referred to 'gallant allies in Europe'. There is, however, no evidence that they had received money, or any other inducement, from Germany. They had succeeded in securing some German arms, but the arrangements for landing the arms in Co. Kerry shortly before the Rising were bungled. This led to the arrest of Sir Roger Casement, who was later hanged for high treason.

The General Post Office, which was a stronghold of the Sinn Féiners,[7] was completely gutted by artillery. The shells were dropped with such marvellous accuracy that, though the whole interior is levelled with the ground, the pillars, the outer walls and even the statues on the top are entirely uninjured.[8]

In my judgment, the revolt is now completely and finally extinguished. As I have said, a very small minority of the people were either engaged in the revolt or were in sympathy with it. The only danger now is in undue severity which may convert general indignation at the mad attempt into sympathy with the leaders.

It is generally recognised, even amongst Unionists in Dublin, that Sir Edward Carson and his preparations for an armed revolt against the constituted authorities are primarily responsible for the disturbance in Dublin. If there had been no Ulster Volunteers raised for the purpose of rebellion, there would have been no Sinn Féin volunteers and no rising in Dublin.

Personally what I should like to see now would be a general disarmament, including the Ulster Volunteers. I was strongly opposed to the repeal of the Arms Act.[9] I think it was a mistake for the Irish Party to press for it, and I said so to Redmond at the time. Instead of repealing it in Ireland, it should have been extended to England. In a civilised country, few men have any legitimate need of rifle or revolver and those few could have no objection to apply[ing] for a licence.

I do not think the Sinn Féin rising will injuriously affect the prospects of Home Rule, for I do not believe that after this disastrous catastrophe any man will dare again to threaten as Carson and his followers did an armed resistance to the law.

All join in very best love,
Ever your affectionate father,
M. McD. Bodkin.

---

7 Note Lyons' comment: '[o]ne of the strangest features of the rising of Easter week was that almost before it had ceased it was being described as a Sinn Féin rebellion. This curious misconception, which was shared by many Irish as well as by British observers, probably derived from the simple fact that whereas the secret springs of the insurrection were known to hardly anyone, the name of Sinn Féin as an open, separatist movement had been familiar for at least a decade. Yet to saddle Sinn Féin with the responsibility, or credit, for what had happened was a travesty of the truth': Lyons, *Ireland since the famine*, p. 380.

8 A photograph of the ruined General Post Office after the Rising, taken from the top of Nelson's Pillar, appears on p. 72. It was previously published in S. Rouse, *Into the light: an illustrated guide to the photographic collections in the National Library of Ireland* (Dublin, 1998), p. 29.

9 The effect of this had been to lift the restrictions on the right of individuals in Ireland to hold guns. The relevant legislation was the Peace Preservation (Ire.) Act 1881 (44 Vict, c. 5).

The careful analysis and lucidity of expression so apparent in this remarkable letter reflect its author's character and experience. The Bodkins were one of the famous 'tribes of Galway',[10] and Judge Bodkin was born in early October 1849 at Tuam, Co. Galway, where his father was a medical doctor. Educated by the Christian Brothers in Tuam and by the Jesuits at St Stanislaus' College, Tullabeg, Co. Offaly,[11] he went on to the Catholic University in Dublin to study classics. Quickly abandoning this endeavour, he joined the *Freeman's Journal* as a junior reporter. One of his earliest assignments was to report a speech made by the young Charles Stewart Parnell at his adoption as a candidate in the Dublin county by-election in 1874; he later wrote that he 'never before or since heard a poorer speech'.[12] Bodkin remained with the *Freeman* until 1880. Meanwhile, he also studied law, was called to the Irish bar in 1877 and began a moderately successful career as a lawyer. The lure of journalism, however, proved too strong – or perhaps the briefs that came Bodkin's way were not plentiful enough. In any event, in 1881 his former colleague on the *Freeman* staff, William O'Brien, later MP, became the first editor of *United Ireland*, a weekly newspaper established by Parnell as his personal mouthpiece, and O'Brien persuaded Bodkin to write for *United Ireland* on a part-time basis. When O'Brien was imprisoned in November 1887 under Balfour's Crimes Act, Bodkin took over as its acting editor. He retained that position until the Parnell 'split', his duties leaving him very little time to devote to the law.

Bodkin played a significant role in the Parnell 'split'. Though the 'split' was provoked by the verdict in the O'Shea divorce case in which Parnell was cited as co-respondent, it did not actually occur until almost three weeks afterwards – not until the Irish party's protracted debate on the question of Parnell's continued leadership, which lasted from 1 to 6 December 1890, in Committee Room Fifteen at Westminster. Acting on instructions from O'Brien who was in America evading a further jail sentence, Bodkin followed the majority view in the party and steered *United Ireland* into the anti-Parnell camp. He declared his position unequivocally in the issue of 6 December, by which time what would be the eventual outcome of the Irish party's deliberations was abundantly clear. When Parnell subsequently returned to

---

Strictly speaking, it was not repealed: it lapsed when the government, at the request of the Irish party, dropped it from the Expiring Laws (Continuance) Bill, 1906. See also p. 81 below.

10 A. MacDermott, 'The tribes of Galway' in *Irish Genealogist*, 2:4 (1946), 99–106.

11 He appears as 'Bodkin, Matthew, Tuam, 1866–1870' in the Tullabeg school list in *The Clongowes record, 1814 to 1932* (Dublin, n.d.), p. 224.

12 M.McD. Bodkin, *Recollections of an Irish judge: press, bar and parliament* (London, 1914), p. 169. Parnell was trounced in the by-election, though he could have had no realistic expectation of success in that constituency: see B.M. Walker (ed.), *Parliamentary election results in Ireland, 1801–1922* (Dublin, 1978), p. 120.

Judge Matthias McDonnell Bodkin. Frontispiece in M.McD. Bodkin, *Recollections of an Irish judge: press, bar and parliament* (London, 1914).

'Ruins of G.P.O., Dublin, as seen from top of Nelson's Pillar'. Valentine Collection, NLI, R.27,448. Reproduced courtesy of the National Library of Ireland.

Ireland (on 10 December), the first thing he did was to re-establish his authority over the paper, forcing his way into its offices with some associates and ejecting Bodkin. One of the Parnellites present described the scene thus: 'I went up to Matty Bodkin. "Matty", says I, "will you walk out or would you like to be thrown out" and Matty walked out.'[13] An attempt by anti-Parnellites, led by T.M. Healy MP, to re-occupy the offices failed. Undeterred, Bodkin used the *Irish Catholic*'s printing facilities to bring out a daily anti-Parnell organ, called '*Suppressed' United Ireland*. After three issues, Parnell got an injunction prohibiting his use of that title. Bodkin immediately replaced it with *Insuppressible*. That survived for about a month, until 24 January 1891. It collapsed when O'Brien, embarrassed by its intemperate criticism of Parnell, withdrew his support.[14]

The anti-Parnellites soon launched a proper daily newspaper, the *National Press*, of which Bodkin was the chief leader writer. This eventually merged with the *Freeman's Journal* in March 1892 under the latter's more venerable title. Bodkin continued to write for the merged paper until elected anti-Parnell MP for North Roscommon in the 1892 general election.[15] Having no independent means, he had been reluctant to stand for parliament and stepped down in 1895 after only one term. He found the routine of parliamentary life dull. With the Liberals in power and the government supported by the anti-Parnell nationalists, Bodkin's 'daily duty was to sit silent and vote', to quote his own words.[16] There may have been another factor in his decision to step down as an MP, for he had become the target of sustained invective in the pro-Parnell newspaper, the *Irish Daily Independent*. This led him to take a libel action against the *Independent* in 1895. Bodkin won but, having sought damages of £2,000, was awarded only £20 – hardly an unambiguous vindication of his reputation.[17] After leaving parliament, he

---

13 See R.B. O'Brien, *The life of Charles Stewart Parnell*, 2 vols (3rd ed., London, 1898), ii, p. 291; O'Brien's informant is not identified by name, but is described as 'one of Parnell's Fenian supporters'. Dr Nicholas Donnelly, titular bishop of Canea and auxiliary to the archbishop of Dublin (and a close friend of Bodkin and his wife; he had officiated at their wedding in 1885), wrote to Mrs Bodkin on 10 December 1890: 'I cannot tell you with what indignation I read in the evening paper [about] the shameful treatment to which your good husband has been subjected today at the hands of that awful scoundrel [i.e. Parnell]. It makes my blood boil. I always felt ... that he was a thousand times too good to be throwing himself away on such a crew and I trust soon that his future lot will be cast where he may achieve the position his ability entitles him to in the pursuit of his chosen profession': F.S. Bourke Collection, NLI, MS 10702/19.

14 F.S.L. Lyons, *The fall of Parnell* (London, 1960), pp. 155–7 and 235–6.

15 See Walker (ed.), *Parliamentary election results in Ireland*, p. 148.

16 Bodkin, *Recollections of an Irish judge*, p. 211.

17 P. Maume, 'Commerce, politics and the *Irish Independent*, 1891–1919', unpublished paper read at the 24th Irish Conference of Historians held at University College, Cork, 20–22 May 1999; I am grateful to Dr Maume for giving me a copy of this paper. A copy of the

returned to the *Freeman* staff and was its chief leader writer until his appointment as county court judge for Clare in November 1907. In this period, he combined journalism with occasional legal work – he had become a queen's counsel in 1894 – and was also a director of Todd, Burns & Co., the Dublin drapery store. Furthermore, in 1904 he represented Irish journalism at the World's Press Parliament, an international gathering of the 'fourth estate', at St Louis, Missouri. While in the United States, he also visited Chicago, Boston, New York and Washington, where he had a private meeting with President Theodore Roosevelt at the White House. Bodkin published a diary of this trip,[18] and wrote about it again in his autobiography, *Recollections of an Irish judge: press, bar and parliament* (1914).[19]

His appointment to the bench in 1907 was part of the policy of the new Liberal government to involve nationalists in the governance of Ireland in anticipation of home rule.[20] It was a controversial appointment, not least because Bodkin, as a former MP, had taken the Irish party's pledge against holding office and had himself previously denounced another former Irish MP, Arthur O'Connor, for accepting an English judgeship in defiance of the pledge.[21] Moreover, Bodkin's qualifications were suspect since he had not seriously practised law since the 1880s. This led to a court challenge to the validity of his appointment, instigated by Alexander Sullivan (afterwards the last serjeant at law in Ireland). The plaintiff, represented by Sullivan, was one Stephen Markham, an illiterate labourer from Ennis, Co. Clare, against whom Bodkin had given judgment in the county court. The case, however, ultimately fizzled out.[22] It was the subject of questions in the house of commons; and, when the chief secretary for Ireland, Augustine Birrell, was asked what had induced the plaintiff to drop the case, he replied that he understood it had been 'a pint of porter'.[23] The attorney general, R.R. Cherry, later wrote to Bodkin that 'Sullivan [had] instituted and financed the whole proceedings'.[24]

    statement of claim in Bodkin's libel action against the *Independent* is in the Timothy C. Harrington papers in the National Library of Ireland: NLI, MS 8932.

18 M.McD. Bodkin, *A trip through the States and a talk with the President* (Dublin, 1907).

19 Bodkin, *Recollections of an Irish judge*, pp. 310–41.

20 See L.W. McBride, *The greening of Dublin Castle: the transformation of bureaucratic and judicial personnel in Ireland, 1892–1922* (Washington DC, 1991), especially pp. 145–6.

21 P. Maume, *The long gestation: Irish nationalist life, 1891–1918* (Dublin, 1999), pp. 91–2.

22 *Freeman's Journal*, 24, 25, and 28–30 January 1908. See also D. Hogan, 'R.R. Cherry, lord chief justice of Ireland, 1914–1916' in D.S. Greer and N.M. Dawson (eds), *Mysteries and solutions in Irish legal history: Irish Legal History Society discourses and other papers, 1996–1999* (Dublin, 2001), p. 180. Bodkin's elder son, Thomas Bodkin, wrote some humorous verse about the case; a printed copy, undated, on a single page, is in the Thomas Bodkin papers: TCD, MS 6913/95.

23 *Hansard's Parl. Deb., 4th ser.*, vol. clxxxiii, cols. 722–3 (4 February 1908).

24 R.R. Cherry to M.McD. Bodkin, 5 February 1908: Bodkin family correspondence, NAI, 1155/1/2/3; Cherry was later a lord justice of appeal and lord chief justice of Ireland: see

Cartoon entitled 'A burden of guilt', *Freeman's Journal*, 15 February 1921

As a judge, Bodkin distinguished himself in February 1921 by reading in open court a statement of his criminal injury awards arising from actions by crown forces, notably in Lahinch, Ennistymon and Miltown Malbay in September 1920. He concluded by saying that '[l]aw and order cannot be restored or maintained by ... a competition in crime'.[25] Asquith and the

Hogan, 'R.R. Cherry'. The Thomas Bodkin papers contain three letters to Thomas Bodkin from Serjeant Sullivan regarding certain pictures, and also a draft of the reply from Thomas Bodkin to one of these letters; they are entirely amicable in tone and make no reference to the proceedings that Sullivan took against Judge Bodkin: TCD, MS 7007/1001–4.

25 *A considered judgment: report of Judge Bodkin forwarded to Sir Hamar Greenwood and read in open court at Ennis, Co. Clare, on Saturday, 5 February 1921* (Dublin, 1921). See also *Another considered judgment: second report of Judge Bodkin* (Dublin, 1921).

archbishop of Canterbury both referred to this statement when criticising in parliament the government's record in Ireland.[26] It received substantial press coverage in Ireland – especially as it came just a few weeks after a damning report by General Strickland on reprisals by crown forces in Cork in December 1920. An unusual feature of this press coverage was the publication of some very sharp cartoons in the *Freeman's Journal*, one of which is reproduced on page 75.[27] It depicts the prime minister, Lloyd George, and the then chief secretary for Ireland, Sir Hamar Greenwood, bearing with difficulty the burdens of the Strickland report and 'Judge Bodkin's indictment'.

In addition to 'press, bar and parliament' – to quote the subtitle of his *Recollections of an Irish judge* – there was a fourth strand to Bodkin's career: he was the author of many popular books, among which *White magic* (London, 1897) was a fictional account of his early years. His *Famous Irish trials* (1918) has recently been reissued, with an introduction by Dr Eamonn G. Hall.[28] Best known during his lifetime were his short stories about detectives Paul Beck and Dora Myrl; these imitated the Sherlock Holmes stories of Sir Arthur Conan Doyle, but are not nearly as good. In Sir Hugh Greene's definitive assessment of Bodkin as a writer of detective fiction, he belongs in the 'twilight world of neglected, but not completely forgotten, writers ... who wrote the occasional story which deserves to be resurrected, if not for its literary quality, then for some ingenuity of plot, some sudden flash of imagination, some light on the late Victorian and Edwardian world'.[29] Bodkin's creation of a male and a female detective is not a unique achievement. Agatha Christie had Hercule Poirot and Miss Marple, as well as Tommy and Tuppence.[30] Moreover, four of the Lord Peter Wimsey novels

26 *Hansard's Parl. Deb.*, *5th ser.*, (commons), vol. 138, cols. 616–9, 629–30 and 704–5 (21 February 1921); *Hansard's Parl. Deb.*, *5th ser.*, (lords), vol. xliv, cols. 86–8 (22 February 1921).

27 *Freeman's Journal*, 15 February 1921. See *The reign of terror: a series of 'Shemus' cartoons printed in the Freeman's Journal during 1920–1* (Dublin, n.d.), p. 9; see also pp. 8 and 30. The cartoonist was Ernest Forbes (1877–1962), later a well-known landscape artist and portrait painter in London and in his native Yorkshire. His full name was Ernest Forbes Holgate, but he dropped the surname when signing his work. He drew for the *Freeman* under the pseudonym 'Shemus'. For an obituary of Ernest Forbes, see the *Yorkshire Post*, 20 February 1962. I am grateful to Mr Alex Robertson of the Leeds City Art Gallery and also to the staff of the Local Studies Library in the Central Library, Calverley Street, Leeds, for information on Forbes.

28 First published in Dublin and London in 1918, reissued in Dublin in 1997.

29 H. Greene (ed.), *The crooked counties: further rivals of Sherlock Holmes* (London, 1973), pp. 12 and 16–7. This volume contains two stories by Bodkin, 'Murder by proxy' (featuring Paul Beck) and 'How he cut his stick' (featuring Dora Myrl).

30 The names 'Tommy' and 'Tuppence' are short for Thomas Beresford and Prudence Cowley. The books in which they feature are *The secret adversary* (London, 1922), *Partners in crime* (London, 1929), *N or M?* (London, 1941), *By the pricking of my thumbs* (London, 1968) and *Postern of fate* (London, 1973).

by Dorothy L. Sayers feature a female writer-turned-detective called Harriet Vane.[31] In our own time, P.D. James has balanced her Adam Dalgliesh novels with a couple of books about Cordelia Gray, a private detective.[32] Like some of the other male and female detectives with an author in common, Paul Beck and Dora Myrl eventually marry. They then have a son who also becomes a detective: his adventures are the subject of *Young Beck, a chip of the old block* (London, 1911), the fifth collection of Bodkin's detective stories published between 1898 and 1911. A sixth – an afterthought, perhaps using material not previously thought worthy of publication – came out in 1929.[33]

Bodkin retired from the bench, aged 74, on the introduction of the Free State court system in 1924, but continued to take a lively interest in current affairs. Thus, in 1929 he wrote to his elder son, Thomas Bodkin, then director of the National Gallery of Ireland: '... the substitution of Gaelic for English would be a curse to the Free State and a fatal obstacle to the reunion of Ireland. It is a comfort that the attempt is bound to fail, but meanwhile it entails the expenditure of a large amount of public money and the obstruction of primary education.'[34] His sound judgment in this matter – like his analysis of the 1916 Rising – is hugely impressive. He died at his home, 52 Upper Mount Street, Dublin, on 7 June 1933.[35] He had married in 1885 Arabella Norman, the daughter of a Dublin solicitor. They had two sons and four daughters, of whom the eldest, Thomas Bodkin, was director of the National Gallery of Ireland from 1927 to 1935 and then Barber professor of fine arts and director of the Barber Institute of Fine Arts at the University of Birmingham (1935–52). Their youngest daughter, Emma Bodkin, was one of the first women chartered accountants in Ireland and reputedly the model for the character Miss Christine Lambert in Lennox Robinson's *Drama at*

---

31 *Strong poison* (London, 1930), *Have his carcase* (London, 1932), *Gaudy night* (London, 1935) and *Busman's honeymoon* (London, 1937). Sayers began another novel about Lord Peter Wimsey and Harriet Vane, which was finished posthumously by J. Paton Walsh as *Thrones, dominations* (London, 1998).

32 P.D. James's novels featuring Cordelia Gray are *An unsuitable job for a woman* (London, 1972) and *The skull beneath the skin* (London, 1982).

33 M.McD. Bodkin, *Paul Beck, detective* (Dublin, 1929). The earlier volumes were *Paul Beck, the rule of thumb detective* (London, 1898), *Dora Myrl, the lady detective* (London, 1900), *The quests of Paul Beck* (London, 1908) and *The capture of Paul Beck* (London, 1909).

34 M.McD. Bodkin to Thomas Bodkin, 31 October 1929: Bodkin family correspondence, NAI, 1155/1/4/5. Thomas Bodkin shared his father's lack of sympathy for reviving the Irish language: see Kelly, Perfect ambition, i, pp. 174–6.

35 Obituaries appeared in the *Irish Independent*, *Irish Press* and *Irish Times* on 8 June 1933. See also *Dod's parliamentary companion, 1893* and *Who was who, 1929–40*. I have written the entry on Bodkin for the Royal Irish Academy's *Dictionary of Irish biography* (Cambridge, forthcoming). For an affectionate portrait by one who knew Bodkin well, see Mrs William O'Brien, *My Irish friends* (Dublin & London, 1937), pp. 95–101.

Inish (1933).[36] Two other daughters became Carmelite nuns. His wife and one of their daughters predeceased him.[37]

The recipient of Judge Bodkin's letter about the 1916 Rising – Matthias McDonnell Bodkin *fils* – was the youngest of the family, and in 1916 was a Jesuit student for the priesthood at his father's *alma mater*, St Stanislaus' College, Tullabeg. Born in Dublin in 1896 and educated at Belvedere College and Clongowes Wood College,[38] he had entered the Jesuit novitiate in 1914 and was ordained in 1932. For many years a teacher in Clongowes, Mungret College and Belvedere, Fr Bodkin later served as a Royal Navy chaplain during World War II in Derry and for a brief period in the Pacific on board HMS *Anson*.[39] Afterwards, his eyesight failing, he undertook mainly retreat work and counselling.[40] Like his father, he was a prolific writer, largely on religious themes but also of adventure stories for boys. So as to differentiate his own from his father's work, Fr Bodkin never used his second Christian name.[41] He died on 2 November 1973 at Milltown Park, Dublin, the last survivor of Judge Bodkin's family.[42] The following passage, in an undated letter from Fr Bodkin to his brother, gives a touching insight into the judge's relationship with his priest-son: '[o]f course, I am worried about the poor old fellow but overjoyed at your news of his talk with you on religious subjects. I always feel that with me he is inclined to imagine that to be a cleric is to have [an] abnormal facility for belief and perhaps [good] conduct, with a consequent inability to understand the difficulties of others. I'm sure you can do far more for him than I.'[43] Sophie O'Brien (*née* Raffalovich, the wife of

36 Emma Bodkin (1892–1973). See C. Ó hÓgartaigh and M. Ó hÓgartaigh, 'A man's trousers on' in *Accountancy Ireland*, 31:5 (1999), 22–3. See also A. Farmar, *A history of Craig Gardner & Co.: the first 100 years* (Dublin, 1988), p. 125.

37 Arabella Bodkin (*née* Norman) died on 17 January 1931, aged 76. Their daughter Norah (in religion, Sister Joseph Agnes of Jesus and Mary) died on 30 October 1929, aged 39.

38 See *The Clongowes record, 1814 to 1932*, p. 254.

39 See Thomas Bodkin's 'Verse to Fr. M. Bodkin in the Far East' (unpublished), in the Thomas Bodkin papers: TCD, MS 6913/76. He contrasts himself 'groping in Birmingham fogs' with Fr Bodkin's situation 'on sunlit eastern seas', and refers to:
   '... the long-gone days when they played together at ball
   In the narrow garden behind their father's house
   And did not dream the world could grow so wide.'

40 Mr Justice Geoghegan has told me that he once attended a retreat for members of the Irish bar conducted by Fr Bodkin.

41 A full bibliography of the Matthias McDonnell Bodkins *père et fils* is to be found in A. Denson, *Thomas Bodkin: a bio-bibliographical survey, with a bibliographical survey of his family* (Dublin, 1966).

42 Obituaries appeared in the *Irish Independent* (3 November 1973), the Jesuit *Irish province news* (January 1974) and *The Belvederian* (1974). His sister, Emma Bodkin, predeceased him by a few months only.

43 Fr M. Bodkin to Thomas Bodkin, undated: Bodkin family correspondence, NAI, 1155/1/4/1.

William O'Brien MP) recalled that Judge Bodkin's 'last joy was being alive for the ordination of his son'.[44]

Fr Bodkin's most substantial book was *The port of tears* (1954), a life of his fellow Jesuit, Fr John Sullivan, which did much to spread Fr Sullivan's reputation for sanctity.[45] Fr Sullivan also had connections with the legal world. Born in 1861, he was the son of Sir Edward Sullivan, lord chancellor of Ireland from 1883 until his death in 1885, and was himself called to the English bar by Lincoln's Inn in 1888. Raised in the Church of Ireland (though with a catholic mother; this was before the *Ne temere* decree), he converted to catholicism in 1896 and entered the Jesuit order four years later. Following ordination in 1907, he spent most of the rest of his life on the teaching staff at Clongowes[46] and died in 1933. The cause for Fr Sullivan's canonisation was opened in 1947. Fr Bodkin had known him well at Clongowes, and so could draw on personal experience in his account of Fr Sullivan's extraordinary life.[47]

Writing to his brother in 1956, Fr Bodkin remembered 'playing cricket [at Tullabeg] in 1916 Easter week',[48] but clearly he was not oblivious of the disturbances in Dublin and soon sent a letter home inquiring how his family had survived 'the ordeal'.[49] Judge Bodkin's letter of 8 May 1916 was his reply to that 'loving letter'.[50] The significance for us of the judge's letter is that it is an immediate, uninhibited response to the Easter Rising from a long-standing Irish party stalwart of repute and some accomplishment in a variety

---

44 O'Brien, *My Irish friends*, p. 101.

45 M. Bodkin SJ, *The port of tears: the life of Father John Sullivan SJ* (Dublin, 1954). An earlier biography of Fr Sullivan, which was superseded by Fr Bodkin's work, was F. McGrath SJ, *Father John Sullivan SJ* (London, 1941). Fr McGrath's book inspired Ethel Mannin to write her novel *Late have I loved thee* (London, 1948). The obscure title of Fr Bodkin's biography is (surprisingly) not explained by him, but Fr Sullivan had attended Portora Royal School in Enniskillen and it may be a play on the name Portora. Christian literature sometimes refers to life in this world as a valley of tears, and Portora means 'harbour of tears' since it is the traditional departure point for funerals to nearby Devenish island in Lough Erne: see Bodkin, *The port of tears*, p. 14.

46 He was, however, rector of Rathfarnham Castle in Dublin from 1919 to 1924.

47 Bodkin, *The port of tears*, p. 113. See also P. Costello, *Clongowes Wood: a history of Clongowes Wood College, 1814–1989* (Dublin, 1989), p. 101.

48 Fr M. Bodkin to Thomas Bodkin, undated but, from internal evidence, written just after Easter 1956: Bodkin family correspondence, NAI, 1155/1/4/10. This may perhaps be seen as a variation on what Dr Conor Cruise O'Brien has identified as the 'Fairyhouse tradition' in relation to the 1916 Rising, i.e. for a substantial body of Irishmen, the focus of interest on Easter Monday 1916 was not the occurrence in the General Post Office in Dublin, but rather horse racing at Fairyhouse: C. Cruise O'Brien, '1891–1916' in C. Cruise O'Brien (ed.), *The shaping of modern Ireland* (London, 1960), pp. 14–5.

49 Unfortunately, this letter is not extant. The quotation is from Judge Bodkin's letter of 8 May 1916.

50 That was Judge Bodkin's characterisation of his son's letter: see p. 67 above.

of spheres. Its publication, therefore, complements the recent work of Professor Paul Bew in reconstructing the constitutional nationalists' critique of the Rising and the events that flowed from it.[51] In addition, it challenges us to look beyond the ongoing debate for or against the Rising, and the related issues of whether, and how, it should be commemorated[52] – and to consider instead what actually happened, why it happened and why it had the effect that it had. Four points in particular should be noted about the letter. First, while Bodkin condemns the Rising as a 'mad attempt', nevertheless he acknowledges the 'desperate courage' of the rebels and praises them for trying to minimise looting by the general public. He thus presages the speech in the house of commons on 11 May 1916 in which John Dillon MP, deputy leader of the Irish party, also spoke of the 'courage' of the insurgents and proclaimed that they had 'fought a clean fight, a brave fight, however misguided'.[53]

Secondly, Bodkin was not alone in assigning blame for the Rising to Sir Edward Carson and his associates, on the basis that their resistance to home rule had reintroduced the gun into Irish politics. For example, the *Freeman's Journal* – under the absolute control of the Irish party leaders in 1916 – referred to 'the licence' that the Unionists had 'arrogated to themselves, and thus extended to every fomenter of civil strife'. That was in the very first issue of the paper after the Rising, on 5 May. Likewise, on 8 May (the date of Judge Bodkin's letter) it stated that 'confidence in peaceable and con-stitutional agitation had first been sapped and ruined by the Carsonite movement in Ulster'. Bodkin may well have read these words in the *Freeman* – his former employer – that morning, before writing to his son. This line was also adopted by the *Irish Independent*, which in 1916 had a much greater circulation and a more diverse readership than the *Freeman's Journal*. It was owned and successfully operated by the Dublin businessman William Martin Murphy.[54] In its first issue after the Rising, on 4 May, it argued that 'Sir Edward Carson's movement in Ulster, with its threat of civil war … set the

---

51 P. Bew, 'Moderate nationalism and the Irish revolution, 1916–1923' in *Historical Journal*, 42:3 (1999), 729–49. A revised version of this essay has appeared as 'Moderate nationalism, 1918–23: perspectives on politics and revolution' in M.J. Bric and J. Coakley (eds), *From political violence to negotiated settlement: the winding path to peace in twentieth-century Ireland* (Dublin, 2004), pp. 62–80.

52 The Taoiseach, Bertie Ahern TD, recently announced the resumption of the traditional military parade past the General Post Office in Dublin on Easter Sunday in commemo-ration of the 1916 Rising (see *Irish Times*, 22 Oct. 2005).

53 F.S.L. Lyons, *John Dillon: a biography* (London, 1968), pp. 380–3.

54 See D. McCartney, 'William Martin Murphy: an Irish press baron and the rise of the popular press', in B. Farrell (ed.), *Communications and community in Ireland* (Dublin & Cork, 1984), pp. 30–8, and A. Bielenberg, 'Entrepreneurship, power and public opinion in Ireland: the career of William Martin Murphy' in *IESH*, xxvii (2000), 25–43. See also Maume, 'Commerce, politics and the *Irish Independent*'.

example which other disaffected elements in the country took as an invitation to arm and drill for their own objects. If there had been no Ulster Volunteers ... there would have been no armed Sinn Féiners or Irish Volunteers.' This last sentence, probably by coincidence, is replicated almost exactly in Judge Bodkin's letter. Moreover, such comments were not confined to Irish sources: on 29 April 1916, even before the Rising was over, the *Glasgow Observer* had asserted that 'Larne begat Dublin', adding the gloss that 'what happened in Dublin ... was simply the consequences of what happened earlier at Larne when the associates and followers of Sir Edward Carson flouted and defied the law of the land, held up its legal guardians and engaged in military operations'.[55]

Thirdly, Bodkin is most prescient in identifying the danger of 'undue severity' in the reaction of the authorities to the Rising. Dillon would say something similar in his speech in the house of commons on 11 May 1916. Two days earlier, on 9 May, the *Freeman's Journal* had warned that 'sympathy is being aroused with the victims [i.e. the executed leaders] where nothing but indignant condemnation of their criminal enterprise previously existed'. In contrast, the *Irish Independent* as late as 12 May was still calling for the execution of 'some of the worst of the leaders [of the Rising] whose cases have not yet been disposed of'. The leaders in question were James Connolly and Seán MacDermott. They were, in fact, shot early on the morning of 12 May, a few hours before most readers would have seen the *Independent's* bloodthirsty editorial.

Finally, Bodkin distances himself from the Irish party leadership on the question of lifting the restrictions on the right of individuals in Ireland to hold guns. This had been done by the new Liberal government in 1906 at the urging of the Irish party, but Bodkin took the view that it was a grave mistake. Now he is confirmed in that opinion. Ironically, his opinion was shared by Serjeant Sullivan, the man who had tried to secure his disqualification as county court judge for Clare. In his *Old Ireland: reminiscences of an Irish KC*, Sullivan wrote: '[t]he foundations of anarchy were laid by an unscrupulous section of the Irish Party who intrigued to procure the dropping of the Arms Act ... The Irish Party and their cause were swept into oblivion in consequence.'[56] Lest there be any confusion: Serjeant Sullivan was not related to Fr John Sullivan, the saintly priest who was the subject of Fr Bodkin's book, *The port of tears*.

In 1914, in the last sentence of his autobiography, Judge Bodkin expressed the hope that he would 'live to administer the laws of an Irish legislature'.[57]

---

55 Quoted in T.P. Coogan, *1916: the Easter Rising* (London, 2001), pp. 136–8.
56 Serjeant Sullivan, *Old Ireland: reminiscences of an Irish KC* (London, 1927), p. 149. Sullivan and Bodkin both refer to the 'Arms Act', but the relevant legislation was the Peace Preservation (Ire.) Act 1881 (44 Vict, c. 5). See note 9 above.
57 Bodkin, *Recollections of an Irish judge*, p. 359.

He did live to see an independent Ireland, but it was not the home rule Ireland of his aspiration. The 1916 Rising had sounded the death knell of home rule. As Bodkin – like most other contemporary observers – was much too close to events to appreciate that fact when writing to his son on 8 May 1916, he could end his letter on an optimistic note, certain that the Rising would not 'injuriously affect the prospects of Home Rule'. That may seem naïve today, but such is the perspective of hindsight.

Legal nationalism: the case of
Lord Cooper

HECTOR L. MacQUEEN*

WESTERN LEGAL SYSTEMS ARE COMMONLY classified in two groups, or families. One is the civilian or civil law group, based ultimately upon the law of the Romans as interpreted and reworked in the middle ages and afterwards, found principally now in continental Europe, and today typically set out in codified form. The other is the Anglo-American common law group, founded upon the laws first developed in medieval England, spread across the world by the growth of the British Empire, and still today uncodified and regarding the decisions of judges in individual cases – precedents – as a major source of law alongside legislation. The Scottish legal system is often said to occupy a mid-position, or to be 'mixed', because the substance of much of its law is, for historical reasons stretching back to the middle ages, a combination of the civilian and the common law. Further, Scots law is uncodified, and precedent is an important source.

Professor Lindsay Farmer of Glasgow University has recently written of 'the strange case of legal nationalism' in Scotland, taking as his starting point the identification of this phenomenon by another Glasgow law professor, John P. Grant, in a collection of essays published in 1976 to consider the place of law in a devolved Scotland (at a time when devolution to Scotland was a distinct possibility). Farmer summarises Grant's analysis thus:

> He considered it to have four principal elements: a belief in the inherent strengths of Scots law; a belief in the exceptional character of the system; that it was a legal system ideally matched to the needs and personality of the Scottish people; and the conviction that the system should be safeguarded against those influences (principally, but not exclusively English) that sought to dilute its identity. The distinctive characteristic of the legal nationalist, however, was that this commitment to a distinctive Scottish legal identity did not necessarily entail any support for nationalist politics.[1]

---

* The slightly revised text of an address to the Society in the Great Hall, Queen's University, Belfast, on 7 May 2003. It represents work in progress, as I hope to complete a much fuller study of the work of Lord Cooper.
1 L. Farmer, 'Under the shadow of Parliament House: the strange case of legal nationalism',

Farmer goes on, however, to discuss the writings of one particular legal nationalist who was also a political nationalist or, if you prefer, a nationalist politician. This was yet another Glasgow law professor, Andrew Dewar Gibb, who held the Regius chair of Scots law from 1934 to 1958. It is, I think, well known that Gibb was prominent in nationalist politics between the wars; perhaps less well known are what Farmer clearly demonstrates to be his sympathies for fascist, anti-semitic and anti-Irish catholic positions, and his support for nationalism as a way of resisting the growth in his lifetime of big government and public social welfare programmes.[2] Maintaining the traditional identity and forms of Scots law and its institutions was one way of resisting the development of new forms of government. So, Farmer suggests, legal nationalism can 'be seen as a reaction to the growth of the role of government with the rise of the welfare state ... However, as we seek a more coherent explanation for its emergence, we should not ignore the more ignoble roots of the tradition [of legal nationalism] in the right-wing, racist and elitist politics of the 1930s.'[3]

It will be apparent, then, that Farmer is out of sympathy with legal nationalism, or at any rate the version of it summarised by John Grant. His article is, however, the latest (and, I should say, one of the most interesting) in what is now a reasonably long list of critical commentaries upon Scottish legal nationalism. The first of these was in fact published in the Grant collection of essays: a paper by Ian Willock,[4] with whom we move away from the Glasgow to the Dundee law school. Willock's contribution, entitled 'The Scottish legal heritage revisited', argued that Scots law had been fitted out with an ideology since the Second World War. This ideology had two prime begetters. One was Professor T.B. (later Sir Thomas) Smith, who had held chairs at Aberdeen and Edinburgh between 1947 and 1972 before going on to become a Scottish law commissioner (a post he still held at the time of Willock's article; he retired in 1982 and died in 1988). The other was the judge, Lord Cooper of Culross, who had died in 1955 but until then had been Smith's 'guide and mentor'. According to Willock:

---

in L. Farmer and S. Veitch (eds), *The state of Scots law: law and government after the devolution settlement* (Edinburgh, 2001), p. 151, summarising J.P. Grant, 'Introduction', in idem (ed.), *Independence and devolution: the legal implications for Scotland* (Edinburgh, 1976).

2 For a detailed analysis of inter-war nationalist politics in Scotland, see R.J. Finlay, *Independent and free: Scottish politics and the origins of the Scottish National Party, 1918–1945* (Edinburgh, 1994).

3 Farmer, 'Under the shadow', pp. 162–3.

4 I. Willock, 'The Scottish legal heritage revisited', in Grant, *Independence and devolution*, pp. 1–14.

Baron Cooper of Culross. Portrait in oils, by W.O. Hutchison, 1956. Reproduced by kind permission of Mr R.E. Hutchison. Photograph reproduced by kind permission of the Faculty of Advocates, Edinburgh.

Lord Cooper was steeped in Scottish legal history and imbued with a sense of the historical mission of Scots law. From his successive positions of eminence as Lord Justice-Clerk (1941–1947) and Lord President of the Court of Session (1947–1954), until his premature death in 1955, he tirelessly proclaimed the virtues of Scots law.[5]

What Willock dubbed the 'Cooper-Smith ideology' he summarised as follows:

1. Scots law is an authentic emanation of the Scottish spirit – a Scottish *Volksgeist*.
2. Its predominant characteristic is an adherence to principle rather than precedent.
3. Contemporary juristic writers as well as judges have a part to play in enunciating these principles.
4. The influence of English law through the United Kingdom parliament, the house of lords (as a final court of appeal in civil matters), and more recently the large Whitehall departments of state, represents a continuous threat to the integrity of Scots law. In the recent past many alien doctrines have thereby been injected into Scots law.
5. The salvation of Scots law lies in drawing upon its own historical roots and upon the experience of other 'mixed' systems, such as those of South Africa and Louisiana, where too a basically Roman civilian system is threatened by infiltration from other legal traditions.
6. Scots law has a destiny to be a bridge between the common law and civilian systems within the European Community.

Willock goes on to attack the ideology as backward-looking, static and elitist, its focus being upon law for lawyers rather than for the people of Scotland, and as a recipe for stagnation, leaving the law out of touch with social developments and popular need. It saw legislation as an interference with the law created by judges and jurists rather than as a tool for the betterment of the law in the service of society as a whole.

Many others have since picked up or indicated their support for such critiques of the Cooper-Smith ideology. 'A distinctive legal system is about as desirable as a distinctive system of weights and measures,' wrote another commentator in the Grant collection,[6] while one of Lord Cooper's successors in the president's chair at the court of session, Lord Rodger of Earlsferry, has suggested that concern with Scots law as a whole is an academic's rather than a practitioner's pursuit and has argued for a pragmatic approach, letting the law develop in accordance with the demands and fashions of the times.[7] But

5 Ibid., p. 2.
6 E.M. Clive, 'Scottish family law', in Grant, *Independence and devolution*, p. 173.
7 A. Rodger, 'Thinking about Scots law' in *Edinburgh Law Review*, 1 (1996), 3–24.

the ideology still has its defenders and proponents, and the debate first prompted by Ian Willock seems likely to run for some time to come.

The debate has so far paid surprisingly little attention to Lord Cooper. Sir Thomas Smith has attracted much more interest, partly because the memory of his vivid personality is still very much alive today, whereas relatively few now have much recollection of Cooper in life; and also because, as befitted a professor even before there was a research assessment exercise, he wrote far more and developed his ideas in much greater depth than was ever possible for a practising advocate, politician and judge. Yet there is a good deal of published material by Cooper, dating from the early 1920s and including one or two posthumous pieces, much of it conveniently gathered in a collection of *Selected papers* published in 1957. From this some attempt can be made to piece together the development of his particular views on Scots law and his contribution to legal nationalism in Scotland.

But let me first return to Lindsay Farmer's article on Dewar Gibb and make some observations on the questions which that raised in my mind with particular reference to Cooper (and, indeed, to T.B. Smith). Farmer drew particular attention to a pamphlet which Gibb published in 1930, called *The shadow on Parliament House: has Scots law a future?* This and other pre-war works by Gibb, as Farmer's analysis suggests, and as I can confirm from my own reading of them, clearly anticipate much of what Willock called the 'Cooper-Smith ideology'. While Cooper was a friend and associate of Dewar Gibb, probably over a long period even before 1930, Smith was still only a schoolboy in 1930 (he was born in 1916). So Willock's ideology appeared at least to be misnamed and misdated so far as concerned its progenitors.

A further point that struck me was that, while Cooper and Dewar Gibb might have been friends, they were not of an identical political persuasion, at least so far as party was concerned. Cooper was a unionist (in modern terms, a conservative) who stood for parliament in that interest in 1930 and was finally elected in 1935, to become a member of the national government as solicitor general for Scotland, and, later, as lord advocate.[8] While this puts Cooper on the political right, he seems much more moderate in his position than Dewar Gibb; and he was certainly not a political nationalist. A contemporary, while noting that Cooper 'took a peculiarly black view of modern economic conditions', also observed that '[i]n his radicalism, he was scarcely a typical Conservative politician and a generation earlier he would certainly have been an Asquithian Liberal.'[9] Cooper (like Smith also, in my view) provides an excellent confirmation of Grant's observation that legal and

---

8 For some context, see I.G.C. Hutchison, 'Scottish unionism between the two world wars' in C.M.M. Macdonald, *Unionist Scotland, 1800–1997* (Edinburgh, 1998), pp. 73–99.

9 *The journal of Sir Randall Philip, OBE, QC: public and private life in Scotland, 1947–57*, ed. F. Craddock (Edinburgh, Cambridge, Durham, NC, 1998), pp. 5, 6.

political nationalism are not necessarily linked. It is worth noting here that, when lord advocate, he advised (correctly) against a Scottish coronation for Edward VIII, on the basis that it would be contrary to the treaty of Union.[10]

A final thought was that Farmer's article seemed to treat legal nationalism as essentially a twentieth-century phenomenon. But, as I attempted to show in an article in the *Scottish Historical Review* in 1995, law has been a badge of national identity in Scotland since at least the thirteenth century. True, the perception of that badge has changed over the centuries: the main thrust of my article was to show how the medieval roots of Scots law had been seen as a major defining characteristic until the nineteenth century, when that began to be overlaid by an emphasis upon the Roman law dimension which distinguished Scots law most sharply from English law.[11] I finished by saying:

> In the twentieth century, this stress on the Civilian tradition became, not just a question of history, but more a programme for the renaissance of a Scots law otherwise doomed to irretrievable Anglicisation. In this perspective, the middle ages had contributed almost nothing to the distinctive character of Scots law, which had essentially been begun anew and on a Civilian basis with the writings of Stair. This may be described as the modern myth of Scottish legal history. Like its predecessor, it contains much which is true, but it is not the whole truth.[12]

The emphasis on the civilian (or non-English) dimension of Scots law as containing its essential character is, of course, another major part of the 'Cooper-Smith ideology', although not explicitly identified as such by Ian Willock. In 1995, I left unexplored the process of the twentieth-century formation of 'the modern myth'; but Farmer's article seemed to demand some further investigation of the subject. Where did the 'Cooper-Smith' ideology come from? How did it develop? Certainly Smith had provided the fullest and most detailed articulation of it, but was Cooper the originator, and whence did he draw his ideas?

It is necessary to begin with some biography. Thomas Mackay Cooper was born in the south side of Edinburgh on 24 September 1892. His father was the burgh engineer of Edinburgh, but there was law in the family on the

---

10 This is revealed in *Journal of Sir Randall Philip*, p. 5. See also ibid., p. 4, reproducing a letter from Cooper to Philip dated 12 July 1936, stating the former's view.

11 See e.g. H. Goudy, *An inaugural lecture on the fate of Roman law north and south of the Tweed* (London, 1894); J. Dove Wilson, 'The reception of the Roman law in Scotland' in *Juridical Review*, 9 (1897), 361; Lord Shaw of Dunfermline, *The law of the kinsmen* (London, 1923), pp. 137, 169–70; J. Mackintosh, *Roman law in modern practice* (Edinburgh, 1934); Lord Normand's foreword to J.S. Muirhead, *Outline of Roman law* (Edinburgh, 1937).

12 '*Regiam majestatem*, Scots law and national identity' in *Scottish Historical Review*, 74 (1995), 1–25, at p. 25.

mother's side: her brothers were solicitors, one in particular being or to become a partner in the well-known Edinburgh court firm, Messrs Macpherson and Mackay WS. Cooper's father died in 1901, and thereafter he was brought up, with his younger brother James, by their mother, living at another address on the Edinburgh south side, 42 St Albans Road. Holidays seem to have been spent on the beaches and golf courses of Fife. The boys were schooled at George Watson's College, and Thomas (or Tommy, as he was known) then went on to take an MA in Classics and an LLB at Edinburgh University, finishing his student days in 1913. After graduation, he embarked upon a bar apprenticeship in his uncle's firm, then devilled before being called to the bar in 1915.

I highlight here Cooper's very middle-class Edinburgh background, because I think it an important element in understanding the man, his work and his ideas. One of the many interesting shafts of insight into Cooper's personality offered in the journal of his advocate contemporary and friend, Sir Randall Philip, is the following: 'Cooper was essentially a product of the middle class backbone of Scotland, the product of a professional man's home, Grammar School and the traditions of Thomas Chalmers and the Free Kirk.'[13] In other words, his upbringing and education take us into a very Scottish, perhaps even a very Edinburgh, world and culture, with little external influence apparently brought to bear in the formation of the man and his socio-political views. Something of the attitudes thus engendered comes through another entry in Philip's diary for 1953, when there was speculation that Cooper was about to be promoted to the house of lords: 'but, as he once said to me, he could not stand the atmosphere of "Westminster and All Souls"';[14] and this from a man who by then had spent many years at the heart of British government, first as a wartime civil servant between 1915 and 1919, and then as lord advocate 1935–1941.

Although I know nothing of the political views of Cooper's father, it seems not unreasonable to suppose that, as a professional man employed in the civic enterprises of a largely self-governing burgh which was also the capital of Scotland, he shared at least some of those nineteenth-century middle-class Scottish attitudes towards their country and its autonomy which have been so interestingly explored by such as Lindsay Paterson and Graeme Morton, and labelled by the latter as 'unionist-nationalism'.[15] Certainly some of these attitudes, I suggest, informed the development of Lord Cooper's legal nationalism. They are nowhere more evident than in an address he gave in 1930, remarkably enough to the Institute of Bankers, which might not

---

13 *Journal of Sir Randall Philip*, p. 2.
14 Ibid., p. 324.
15 L. Paterson, *The autonomy of modern Scotland* (Edinburgh, 1994); G. Morton, *Unionist-Nationalism: governing urban Scotland 1830–1860* (East Linton, 1999).

have been thought the most receptive of audiences for this message,[16] even if their speaker assured them that it was not the election address of a nationalist candidate:

> ... there never was a time when there was greater need to stimulate and to foster all that is best in Scottish ideals, Scottish sentiment, and Scottish traditions, if the spirit of Scotland is to survive and to rise superior to the material influences which are at present combining to stifle our independent national life. In matters commercial, industrial, financial and political, we are rapidly succumbing to a process which can only end, if unchecked, in degrading Scotland to the level of a minor and decaying English province.[17]

Cooper began to write almost immediately upon commencing practice in 1919, but not on the traditional core areas of private law which have been at the heart of the Cooper-Smith ideology in its modern form. Instead, he was the junior partner with Sir William E. Whyte in a book on the very modern subject of housing and town planning, published in 1920.[18] His earliest article was a fairly severe critique of legal education in Scotland, published in 1922,[19] but the criticism rested, not on the basis of the law faculties' failure to respect or develop the traditions of Scots law, but upon the inertia of the curriculum, which was both 'palpably illogical, and wholly out of touch with modern conditions and requirements'.[20] There were 'whole continents [of law] of which Stair and Erskine never dreamt';[21] while the 'haphazard arrangement' of the curriculum, 'founded upon the principle of unequal emphasis', meant that civil law received as many lectures as the whole of Scots law.[22] Apart from an observation that 'it is essential that the law student in his early days should view the jurisprudence of Scotland as an organic whole',[23] nothing much here conjures up the 'Cooper-Smith ideology'.

In 1933 Cooper published a short but critical note on the decision of the house of lords in the celebrated 'snail in the bottle' case, *Donoghue v.*

---

16 But *cf.* R.J. Finlay, 'National identity in crisis? Politicians, intellectuals and the "end of Scotland"' in *History*, 79 (1994), 242, showing that as the Great Depression bit deeply in Scotland after 1929, so traditional unionists turned more and more to nationalist rhetoric of the type exemplified in Cooper's remarks quoted below.

17 *Selected papers*, p. 38.

18 T.M. Cooper and Sir William E. Whyte, *The law of housing and town planning* (Edinburgh, 1920). In 1926 there was a second edition of this work, which contained the texts of the legislation with a commentary thereon, but Cooper does not seem to have been involved.

19 Compare A. Dewar Gibb, *The shadow on Parliament House: has Scots law a future?* (Edinburgh, 1930), p. 6: '[a] Scottish law-school of today gives little more encouragement to true legal scholarship than a Baptist church seminary.'

20 *Selected papers*, p. 7.   21 Ibid., p. 4.

22 Ibid., pp. 6–7.   23 Ibid., pp. 5–6.

Stevenson,[24] arguing that the judicial creativity there on display, going beyond any recorded precedent, was illegitimate:

> The law of Scotland and England and of the countries which have derived their law from England has developed primarily as a system of case law, founded upon respect for the common law and for the judicial precedents which constitute its most important source ... [T]he fact remains that judicial precedent is the heart and core of our jurisprudence, and that, if we ceased to be case lawyers, we should cease to be lawyers at all ... [I]f amid the wealth of precedents ... no answer is given to the question whether a given right or remedy exists, it would seem a reasonable assumption that the common law does not recognise the right nor afford the desired remedy, and that it is to the Legislature that the aggrieved party must look.[25]

There are many grounds on which legal nationalists have since criticised *Donoghue v. Stevenson*, but the failure to follow precedent has not been one of them. Again, it does not appear that a concern to follow principle rather than precedent was as yet dominant in Cooper's thinking.

What really seems to have concerned the inter-war Cooper, and to have continued to concern him after 1945, was the growth of the state and government at the expense, as he saw it, of the individual, with a corresponding reduction in the role of law, lawyers and the courts. An interest in such public law questions may have sprung from the nature of some of his practice, concerned with private legislation procedure enabling public works to take place, usually at the behest of local authorities or those opposing what the bill proposed.[26] His concerns thus tie in with the thinking of Dewar Gibb already discussed, inasmuch as he saw 'a remarkable and increasing tendency by the Executive to encroach farther and farther upon the legislative and judicial functions of government'.[27] But unlike Dewar Gibb, Cooper seems to have accepted the inevitability of the growth of the state in the social and economic conditions prevailing after 1918, the question being for him how to find and maintain a balance between government and the individual in the altered circumstances of the modern world. In this he thought that both private and public law and the judicial system had a role to play. And later on in his public career, in 1942, he was to head the committee of inquiry which recommended the establishment by the state of the North of Scotland

---

24 1932 SC (HL) 31. 25 *Selected papers*, p. 57.

26 See JMC, in *Selected papers*, p. xv; J.A. Lillie, *Tradition and environment in a time of change* (Aberdeen, 1970), p. 82. Further on Cooper's practice in company law, see ibid., p. 109; and for other cases, pp. 133–4. On the nature of parliamentary private bill practice, see Lord Macmillan, *A man of law's tale: the reminiscences of the Rt Hon Lord Macmillan* (London, 1952), pp. 51–76.

27 *Selected papers*, p. 26 (written 1929).

Hydro-Electric Board, to dam Highland rivers and utilise the water resources thus obtained to provide electricity in the Highlands; the aim being, as his report expressed it, 'to give the Highlands and the Highlanders a future as well as a past'.[28]

At the heart of his concerns was the proliferation – or, as Cooper put it, the 'perplexing variety and lack of system'[29] – of administrative tribunals discharging judicial and quasi-judicial functions in the new dispensation, as opposed to the courts. The overall theme was a familiar one, given focus for lawyers by the English lord chief justice, Lord Hewart, in his book *The new despotism*, published in 1929. But the interest of Cooper's contribution to the debate is its attack upon the use of administrative officials to perform judicial functions part-time. Two solutions lay to hand: one, the use instead of officials of the full-time, legally qualified Scottish sheriff in the role of administrative judge ('on the score of efficiency the probabilities are all in favour of the experienced professional judge and against the casual amateur'[30]); the other, the development of a British *droit administratif*, comparable to the French system, by which the courts would regulate the conduct of tribunals and officials. All of this would have great resonance in his later work on legal history.

In subsequent years Cooper also came to see a further challenge to the judicial system in the resort to arbitration by private parties in preference to having their disputes resolved by the courts.[31] For him this was the ultimate reproach to the legal system itself. In 1947 he wrote that, 'we [i.e. lawyers] have forgotten that the law was made for the citizen, not the citizen for the law'.[32] If the individuals for whom the courts and the rule of law existed were rejecting what they had to offer, reform was necessary. How could judicial process be made cheaper and quicker? Cooper argued for what we would now call judicial case management to ensure that litigation kept moving, and also for a simplification of the court hierarchy, leaving the judge of first instance as final on matters of fact, with limited appeal on matters of law to the next level, and a further appeal to the house of lords only by leave of the court.[33]

Again, the law might be made easier to determine and apply if it was codified rather than left dependent on an ever-growing body of precedent.[34] In any event, the substantive law in some parts at least cried out for reform.[35]

---

28 *Report of the committee on hydro-electric development in Scotland* [Lord Cooper, *chairman*], 1942 [Cmd. 6406]; see further J. Hunter, *Last of the free: a millennial history of the Highlands and Islands of Scotland* (1999), p. 345.
29 *Selected papers*, p. 28 (written 1929).
30 Ibid., p. 36.   31 Ibid., pp. 154–5, 246–7.
32 Ibid., p. 156.   33 Ibid., pp. 157–8, 251–7.
34 Ibid., p. 157; *cf.* ibid., pp. 205–6, 249–50. Note that Dewar Gibb also favoured codification: *Shadow on Parliament House*, pp. 33–6.
35 *Selected papers*, pp. 148–51, 159.

This was not merely an academic view. When lord advocate, he helped to promote legislative reform of both marriage (ridding Scots law of the irregular 'Gretna Green' marriage *per verba de praesenti* and of marriage *per verba de futuro subsequente copula*), and divorce (amending the law relating to the grounds of divorce). He was also responsible for the first modern Law Reform (Miscellaneous Provisions) (Scotland) Act in 1940, enacting some of the proposals of a law reform committee which, following an English model set up in 1934, Cooper had established in December 1936.[36] His writings indicate that he would also have liked to use his opportunities as a law officer to abolish the feudal land law system and to reform the law of intestate succession, a bill to the latter end apparently failing to reach parliament in 1938 only because of the deteriorating international situation.[37] As a judge, he gave the leading opinion in 1950 in *Beith's Trs v. Beith*,[38] which some view as authority for the maxim in Scots law, *cessante ratione legis cessat lex ipsa*, and which shows Cooper's court not following a weighty precedent of 1875 on married women's property, on the grounds that the legislative background to that case had since been changed significantly.

All this seems to show that, whatever else his conservatism may have entailed, Cooper was not a reactionary preserver of either the good old Scots law or the established ways of doing judicial business. Nor, I think, is it fair to see his concern with the law as 'elitist', or at any rate consciously so. A revealing passage in his Saltire Society pamphlet, *The Scottish legal tradition*, published in 1949, shows his perception of the close relationship between private law and the people of Scotland:

36 For the initial establishment, membership and remit of the Law Reform Committee, see 1937 SLT (News) 8. The first topics were (1) the use of holograph wills as links in title to heritage; (2) the enforcement of decrees *ad factum praestandum*; (3) the law and practice of edictal citation; (4) title to sue for solatium; and (5) contribution between joint delinquents. The first of these was dealt with by the Conveyancing Amendment (Scotland) Act 1938; the 1940 Act's eleven sections reformed the law on (2), (4) and (5) above, as well as on prorogation of the jurisdiction of the sheriff court, extension of the Intestate Husbands (Scotland) Acts, the Crown as *ultimus haeres*, certain international conventions affecting jurisdiction, and aspects of criminal procedure and summary jurisdiction. For a contemporary comment (by J.R. Philip, a member of the Law Reform Committee), see 1940 SLT (News) 93.

37 *Selected papers*, pp. 150, 187, 189. See also ibid., p. 255: '[l]aw reform, whether affecting procedure or substantive law, is a heart-breaking enterprise. *Experto crede*. It has no vote-catching value, least of all when it is technical as it usually is, and it makes no appeal to either Government or Opposition. With infinite difficulty it may be possible to secure the appointment of a Committee; but too often that Committee's report when at long last it appears is left to languish in a pigeon-hole to await that most elusive of all commodities – Parliamentary time. And Parliamentary time will rarely be allotted to such a subject except for an agreed measure, which means that one determined opponent can veto action' (written 1953.)

38 1950 SC 66; 1950 SLT 70.

[W]hen we speak of a legal system let us think rather of the body of principles and doctrines which determine personal status and relations, which regulate the acquisition and enjoyment of property and its transfer between the living or its transmission from the dead, which define and control contractual and other obligations, and which provide for the enforcement of rights and the remedying of wrongs. These are the matters which inevitably touch the lives of all citizens at many points from the cradle to the grave, and their regulation is a function of government with which no civilised community can dispense and on the due administration of which the well-being of every society depends.[39]

The first published indication of Cooper's interest in legal history came in 1930, when he gave a lecture celebrating 'Some classics of Scottish legal literature' for an audience of bankers.[40] In this he highlighted the institutional works of Stair, Erskine and Bell, but the point of interest is the way in which Cooper gives the palm to Stair and Bell rather than Erskine, as jurists who could be seen to have helped bring the law into line with the requirements of their times and the times which followed, using external sources as necessary for the purpose. But Roman law and the civilian tradition, it should be noted, were not specifically mentioned in this context. It was other lawyers of the period, notably Cooper's colleague at the bar, Wilfred Normand KC, who were arguing for the use of the civilian tradition to develop Scots law. Normand, who became lord president of the court of session in 1935, wrote in 1937:[41]

... there are chapters in Scots Law today in which we may feel confident that a decision in harmony with the texts of the great Roman jurists will harmonize also with the genius of our law ... We have in the tradition of Roman Law a vast and unexhausted treasure house of principle, highly rationalized and deeply humanistic, which we must not neglect if we are to maintain the identity of Scots Law in the necessary changes and modifications of the future. For unless our law continues to grow in accordance with that tradition it will run a grave risk of becoming a debased imitation of the Law of England, stumbling and halting before every new problem where we have no English precedent to guide us. From that fate our law students and future practitioners can save us by a right appreciation of the Roman tradition in the Law of Scotland and by accepting it as an active principle of natural growth and development.

39 *Selected papers*, p. 174.   40 Ibid., pp. 39–52.
41 Foreword to Muirhead, *Outline of Roman law*.

This may be contrasted with Cooper, writing for the first time in 1936 about the medieval law which would later become his major field of study outside his ordinary legal work:[42]

> There is here a rich and almost unexplored field for the investigator – the law of Scotland as it was before it became deeply permeated by the law of Rome, the Canon Law, and the law of the feus ... There is indeed a sense in which Stair is open to the criticism which Dutch lawyers have directed against Grotius and Voet – that he enslaved his country to an alien system, or at least that he largely discarded or ignored its native rules, and sought to break the natural continuity of their development.

There is a striking contrast between Cooper's enslaving alien system and Normand's treasure house.

Two years before these words were published, Cooper was amongst a distinguished group of lawyers and historians (interestingly, not including Normand) who published proposals for the formation of a Scottish legal history society to be known as the Stair Society.[43] Their numbers did include the Scottish law lord, Lord Macmillan, who actually seems to have been the prime mover in drawing up the scheme.[44] The real significance of the proposal in the history of legal nationalism lies in its clear identification of the principal interest in the history of Scots law being the 'mixed' character of the Scottish legal system, and the importance of this for comparative legal science. The proposal contains the following passage about Scots law, which embodies some central tenets of the 'Cooper-Smith ideology':

> It is also of unique interest among the legal systems of the world in that it affords the only instance of the combination in theory and practice of the Civil Law and the Common Law, the two great rivals for supremacy in the legal world. On the one hand, it has drawn its inspiration largely from the law of Rome, yet unlike the continental nations under the Civil Law it has no code: on the other hand, while it shares the respect for precedents distinctive of the Common Law, it has also been systematised in the works of authoritative institutional

---

42 T.M. Cooper, '*Regiam majestatem* and the auld lawes' in *The sources and literature of Scots law*, Stair Society, vol. 1 (Edinburgh, 1936), p. 77.

43 For the text of the proposal see *Juridical Review*, 46 (1934), 197–201.

44 See Lord Macmillan, *Man of law's tale*, pp. 214–16; also his *Law and other things* (Cambridge, 1937), pp. 130–2. See also Viscount Dunedin, *Divergencies and convergencies of English and Scottish law*, 5th David Murray lecture (Glasgow, 1935), p. 10.

45 *Juridical Review*, 46 (1934), 197.

writers. As a practical compromise between code law and case law it is a characteristic product of the Scottish genius.[45]

But when Cooper came to promote the Stair Society to his professional colleagues in a short note in the *Scots Law Times*, he did not choose to dwell on this comparative law perspective, but rather once again on the need to engender legal renaissance in modern Scotland itself:

> ... it is possible to detect in Scotland a relaxation of effort and a weakening of interest in the broader and deeper aspects of legal research, a growing disinclination to participate in the wider problems of comparative jurisprudence and legal reform, and an increasing tendency to find in the latest precedent or departmental regulation a substitute for the fundamental principles of law and equity ... If accepted and prosecuted with enthusiasm, this project may pave the way to an expansion of beneficent activities in many directions – leading, perhaps, with the assistance of the universities and the legal societies, to an improved system of legal education, to large-scale legal reforms, and eventually to a Scottish legal renaissance, under the inspiration of which the Scottish lawyer, as the exponent of a system unique in its development and characteristics, may be able to make contributions of permanent value to the jurisprudence of the civilised world.[46]

The proposal for the Stair Society also cited a paper published a decade before by the French comparative lawyer, Henri Lévy-Ullmann, in which he had discussed the varied historical sources and development of Scots law and concluded, in a passage quoted by the Stair Society proposal, that 'Scots law as it stands gives us a picture of what will be some day (perhaps at the end of this century) the law of the civilised nations, namely a combination between the Anglo-Saxon system and the continental system'.[47] A translation by F.P. Walton of this paper, first delivered in French in Paris in 1924, had been published in the main Scottish academic law journal, the *Juridical Review*, in 1925; the paper, it may be noted, was also cited by Dewar Gibb in his 1930

---

46 T.M. Cooper, 'The Stair Society' in SLT (News) (1934), 113.

47 The idea that Scots law might be a model for the international unification of law was not a wholly new one in the 1920s, however. A prefatory note by the editors of the first issue of the *Juridical Review* in 1889 commented: '[t]he Law of Scotland owes a large debt to the jurisprudence of other countries, especially to the Roman and the English Law, and to the works of the Jurists of France, Holland, Germany and America. Scotland may, perhaps, repay a small part of that debt by showing, by means of practical examples, how principles derived from foreign as well as native sources have been combined in a good working system by her own eminent judges and legal writers': *Juridical Review*, 1 (1889), 1.

pamphlet.[48] Lévy-Ullmann was the leading French figure in the rapidly developing academic field of comparative law, which was increasingly focusing upon the ways in which, as a result of their histories, legal systems differed in their approach to, but not necessarily their solutions of, concrete problems. The comparative lawyers had in particular identified the vital divide which lay between the common law of England and the civil law of the European continent. The common law of England and, significantly, its history were at the centre of Lévy-Ullmann's researches,[49] and it was in the course of this that he had discovered Scots law and its mixture of the two traditions previously thought to be so sharply distinct.[50] Other French academic lawyers had followed in his footsteps,[51] while the theme of Scots law as a mixed system worthy of comparative study in an international context had been picked up by Lord Macmillan in an address to the International Congress of Comparative Law at The Hague in August 1932, and also featured in his Rede lecture, 'Two ways of thinking', delivered in Cambridge in May 1934.[52]

I would therefore suggest that, although much of what we have come to know as the 'Cooper-Smith ideology' had been developed in at least embryonic form before the Second World War, Cooper himself had not played a direct or leading part in these initial formulations. The seed was the well-known Roman law or civilian dimension of Scots law, which continued to differentiate it from the law of England, but a topic on which Cooper had written very little indeed. What especially propagated the seed, I would suggest, were the writings of a French comparative lawyer concerned with

---

48 *Shadow on Parliament House*, p. 38.

49 His major work on the subject, *Éléments d'introduction générale à l'étude des sciences juridiques: le système juridique de l'Angleterre. Tome premier, Le système traditionnel* (Paris, 1928), appeared in translation in 1935, as *The English legal tradition: its sources and history*. There are brief references to Scots law at pp. xxiii–iv, and 132–3.

50 See K.G.C. Reid, 'The idea of mixed legal systems' (the Eason-Weinman lecture) in *Tulane Law Review*, 78 (2003), 5–40, at pp. 8–10. Reid points out that the existence of mixed systems had been recognised by F.P. Walton in the late 1890s (see 'The civil law and the common law in Canada' in *Juridical Review*, 11 (1899), 282 at p. 291), and the term itself apparently coined and explored in some detail by R.W. Lee in an article published in 1915: 'The civil law and the common law – a world survey' in *Michigan Law Review*, 14 (1915), 89. But Lévy-Ullmann, under the stimulus provided by the First World War and the foundation of the League of Nations, seems to have been the first to detect the potential of a mixed system for global unification of law.

51 See e.g. A. Bérard, *La survivance du droit romain en Écosse* (*Thèse*, Paris, 1925).

52 Lord Macmillan, 'Scots law as a subject for comparative study' in *LQR*, 48 (1932), 477–87, reprinted in idem, *Law and other things*, pp. 107–17; for the Rede lecture, see *Law and other things*, pp. 76–101. See also Mackintosh, *Roman law in modern practice*, pp. 30–1, referring in 1934 to the 'composite nature' of Scots law, and adding that 'our Scots Law is a knitting together of many scattered threads as variegated in hue as the national tartan'.

the international unification of law as a means to a more peaceful and orderly world in the aftermath of a long-lasting European war. In other words, its roots lie much more in the ideals of the essential brotherhood of man than in those of fascism.

Possibly the principal tender of the new plant in Scotland was Lord Macmillan, whose role in this period deserves fuller exploration. The idea of Scots law as a model for unification of law was discussed by Cooper in some of his later writings, but does not seem ever to have enthused him, because, like Dewar Gibb before him, he felt that Scotland was too small to play a major part in world movements.[53] Cooper was undoubtedly already deeply concerned with the state of Scotland and the survival and development of Scots law; but in his view this was essentially an internal matter for the Scots, not something fit for export abroad. The law had not been designed or operated on a large stage, and so would likely prove inappropriate in that context. And equally, before 1939 there is little sign that he saw much assistance coming from abroad for Scots law, or from the civilian tradition, in the legal renaissance he sought. The Savigny-esque link between law and people should not be broken, at least in a small country like Scotland.

This is not to say that some roots of the later ideology described by Ian Willock are invisible in the writings of the inter-war Cooper. Clearly he was a patriotic Scots lawyer, and the idea of Scots law as a truly Scottish product under threat from external influences was firmly established in his mind. But this Scottish-ness was not yet found in the civilian or mixed characteristics of the law, and the solutions to the problems of the system were not to be found in comparative law or legal history. This angle would emerge instead after the experience of another world war, during which Cooper began his serious work on Scottish legal history – significantly, medieval, pre-Reception, Scottish legal history, and the 'native' tradition which it might be thought to embody. As I hope to show elsewhere, much of this work was coloured by the concerns which Cooper had expressed before 1939, but in turn it led him to new insights into the development of Scots law from its beginnings in the twelfth century. There never had been much indigenous Scots law; it had always developed by borrowing from other systems, and that borrowing had been characterised by 'effort ... to attain simplicity, flexibility and directness, and to attain these things systematically'.[54] As a result, Cooper began to be able to join up his earlier thought with those who had promulgated Scots law as a civilian or mixed system, with all that that entailed by way of positioning the law for further development. These were the foundations upon which, for good or ill, the full-blown Cooper-Smith ideology would be built.

53 *Selected papers*, pp. 145–7; also pp. 182, 198.   54 *Selected papers*, p. 178.

Prevention and detection of crime in nineteenth-century Ireland

BRIAN GRIFFIN*

ONE OF THE MOST IMPORTANT features of the constabulary of nineteenth-century Ireland, and of the Dublin Metropolitan Police (DMP), who first took to the streets of Dublin in January 1838, was that their recruits were repeatedly informed that the primary function of a policeman was the prevention and detection of crime, with the emphasis placed on his preventive role.[1] This point has been somewhat obscured by those historians who emphasise the military character of the Irish police, and especially of the Royal Irish Constabulary (RIC).[2] Both major nineteenth-century Irish police forces, by their preliminary training of recruits, went to great pains to impress on new members the concept of the policeman as a person dedicated to combating crime. In this the Irish police authorities were considerably in advance of their counterparts in Britain. In nineteenth-century England many recruits were sent out on the beat with only a hazy notion of what was expected of them as policemen. An English police historian has described the nineteenth-century policemen as 'working class men with no training, dressed up in uniform'.[3] W.J. Lowe qualifies this somewhat by showing that mid-century Lancashire policemen, at least, spent some time in learning 'routine military drill'. In the 1850s the Liverpool Borough Police had a month-long probationary training period, during which recruits spent their time observing the routine of the police courts and accompanying experienced

---

* [Editor's note: this paper was submitted to the Society in the 1990s for inclusion in a volume, planned but not completed, on the theme of criminal justice in Ireland in the nineteenth century. The author has revised the paper to take account of work published in the interim.]

1 *Standing rules and regulations for the government and guidance of the constabulary force of Ireland; as approved by his excellency the earl of Mulgrave, lord lieutenant general and governor general of Ireland* (Dublin, 1837), p. 2 (hereafter, *1837 constabulary rules*); *Dublin Metropolitan Police, Instructions, orders, &c, &c, &c* (Dublin, 1837), pp. 3–4 (hereafter, *1837 DMP instruction book*).

2 See e.g. G.J. Fulham, 'James Shaw Kennedy and the reformation of the Irish constabulary, 1836–38' in *Éire-Ireland*, vi:2 (1981), 93–106; C. Townshend, *Political violence in Ireland: government and resistance since 1848* (Oxford, 1983), pp. 72–7; K.T. Hoppen, *Elections, politics and society in Ireland 1832–85* (Oxford, 1983), p. 409.

3 J. Hart, 'Police' in W.R. Cornish et al. (eds), *Crime and law in nineteenth century Britain* (Dublin, 1978), pp. 208–9.

policemen on the beat for first-hand observation of how to perform the job.[4] Liverpool policemen were probably the best trained in England. In contrast, in the 1860s London Metropolitan Police recruits spent only about two weeks learning drill before they were sent to the streets as constables. Even as late as the 1890s only one month's training in police duties and criminal law was normal in large English police forces, while as late as 1918 many English police establishments had no formal training schemes for recruits.[5]

The contrast with the DMP and the Irish Constabulary is striking. The DMP placed its recruits in a special supernumerary class at the Kevin Street training depot, where the men spent their time drilling and, more importantly, learning police duties from the DMP instruction book or 'catechism', under the tuition of a 'schoolmaster' policeman.[6] Recruits normally spent from four to six months at the depot; six months was the norm in the last third of the century.[7] Once they had satisfied the chief commissioners of their knowledge of the duties and powers of policemen (as well as their proficiency in drill, acquaintance with the police code and familiarity with the geography of Dublin), recruits were accepted as constables and absorbed into a force whose organisational structure and mode of operation were designed, theoretically at least, to provide 24-hour protection against crime. A round-the-clock police presence on the streets was a feature of the 'new police' introduced to Britain by Sir Robert Peel, and the DMP's beat system was also modelled on that of the London Metropolitan Police[8] and considered the first line of defence against crime. The hierarchy of constable, sergeant and superintendent was designed to instil vigilance in the subordinate ranks and to provide maximum protection to the public. Men and officers were told to 'distinguish themselves by such vigilance and activity, as may render it extremely difficult for any one to commit a crime within that portion of the district under their charge'.[9] Superintendents were reminded that when watching 'loose and disorderly persons' or 'people whose behaviour is such as to excite just suspicion', the best way to proceed was to make it clear to the

4 W.J. Lowe, 'The Lancashire constabulary, 1845–1870: the social and occupational function of a Victorian police force' in *Criminal Justice History*, iv (1983), 43, and T.A. Critchley, *A history of police in England and Wales, 900–1966* (London, 1967), p. 149.

5 J.J. Tobias, *Crime and police in England, 1700–1900* (Dublin, 1979), p.102; J.P. Martin and G. Wilson, *The police: a study in manpower: the evolution of the service in England and Wales, 1829–1965* (London, 1969), p. 24.

6 N.I. Cochrane, 'The policeman's lot was not a happy one: Dublin, c. 1838–45' in *Dublin Historical Record*, xl:3 (1987), 95.

7 For a detailed account of the routine at the Kevin Street depot, see B. Griffin, 'The Irish police, 1836–1914: a social history' (unpublished, Ph.D. thesis, Loyola University of Chicago, 1991), pp. 13–16.

8 *Freeman's Journal*, 8 Sept. 1836.

9 *1837 DMP instruction book*, pp. 3–4, 18–19.

'Study of an Irish peace officer' from *Zoz*, 7 September 1876. (This cartoon highlights the volume of rules and regulations with which an RIC constable had to be familiar. The author thanks Professor Gary Owens for bringing it to his attention.)

suspects that 'they are known and strictly watched, and that certain detection will follow any attempt to commit crime'.[10] In making the rounds of his beat the constable was required to be 'perfectly acquainted' with the streets and courtways of his section, and to 'possess such a knowledge of the inhabitants of each house, as will enable him to recognize their persons'; at night he was told to check routinely that doors and windows were properly closed 'so that deprecators may not take advantage of any door or window being left insecure'.[11] Constables who failed to notice broken windows on their beat were fined heavily.[12]

As with the constabulary stationed in ports, the DMP also regularly placed policemen who were familiar with suspects' descriptions in the *Hue and Cry*, the police gazette, along the docks in the hope of spotting fleeing suspects. DMP port surveillance was considered to be more stringent than that operated in British cities. As the *Freeman's Journal* commented in January 1852, '[o]ne is struck at the rarity of the police on the quays of Liverpool, while every person is equally struck at the suddenness with which a blue coat appears on our quays when anything's "in the wind".'[13]

At first the DMP authorities tried to boost their force's crime-fighting efficiency by offering the prospect of promotion to sergeant or officer rank for exceptional duties performed. An unusual example of promotion for efficient duty involved Inspector James Mullins, who had been appointed to the DMP from the London Metropolitan Police. In 1840 he was selected by the chief commissioners to infiltrate a meeting of 'Ribbon' delegates from England and Ireland in Ballinamore, Co. Leitrim. For successfully prose-cuting the parties involved, Mullins was promoted and rewarded with £50.[14] However, practically all early promotions were for police work performed within the DMP district, and indeed the early emphasis on rewarding detective rather than preventive duty led to some controversy in the 1840s that members of the DMP made an inordinate number of apprehensions for minor offences in order to boost their arrest record.[15]

One man who seems to fall into this category was Constable Kevlin, 58A, who had, according to Inspector Campbell in January 1840, 'made himself unusually active of late in bringing charges against the car-drivers, and in consequence had become an object of enmity among them'.[16] In March

---

10 Ibid., pp. 19–20.
11 Ibid., p. 38, and *Manual relative to the duty of the Dublin Metropolitan Police; and the carriage regulations within the police district of the Dublin metropolis* (Dublin, 1840), pp. 8–9.
12 *Report of the committee of inquiry into the Dublin Metropolitan Police; with evidence, appendix, and maps*, H.C. 1883 [C. 3576] xxxii, 1, 125–6, 172–3 (hereafter, *1882 DMP inquiry*).
13 *Freeman's Journal*, 10 Jan. 1852.
14 Chief Commissioner Browne to Chief Secretary Herbert, 30 Dec. 1857: NAI, CSO Registered papers, 10934 on 1858/11753.
15 Cochrane, 'Policeman's lot', p. 101. 16 *Freeman's Journal*, 1 Feb. 1840.

1841, the Dublin carmen held a meeting to protest at what they considered excessive police interference with their trade. One disgruntled driver claimed that the DMP watched them as if they were 'midnight assassins'.[17] After a number of trivial car cases in February 1843, the *Freeman's Journal* commented that unless drivers were compensated for loss of time over such cases they would be subject 'not to regulations, but to persecution, and the police, in their zeal for the acquirement of a character for activity, will sink into informers'.[18] Dublin publicans were also unhappy with the close scrutiny of the DMP. In January 1840 the Licensed Grocers and Vintners Society, trying to account for the unwonted zeal displayed by the police towards them, erroneously alleged that sergeants received £5 reward for every forty publicans that they successfully prosecuted for infringements of the licensing laws.[19] The basis for the allegations of excessive arrests to secure rewards or promotion was removed in 1852 when promotions beyond constable rank were restricted to candidates selected by seniority for a competitive examination. Thereafter some form of examination, whether qualifying or competitive, formed the basis for DMP promotions for the next 30 years, after which most promotions were by seniority.[20]

The constabulary had four training depots initially – at Philipstown, Ballincollig, Ballinrobe and Armagh – but these were replaced by a single training depot at the Phoenix Park, Dublin, in 1840. Part of the reason for the establishment of a single depot for the force was the desire to promote a uniform standard of discipline, and there is no doubt that the infantry-regiment atmosphere of the Phoenix Park depot inculcated a unique *esprit de corps* in the constabulary.[21] There was another side to the depot, however, which placed the Irish Constabulary far ahead of its British counterparts in preparing recruits for police life, and that was the school in which sub-constables (designated 'constables' after 1883) were given a solid grounding in what was expected of them as policemen. As the constabulary was an armed force it placed more emphasis on drill and weapons training than the DMP did, but its recruits also received what was probably the best instruction in police duties and criminal law in the United Kingdom. Foreign visitors and the heads of English police forces greatly admired the constabulary's course of preparation: in 1872 Inspector-General John Stewart Wood

---

17 Ibid., 8 Mar. 1841. 18 Ibid., 3, 6, 7, 15, 17 Feb. 1843.
19 Ibid., 29 Jan. 1840.
20 The various promotion regulations are outlined in Griffin, 'Irish police', pp. 154–63.
21 For the military atmosphere of the Phoenix Park depot, see Constabulary circular, 23 Mar. 1840: NA, HO 184/111; Sir Francis B. Head, *Fortnight in Ireland* (London, 1852), pp. 56–64; C.P. Crane, *Memories of a resident magistrate* (Edinburgh, 1938), pp. 16–17; G. Garrow Green, *In the Royal Irish Constabulary* (London, 1905), pp. 10–12; J.A. Gaughan (ed.), *Memoirs of Constable Jeremiah Mee, RIC* (Dublin, 1975), pp. 12–14; T. Fennell, *The Royal Irish Constabulary: a history and personal memoir* (ed. R. Fennell) (Dublin, 2003), p. 11.

claimed that because RIC recruits were 'well tutored' at the depot school, they were 'much sought after in England'.[22]

When posted to a station from the depot, the new sub-constable's main activity was that of the patrol in rural areas or the beat in towns. Like his DMP counterpart, the constabulary man was expected to be scrupulously courteous to everybody he met on his rounds; in the early 1880s the sub-constable was told that '[i]n his walks and whenever he has an opportunity he should have a friendly greeting and a kind cheery word for everyone he meets'. The reasoning behind this was that '[a]s a rule an unpopular police-man is useless as a detective',[23] whereas the policeman who treated his neighbours in a friendly manner, thus 'impressing upon their minds that the police are their friends and protectors', opened up avenues of information and made himself 'useful and efficient in the prevention of crime'.[24]

Inspector-General Andrew Reed, mindful of the damage done to the force's image by policemen strictly enforcing the various laws and bye-laws which restricted children's street games, cautioned his men that '[s]eizing and confiscating a boy's kite, top, or ball makes the pantomime policeman'.[25] It is no coincidence that Belfast detectives in the early twentieth century were forbidden to prosecute publicans for breaches of the licensing laws or boys for playing football in the streets, for fear that valuable channels of infor-mation might be closed as a result of over-officious police interference.[26] Similarly, in rural areas the RIC found that farmers who were prosecuted for minor offences such as allowing their animals to stray on the road or not having their dogs licensed or muzzled, proved unco-operative when it came to investigating serious crimes.[27] The police authorities suggested that one

22 Head, *Fortnight*, pp. 64–65; J. Morley, *What I have seen and heard*, 2 vols (London, 1917), i, p. 378; *Report of the commissioners appointed by the lords commissioners of her majesty's treasury to enquire into the condition of the civil service in Ireland on the Royal Irish Constabulary: together with the minutes of evidence and appendices*, H.C. 1873 [C. 831] xxii, 131, 132 (hereafter, *1872 RIC commission*). In 1837 recruits trained at the provincial depots for one month before being posted to a county. By the early 1870s the training period had stretched to four months, and by the early twentieth century the trainee had six months' preparation at the Dublin depot: *1837 constabulary rules*, p.108; *Standing rules and regulations for the government and guidance of the Royal Irish Constabulary* (3rd ed., Dublin, 1872), p. 264 (hereafter, *1872 RIC rules*); C. Budding, *Die polizei in Grossbritannien und Irland* (Berlin, 1908), p. 190.

23 *1837 constabulary rules*, p. 2; A. Reed, *The policeman's manual, intended for the use of the sub-constables of the Royal Irish Constabulary* (Dublin, 1883), pp. 6, 48 (hereafter, *1883 RIC manual*).

24 A. Reed, *The policeman's manual; or, guide to the discharge of police duties* (4th ed., Dublin, 1888), p. 80 (hereafter, *1888 RIC manual*).

25 *1883 RIC manual*, p. 10.

26 Belfast police commission, 1906. *Appendix to report of the commissioners. Minutes of evidence, appendices, and index* (Dublin, 1907), p. 11.

27 Resident magistrate William O'Hara, Tulla, to Chief Secretary Fortescue, 8 Feb. 1870 and resident magistrate Benjamin Hill, Tuam, to Chief Secretary Fortescue, 4 Feb. 1870: NAI, CSO Registered papers, 1870/2757; *Report from the select committee on Westmeath, &c.*

way of engaging in seemingly casual, friendly conversation with local people was for a policeman always to have a pipe and tobacco on his person and to use the pretext of lighting the pipe as a means of entering a house and, hopefully, picking up useful scraps of information.[28]

A close knowledge of all the 'roads, passes, residences and characters' in the neighbourhood was also deemed essential for the efficient sub-constable. Policemen were not allowed to serve in their native county, and while this might appear to have made it more difficult for a policeman to become acquainted with local residents, the acquiring of local knowledge was facilitated by the constabulary practice, since 1823, of keeping a list of the householders in each sub-district. This register, compiled by the senior policeman at each station, included the names of the inhabitants of each house, as well as a list of public houses, forges, sellers of gunpowder and arms, and the names of people licensed to keep firearms. There was also a 'private register' which contained the names of all persons considered 'likely to commit crime', as well as the names of ticket-of-leave convicts and prostitutes in the area. When a new man joined a station the people on the private list were to be pointed out to him 'without exciting observation'.[29] The RIC authorities even made it mandatory in 1890 that a transferred man was to become 'personally acquainted' with the inhabitants of his sub-district within three months of joining his station, and his officer had to test him on his local knowledge.[30] Men on patrol were advised that they should 'frequently traverse the fields and bogs, and conceal themselves near suspected passes, or other localities favourable to the detection of night walkers'. Such 'ambush patrols' were particularly common in times of agrarian disturbance. When on the roads the men were expected to stop frequently and listen for sounds of people approaching: the method of listening through a ramrod placed on the ground was especially recommended.[31]

While an acquaintance with the 'individual character' of the people of his area was considered vital for the efficiency of the rural policeman, it was deemed to be 'doubly essential' in cities and towns 'from the greater degree of vice that exists in them, and from the adroitness with which delinquents endeavour to evade detection'. Police stationed in villages were enjoined to be particularly active, 'the idle lounging of the men at their barracks being

(*unlawful combinations*); *together with the proceedings of the committee, minutes of evidence, and appendix*, H.C. 1871 (147) xiii 547, 695, 698 (hereafter, *1871 Westmeath select committee*).

28 *Report of the committee of inquiry into the Royal Irish Constabulary; with evidence and appendix*, H.C. 1883 [C. 3577] xxxii, 255, 377 (hereafter, *1882 RIC committee*).

29 Chief Secretary Lord Eliot to Inspector-general McGregor, 4 Sept. 1844; McGregor to Lord Eliot, 10 Oct. 1844: BL, Add. MS 40480; *Nation*, 29 Aug. 1846; *1872 RIC rules*, pp. 267–68; *Freeman's Journal*, 2 June 1881; Fennell, *Royal Irish Constabulary*, p.15.

30 RIC circular, Sept. 1890: NLI, Royal Irish Constabulary circulars 1882–1900 [IR 3522 r 3].

31 *1872 RIC rules*, pp. 223–4; *Freeman's Journal*, 8 Apr. 1882; *1882 RIC committee*, p. 69.

calculated to give the public an unfavourable impression of their zeal and vigilance'.[32] It is clear from the above that the constabulary authorities sought to create the impression of their force as an omniscient, ever-alert presence in Irish society, representing both a deterrent to crime and forming the basis for an impressive source of local information which should be invaluable in prosecuting offenders. Even such innocuous activity as the annual collection of agricultural statistics after 1847 was turned into an intelligence-gathering exercise: this duty was frequently given to newcomers at a station so that they could discreetly and quickly acquire a close knowledge of the area and the local inhabitants.[33]

Neither the constabulary nor the DMP authorities formally trained their men in detective work. Instead, the men were instructed as to the various acts of parliament which they were expected to enforce but once they left the training depot it was largely a matter for their own common sense as to how they went about bringing offenders to justice. Most non-indictable offences required little or no sophisticated detective work anyway; it was usually no great test of a literate constable's ingenuity to successfully prosecute a case of drunkenness, assault, begging or driving a cart that had not got the owner's name painted on it. When the constable was an eye-witness to the offence, all that was normally required was that he present his evidence clearly in court in order to secure a conviction.

The police found that in 'ordinary' cases, that is, cases in which inform-ants were not deemed to have transgressed against an unwritten communal or agrarian code in helping the authorities, there was usually no shortage of information from the public.[34] Even in the most private of crimes, such as concealing the birth of children, the police often received assistance from the public – for example, in the 1840s the parish priest of Clontibret kept the local head constable informed of several such instances.[35] Drunks were a useful source of information, as were 'corner boys and loafers' in towns and villages; indeed, the success of Father Mathew's temperance crusade caused a dramatic if temporary decline in information and confessions from drunks.[36] In general, the authorities expressed their satisfaction at the constabulary's handling of 'normal' criminal cases. In 1864 Echlin Molyneux, chairman of Meath quarter sessions, stated that:

32 *1837 constabulary rules*, p. 66; *1872 RIC rules*, pp. 74–5.
33 Recollections of Martin Nolan, RIC, p. 220: University College Dublin, Dept. of Irish Folklore, MS 1264.
34 É. Hickey, *Irish law and lawyers in modern folk tradition* (Dublin, 1999).
35 *Nation*, 27 Jan. 1844.
36 Head, *Fortnight*, p. 50; *Freeman's Journal*, 5, 6, 15 Mar. 1880; T. Garvin, *Nationalist revolutionaries in Ireland 1858–1928* (Oxford, 1987), p. 151.

... in all instances of ordinary crime, such as private murders & assaults, casual riots, larcenies etc which are all unconnected with the dangerous secret confederacies in Ireland, the criminals are made amenable to justice through the instrumentality of the constabulary, with a zeal, acuteness, and activity, such as is not excelled by any police in Europe ... In all such cases, as far as my experience enables me to judge, the people readily look upon the police as their protectors.[37]

Molyneux pointed out, however, that the situation was very different with agrarian crimes: when the latter cases were involved sources of information dried up, and the attitude of most people was that 'silence is safety – revelation is death'.[38]

The police were hampered in investigating agrarian and, often, other serious crime due to the fear of key witnesses and even of victims of giving information or testifying in court.[39] Another undoubted factor was the widespread sympathy often accorded to perpetrators of agrarian crime.[40] Blatant perjury in court, and particularly in agrarian cases when false alibis were sworn to, made the task of the constabulary even more difficult.[41] To break through the veil of silence which usually surrounded agrarian cases the authorities relied firstly on the local sub-inspector.[42] Most of these were gentlemen who were directly commissioned as cadets, an officer appointment system that was maintained in the constabulary from 1842 onwards.[43] The

37 Echlin Molyneux to Sir Thomas Larcom, 28 Mar. 1864: NLI, Larcom papers, MS 7619.

38 Ibid.

39 *Daily Express*, 2 June 1862; H.J. Brownrigg, *Examination of some recent allegations concerning the constabulary force of Ireland, in a report to his excellency the lord lieutenant* (Dublin, 1864), pp. 41, 46, 51–2, 55–6, 60–1, 63, 67, 82, 84; Report of Sub-inspector Hickson, Castlepollard, 19 Jan. 1870: NAI, CSO Registered papers, 1870/1283 on 2808; *Special Commission Act 1888. Reprint of the shorthand notes of the speeches, proceedings, and evidence taken before the commissioners appointed under the above-named act*, 12 vols (London, 1890), ii, p. 518.

40 See e.g. resident magistrate Tracy to Under-secretary Redington, 26 Oct. 1847: NAI, Outrage reports, Limerick 1847/17/1764; *Daily Express*, 25 July 1862; Brownrigg, *Examination of allegations*, pp. 41, 67; resident magistrate Bodkin, Tipperary, to Chief Secretary Fortescue, 1 Feb. 1870: NAI, CSO Registered papers, 1870/2757; Crane, *Memories*, p. 38.

41 *Report from the select committee on outrages (Ireland); together with the proceedings of the committee, minutes of evidence, appendix and index*, H.C. 1852 (438) xiv, 1, 15, 32 (hereafter, *1852 select committee on outrages*); Crane, *Memories*, pp. 193–95; J.A. Curran, *Reminiscences of John Adye Curran KC, late county court judge and chairman of quarter sessions* (London, 1915), p. 228; A.M. Sullivan, *The last serjeant: the memoirs of Serjeant A.M. Sullivan QC* (London, 1952), pp. 65–6, 72, 109.

42 Until 1839, the designation 'chief constable' was used to describe the lowest officer rank; in 1883 the term 'district inspector' replaced 'sub-inspector'.

43 For the controversy surrounding the cadet officer class, see Griffin, *Irish police*, pp. 273–82. As the nineteenth century progressed, the number of head constables promoted to the rank of sub-inspector or district inspector increased, but officers promoted from the ranks were still in a minority before the outbreak of the First World War.

cadet system was defended on the grounds that it boosted the confidence of
the landed gentry in the police force. Constabulary regulations stipulated that
officers had to cultivate friendly relations with the local gentry, and defenders
of the cadet system argued rather dubiously that gentlemen officers secured
valuable information from justices of the peace drawn from the landed gentry
that would not have been divulged to officers of a lower social class.[44] The
utility of friendly relations between gentlemen officers and the gentry – and,
by extension, of the cadet system – can be assessed by Inspector-General
Brownrigg's admission in 1859 that despite the facilities which local
magistrates and landlords had at their disposal for acquiring information, for
example through their agents and tenantry, 'they have not, even in a single
instance, that I can call to mind after an experience of 33 years, been able to
detect any crime of an agrarian or serious character, or even been able to
afford the constabulary the slightest hint useful for the discovery of the
perpetrators, or their whereabouts'.[45]

Efforts to improve the detection rate through the offer of monetary
rewards to informers generally proved unsuccessful. For example, the
rewards offered in the case of 520 outrages in 1836 and 1837 yielded paltry
results; only 19 cases, or less than four per cent of the total, were successfully
solved as a result of private information (see Table 1). The results were not
much better in the early 1840s. Some 1,048 cases of murder or attempted
murder were recorded from January 1842 to February 1846 (although, of
course, not all of these were agrarian crimes). Rewards for information were
offered in some 406 cases, but in only 20 instances were the rewards claimed
and convictions obtained as a result.[46] Not surprisingly, in March 1852 the
deputy inspector-general of the Irish Constabulary stated of the offers of
rewards that 'we seldom if ever find they produce any result', and that they
sometimes tempted people either to give false information or even to
fabricate crimes in the hope of claiming rewards.[47]

---

44 *Report of the commissioners directed by the treasury to inquire into the state of the constabulary*
   force of Ireland, with reference to their pay and allowances, strength and organisation, conditions
   of service, and system of superannuation, H.C. 1866 (9365) xxxiv, 167, 179; *1872 RIC rules*, p.
   245; *1872 RIC commission*, pp. 61–2, 65, 70, 80, 119.
45 Report of Sir Henry John Brownrigg, CB, inspector-general of constabulary, for the year
   1859: NLI, Larcom papers, MS 7618.
46 *A return of all murders that have been committed in Ireland since the 1st day of January 1842;*
   specifying the county, and the barony of the county, where such murder[s] had been committed;
   the name and condition of the person so murdered; also, a return of the rewards offered in each
   such instance; where the rewards have been claimed; and when conviction has followed; the
   different queries to be arranged in columns; similar return of attempts to murder, attended with
   bodily injuries, arranged in columns; similar return of attempts to murder, not attended with
   bodily injuries, arranged in columns, H.C. 1846 (220) xxxv, 293.
47 *1852 select committee on outrages*, pp. 188–9. For an assertion that the availability of rewards
   also prompted informers in Dublin to give false information to the DMP and even to

Table 1. Number of outrage cases in which private information led to a conviction and reward, 1836–1837

Offences for which reward offered	Number of offences	Number of convictions rewarded
Murder	139	5 (3.6%)
Assault	104	5 (4.8%)
Arson	77	–
House attack	72	4 (5.6%)
Attempted murder	24	–
Robbery	19	3 (15.8%)
Threatening notices	13	–
Killing/maiming animals	13	–
Attack on church building	6	–
House levelling	5	–
Other destruction of property	23	–
Other crimes	25	2* (8%)
Total	520	19 (3.7%)

* one case of manslaughter and one case of obstructing the transport of potatoes.
[Source: *A return of all rewards offered by proclamation of the lord lieutenant or lords justices of Ireland, for the discovery of the perpetrators of murders and other outrages, from the 1st of January 1836 to the 12th December 1837 with the dates of the proclamation; and distinguishing which of such rewards (if any) have been claimed and paid by the Irish government, in consequence of information given pursuant to such proclamations*: H.C. 1837–38 (157) xlvi, 427.]

The upsurge in serious crime during the Famine, particularly crimes against property, prompted the government to employ constabulary detectives in 1847 in an attempt to alleviate the situation. This was a controversial decision, given the disreputable image that the term 'detective' evoked in the British imagination. Lord Lieutenant Carlisle explained in 1864 that when the Irish Constabulary was reformed in 1836, detectives were 'studiously

commit crimes for which others would be unjustly convicted, see 'An informer', *Report of a meeting of the informers of Dublin, held on Sunday evening, Feb. 6th, 1842, being the day after the execution of John Delahunt for the murder of the boy Thomas Maguire* (Dublin, 1842). Delahunt had sworn falsely against a husband and wife who were charged with the murder of an Italian organ boy, and also against a number of coal porters who were charged with assaulting a Captain Cradock. Delahunt murdered Thomas Maguire, an eight-year-old boy, with the intention of swearing falsely against an innocent person and securing a reward on this person's conviction for young Maguire's murder. In the meantime, he had hoped to be lodged in comfort in Dublin Castle.

excluded from it, as the apprehension then was that any approach to the system of espionage would revolt the public, & endanger the existence of the force itself'.[48] In the United Kingdom a considerable body of opinion felt that even permanent uniformed police smacked of 'Bourbon' despotism; the creation of a non-uniformed detective police undoubtedly held sinister overtones of the European secret police systems.[49] The constabulary authorities, therefore, proceeded cautiously with their employment of detective police. Significantly the term 'detective' was avoided at first, and the men were described as 'disposable men' instead.[50] Not more than six disposables were to be selected in each county, 'on account of their respectability, intelligence, and tact in the investigation of crime'. They were not full-time detectives, however. Normally they performed the usual duties of the force in uniform but on the commission of 'any grave offence', at least two disposables dressed in plain clothes could be sent to the scene of outrage to make enquiries about the offenders. Inspector-General McGregor, no doubt mindful of the prejudice against detective police, stressed that:

> ... however anxious the government are for the conviction of criminals the greatest delinquents, even, are not to be brought to justice by unjustifiable means. Should any disposable policeman, therefore, be convicted of practices in the discharge of his duties, whatever may be the amount of his success, that are inconsistent with the course to be fairly expected of every honest man, he will be dismissed with disgrace from the public service.[51]

The inspector-general's caution was justified, given the eagerness of certain newspapers to criticise detectives as *agents provocateurs*. For example, in June 1848 the *Freeman's Journal*, commenting on a murder case near Kilbeggan, suggested that the murderer 'may be some idle, well dressed ruffian, who, prowling about for something to *detect* and report, makes the crime he cannot find'.[52]

Inspector-General Brownrigg wrote in 1859 that the disposables were 'always ready to mount the frieze, to assume the short pipe, to converse –

---

48 Lord Lieutenant Carlisle to Earl Grey, 26 Mar. 1864: NLI, Larcom papers, MS 7619.

49 R. Hawkins, 'Government versus secret societies: the Parnell era' in T.D. Williams (ed.), *Secret societies in Ireland* (Dublin, 1973), p. 104; D. Knight (ed.), *Cobbett in Ireland: a warning to England* (London, 1984), pp. 154, 241, 262, 269–70; S.H. Palmer, *Police and protest in England and Ireland, 1780–1850* (Cambridge, 1988), passim.

50 In 1872 the term 'detective' began to be employed. See E. Malcolm, 'Investigating the "machinery of murder": Irish detectives and agrarian outrages, 1847–70' in *New Hibernia Review/Iris Éireannach Nua*, 6:3 (2002), 90.

51 Inspector-General McGregor's instructions on the use of disposable men, 6 Jan. 1847: NAI, Official papers, OP 1847/146.

52 *Freeman's Journal*, 20 June 1848 (original emphasis.)

YOU NEVER CAN TELL, CAN YOU?

FIRST PLAIN (?) CLOTHES OFFICER TO SECOND DITTO—
" Here they come ; they'll never guess we're policemen watching them."

[Plain Clothes Police Officers have been told off to do duty outside some houses in the City where Suffragettes are staying. Judging by some " loithering men " we've seen, we fancy (of course it's only fancy) that they would be less conspicuous if they did their duty disguised as policemen.]

'You never can tell, can you?' Cartoon by 'Shy', *The Lepracaun*, October 1912. Not all contemporaries were impressed with the DMP's plain-clothes police.

many of them – in the Irish language, and to employ other devices, as an Irishman knows how, to come at the knowledge they are in quest of.[53] Their success in agrarian cases was slight, but Brownrigg remained as wary as his predecessor about the possibility of a 'disposable' using unscrupulous methods to improve the detection rate.[54] Contemporaries felt (with some justification, given the police success against the largely urban-based Fenian conspiracy) that detectives were more effective in towns and cities than in rural areas, where the sudden appearance of strangers after an outrage was bound to give rise to suspicions as to their identity.[55] Inspector-General John Stewart Wood stated in March 1871 that 'a detective is very well in large towns, but in country districts in Ireland, whenever a stranger goes into the country, the children of eight years will say, "Bedad, that's a paler", and he is put in Coventry'. Not surprisingly, Wood admitted 'ignorance of Ribbonism, which is about the only thing I cannot master'.[56]

Public criticism of the constabulary's tackling of serious crime, so common in the early 1860s, was muted by the force's success against the Irish Republican Brotherhood in the mid-1860s; however, the spate of agrarian outrages in the late 1860s and early 1870s, especially in Westmeath, revived the accusations of inefficiency and prompted a further reform of the detective system. In June 1872 a permanent detective director was appointed at the Dublin depot, along with a small team of assistants. They concentrated on 'special crimes', which largely meant keeping tabs on nationalist secret societies and the more shadowy incidences of 'Ribbonism'. While the latter remained as difficult a problem to tackle as ever, the extensive files on nationalist agitators in the National Archives are evidence of their successful surveillance of the former.[57]

Most RIC disposables remained part-time sleuths, performing the regular duties of the force until sent by the detective director or their county inspector to investigate a crime. In Belfast from six to eight detectives were employed at first, and these were replaced at intervals 'in order that the most intelligent men of the Belfast force may be practised in detective duties'. Following the 1886 riots their number was increased to 20, and they were particularly enjoined that 'nothing in the slightest degree affecting the peace of the town should escape their observation'. Guidelines issued in 1888 to

53 Report of Sir Henry John Brownrigg, CB, inspector-general of constabulary, for the year 1859: NLI, Larcom papers, MS 7618.
54 Brownrigg, *Examination of allegations*, pp. 8–29. For a discussion of the efforts of a number of disposable men in agrarian cases in the 1850s and 1860s, see Malcolm, 'Machinery of murder', pp. 73–91.
55 *Daily Express*, 10 June 1862; T.W. Moody and R. Hawkins (eds), *Florence Arnold-Forster's Irish journal* (Oxford, 1988), p. 32.
56 *1871 Westmeath select committee*, pp. 141, 143.
57 Hawkins, 'Government versus secret societies', p. 101.

RIC officers when selecting men for detective duty continued the *leitmotif* of the need for honest men:

> Mere cunning and ability to prepare a good report do not of themselves form sufficient qualifications for a good detective; there ought, if possible, to be, along with respectability, intelligence, and tact, an aptitude by practice to gain an influence over others, cleverness, shrewdness, self-reliance, self-control, good judgment, indomitable patience and courage, and strict integrity.[58]

It is doubtful whether the police authorities considered that the first detective director, James Ellis French, had all of these qualities after he became involved in a sodomy scandal in the mid-1880s.[59] However, the evidence suggests that at least town-based detectives met their superiors' expectations. One of these was a Sergeant Byrne, who by 1913 had served for over 18 years as a detective in Queenstown, arresting more than 300 suspects in the course of his duties there. In 1911 the king awarded him the Distinguished Service Medal for his 'exceptional ability in the detection and prevention of crime', as many criminals 'who managed to elude the vigilance of the police authorities on the continent, in Great Britain, and in America fell into the hands of Sergeant Byrne at this port when fleeing from justice'.[60]

Detectives or disposable men were not the only RIC men to wear plain clothes on duty. Non-detective policemen frequently wore so-called 'coloured clothes', the constabulary term for plain clothes, as the Irish Constabulary considered a suit of plain clothes as much a part of a policeman's equipment as his truncheon or uniform. The *Waterford Chronicle* suggested in April 1842 that disguises were not limited to a mere suit of plain clothes, when it claimed that the constabulary were 'prowling through the country in all sorts of Protean disguises, attired in the various costumes of tinkers, ballad singers, beggarwomen, and quack doctors'.[61] Plain-clothes policemen were mainly used for catching publicans in breach of the licensing laws, or shadowing suspects. Some of the prejudice against detectives attached itself to the plain-clothesmen. In August 1862 a Cork magistrate dismissed a case against a Toormore shebeen keeper brought by a plain-clothes sub-constable. Despite Sub-Constable Tracy's protest that it was frequent police practice to wear coloured clothes in such cases, Magistrate Davys denounced the 'act of low chicanery'. According to Davys, '[s]uch proceedings would be perfectly

---

58 *Belfast police manual, compiled for the use of the Royal Irish Constabulary serving in the town of Belfast* (Belfast, 1888), pp. 6, 21, 23; *1888 RIC manual*, p. 19.
59 L. Ó Broin, *The prime informer: a suppressed scandal* (London, 1971), pp. 26–8.
60 *Irish Times*, 4 Jan. 1911; *Constabulary Gazette*, 12 July 1913.
61 *Nation*, 22 Apr. 1842, quoting recent *Waterford Chronicle* article.

justifiable in cases of murder, or in detecting culprits charged with serious crimes; but here I say it was wrong, and I will not countenance such acts of low cunning'.[62]

Nevertheless, plain-clothes public house and shebeen duty remained a regular activity of the force. In Cork city in the late 1870s from six to ten men were usually so employed, while in Belfast the plain-clothesmen watching shebeens 'are changed so often, that most of the steady men in the force get their turn at it from time to time'.[63] In Belfast in the 1880s plain-clothesmen were also detailed to 'go about and meet desperadoes, swell mobs-men, and others of that sort who come into the town to rob'.[64] Also in the 1880s Inspector-General Andrew Reed ordered that whenever 'any suspicious stranger' appeared in a constabulary sub-district, one of the station party was to immediately change into plain clothes, engage the stranger in conversation and with 'tact and caution' try to ascertain where he came from and his destination, at the same time noting the stranger's description, which was to be sent to the next district so that his movements might be watched.[65] Perhaps the most ludicrous constabulary plain-clothes duty occurred on the occasion of Edward VII's visit to Ireland early in the twentieth century. When the king was travelling through Connacht 'an enormous force' of plain-clothesmen disguised as cycling tourists was positioned along the route. Each man had a bicycle and was dressed alike in Norfolk jacket with watch-chain from breast pocket to buttonhole, straw hat and knickerbockers. The men were positioned 'exactly the same distance apart', and 'all were lying in a carefully rehearsed loose and careless attitude beside the road in the character of the weary cyclist'. When the king's car passed, each 'tourist' sprang to attention and saluted, much to the monarch's astonishment, and then resumed his lounging until the king's car was out of sight.[66] Would-be assassins would have had little difficulty in spotting the king's minders.

In summing up the constabulary's measures for preventing and detecting crime, one should bear in mind the primitive state of forensic procedure. Fingerprints, for example, were not used for police purposes until the early twentieth century. Before 1850 blood stains could not be positively identified as such, and it was not until 1895 that human blood could be distinguished forensically from animal blood.[67] In such circumstances progress in

---

62 *Freeman's Journal*, 16 Aug. 1862.
63 *Report from the select committee on sale of intoxicating liquors on Sunday (Ireland) bill; together with the proceedings of the committee, minutes of evidence, and appendix*, H.C. 1877 (198) xvi, 1, 215, 249.
64 *Belfast riots commission, 1886. Report of the Belfast riots commissioners. Minutes of evidence, and appendix*, H.C. 1887 [C. 4925] xviii, 1, 266.
65 *1888 RIC manual*, pp. 17–18.
66 Sir Henry A. Robinson, *Memories: wise and otherwise* (London, 1923), p. 153.
67 Palmer, *Police and protest*, p. 533; *Freeman's Journal*, 26 May 1911. By the 1880s police

investigations depended on factors such as a policeman's familiarity with the people of his area, his skill at making enquiries, his intuition or his ability to 'read' a suspect's face.[68] Simple good fortune with the evidence was also a factor, as proved to be the case in the police investigation of the murder of Charles Wilgar at Ballylesson, near Belfast, on 10 May 1862. A stopped watch proved to be the vital clue which put the police on the trail of Daniel Ward, Wilgar's friend. The trial details show that Wilgar and Ward paid a visit to William Wright, Wilgar's uncle, on 10 May. When his guests were leaving Wright, unknown to Ward, gave his nephew a watch to give to another one of his nephews. On their way home, Ward killed Wilgar with a blow to the head from a stone wrapped in a handkerchief, stole a watch which he knew Wilgar possessed, but overlooked the watch which Wilgar's uncle had recently given to him. He then dumped Wilgar's body in the river Lagan, but unfortunately for Ward the water stopped the action of the watch almost immediately, thus giving the police an approximate time of death. After that it was simply a matter of ascertaining Ward's whereabouts at that time. A string of witnesses placed him near the scene of the crime and, more damning still, in Lisburn pawning Wilgar's other watch for £2.[69]

Given the poor state of forensic science, it is perhaps understandable that in times of disturbance, as for instance during the land war when pressure on the RIC to secure convictions or prisoners was intense, the constabulary frequently considered their duty done in serious crime cases when they merely reported those whom they suspected of the offences, thus leaving them open to arrest under the 'coercion laws'.[70] In the virtual absence of forensic science, and given the fact that the police often knew the guilty parties but were unable to produce corroborating evidence,[71] it is difficult to see what alternatives they had.

The daily barrack ritual of examining the men's knowledge of their powers and obligations under the various acts of parliament and of the descriptions in the *Hue and Cry* at least ensured that the men knew what was expected of them in general terms, and also held out the hope that a fugitive or suspect might be recognised by his description. An interesting example

procedure at the scene of a burglary had advanced to the stage of making paper cut-outs of footprints in the area, with the number of nail prints being carefully recorded. By the mid-1890s the RIC had adopted the practice of making plaster cast impressions of footprint evidence: *1888 RIC manual*, p.21; Inspection book of Timooney RIC station, Aug. 1893 to Aug. 1900, entry for 17 July 1896 (MS in possession of Dr David Fitzpatrick).

68 *Freeman's Journal*, 28 Jan. 1852; Memoirs of District Inspector John Regan, p. 50: PRONI, D3160.

69 *Belfast Newsletter*, 6, 7, 9 Mar. 1863.

70 C.D. Clifford-Lloyd, *Ireland under the Land League: a narrative of personal experiences* (Edinburgh and London, 1892), p. 226; Robinson, *Memories*, pp. 31–3. For a useful annotated list of coercion legislation, see V. Crossman, *Politics, law and order in nineteenth-century Ireland* (Dublin, 1996), pp. 199–230.

occurred in July 1843. While the entire Kilrea station party were absent on duty at a fair, a man called at the barracks and asked the sergeant's wife for permission to light his pipe inside. The wife, recognising the smoker from his description in the *Hue and Cry* as a man wanted by the police for a murder committed in March, managed to trick him into the lock-up, and he ended up as a prisoner.[72] Eloping couples, particularly when the woman robbed her family or her husband to finance her and her lover's new life overseas were sometimes recognised at ports or on steamers, as were other young countrywomen 'on the run' after theft.[73] In towns, 'an active, intelligent and discreet policeman' who had memorised the descriptions in the *Hue and Cry* routinely attended the arrival and departure of public transport. We have no comprehensive figures of the arrests made as the result of such routine surveillance except for the one-year period from July 1879 to July 1880, when some 68 suspects were arrested by the RIC at railway stations.[74]

The use of the telegraph to transmit descriptions of suspects arriving at ports or railway stations is one of the few examples of technology proving useful to the police in the period.[75] A less important technological aid was the provision of binoculars in disturbed districts in 1890. The author is not aware of binoculars proving useful in detecting or preventing agrarian crime, but a Bray sergeant did make use of a pair in January 1905 to catch two poachers in the act.[76] Also in the 1890s, RIC detectives who were assigned to shadow political suspects began to use cameras as part of their surveillance work. In April 1890, C.P. Crane, a district inspector attached to the Special Crime Branch, recommended the 'Luzo' portable camera for such work. The 'Luzo' could be carried in a thick leather case by means of a strap over one's shoulder; a hole cut in the case allowed one to take furtive photographs of suspects. In the same month David Harrel experimented with a number of

---

71 See e.g. the assertion of resident magistrate George Fitzmaurice of Crossmaglen in March 1852: 'there is scarcely a murder that has occurred in which we did not know the people [responsible]; but we cannot get such evidence as will enable us to bring them to trial': *1852 select committee on outrages*, p. 62.

72 *Freeman's Journal*, 11 July 1843.

73 Ibid., 8 Mar. 1844, 18 Jan. 1849, 28 Aug. 1849, 19 June 1854, 15 May 1857; *Ulsterman*, 24 Apr. 1857.

74 *Copies of instructions to the Irish Constabulary, in force in January 1858, with regard to the protection, during the night, of life and property where no local police exists; and, of instructions on the same subject issued between that date and January 1864*, H.C. 1864 (112) xlix, 855, 856; *Freeman's Journal*, 4 June 1880; *Return of the number of criminals arrested by members of the Royal Irish Constabulary at railway stations in Ireland within the past twelve months, specifying the stations at which the arrests were made*, H.C. 1880 (340) lx, 395; *1883 RIC manual*, p. 53.

75 *Belfast Daily Mercury*, 30 June 1859; *Belfast Newsletter*, 26 Mar. 1861, 16 Sept. 1862; *Freeman's Journal*, 24 Nov. 1871.

76 RIC circular, 18 Sept. 1890: NLI, RIC circulars 1882–1900 [IR 3522 r 3]; *Irish Times*, 3 Jan. 1905.

cameras and found that a buttonhole camera manufactured by a Berlin firm and used by various continental police forces could be used successfully under favourable light conditions.[77] The use of the bicycle in the late nineteenth century was another modest technological advance. Constabulary men saved up for bicycles in the hope that their use would increase their chances of catching criminals and thus boosting their prospects of promotion or of an award from the force's reward fund.[78] On many occasions policemen on bicycles were able to arrest suspects, particularly tramps, who had travelled miles from crime scenes.[79]

To encourage the preventive and detective exertions of their men the constabulary authorities maintained a fund to reward exceptional instances of police duty. Initially applicants were paid shortly after a special committee of officers at headquarters recommended a reward, but the rules governing the fund were changed in 1842 when it became obvious that the men were applying to be rewarded for performing quite trivial duties. Thereafter the men received a monetary award only after their retirement.[80] The frivolous applications for rewards continued into the 1860s, to the inspector-general's annoyance.[81] Nevertheless, the incentive of a reward sometimes proved the vital spark needed to spur the men to added and successful exertions against offenders. For example, early in 1850 the Granard constabulary were unable to stop a spate of petty thefts in the area, especially of grain, despite knowing the receiver of the stolen property. When the sub-inspector announced that the first man to make a capture in the case would be warmly recommended to the county inspector, he galvanised the efforts of his promotion-hungry men. Sub-Constables Robert Dunlop and John Hickey were fortunate enough while on 'ambush patrol' one night to stop an old man and his wife and son, 'all loaded down with plunder which they had stolen during the night'. The trio had a dead goose, two young goats, a tin can, a spade, a horse's ploughing chains, cabbages and women's caps in their possession. The sub-inspector made out 'a splendid report' in his men's favour and shortly thereafter Dunlop was promoted.[82]

---

77 Crime Branch Special reports: NAI, CBS 1890 130/S. For some examples of surreptitiously taken photographs in October and November 1894, see NAI, CBS 1894 9301/S.

78 *Royal Irish Constabulary. Evidence taken before the committee of enquiry, 1901. With appendix*, H.C. 1902 [Cd. 1094] xlii, 313, 330, 412, 422.

79 For some examples of policemen using bicycles to track down fleeing suspects, see *Irish Cyclist*, 29 Oct. 1890, 19 July 1893, 14 Mar. 1894; *Ulster Cycling News*, 26 July 1893; *Constabulary Gazette*, 29 May 1897, 5 June 1897, 6 Nov. 1897; *Irish Wheelman and Automobile Review*, 8 Jan. 1901, 11 June 1901.

80 Constabulary circular, 15 Apr. 1842: NA, HO 184/111.

81 Constabulary circular, 5 Sept. 1862: NA, HO 184/113; Brownrigg, *Examination of allegations*, pp. 91–3.

82 Reminiscences of Head Constable Robert Dunlop: PRONI, T2815/1.

A series of fishery acts from 1842 to 1891 made the constabulary responsible for enforcing close seasons and suppressing poaching on public rivers, and the fact that the police were entitled to a portion of the fines imposed on offenders proved an unexpected problem for the constabulary authorities. According to Inspector-General Wood in 1871, '[w]hen any policeman has a chance of getting a reward, it leads him to look more after the fisheries than after the peace of the neighbourhood'.[83] When the revenue police were abolished in 1857 and the Irish Constabulary took over their duties, the prospect of rewards from the inland revenue commissioners was sufficient to ensure remarkable diligence in the arduous duty.[84] The reward system might have proved a double-edged sword, as there is some suspicion that it prevented the RIC from stamping out the poteen trade entirely and thus killing off the goose that laid the golden egg. To qualify for a reward the police had to produce still parts or quantities of poteen. In 1900 there were some 1,828 detections but only 20 prosecutions. The tiny number of prosecutions makes the claim of one excise commissioner, that the RIC did not press illicit distillers too closely for fear that they would cease production, seem less fantastic than it might otherwise appear.[85] In addition to awards from the revenue commissioners and the constabulary reward fund, RIC men could also collect comparatively massive rewards from the government or magistracy for solving serious crime. Some examples include the £52 awarded to Sub-Inspector Heard in October 1847 for arresting William 'Puck' Ryan on a murder charge in Limerick; the £51 granted to Constable Smyth of Legan for the arrest of a murderer who was executed in August 1863, and the £50 received by Constable Supple of Westmeath in January 1871 for arresting an armed assailant despite having his face 'tattooed' by a revolver blast.[86]

Given the quite substantial rewards available for successful prosecutions, it is a testimony to the integrity of the constabulary that it was almost unknown for a policeman to act as an *agent provocateur* or 'manufacturer of crime' in order to qualify for promotion or rewards. Allegations that the constabulary fabricated crimes, especially agrarian crimes, were frequently made,[87] but there is little evidence to substantiate these allegations. They were usually made in times of social disorder when the force was out of favour with the public, and should be seen more as an indication of the

---

83 *1871 Westmeath select committee*, p. 142.
84 See *Return of revenue commissioners' rewards to constabulary men for July to December 1857*: Trinity College Dublin, Goulden papers, MS 7376, no. 280.
85 E.B. McGuire, *Irish whiskey: a history of distilling, the spirit trade and excise controls in Ireland* (Dublin, 1973), pp. 428–9.
86 Dublin Castle memorandum, 21 Oct. 1847: NAI, Outrage reports, Limerick 1847/17/1401; *Daily Express*, 23 Nov. 1863; *The Times*, 21 Jan. 1871.
87 Griffin, *Irish police*, pp. 470–2.

constabulary's temporary unpopularity than as proof of corruption. The most publicised exception to the rule, which was raised in the house of commons in 1904, was the case of Sergeant Sheridan. Sheridan, who joined the RIC in December 1880, served in Limerick until May 1898 and spent the last three years of his service in Leitrim and Clare. During his career he 'dazzled' his colleagues by his detective ability, especially in cases of agrarian crime. It was not until 1901 that suspicion was cast upon Sheridan's record, when he gave perjured evidence in a court case in Clare that he had seen a tramp posting threatening notices, it being physically impossible for the handicapped tramp to behave as Sheridan alleged. A subsequent investigation of Sheridan's career showed that his unusual ability was due to the fact that he and three accomplices committed the crimes themselves and framed innocent men for the offences.[88]

DMP men, like their constabulary counterparts, were also required to familiarise themselves with the details of stolen property or wanted persons published in the police gazette, the *Hue and Cry*. An examination of the number of arrests of people mentioned in the gazette shows that their success rate improved steadily throughout the century, despite a rather inauspicious start: from 1842 to 1844 the police apprehended people in only 5.5 per cent of the cases of robbery reported in the DMP area.[89] Part of the reason for the low capture rate was undoubtedly the extreme number of cases advertised, with 615, 656 and 725 robberies alone listed in 1842, 1843 and 1844 respectively: it was asking rather a lot of the average constable to expect him to remember the details of so many incidents. From 1845 the number of robberies and other crimes in the DMP area reported in the *Hue and Cry* was dramatically curtailed, and never exceeded the 76 advertisements for 1853. The result was a considerable improvement in the arrest rate of suspects: arrests were made in 33.9 per cent of *Hue and Cry* cases from 1845 to 1849; the figures for the 1850s, 1860s, 1870s and 1880s were 22.5 per cent, 36.5 per cent, 42.5 per cent and 41.9 per cent respectively, while from 1890 to 1894 (the last years for which statistics are available) the DMP caught suspects in 63.6 per cent of the *Hue and Cry* cases affecting their district.[90]

88 RIC reports on the case of Sergeant Sheridan: NAI, CBS 1901/25413/S; *Freeman's Journal*, 9 Oct. 1901; *Hansard's Parl. Deb.*, 4th ser., vol. cxxxviii, cols. 124, 255, 1032, 1034, 1038–39 (22–23 July 1904); H. Sutherland, *Ireland yesterday and tomorrow* (Philadelphia, 1909), pp. 99–100.

89 *Statistical returns of the Dublin Metropolitan Police, for the year[s] 1842 [–1844]* (Dublin, 1843–1845). These figures do not include the number of cases where suspects were arrested after the robbery was committed, but before the particulars appeared in the *Hue and Cry*, as obviously the *Hue and Cry* entry played no part in these arrests.

90 *Statistical returns of the Dublin Metropolitan Police, 1845–1894* (Dublin, 1846–1895). The title of the annual returns varied slightly in this period; the author was unable to locate the returns for 1851, 1854 and 1880.

The men of the Dublin force, like the constabulary, were required to own a decent suit of plain clothes and they often had to wear them on duty. Some went beyond the wearing of mere plain clothes. For instance, in December 1841 two DMP constables disguised themselves as women and secured a conviction against a North Earl Street grocer for illegally selling porter and whiskey.[91] Magistrates did not initially wholeheartedly endorse the activities of the plain-clothesmen. For example, in April 1843 a number of cases brought against shebeen keepers by plain-clothesmen were dismissed by Police Magistrate Kelly after the police admitted that they had first ordered drink on the premises. Kelly told them that he would 'never convict persons offending under such circumstances', as the police 'created the offences themselves, and then seek to punish the parties whom they had induced to violate the law'.[92] He dismissed several similar cases in 1847, despite police protests that the only way in which they could catch shebeeners in the act was for plain-clothes policemen to order drink from them.[93] Magistrate opinion had changed somewhat by the late 1850s, to judge from the verdict of Police Magistrate Porter in February 1858. On Constable 83B's admitting that he had borrowed a carman's clothes and ordered whiskey for consumption on the premises of a Johnson's Court spirit grocer, Porter remarked that the evidence had been 'obtained by unworthy means', but he nevertheless convicted the offender.[94]

Plain-clothesmen were not used merely to police erring drink traders. They were also employed to catch beggars, disperse prostitutes who congregated in the streets or to prevent boys from playing hurling or other unruly street games. In September 1858, the *Freeman's Journal* published a sarcastic sketch of Constable 61D walking through Great Britain Street 'attired in the garb of an unsophisticated countryman'. It stated that he was:

> … highly successful in making sudden descents on any of the unsus-
> pecting juveniles of the locality who happened to be engaged in the
> laudable undertaking of flying a kite, which said kite the said constable
> would forthwith demolish with an air of grave authority, eminently
> calculated to create in the mind, even in the luckless owner of the kite, a
> high respect for the law, of which 61D was a distinguished upholder.[95]

In addition to plain-clothes police, who were merely ordinary constables clad in mufti, the DMP had a section of permanent, non-uniformed detectives from November 1842 onwards. This was the G division, based at the Exchange Court. By 1865 it consisted of 31 officers and men, which number

91 *Freeman's Journal*, 31 Dec. 1841.
92 Ibid., 28 Apr. 1843.
93 Ibid., 11, 20 Feb. 1847; *Nation*, 13 Feb. 1847.
94 *Freeman's Journal*, 9 Feb. 1858.
95 Ibid., 25 Sept. 1858.

had increased to 44 by 1890.[96] Detective police were, as stated earlier, viewed with suspicion by many in the United Kingdom when they were first employed. The *Nation* newspaper was one of the most prominent early critics of the G division. In September 1844 it attacked the 'frightful gang' of 'detective scoundrels', commenting that '[i]t is amazing to us that they dare rot this pure air of ours with their presence'.[97] This was rather mild compared with its leading article in the following month:

> ... there is no man, however high, virtuous, and honorable, that is not liable to have a frightful crew of harpies sliming his steps, following him into every corner, noting down his doings, eaves-dropping in his path, malignantly constructing his words and actions, and, like loaded bees, returning to a certain hive of iniquity every night with their thighs full of malicious conjecture, perverted fact, and lying conclusions. A wealthy man, a firm man, can defy the machinations of the detective villains. Such a man can awe the rascals into silence and humility. But the poor man ... is crushed at once by the leech, the blood-sucker, the vampire policeman. The poor man may have no home – the detective spy is authorised to drag him to one of those dens that are every day swelling their proportions to meet the demands of constructive crime; the poor man may have been guilty of some petty theft, some sixpenny larceny – the detective spy is authorised to dog his steps, to arrest him whenever sunset sees him without a shelter, and to remit him to gaol ... It is bad enough to be torn by the lion or to be gnawed by the wolf; but to be destroyed by vermin – to be crawled to death – to be infested with these base and obnoxious creatures, is what no man of honor or spirit will or ought to endure.[98]

Once the novelty of the detective division had worn off, the fears of the G man as an obnoxious spy abated. Nevertheless, as late as 1865 the DMP authorities remained wary that the activities of the G division might be identified with those of European secret policemen. They insisted that their detectives were 'not to be used as spies, nor to employ persons for that purpose'. Plain clothes only were to be worn in normal circumstances, but if detectives felt that this would be insufficient to detect crime or to prevent a crime of which they had received advance information, they could apply to the G division superintendent for permission to use a disguise.[99]

96 *Instruction book for the Dublin Metropolitan Police* (Dublin, 1865), p. 66 (hereafter, *1865 DMP instruction book*); *Reprint of general orders issued to the [DMP] force since the publication of the police code (1889–1902)* (n.d.): NLI, I 3522 d 8, p. 21 (hereafter, *Reprint of [DMP] general orders*).
97 *Nation*, 28 Sept. 1844.   98 Ibid., 5 Oct. 1844.
99 *1865 DMP instruction book*, p. 68.

DMP detectives were rarely used as 'spies' in the political sense, although the activity of some of the division against the Fenians in the 1860s, 'the Invincibles' in the early 1880s, and the IRA during the Troubles, has helped to create a distorted image of the customary role of the G men. Their activities normally involved much more routine police work, such as enforcing Dublin corporation's carriage bye-laws, executing warrants from the RIC and other police forces as well as warrants from Dublin courts for persons suspected of larceny, embezzlement or bigamy, investigating serious crimes such as murder and burglary, and supervising ticket-of-leave convicts. One of their most common and important duties was visiting the various pawnshops in the city. Dublin's pawnshops were not merely resorts of the poor in times of need; they were also used by thieves, pickpockets and other professional criminals as a means of getting ready cash for their variously-acquired property. Most indictable crime in Dublin consisted of larcenies, and probably most of these were committed by pickpockets. As in England, gentlemen's silk handkerchiefs or 'wipes' were popular targets of the 'light-fingered gentry,' as they could easily be disposed of in pawnshops.[100]

How did the DMP tackle Dublin's pickpockets? Their task was made somewhat easier by the fact that the 'gentry' were notoriously creatures of habit. Pickpockets, as well as burglars, thieves, and army deserters frequently sought shelter for the night in lime kilns, and thus sometimes fell easily into the hands of the police.[101] A more important and effective method of thwarting pickpockets was to observe them in action and catch them red-handed, especially when engaging in a favourite tactic of dipping into the pockets of window-shoppers. Observant policemen proved effective discoverers of pickpockets in fashionable streets such as Grafton Street, Nassau Street, Dame Street and Sackville Street, or other areas frequented by the well-to-do, such as Stephen's Green or the zoo.[102] A considerable part of the DMP's haul of arrested pickpockets was made at the various crowded meetings of the Dublin social or business calendar: crowds at Donnybrook fair, Smithfield market, the Phoenix Park races, and at elections, auctions, exhibitions and regattas were regularly and fruitfully watched over by detectives and plain-clothesmen.

Part of the reason for the DMP's success against pickpockets was that many of them were 'swell mobsters,' English pickpockets who followed their accustomed targets to Ireland. Members of the 'swell mob' were distin-

100 The Dublin pickpocket problem is described in Griffin, *Irish police*, pp. 434–44. For a discussion of Belfast criminals using pawnshops to 'fence' stolen property, see B. Griffin, *The Bulkies: police and crime in Belfast, 1800–1865* (Dublin, 1997), pp. 79–80.
101 *Freeman's Journal*, 12 June 1857, 10 July 1858, 13 Mar. 1862, 25 Aug. 1862, 1 Sept. 1871, 22 Nov. 1880.
102 For some examples see ibid., 12 June 1854, 17 Aug. 1854, 11 Nov. 1854, 1 Jan. 1858, 5, 9 Feb. 1858, 17 Apr. 1858, 11, 25 May 1858, 16 Oct. 1858.

guished by their elegant taste in clothes and jewellery and were often mistaken for ladies and gentlemen; they were easily spotted by detectives.[103] The G division had a regular mode of procedure when informed that members of the swell mob were in Dublin:

> Immediately that their arrival is known two or more of the lynx-eyed force are appointed to the duty of discovering, first, their whereabouts, and then of watching the locality until some of them come forth; their duty then is to follow them through street and square, to concert, theatre, and saloon, never to lose sight of them – to pick them up on every possible occasion, and have them searched thoroughly; until at length literally hunted down, their occupation gone, and their hopes blighted, they are obliged to take their departure to some other locality. In the present instance the 'professors', five in number, took up their residence in Mabbot Street, and previous to being waited on by the police had transacted a little business at Jullien's concerts, of which fact many parties were, no doubt, made painfully aware by the disappearance of purses, brooches, silk handkerchiefs, &c. As soon as their presence in the city was known two of the detective force were appointed to wait on them, which they did most assiduously, doing just as they did, walking when they walked, and driving when they drove, until at length they were forced to admit that they were conscious of being 'spotted', as one of them expressed it, and, finally, were constrained to take their departure in [the] presence of their indefatigable attendants.[104]

For most of the period covered by this article, pickpockets were a major preoccupation for the DMP but by 1881 the chief commissioner expressed his confidence in his force's ability to handle the visits of English swell mobsmen and other criminals. This confidence was increased in 1890 by the G division's practice of providing the 54 pawnbrokers in the DMP district with daily lists of articles of property reported stolen or lost, thus making it more difficult for professional criminals to operate.[105]

Although they were an extremely important part of the DMP, the detectives did not receive any special instruction in detective work before their appointment to the G division. Instead, '[a]ctivity of body, corporeal strength, general mental intelligence, and moderate educational requirements' were considered 'sufficient qualifications for the discharge of detective duties, and

---

103 Ibid., 31 Aug. 1854, 26 Dec. 1871; Thomas Clarke Luby's recollections of Fenianism, p. 174: NLI, MS 331; J.J. Tobias, *Urban crime in Victorian England* (New York, 1972), pp. 64, 72, 105.

104 *Freeman's Journal*, 9 Mar. 1855.

105 *Statistical tables of the Dublin Metropolitan Police, for the year 1881* (Dublin, 1882), p. viii; *DMP circular*, 10 June 1890, in *Reprint of [DMP] general orders*, p. 27.

further teaching is left to be acquired by future experience.'[106] Their task was complicated by the hostility sometimes shown towards police informers.[107] James Joyce, through his fictional character Leopold Bloom, offers what is probably an accurate insight into how detectives acquired some of their information:

> Why those plain clothes men are always courting slaveys. Easily twig a man used to uniform. Squarepushing up against a door. Maul her a bit. Then the next thing on the menu. And who is the gentleman does be visiting here? Was the young master saying anything? Barmaids too. Tobacco shopgirls.[108]

Superintendent John Mallon detailed in 1882 the qualities looked for in a new detective. No constables reported for intoxication, insubordination or impertinence were ever allowed to join, and those who were admitted were 'supposed to be more intelligent and better trained men than the men employed on ordinary duty'. In the G division, 'the moral character of a man is of infinite importance, because if a man was untruthful he would be a dangerous man to have in the department, or if he was corrupt': there are echoes here of the concern voiced by the constabulary authorities that the disposable men should be above reproach in their behaviour. G men joined the division by selection only, usually after attracting the superintendent's notice by the manner in which they gave evidence in court. The new detectives were first sent on carriage duty. This gave them 'the knack of making enquiries', as they were constantly asked by gentlemen who had lost their luggage in cabs to trace their property. After carriage duty detectives graduated to pawnshop duty, and by the time they mastered that they were considered 'pretty well up' in detective work. According to Mallon, it took at least seven or eight years of carriage and pawnshop duty before a detective investigated an important case, and even then he was always accompanied by a senior colleague.[109]

The DMP detectives were generally more successful than the constabulary disposable men, but it seems unfair to juxtapose their respective achievements as the G men benefited from certain factors which made it more likely that they would out-perform the RIC sleuths. First, in the nineteenth century Dublin had the highest number of police to civilians in the United Kingdom, which inevitably gave the DMP an edge when it came to

---

106 F.T. Porter, *Twenty years' recollections of an Irish police magistrate* (8th ed., Dublin, 1880), p.141.
107 Ibid., pp. 91–2.
108 J. Joyce, *Ulysses* (London, 1969 Penguin edition), p. 163.
109 *1882 DMP inquiry*, pp. 53–5.

preventing and detecting crime. Secondly, the capital city had a nucleus of professional criminals or offenders, ranging from prostitutes, child-strippers,[110] and burglars to pickpockets and receivers of stolen goods: the fact that they inevitably went to pawnbrokers to dispose of the proceeds of their crimes improved the DMP's chances of identifying and apprehending suspects. Finally, the G men were full-time detectives who generally investigated crimes of a much less serious nature than those investigated by the part-time disposable men and detectives of the RIC. Even to a layman it seems an easier task to track down the person responsible for picking a gentleman's watch from his pocket (the usual procedure involved getting a description from the pawnbroker who accepted the watch in pawn, and searching the suspect for incriminating pawn tickets) than to find the people responsible for houghing cattle or committing a murder at night in a rural area.

---

110 Child-strippers specialised in enticing young children to secluded areas, stripping them of some or all of their clothing and pawning the stolen articles.

Open court: law and the expansion of magisterial jurisdiction at petty sessions in nineteenth-century Ireland

DESMOND McCABE*

IN MID-NINETEENTH-CENTURY IRELAND, someone walking one afternoon into a typical rural petty sessions, would have been struck by the simplicity of the usual hired room and by the informality of proceedings. The visitor might first have noticed an expanse of bare floorboards, scant furniture, unevenly whitewashed walls and (in winter) a fuming turf fire. There were likely to have been a few police constables standing in the room, attentive to the wishes of one or two gentlemen evidently in the office of magistrate (though in casual dress) seated at a raised bench, facing a number of roughly-clothed men and women. In time the visitor would have seen these men and women, obviously litigants, either speaking to a clerk sitting near the magisterial bench, or severally stepping forward to get up on a table and testify on oath as cases were called. The mood was often boisterous as cases got underway. In most particulars, this was a familiar scene, weekly or fortnightly, in the 550-odd rooms in regular use for the conduct of petty sessions in Ireland in the nineteenth century.[1]

The petty sessions consisted of a regular and voluntary meeting of magistrates, jointly to consider and adjudicate on civil and criminal matters

---

* [Editor's note: this paper was submitted to the Society in the 1990s for inclusion in a volume, planned but not completed, on the theme of criminal justice in Ireland in the nineteenth century.]

1 For a general review of petty sessions see D. McCabe, 'Magistrates, peasants and the petty sessions courts, Mayo 1823–50', in *Cathair na Mart*, v (1985), 45–53; and D. McCabe, 'Law, conflict and social order: County Mayo, 1820–45' (unpublished, Ph.D. thesis, National University of Ireland, 1991), ch. 6. See also P. Bonsall, *The Irish RMs: the resident magistrates in the British administration in Ireland* (Dublin, 1997); W.N. Osborough, 'The Irish legal system, 1796–1877', in idem, *Studies in Irish legal history* (Dublin, 1999), pp. 239–69, at pp. 253–5, and R. McMahon, 'The regional administration of a central legal policy', in L. Litvack and G. Hooper (eds), *Ireland in the nineteenth century: regional identity* (Dublin, 2000), pp. 156–68.

within their jurisdiction.[2] The Irish justice of the peace had administered summary proceedings according to statute, as an individual or in concert with others, from the 1300s.[3] But the petty sessions had not been generally instituted in the Irish country parish as it had been in England from the early 1500s.[4] Eventually, it took judicial exhortation and widespread local initiative to bring a network of petty sessions into being in Ireland between 1823 and 1825. This extension of summary facilities rapidly changed the character of petty litigation. By the end of the decade it was clear that the petty sessions had displaced in routine authority the older manor courts, which had, in many parts of the country, offered a limited forum for civil litigation in minor matters from the 1620s or earlier. Magistrates now rarely acted outside the petty sessions framework. Moreover, both rural and urban litigation substantially increased as a result of the efficiency of petty sessions, and the expansion of summary prosecution by the constabulary from the later 1820s.[5] It is notable that close to 80 per cent of those confined in county gaols in the later nineteenth century had been summarily convicted at petty sessions.[6] For most purposes the common law was represented to the small litigant and offender by the authority of the local magisterial bench.

Following a brief inquiry into the administration of petty sessions, the main body of this paper comprises a survey of the legislation relating to summary jurisdiction in force in Ireland between 1800 and 1900. The paper concludes with a preliminary analysis of patterns of petty sessions usage by litigants and of long-term trends in magisterial decision-making.

INTRODUCTION

The whole body of criminal and civil law was administered at several levels in Ireland throughout the nineteenth century. Initial investigation into serious crime was carried out by magistrates assembled at petty sessions. Depending on the magisterial decision, prosecution on indictment to crown court at quarter sessions or assizes, in the county concerned, then took place. Less serious cases of crime were determined summarily at petty sessions after 1823. Certain kinds of assault, larceny and rescue cases were transferred from indictable to summary jurisdiction at different stages (1829, 1843, 1857, 1861: see Table 1). The range of criminal offences open to summary

---

2 R. Nun and J. Walsh, *The powers and duties of the Irish justice of the peace* (Dublin, 1844), p. 76.
3 R. Frame, 'Commissions of the peace in Ireland, 1302–1461' in *Analecta Hibernica*, xxxv (1992), 1–44.
4 F. Milton, *The English magistracy* (London, 1967), pp. 10–12. A sitting of two justices of the peace was somewhat facetiously known as 'double justice'.
5 McCabe, 'Law, conflict and social order', ch. 6.
6 *Judicial Statistics, Ireland*, H.C. 1865 (C.3563) lii, xxxi.

adjudication widened greatly in any event. Cases indicted to crown court underwent an involved, formal process of inquiry, before being tried by jury. Magisterial powers of adjudication in summary law intentionally minimised such formalities without sacrificing the integrity of statutory rules of evidence. Major disputes in civil law were dealt with at the superior courts in Dublin, or at the record court at assize. The court of the assistant barrister at quarter sessions possessed jurisdiction in cases of debt in amounts up to £20. Magistrates at petty sessions summarily adjusted a narrow range of civil matters – essentially master/apprentice/servant disputes, wage disputes in limited amounts, cases of trespass and damage, and certain cases of debt. The debt jurisdiction was inferior to that exercised until 1858 by seneschals at manor courts.[7]

Summary jurisdiction, then, provided for the settlement or adjudication of specific minor injuries and offences. Although the court of petty sessions was the normal arena for the exercise of summary jurisdiction from the mid-1820s, that jurisdiction was not restricted by statute to petty sessions. Whereas indictable crime could only be dealt with at the assize or quarter sessions (a judge, bench of magistrates or assistant barrister had no judicial authority in this regard outside the court as duly appointed), magistrates were empowered to carry out summary adjudication, once the relevant statutory conditions were fulfilled, at any time or place.[8] Though in practice this seldom occurred, as the lord chancellor and the judiciary took a dim view of the exercise of summary powers in cases outside sessions, magisterial freedom in this connection was never revoked. The petty sessions was not, strictly speaking, a court of law, rather a 'mere voluntary association of magistrates', or no more than a sensible, public-spirited arrangement for the provision of access to summary authority.[9] Purists even doubted whether the executive was 'constitutionally authorised' to ask for returns on the conduct of petty sessions.[10]

The amphibious character of the early petty sessions was congruent with the view that the procedures of summary law ought to show more elasticity

7 The enlargement of summary jurisdiction is treated in the third section of this paper. For the administration of courts of assize, see D. McCabe, '"That part that laws or kings can cause or cure": crown prosecution and jury trial at Longford assizes, 1830–45', in R. Gillespie and G. Moran (eds), *Longford: essays in county history* (Dublin, 1991), pp. 153–72. For an account of quarter sessions, see *Seventeenth report of the commissioners appointed to inquire into the duties, salaries and emoluments of the officers, clerks and ministers of justice ... in Ireland ... in the courts of quarter sessions and of assistant barristers*, H.C. 1828 (144) xii, 161 (hereafter '*Report on quarter sessions*'); for manor courts, see McCabe, 'Law, conflict and social order', ch. 6.

8 Statutes did not refer to the summary jurisdiction of magistrates specifically assembled at petty sessions until the consolidation act of 1851 (see Table 1).

9 Nun and Walsh, *Powers and duties*, p. 76.

10 *Report of the select committee appointed to inquire into the operation of the small debt jurisdiction of manor courts in Ireland*, H.C. 1837–8 (648) xvii, 60.

than those of the higher courts, 'to reconcile such private disputes, as the peace of the country may better be consulted by accommodating than by making the subject of a public prosecution'.[11] Once the ordinary civil and criminal business of petty sessions was despatched, the magistrates now and then convened special sessions to study lists of registered freeholders, or barony panels of petty jurors for the quarter sessions. At the same time, the petty sessions gradually took on certain legal functions which made the gathering assume increasing resemblance to a statutory court. From the early 1830s, justices of the peace were required to assemble at petty sessions in order to appoint, admonish, or discharge parish appraisers, pound keepers, summons servers and special constables.[12] Dog licences were issued by the clerk at the sessions from 1865.[13] The petty sessions administered perhaps 95 per cent of civil and criminal cases taken in the country, and sorted out a wide 'mixum-gatherum' of other matters of local significance, but remains curiously inaccessible to exact definition.

SUMMARY PROCEEDINGS AND PERSONNEL

Petty sessions were not unknown in Ireland before the 1820s: in a sense, every meeting of more than one justice of the peace outside quarter sessions or assizes constituted a petty sessions. As a rule, however, prospective litigants set out, in eighteenth-century Ireland, to make their complaints at the private residence of their local magistrate. While some magistrates made themselves available at regular intervals for the adjudication of disputes, many did not trouble themselves to deal with minor problems unless harassed at length, and altogether disclaimed magisterial responsibility for any but the disputes of their own tenantry.[14] Examinations took place, either in an open yard, or, occasionally, in serious cases, in the magistrate's living quarters: in May 1817, as Richard Chaloner of Moynalty, Co. Meath, wrote out a committal upon a suspected meal-thief, 'the tender-hearted cook and kitchen maid favoured his escape through the kitchen'.[15] Commonly, magistrates were used as arbitrators in a wide range of cases in which they had no legal authority to adjudicate and domestic servants were 'employed' as clerks and constables. Fees for legal services (orders, summonses, committals and so on) were

11   Nun and Walsh, *Powers and duties*, p. 76.
12   McCabe, 'Law, conflict and social order', ch. 6.
13   28 & 29 Vict, c. 50 (1865).
14   E. Wakefield, *An account of Ireland, statistical and political*, 2 vols, (London, 1812), ii, pp. 334–40, 752–4; *Hansard's Parl. Deb., 2nd ser.*, vol. vii, col. 850 (7 June 1822); *Report from the select committee appointed to inquire into the state of Ireland*, H.C. 1825 (129) viii, 749, 758.
15   V. Farrell, *Not so much to one side* (Cavan, 1984), p. 63.

subject to no outside control, and were known to have been routinely pocketed by certain magistrates. Where there was a shortage of specie, and fees were paid in kind, magistrates were open to blandishment by gifts of fowl, oysters or other delicacies, or assistance in drawing turf in due season.[16] As in parts of contemporary England, gentry in straitened circumstances were said to have made a living as 'trading justices'.[17]

The hypothetical benefits of informality and discretion aside, the executive was determined by the early 1820s to remodel the exercise of summary procedure 'to give regularity and publicity to the discharge of magisterial duties'.[18] An act of 1822 facilitated summary process. The lord lieutenant, the marquess of Wellesley, invited magistrates by circular, in early 1823, to set up regular petty sessions, and the judiciary spoke on the merits of the system at spring and summer assizes.[19] Magisterial goodwill was displayed in the alacrity with which petty sessions were organised. By 1824–25 only the most remote areas in the country lacked a regular sessions (in theory if not always in practice).[20] Peasant apprehensions with regard to the conduct of law were not immediately dispelled, but there was an observable increase in summary litigation in the country by the later 1820s. In places this increase led to busier quarter sessions and assize courts; elsewhere it may have reduced court pressure.[21] In 1827, magistrates in Louth and Cavan were said to have got into the habit of forwarding an excess of cases to higher courts, 'without permitting the compromise of trifling assaults, which previously was practicable'.[22] Galway magistrates proved more restrained in summary practice now that cases received 'more discussion' than formerly.[23] Differences now becoming apparent in the character of summary jurisdiction around the country related to regional variations in summary practice as it had existed before the introduction of petty sessions, which had itself often been linked to variations in the number of magistrates resident in each area (something which changed very little before the Famine). The new system appeared to enhance the quality of summary investigation into complaints ('parties confronted before the magistrates at petty sessions are less emboldened to falsify or more likely to be detected in the act'),[24] to lessen the number of so-called 'cross-cases' arriving at quarter sessions or even assizes, and to regularise somewhat the transmission of informations to the higher courts.

16 *Minutes of evidence taken before the select committee appointed to examine into the nature and extent of the disturbances which have prevailed,* H.C. 1825 (20) vii, 109, 183, 256, 336–7.
17 Milton, *English magistracy,* pp. 14–17.
18 *Report on courts of quarter sessions,* p. 22.
19 3 Geo IV, c. 23 (1823); McCabe, 'Law, conflict and social order', ch. 6.
20 NAI, CSO Registered papers, 1825:12/288.
21 *Report on courts of quarter sessions,* pp. 55, 69, 71, 78, 95, 98.
22 Ibid., pp. 81, 90.   23 Ibid., p. 63.
24 Ibid., p. 61.

Table 1: Select table of statutes relating to petty sessions

Date	Act	Summary description
1696	7 Wm III, c. 17 (Irish)	Lord's Day observance
1698	10 Wm III, c. 8 (Irish)	Game preservation
1756	29 Geo II, c. 8 (Irish)	Master/servant disputes
1771	11 & 12 Geo III, c. 30 (Irish)	Mendicancy
1786	26 Geo III, c. 24 (Irish)	Licensing hours
1787	27 Geo III, c. 35 (Irish)	Game preservation
1793	33 Geo III, c. 55	Apprenticeship disputes
1813	54 Geo III, c. 116	Recovery of wages, Ireland
1822	3 Geo IV, c. 23	To facilitate summary proceedings
1822	3 Geo IV, c. 71	Prevention of cruelty to cattle
1823	4 Geo IV, c. 34	Master/servant disputes
1827	7 & 8 Geo IV, c. 67	Administration of justice at petty sessions, Ireland
1828	9 Geo IV, c. 54	Administration of criminal justice, Ireland
1828	9 Geo IV, c. 55	Larceny, Ireland
1828	9 Geo IV, c. 56	Malicious injuries to property, Ireland
1829	10 Geo IV, c. 34	Offences against the person, Ireland
1832	2 & 3 Wm IV, c. 77	Regulation of linen and hempen trade, Ireland
1833	3 & 4 Wm IV, c. 103	Labour of children, young people in mills, UK
1834	4 & 5 Wm IV, c. 93	Appeals against summary convictions, Ireland
1835	5 & 6 Wm IV, c. 63	Weights and measures, UK
1836	6 & 7 Wm IV, c. 34	Administration of justice, petty sessions, Ireland
1836	6 & 7 Wm IV, c. 38	Sale of beer, wine, spirits, Ireland
1838	1 & 2 Vict, c. 56	Relief of the destitute poor, Ireland
1838	1 & 2 Vict, c. 99	Fines and penalties, Ireland
1839	2 & 3 Vict, c. 77	Punishment of assaults, Ireland
1842	5 & 6 Vict, c. 106	Regulation of Irish fisheries
1843	6 & 7 Vict, c. 56	Better collection of fines, penalties and issues
1844	7 & 8 Vict, c. 24	Abolition of offences of forestalling etc.
1847	11 & 12 Vict, c. 59	Speedy trial of juvenile offenders, Ireland
1849	12 & 13 Vict, c. 70	Summary convictions, Ireland
1850	13 & 14 Vict, c. 102	Summary jurisdiction, Ireland
1851	14 & 15 Vict, c. 92	Summary jurisdiction, consolidation, Ireland
1855	18 & 19 Vict, c. 126	Criminal justice, England and Ireland
1857	20 & 21 Vict, c. 43	Improvement in summary proceedings
1858	21 & 22 Vict, c. 100	Clerk of petty sessions, Ireland
1858	21 & 22 Vict, c. 103	Reformatory schools, Ireland
1859	22 Vict, c. 14	Small debts, abolition of manor courts, Ireland
1861	24 & 25 Vict, c. 96	Larceny, England and Ireland
1861	24 & 25 Vict, c. 97	Malicious injuries to property, England & Ireland
1861	24 & 25 Vict, c. 100	Offences against person, England and Ireland
1864	27 & 28 Vict, c. 35	Sale of beer, Ireland
1868	31 Vict, c. 25	Industrial Schools (Ire.) Act
1875	38 & 39 Vict, c. 90	Employers and Workmen Act
1878	41 & 42 Vict, c. 52	Public Health (Ire.) Act
1878	41 & 42 Vict, c. 69	Petty Sessions Clerks & Fines (Ire.) Act
1884	47 & 48 Vict, c. 19	Summary Jurisdiction over Children (Ire.) Act
1894	57 & 58 Vict, c. 41	Prevention of Cruelty to Children Act

A legislative basis for the administration of petty sessions was provided by a series of enactments between 1827 and 1851 (see Table 1). The Petty Sessions (Ire.) Act 1827 consolidated in law the arrangements already undertaken by assembled magistrates since 1823. County grand juries were empowered to present a sum for the rent of rooms for use as petty sessions. Under the act, petty sessions districts were delimited by magistrates at quarter sessions. Clerical fees were prescribed, and it was required that informations be sent up to the offices of the crown and peace monthly. Note was to be taken of all magisterial activity outside petty sessions, placing the solitary doings of a magistrate 'under a suspicious vigilance'. Acts of 1828 and 1834 provided for the estreatment of recognisances and for procedures of appeal from petty sessions to the assistant barrister's court at quarter sessions. An act of 1836 detailed clerical duties more fully, and allowed for the punishment of recalcitrant witnesses in summary cases. The Fines Acts of 1837 and 1843 enlarged police responsibilities in the collection of levy warrants. Finally, acts of 1849, 1850 and 1851 dealt comprehensively with every aspect of the role and duties of magistrates at petty sessions with respect both to indictable and summarily triable offences. Legislation of 1858 and 1878 primarily concerned the fees and salaries of petty sessions clerks.[25]

By the mid-1830s the country was served by a total of 536 petty sessions, weekly, fortnightly and monthly. This approximated to about 13,900 actual sessions due to be held annually.[26] The system was weakest in Monaghan and Tipperary and at its most ambitious in Wicklow, Westmeath, King's Co. and Queen's Co.[27] The number of petty sessions rose gradually to 595 in 1849 and 610 in the early 1880s: access to summary justice improved considerably after the Famine.[28] Before small public courthouses were erected towards the end of the century, magistrates made do with rooms in market houses, hotels or other civic or public buildings, in the smaller towns and villages outside the quarter sessions and assize circuits.[29] The body of magistrates required

25 See Table 1: 7 & 8 Geo IV, c. 67 (1827); 9 Geo IV, c. 54 (1828); 4 & 5 Wm IV, c. 93 (1834); 6 & 7 Wm IV, c. 34 (1836); 6 & 7 Vict, c. 56 (1843); 12 & 13 Vict, c. 70 (1849); 13 & 14 Vict, c. 102 (1850); 14 & 15 Vict, c. 92 (1851); 21 & 22 Vict, c. 100 (1858); 41 & 42 Vict, c. 69 (1878).

26 *Report on the small debt jurisdiction of manor courts in Ireland*, H.C. 1837–8 (648) xvii, 74; the calculation assumes an average of 26 sessions held yearly at each location.

27 There were seven sessions in Monaghan and twenty in Tipperary: this converts into 182 and 520 sessions held annually in the respective counties (see above). Finally, this translates into 91 sessions per 100,000 population in Monaghan and to 119 sessions per 100,000 population in Tipperary, compared to a national rate of 170 per 100,000, and rates of between 290 and 305 per 100,000 in the stronger counties mentioned. There was a paucity of magistrates resident in Tipperary before and after the Famine.

28 *Returns showing the number of petty sessions clerks and the amount of fees received by them, in each county of Ireland, in the year 1849*, H.C. 1850 (304) li, 527; *Returns showing for the year 1883 the total number of petty sessions districts in Ireland etc.*, H.C. 1884–5 (23) lxiv, 669.

29 McCabe, 'Law, conflict and social order', ch. 6.

to officiate at petty sessions rose from about 3,500 in 1821 to perhaps 4,000 in 1830, was shorn to 3,500 again by the later 1830s, climbing to 5,000 in the 1880s, and 6,000 in the early 1900s.[30] Accordingly, the proportion of magistrates on the county benches, per head of population, climbed from one to 1,943 in 1821 to one to 730 in 1912. Magistrates were most sparse and scattered before the Famine in Donegal, Monaghan, Kerry and Mayo, and most abundant in the counties of Leinster. Throughout the century, the bench was predominantly landed and protestant. However, the proportion of clerical (episcopalian) office holders fell from ten per cent in the 1830s to less than one per cent in the 1880s. By the 1880s, 24 per cent of the bench was catholic, 66 per cent episcopalian, and ten per cent of dissenting faiths. Landed gentry and land agents still occupied 63 per cent of commissions, despite encroachments by merchants (13 per cent), farmers (seven per cent), and others (police, lawyers, doctors).[31] Fewer honorific commissions were tolerated by the end of the century than was the case before the administrative surgery carried out in the 1820s and 1830s.[32] Nevertheless, stipendiary magistrates (never more than approximately 1.5 per cent of the bench) shouldered an increasingly heavy burden of county business by the 1860s and 1870s, though suffering lingering distrust from their unpaid colleagues.[33]

Sessions personnel were appointed by the assembled local magistracy. The turnover of summons servers tended to be high,[34] but the petty sessions clerk was a powerful and enduring local presence. Early on at least, many clerks of petty sessions were also local stewards, bailiffs or tax collectors of some description:[35] however the Summary Jurisdiction (Ire.) Act 1851 regarded these and similar occupations as inconsistent with the responsibilities of the position. Clerks entered, at the time of their appointment, into a recognisance before the

---

30 It is no easy matter to differentiate between live and redundant commissions. Census figures are not a sure guide. *Numbers and names of magistracy in the commission of the peace in Ireland*, H.C 1830–31 (171) viii, 291; *Return of the number of warrants for the commission of justices of the peace*, H.C. 1831–32 (93) xxxv, 339; *Return of the names and residences of the deputy lieutenants and magistrates included in the commission of the peace in Ireland*, H.C. 1836 (318) xliii, 299; *A return of the number and names of gentlemen appointed to the commission of the peace in each county in Ireland*, H.C. 1876 (339) lxi, 347; *Returns, as to each county in Ireland, stating the names of lieutenants and the names of the local magistracy*, 1882 (123) lv, 489; F.S.L. Lyons, *Ireland since the Famine* (London, 1971), p.74.

31 *Returns for each county, city and borough in Ireland, of the names of persons holding the commission of the peace*, H.C. 1884 (13) lxiii, 331.

32 McCabe, 'Law, conflict and social order', ch. 6.

33 K.T. Hoppen, *Elections, politics and society in Ireland: 1832–1885* (Oxford, 1984), p. 408; F.S.L. Lyons, *Ireland since the Famine*, p. 75; by the third quarter of the century, statutes frequently entrusted single stipendiary magistrates with the summary authority of two local magistrates. Local magistrates often came to sessions for criminal business, and then left the civil business to the stipendiary magistrate, if one was in attendance.

34 McCabe, 'Law, conflict and social order', ch. 6.

35 Ibid.

magistrates for the 'due discharge' of their duties, and held office at the pleasure of the petty sessions bench.[36] The given amount of such recognisance was not specified until 1858.[37] Clerical duties embraced the maintenance and supervision of a register of civil and criminal proceedings, keeping accounts of all fines meted out and paid to his charge, and the preparation, under magisterial direction, of informations, summonses, warrants and other court instruments, and the transmission of documentation appropriate to cases of indictment to the offices of the county clerks of the peace and crown. These duties were first stated in law in 1836.[38] Until 1858, Irish clerks were paid by fee, charging from six pence to two shillings (according to tables of fees in the acts of 1827 and 1851) for the preparation and issue of orders, summonses, convictions and other legal instruments. On foot of the act of 1858, the lord lieutenant fixed a half-yearly salary (and a pension on termination of office) for each clerk according to the extent of local petty sessions business.[39] This did not mean that the fees of litigation disappeared: instead, the fund out of which clerical salaries were paid was henceforth amassed out of the aggregate of 'the produce of the petty sessions stamps' and the amount of summary fines imposed by the Irish magistracy on criminal offenders. (Indeed, there was suspicion by the 1870s that the Irish magisterial preference for punishment by fine rather than imprisonment was not unrelated to 'the direct interest' of the Irish petty sessions clerk 'in a very large number of cases in the amount of fines imposed'). Every three years the clerical salaries in each district were revised according to the takings of the previous period: in January 1875 the registrar of Irish petty sessions clerks innocently thought to remind his officers that 'the amount of your salary largely depends upon your own efforts to increase the fund arising from fees and fines'. The majority of English petty sessions clerks continued to be paid directly by fee until a system of salaries paid out of county rates was introduced in 1877.[40] Unlike England, where the petty sessions clerk was traditionally often more skilled in legal matters than the local magistrate, the rural Irish clerk did not usually rise above administrative competence.[41] This, however, was frequently enough to ensure that the clerk was able to manage or run each sessions, and could exploit such power to personal advantage. The embezzlement of fines collected was often a temptation if not a sore reality. Up to 1858, complaints were intermittently made of extortionate and unlawful fees for clerical services.[42] Delays in the transmission of informations and other documents

36 14 & 15 Vict, c. 93 (1851).   37 21 & 22 Vict, c. 100 (1858).
38 6 Wm IV, c. 34 (1836).   39 21 & 22 Vict, c. 100 (1858).
40 C. Molloy, 'Report of the charity organisation committee on the organisation of the courts
    by which drunkenness is punished, in connexion with suggested extension of the Justices
    Clerks Act, 1877, to Ireland' in *JSSISI*, vii (1877–8), 213–7.
41 Milton, *English magistracy*, pp. 44–8.
42 McCabe, 'Law, conflict and social order', ch. 6.

were common to the 1840s. To compound matters, until the passing of the Summary Jurisdiction (Ire.) Act in 1851, the local petty sessions bench (of course an interested body) was the only authority that could dismiss a clerk for breach of duty.[43]

By convention, petty sessions commenced at noon, on the day appointed, at weekly to monthly intervals. An impressive system on paper was in places undermined by an irregularity in magisterial attendance or even by continual absenteeism. Until a remedy was provided under an act of 1858, all of the summonses to a particular sessions lost legal force were no magistrate formally to open that sessions, and disappointed litigants might therefore be compelled to pay for a fresh summons to the next sessions. The sessions clerk was accordingly authorised in 1858 to adjourn all matters to the next sessions if no magistrate appeared.[44] On a national level, the rate of absenteeism declined from 12 per cent in the 1840s to about five per cent in the 1890s.[45] Magistrates were at their least reliable in the province of Connacht (where rates of absenteeism could rise to over 20 per cent) and at their most punctual in eastern Ulster. There was no collapse in attendance figures in western counties during the land war of 1879–82, though admittedly rates of absenteeism were persistently high in the counties of Mayo, Roscommon and Galway from the 1840s to the 1890s, despite periodic censure by county and lord lieutenants.[46] Realistically, absenteeism rates of three to four per cent were as low as could reasonably be expected of any bench (allowing for causes such as illness, funerals, quarter sessions and assize business, inclement weather and so on). Although in certain districts a single magistrate presided over a very high proportion of sessions (essentially limiting available jurisdiction to civil cases), about 40 per cent of sessions were manned by two magistrates, and 45 per cent of sessions attended by three or more magistrates.[47] It was apparent, moreover, that over 60 per cent of active magistrates attended petty sessions more than five times each year: work was thus fairly evenly distributed within this group.[48]

---

43   14 & 15 Vict, c. 92 (1851).

44   21 & 22 Vict, c. 100 (1858); McCabe, 'Magistrates, peasants and the petty sessions courts', p. 48.

45   See Table 2; *Return from every petty sessions in Ireland, showing the number of days and date thereof, on which petty sessions were or ought to have been held in 1842*, H.C. 1843 (543) li, 181 (the rate for 1842 was calculated from a sample of 12 counties).

46   The matter was raised in parliament in 1879: *Judicial Statistics, Ireland*, H.C. 1880 (C. 2698) lxxxvii, 77.

47   *Return from every petty sessions in Ireland in 1842*.

48   *Returns showing for the year 1883 the total number of petty sessions districts in Ireland*, H.C. 1884–5 (23) lxiv, 669.

Table 2: Petty sessions – % magisterial non-attendance by province,
Ireland, 1863–90

	1863–70	1871–78	1879–82	1883–90
Leinster	8.3	6.9	5.9	4.2
Munster	7.4	6.6	5.7	4.9
Ulster	6.3	4.4	2.8	2.1
Connacht	15.2	14.9	12.5	10.6
Totals	9.3	8.2	6.1	4.9

During the 1830s and 1840s, litigants in summary jurisdiction were normally granted up to three months from the date of a dispute or alleged offence to make complaint.[49] Under the Summary Jurisdiction (Ire.) Act 1851, time limits for most civil and criminal prosecutions were extended to six months. In the case of wage disputes the time limit was raised to one year.[50] The litigant generally took out a summons at petty sessions, in the district in which the alleged offence occurred. The clerk completed and issued the summons, signed by a magistrate present, for a fee of six pence (doubled in 1878 to one shilling, in certain circumstances).[51] The summons was delivered by a district server, either personally, or to the 'usual place of abode' of the named defendant. Magistrates were authorised to deal *ex parte* with most summary cases, upon proof of service of summons, where a defendant failed to appear, and were enabled, if necessary, to issue a warrant for the apprehension of a defaulter on the basis of sworn informations. Complaints were usually dismissed upon the non-appearance of a complainant.[52]

The structure of the criminal hearing changed little over the century. Initially the substance of the complaint was stated to the defendant, who was asked if there was cause 'to show why he should not be convicted'.[53] If the defendant admitted to no cause, the bench made out either a conviction or an order, at their discretion. If the substance of the complaint was denied, then the magistrates proceeded to hear, first, the prosecutor and his witnesses, then the defendant and his. The complainant and defendant were entitled to cross-examine the opposing party and witnesses, but not to 'make

---

49   For instance, see 9 Geo IV, c. 56 (1828), 9 Geo IV, c. 55 (1828) and 10 Geo IV, c. 34 (1829).
50   14 & 15 Vict, c. 93 (1851).
51   Ibid.; 41 & 42 Vict, c. 69 (the cost of summons in England was one shilling throughout the nineteenth century).
52   12 & 13 Vict, c. 70 (1849); 14 & 15 Vict, c. 92 (1851).
53   12 & 13 Vict, c. 70 (1849); J. O'Donoghue, *The summary jurisdiction of magistrates* (Dublin, 1835), pp. 203–10.

observations' upon their testimony.[54] Magistrates were entitled to adjourn cases at any time to allow for the summons of additional witnesses. Though the immediacy and flexibility of summary procedure was a major strength of the system, it was not acceptable for statutory rules of evidence to be at all compromised in the course of the hearing.[55] There was some uncertainty as to the power of magistrates to summon witnesses in summary cases, except under particular statutes.[56] Once in court, witnesses could be committed for 24 hours for contempt, or, after 1851, committed for up to one month for refusal to be examined.[57] During the 1820s and early 1830s, magistrates often challenged the right of attorneys to represent parties at petty sessions, in the belief that summary trial could best do without 'that nicety of discussion, or subtlety of argument, which are likely to be introduced by persons more accustomed to legal questions'.[58] It seems that the interpretation of the Irish lord chancellor was more lenient to attorneys than that of his English counterpart. The matter was eventually resolved by an act of 1836 which permitted the provision of counsel on both sides, at all levels of the law.[59]

Ultimately the magistrates consulted and determined the matter. Convictions were entered in the petty sessions book. Otherwise, defendants received a certificate of dismissal as a bar to further prosecution for the same complaint.[60] The lawful forms of conviction and dismissal were specified in acts of 1822 and 1849.[61] Summary legislation provided for a range of penalties: the award of fines together with medical or legal costs and/or compensation; commitment to gaol for periods of up to six months, or, very occasionally, one year, with or without hard labour; committal of children and young adults to reformatory or industrial school from the later 1850s; requirement to take recognisances or sureties to keep the peace; orders of various sorts, or, exceptionally, the discharge of an offender.[62] From 1828, in cases of theft or malicious injury, magistrates could discharge offenders 'on payment of recompense'.[63] From 1887, magistrates received broader powers to release juvenile offenders 'on probation of good conduct'.[64] In practice, magistrates generally exercised the options of fine or committal. The chances of committal tended to depend on ability to pay the fine imposed. It was unusual for magistrates to insist upon committal where the offender professed sufficient means to

---

54 Ibid., p. 210.   55 Ibid., p. 203.   56 Ibid., p. 209.
57 14 & 15 Vict, c. 92 (1851).
58 Milton, *English magistracy*, p. 49; McCabe, 'Magistrates, peasants and the petty sessions courts', pp. 50–1.
59 6 & 7 Wm IV, c. 114 (1836).   60 12 and 13 Vict, c.70 (1849).
61 3 Geo IV, c. 23 (1822); 12 and 13 Vict, c.70 (1849).
62 The third section of this paper gives a summary of the penalties attached to the different statutes examined.
63 9 Geo IV, c. 55 (1828); 9 Geo IV, c. 56 (1828).   64 50 & 51 Vict, c. 25 (1887).

pay a fine.[65] The duration of the prison sentence was scaled according to the weight of the fine incurred.[66] Magistrates ordinarily fixed a time for payment of a given fine and if it was not paid voluntarily it was later collected or levied under warrant of distress by the constabulary. Enactments in 1851, 1863 and 1888 prohibited the distraint of growing crops, 'wearing apparel', or trades-men's tools to the value of £5, for payment of summary fines and small debts.[67] The archaic punishment of the pillory was abolished for every offence save that of perjury in 1816, then abolished unconditionally in 1837. The public whipping of female offenders was abolished in 1820. Minor offenders continued now and then to be placed in the stocks up to the early 1830s.[68]

Appeal to the assistant barrister at quarter sessions against convictions at petty sessions was allowed under certain conditions. From 1820 to 1850, appeals were permitted where a fine exceeded £5, a term of imprisonment exceeded one month, or where a justice had acted alone.[69] The assistant barrister for Cavan testified in 1827 that appeals were 'not very frequent ... generally from convictions under the game laws and for selling spirits without license'.[70] Appeal was costly and onerous: the appellant was required, within days, both to enter a recognisance to the value of double the amount of the fine imposed, with the clerk of petty sessions, and to nominate two solvent persons as security for the appeal. The conditions of appeal were amended in 1851 to include cases where fines exceeded £1.[71] The machinery of appeal was simplified in 1858.[72] Over the period from 1863 to 1890, however, appeals were never taken in more than 0.5 per cent of convictions and the original verdict was consistently affirmed in half of appeals taken.[73]

SUMMARY JURISDICTION

Knowing what to expect of a summary hearing at petty sessions, it remains to give an account of the scope of summary jurisdiction. What kind of case could be taken before magistrates and what powers of adjudication did they

65   Indeed, there was criticism of the partiality of Irish magistrates to use of the fine rather than imprisonment. English magistrates were less amenable, sentencing to prison about 22 to 25 per cent of criminal offenders: *Judicial Statistics, Ireland*, H.C. 1876 (C.1563) lxxix, 24.

66   For instance, the act of 36 & 37 Vict, c. 82 (1873) modified the act of 14 & 15 Vict, c. 92 (1851), in specifying that fines of up to ten shillings might translate into sentences of up to seven days; fines of from ten shillings to £1, into terms of seven to 14 days; fines of £1–2, into terms of 14 days to one month; and fines of £2–5 into terms of one to two months.

67   11 & 12 Vict, c. 28 (1851); 26 & 27 Vict, c. 62 (1863); 51 & 52 Vict, c. 47 (1888).

68   56 Geo III, c. 138 (1816); 1 Vict, c. 23 (1837); 1 Geo IV, c. 57; Milton, *English magistracy*, p. 78.

69   For instance, see 9 Geo IV, c. 55 (1828) and 10 Geo IV, c. 34 (1829).

70   *Report on courts of quarter sessions*, p. 90.

71   14 & 15 Vict, c. 92 (1851).   72   21 & 22 Vict, c. 103 (1858).

73   *Judicial Statistics, Ireland*, 1863–90, see note 99 below.

possess during each quarter of the nineteenth century? The clearest way that suggested itself of dealing with the tangle of laws appearing on the statute-book over such a long period was to gather associated pieces of legislation together in order of enactment under common-sense explanatory headings (as '*wages & hire*' and so on). A simple outline under each heading of the content of the principal pieces of legislation in force at different times during the century will then support analysis of the statistical data tabulated under similar headings in the fourth section of this paper. Overall, the intricacies of change and development in summary jurisdiction are described according to an intuitive thematic order: for example, laws dealing with matters of employment and wages and hire are discussed in sequence.

Although civil cases were not recorded as well as criminal cases in the official statistical data, it seemed best to include an analysis of civil summary jurisdiction in order to give a rounded picture of the nature and extent of petty sessions business. Civil cases are those in which one person sues another on the basis that he, as an individual, has been wronged by that other; usually, compensation for damage of some description is claimed. Actions 'deemed to be contrary to the welfare of the community' are at issue in criminal prosecutions. The volume of civil case work at petty sessions averaged out at 17 to 25 per cent of the volume of criminal offences deter-mined, and the scope of summary civil law was rather confined. Criminal and civil cases were randomly interspersed for determination at petty sessions. Unresolved conflict in civil matters was believed to be conducive to increase in crime, and there was some public anxiety to widen the range of cheap civil options open to the litigant at summary level.[74]

There was an immense difference between the legal and social environ-ment in which petty litigation was pursued at the start and end of the nineteenth century. In the early 1800s, the Irish magistrate, alone or with one of his fellows, was expected to 'conserve the peace' of his neighbourhood, to inquire into all local complaints of crime, and if necessary, to indict those accused to trial. Their summary powers broadly encompassed certain wage disputes; problems in the master/apprentice/servant relationship; certain thefts of timber; poaching of game and fish; drink licence offences; Sabbath breach; certain disputes at fairs and markets; nuisance and carriage offences; certain excise and revenue offences related to illicit distillation; constabulary discipline; trespass; vagrancy; and certain powers under the coercion acts of the 1790s and 1800s. By the 1890s, legislation on all of these matters had evolved and ramified. The scope of criminal and civil summary jurisdiction had been hugely extended. Regulation of public life by state personnel, such as poor law guardians, sanitary inspectors, town commissioners, and constabulary police, among others, was enforced at petty sessions under

74 Milton, *English magistracy*, pp. 56–7; *Judicial Statistics, Ireland*, H.C. 1874 (C.1034) lxxi, 95.

public health, poor law, sanitary and police legislation. The maltreatment of animals was liable to summary prosecution from 1820. Common assault became open to summary prosecution in 1829. The consumption and sale of alcohol was regulated more thoroughly from the mid-1830s. From 1856 larcenies under five shillings (and, in special circumstances, above that amount), attempted larcenies, and larcenies from the person, might be taken up at petty sessions. Sums open to civil proceedings under the wages acts were steadily increased. Summary jurisdiction in cases of distress and replevin of livestock was haltingly introduced in the 1820s. From 1858, the petty sessions acquired a limited jurisdiction in the recovery of small debts. Incremental changes in the law were manifold (see Table 1 for important additions to summary jurisdiction between 1820 and 1900).

Master/servant legislation

Magistrates had been entrusted with summary jurisdiction in master/apprentice relations from the sixteenth century. A statute of 1793 (which superseded acts of 1756 and 1760) empowered two or more justices of the peace to examine the complaints of apprentices, bound out in sums up to £10, against their masters, and *vice versa*. If the finding was for the apprentice, the magistrates could discharge him and fine his master in sums up to 40 shillings. Complaints found in favour of the master might result in imprisonment of the apprentice in terms up to one month. An act of 1823 enabled magistrates to resolve such complaints in the case of apprentices bound out in sums of up to £25. Another act of the same year provided a summary remedy for failure to honour or fulfil contracts entered into by a classified range of artisans and servants: wages could be abated and/or the culprit imprisoned for a term of up to three months. An act of 1851 reaffirmed these penalties, and added a fine of £5 for entering into contract under 'false or forged' certification. An act of 1867 introduced (and defined) the terms 'employer' and 'employed' into the contractual relationship, and enabled the magistrate to order the payment of amounts of up to £20 as recompense for breach of contract. The Employers and Workmen Act 1875 provided for the setting off of claims by both parties to a contract. The instrument of apprenticeship was from then on treated as a contract of employment.[75]

Wages and hire

From 1813, a single justice of the peace was empowered to hear and determine the complaints of 'servants, artificers and labourers' for non-payment

---

75   Master/servant disputes: 2 Geo I, c. 17 (1716); 25 Geo II, c. 8 (1752); 29 Geo II, c. 8 (1756); 33 Geo II, c. 10 (1760); 33 Geo III, c. 55 (1793); 4 Geo IV, c. 34 (1823); 4 Geo IV, c. 39 (1823); 14 & 15 Vict, c. 92 (1851); 30 & 31 Vict, c. 141 (1867); 38 & 39 Vict, c. 90 (1875).

of wages in sums up to £6, and to order payment, with up to £2 in costs, and in default of payment, issue a levy warrant on the 'goods and chattels' of the employer. An act of 1819 extended the summary jurisdiction of magistrates to the complaints of seamen trading from United Kingdom ports, as to amounts of wages up to £20. In 1823 it was provided that apprentices might sue before a single justice for wages up to the amount of £10 (other categories of workmen were confined to pleas for amounts up to £6). An act of 1844 stated that sums recoverable by school teachers came within the Wages Act 1813. In 1849 sums recoverable on task work were included within the terms of earlier wages legislation, in addition to sums agreed for the hire of vehicles for uses other than passenger transport. Wage disputes on amounts up to £10, between employer and labourer, and for tuition, day work, task work and cart hire, was legislated for in 1851. An act of 1871 arranged for wage complaints to be taken to any Irish petty sessions in the country (that is, no longer solely to the defendant's home petty sessions), allowing for the needs of the migratory labourer.[76]

Conditions of employment

Various Acts of 1819, 1820, 1825, and 1829 established a legal code for the protection of the health and safety of young persons employed in cotton and other factories. Hours of work were limited (to no more than 12 hours in one day and nine on a Saturday), the duration of times of rest and refreshment was stated, and the minimum age of employees prescribed. Two justices of the peace were enabled to fine offences in sums of £10 to £20. An act of 1833 extended legislation to all 'mills and factories' and enabled a single magistrate to determine complaints and fine in amounts of £1 to £10. Mines and collieries were dealt with in 1842: the labour of male and female children under the age of ten was prohibited. In 1844 the legal requirements for the employment of children were made more comprehensive to allow for their schooling. Women of any age were classified as 'young persons' for the purposes of this legislation. The act also directed the maintenance of factory cleanliness, the fencing off of dangerous machinery, and renewed the condition that adjudication under the factory acts was by two or more magistrates. Later acts (passed in 1848, 1850, 1853, 1856, 1861, 1862 and 1863) variously addressed the maximum hours of paid daily work permissible, and acceptable times and periods of daily employment, to eliminate loopholes in the legislation being exploited in industrial practice. The factory acts were extended to lace factories, and, in 1863, to bakehouses. The sanitary conditions of factories and workshops, together with the security of working

76 Wages and hire: 54 Geo III, c. 116 (1813–14); 59 Geo III, c. 58 (1819); 4 Geo IV, c. 29 (1823); 7 & 8 Vict, c. 8 (1844); 12 & 13 Vict, c. 15 (1849); 14 & 15 Vict, c. 92 (1851); 34 & 35 Vict, c. 76 (1871).

machinery made up the burden of acts passed in 1864, 1878 and 1891. The age limit for employment in 'dangerous performances' was raised in 1897. Between 1886 and 1895, employment in shops began to come under legislative provision, to the effect that shop-workers should not work more than 74 hours weekly, family members excepted. Irish prosecutions under the factory acts were fewer, for obvious reasons, than in England, but the acts had a certain impact.[77]

Fairs and markets

The marketing of produce had been governed by a series of statutes leading back to the fifteenth and sixteenth centuries. Patents provided for the creation of market juries to settle disputes of sale, adulteration of food, fraud in the purchase or sale of commodities, and wrongful toll charges, and to limit sales to the defined marketplace, invariably to operate in conjunction with summary magisterial authority. The linen trade was especially well served by statutory legislation under the Irish parliament of the later eighteenth century: summary penalties were fixed for abuses in reeling and counting yarn, or deceit in the preparation or presentation of linen cloth of different qualities. Conditions for the regulation of linen and hempen manufactures were restated and amended in 1832, and no less than six times in the 1840s. Legal regulation of the butter trade in Ireland rested on late eighteenth-century enactments deemed too strict or elaborate by the 1870s. Under an act of 1818, fines of up to 40 shillings (imposed by two justices of the peace) were prescribed for adulteration of grain offered for sale. From 1832 the range of ingredients used in the baking of bread was made subject to statute, and bread was required to be sold by weight, not measure: maximum penalties were raised in 1838 from £5 to £50. An act of 1844 firmly put a period to vague magisterial tolerance of a system of moral economy (in force under acts of the 1770s and earlier), by abolishing the offences of forestalling, regrating and engrossing, cancelling prohibitions on the grazing of livestock for sale by licensed butchers, and removing the legal basis for market juries, on the ground that such rules amounted to an unnecessary 'restraint of trade'. Consolidation acts of 1847 and 1850 set out penalties of up to £5 in fines for abuses of all kinds at markets and fairs, detailed in bye-laws or in

77 Conditions of employment: 59 Geo III, c. 66 (1819); 60 Geo III, c. 5 (1820); 6 Geo IV, c. 63 (1825); 10 Geo IV, c. 51 (1829); 10 Geo IV, c. 63 (1829); 3 & 4 Wm IV, c. 103 (1833); 5 & 6 Vict, c. 99 (1842); 7 & 8 Vict, c. 15 (1844); 10 & 11 Vict, c. 29 (1848–9); 13 & 14 Vict, c. 54 (1850–1); 16 & 17 Vict, c. 104 (1853–4); 19 & 20 Vict, c. 133 (1856–7); 24 & 25 Vict, c. 117 (1861); 25 & 26 Vict, c. 8 (1862); 26 & 27 Vict, c. 38 (1863); 26 & 27 Vict, c. 40 (1863); 27 & 28 Vict, c. 48 (1864); 41 & 42 Vict, c. 16 (1878); 49 & 50 Vict, c. 55 (1886); 54 & 55 Vict, c. 75 (1891); 55 & 56 Vict, c. 62 (1892); 56 & 57 Vict, c. 67 (1893); 58 & 59 Vict, c. 29 (1895); 60 & 61 Vict, c. 52 (1897).

regulations determined by magistrates at petty sessions, and provided that magistrates could make awards as to disputes over sales, where the value of the articles concerned did not exceed £5.

From 1835, 'local or customary' measures were abolished, and grand juries required to appoint inspectors of weights and measures, responsible for the prosecution of merchants and traders using non-standard measures, or 'light or unjust measures', on penalties of up to £5 or two months' imprisonment, before two justices of the peace. The Irish constabulary was authorised to inspect weights and measures from 1850. The remaining office of county inspector under the grand jury was abolished in 1862. Statutes in 1878 and 1889 increased penalties for use of unjust weights and measures, on a second conviction, to up to £10, and/or up to two months' imprisonment.[78]

Small debts

Though facilities for summary proceedings for debts outstanding up to £10 due to charitable loan societies, and for the recovery of small loans to the same amount due to the commissioners of Irish fisheries, were made available in 1823 and 1829 respectively, there was no further addition to petty sessions jurisdiction in debt until the abolition of manor courts in 1858, when one or more magistrates could hear and determine cases for the recovery of debts not exceeding £2. This did not impinge greatly upon the jurisdiction of the court of the assistant barrister at quarter sessions, which, together with the manor courts, had monopolised small debt proceedings until that date. When imprisonment for debt was abolished in Ireland in 1872, exception was made in the case of default from sums recoverable summarily.[79] Acts of 1851 and 1860 provided for summary proceedings at petty sessions for the recovery of possession of tenements occupied by weekly and cottier tenants, on grounds of waste of land, non-payment of rent, or overholding.[80]

Nuisance and highway offences

Summary prosecution of the general run of nuisances common to rural and small urban settings was well provided for by statute from the eighteenth century. Such annoyances as letting pigs, horses or cattle loose on public

78 Fairs and markets: E.P. Thompson, 'The moral economy of the English crowd in the eighteenth century', in *Past and Present*, 99 (1983), 41–64; W.H. Crawford and B. Trainor (eds), *Aspects of Irish social history, 1750–1800* (Belfast, 1969), pp. 126–131; 58 Geo III, c. 82 (1818); 7 & 8 Geo IV, c. 61 (1827); 2 & 3 Wm IV, c. 77 (1832); 7 & 8 Vict, c. 47 (1844); 2 & 3 Wm IV, c. 31 (1832); 1 & 2 Vict, c. 28 (1837–8); 7 & 8 Vict, c. 24 (1844); 10 Vict, c. 14 (1847); 13 & 14 Vict, c. 102 (1850). Weights and measures: 5 & 6 Wm IV, c. 63 (1835); 13 & 14 Vict, c. 102 (1850); 25 & 26 Vict, c. 76 (1862); 41 & 42 Vict, c. 49 (1878); 52 & 53 Vict, c. 21 (1889).
79 Small debts: 4 Geo IV, c. 32 (1823); 10 Geo IV, c. 33 (1829); 22 Vict, c. 14 (1858); 35 & 36 Vict, c. 57 (1872).
80 Tenancies: 14 & 15 Vict, c. 92 (1851); 23 & 24 Vict, c. 154 (1860).

roads; driving cattle without regard for common safety; setting off fireworks; abandoning ploughs on the roads, dumping dung or 'scourings' of any sort on any public way; lighting bonfires or beating flax on the roads, and numerous other offences, were liable to summary fines of up to ten shillings on conviction before one justice. Sanitary and public health acts (1848, 1855, 1874, 1878) made room for the prosecution of nuisances arising in the industrial and increasingly urbanised world in which manufacturing concerns frequently neighboured residential areas. Equally, carriage and highway offences were well catered for by statute from the early nineteenth century, but required continual overhaul, to catch up with transport developments. Police prosecutions at summary level were normally directed at misconduct such as, obstructing passages with carts, leaving carts unattended, driving 'furiously' or with culpable negligence, or permitting an excess of passengers, or an excessive quantity of luggage, to be laden on a carriage. Fines reached 20 shillings for most such offences, and could rise to £5 for offences in the field of public transport (reduced to a maximum of 40 shillings in 1851).[81]

Alcohol

Whatever the moral prejudices of contemporary pundits and public officials on the subject, the scale of the problem of drink in pre-Famine Ireland was considerable. An act of 1833 aimed to straighten out laws which had become 'confused, doubtful and complicated'. Public houses were required not to sell beer, spirits or other alcoholic beverages after 11.00 p.m. and before 7.00 a.m. on weekdays, and before 2.00 p.m. on Sundays. Persons present on the premises during these hours were liable to summary fines of five to ten shillings and offending publicans were liable to fines of from £2 to £10. Justices at petty sessions now certified publicans prior to application for new or renewed licences at quarter sessions. An act of 1836 subjected the public licence to greater scrutiny, giving the local chief constable authority to certify the character of publicans in each police district, before licences could be renewed. This act regulated consumption of alcohol at fairs, requiring that booths and tents close between 6.00 p.m. and 9.00 a.m. in summer, and from 3.00 p.m. to 9.00 a.m. in winter. Finally, the act stated that any person found intoxicated 'at any hour of the day or night in any street, square, lane or roadway' was liable to arrest and summary fine in amounts up to five shillings and/or 12 to 48 hours' imprisonment. This act was the cornerstone of drink legislation for the rest of the century. In 1839, summary fines of up to £2 were imposed in statute on persons selling beer in unlicensed premises. Acts

---

81 Nuisance and highway offences: E. Bullingbroke, *The justice of the peace* (Dublin, 1788), pp. 398–416; 13 & 14 Geo III, c. 32 (1773–4); 11 & 12 Vict, c. 123 (1848); 18 & 19 Vict, c. 116 (1855); 37 & 38 Vict, c. 93 (1874); 41 & 42 Vict, c. 52 (1878); 2 & 3 Wm IV, c. 120 (1832); 14 & 15 Vict, c. 92 (1851).

of 1854 and 1855 consolidated legislation on the sale of beer and spirits in shebeens, raising penalties to fines of up to £10 (on previous conviction), and in default of payment, terms of imprisonment of up to six months. The Beerhouses Act 1864 enabled sub-inspectors of police to object to more decisive effect to the issue of certificates to publicans by magistrates at petty sessions. By mid-nineteenth century, drink laws were significantly more severe in Ireland than in England. An act of 1874 raised fines on persons drinking out of hours to 40 shillings, introducing to the summary code the legendary exemption from prosecution of the *bona fide* traveller. In 1878, a statutory requirement was enacted that public houses outside the cities of Dublin, Cork, Limerick, Waterford and Belfast close on Sundays.[82]

The Sabbath

One of the moral counterparts to legislation on the sale and consumption of alcohol was legislation on the purity of the Sabbath. Prosecutions for profanation of the Sabbath derive ultimately from an act of 1696, which prohibited the pursuit of 'ordinary callings' on a Sunday by tradesmen, labourers and others over the age of 14, together with a ban on the sale of goods, crying of wares, carriage of goods, and 'disorderly meetings', on pain of fines up to five shillings or two hours in the stocks. Amended in 1781, this act remained on the statute-book throughout the nineteenth century, though increasingly obsolete in practice.[83]

Vagrancy

Vagrancy frequently awoke something of the same moral indignation in the heart of the scrupulous magistrate (though the problem of vagrancy was associated in Ireland and in England from the 1650s with the repression of disturbances). Whippings, expulsions, the use of stocks or the house of correction were all employed against the beggars and 'incorrigible rogues' of the Tudor statute-book. Irish legislation was more tangled than English law: the seminal English Vagrancy Act of 1723 was not re-enacted in the Irish parliament. Under the Irish statute of 1771, which set up a system of badged mendicancy in Ireland, a justice of the peace was enabled to commit to the stocks men over 15 found begging without licence. The system was not widely adopted, however, and the law was not given much effect. Brief committal of the 'mere vagrant' was provided for in 1810. Under an act of

82 Alcohol: Bullingbroke, *Justice of the peace*, pp. 18–28; 33 Geo II, c. 10 (1759–60); 26 Geo III, c. 24 (1786); 3 & 4 Wm IV, c. 68 (1833); 6 & 7 Wm IV, c. 38 (1836); 2 & 3 Vict, c. 79 (1839); 17 & 18 Vict, c. 89 (1854); 18 & 19 Vict, c. 62 (1854–5); 27 & 28 Vict, c. 35 (1864); 37 & 38 Vict, c. 69 (1874); 41 & 42 Vict, c. 72 (1878).
83 Sabbath: 7 Wm III, c. 17 (1696); 21 Geo III, c. 49 (1781); 38 & 39 Vict, c. 80 (1875); *Judicial Statistics, Ireland*, H.C. 1871 (C. 443) lxiv, 17.

1819, a magistrate was empowered to commit 'all idle poor persons' found begging, for up to 24 hours. Such unfortunates faced terms of up to one month under an act of 1847 (which also provided specific penalties for desertion of wife and children). The Larceny Act 1861 covered those suspected of loitering with intent to steal. The terms of the English act of 1723 were incorporated into Irish legislation under a statute of 1871.[84]

Agricultural trespass, injury and rescue

Acts of trespass and damage to mature or growing crops featured incessantly in the agricultural cycle. In cases of the trespass of animals, the law required that the offending beast first be returned to its owner, who was liable to pay on request the appropriate rate for trespass to the occupier (ranging from six pence for a cow or pig to three shillings for a goat, on pasture or arable uncropped land, and twice these rates for trespass on cropped land). If the parties disagreed, the owner might be summoned to petty sessions, and a parish appraiser ordered to assess the damage inflicted. Only if the ownership of the offending animal was unknown was the complainant entitled to put it in pound. Malicious injuries to trees, shrubs, vegetables, fruit, fences and stiles were summarily punishable, according to acts of 1828 and 1850, in fines of up to £5 or imprisonment for terms up to six months, or even, occasionally, one year. Certain of these offences were made felonies (not triable at petty sessions) if committed twice or more (or the option of summary fine was removed by the act of 1861). An act of 1862 made the owner liable for injuries to sheep committed by a dog. Acts of 1826 and 1827 provided a somewhat cumbersome facility for the summary replevin of animals impounded for rent of less than £10 in amount. On the other hand, in 1843 a bench of two magistrates was enabled for the first time to convict summarily for rescue or attempted rescue of animals in pound, and to impose fines of up to £5 or prison terms of 14 days to three months.[85]

Cruelty to animals

'Martin's Act' of 1820, which first provided for the summary prosecution of acts of cruelty to animals (initially horses) met for a time with uncomprehending derision in many localities, but the number of prosecutions picked

---

84 Vagrancy: see D. Dickson, 'In search of the old Irish poor law', in R. Mitchison and P. Roebuck (eds), *Economy and society in Scotland and Ireland 1500–1939* (Edinburgh, 1988), pp. 149–59; 33 Henry VIII, c. 15 (1542); 10 & 11 Chas I, c. 11 (1635–6); 11 & 12 Geo III, c. 30 (1771–2); 50 Geo III, c. 102 (1810); 1 & 2 Vict, c. 56 (1838); 10 & 11 Vict, c. 84 (1847); 24 & 25 Vict, c. 97 (1861); 34 & 35 Vict, c. 141 (1871); 36 & 37 Vict, c. 38 (1873).

85 For civil procedure in the case of trespass of animals, see 7 Geo IV, c. 42 (1826); 7 & 8 Geo IV, c. 69 (1827); 9 Geo IV, c. 56 (1828); 6 & 7 Vict, c. 30 (1843); 13 & 14 Vict, c. 102 (1850); 14 & 15 Vict, c. 92 (1851); 24 & 25 Vict, c. 97 (1861); 25 & 26 Vict, c. 59 (1862).

up in the 1830s. In 1822 summary penalties of from ten shillings to £5, or terms of imprisonment of up to three months, were imposed on conviction for 'cruel and improper treatment of cattle' (that is, horses, cows, donkeys and so on). An act of 1837 (equivalent to English legislation of 1835) specified summary penalties of five to 40 shillings, or 14 days' imprisonment, for cruelty in driving cattle to fair or market, and rendered dog-fighting, cock-fighting, and bear- or badger-baiting unlawful, and punishable summarily in fines of ten shillings to £5. Regulations on the care of cattle before slaughter were enacted in 1849. Finally, in 1876, vivisection was banned except in the case of supervised medical research.[86]

Game laws

Given the reputed fixation of country gentlemen in Ireland and England with the excitements of hunting and fishing, it is not surprising that summary jurisdiction in the case of offences against the game and fishery acts was well advanced by the later eighteenth century, and was in fact little revised until the 1840s. Under an Act of 1698, qualification to shoot game was restricted to those holding an annual freehold estate of £40 or a personal estate of £1,000. An act 'for the preservation of the game', enacted in 1787, established close seasons for the sale, purchase or hunting of game fowl between December and August, and for hares between November and July, with summary fines, before one justice of the peace, of up to £5 for violation. This penalty was also incurred for destruction of game on Sundays or at night at any time of year. Trespass by day in pursuit of game was summarily punishable in sums up to ten shillings. Summary conviction for trespass by night with gun dogs on preserved land was punishable in sums up to £10, or indictable to quarter sessions, as the justice recommended. Two acts of 1797 in close succession modified the close seasons for pheasant and partridge. In 1817 the offence of poaching by night by an armed party was made punishable before two justices in terms of imprisonment of from three to six months: in 1828 a third offence of this nature was made a misdemeanour liable to transportation at assizes. Legislation in 1842 entirely restructured the antiquated licence system: henceforth the board of excise issued game certificates. Possession and/or use of a gun dog without a certificate was penalised in fines of £20 to £50. Game legislation was applied to rabbits and game on the public roads in 1844. The constabulary were empowered to detain and search persons under suspicion coming from preserved lands, and to prosecute for possession of game to petty sessions in 1862. Later acts controlled the use of poison on lands (1864); reduced the penalty of

86 Cruelty to animals: S. Lynam, *Humanity Dick: a biography of Richard Martin, MP, 1754–1834* (London, 1975), pp. 204–9; 3 Geo IV, c. 71 (1822); 1 Vict, c. 66 (1837); 12 & 13 Vict, c. 92 (1849); 39 & 40 Vict, c. 77 (1877).

imprisonment for trespass on preserved land to one month; protected sea and inland birds and their eggs (1876, 1880, 1894), and amended times of close season for pheasants, partridges and hares (1863, 1865, 1892, 1898).[87]

River fisheries

Fishery legislation, for the protection of stocks of salmon, trout, eels, herring and shellfish, was truly labyrinthine. The accumulated legislation in force in the 1780s, like that of the game laws, was barely touched until the 1840s. The property qualification for ownership of a salmon or trout fishery was the same as that for a game licence. Under an act of 1716, various penalties could be imposed: fines of up to 20 shillings, imprisonment for up to one month, or whipping in the public market place, upon conviction for use of spears, lights or unlawful use of nets. The period from August to February defined the close season for salmon. Times of ocean and estuary fishing, the legitimate form and mesh size of nets, and other matters were governed by a series of acts in the 1730s and 1740s. An act of 1777 provided for the summary prosecution of persons taken fishing for trout and salmon in rivers or lakes without the owner's permission, with fines on conviction of from £5 to £10, or three to six months' imprisonment. Night fishing or the use of poison was punishable by fines of up to £5 or prison terms of up to six months. In 1783 legislation was enacted to govern the administration of weirs and salmon runs, to the effect that the illegal erection of weirs, the use of baskets or hoop-nets on weirs, or otherwise checking all free passage for salmon, was prohibited, on foot of fines of up to £5, or terms of imprisonment of up to three months. Use of fixed nets to catch salmon was punishable in fines up to £10 or by between three and six months' imprisonment. The next major fishery act, in 1842, gave detailed consideration to the use of fixed nets from shore; the mesh size of nets to be employed in the sea; removal of floating nets in the daytime; registration of sea-going fishing vessels; the proper size of drag, stake and bag nets in the salmon fishery; fishing seasons for eels and oysters; sale or possession of salmon or trout out of season, and the correct mesh-size of inland water nets, among other questions. Offences were triable before one or more justices, who could convict in fines of £10 to £20, and prison terms of up to six months, in most cases. An act of 1845 imposed a new set of summary penalties for the use and erection of illegal weirs and

---

87 Game: 10 Wm III, c. 8 (1698–9); 25 Geo III, c. 5 (1752); 3 Geo III, c. 25 (1763); 27 Geo III, c. 35 (1787); 37 Geo III, c. 21 (1797); 37 Geo III, c. 35 (1797); 57 Geo III, c. 90 (1817); 9 Geo IV, c. 69 (1828); 5 & 6 Vict, c. 81 (1842); 7 & 8 Vict, c. 29 (1844); 25 & 26 Vict, c. 114 (1862); 26 & 27 Vict, c. 19 (1863); 27 & 28 Vict, c. 67 (1864); 27 & 28 Vict, c. 115 (1864); 28 & 29 Vict, c. 54 (1865); 36 & 17 Vict, c. 82 (1873); 39 & 40 Vict, c. 29 (1876); 42 & 43 Vict, c. 23 (1879); 43 & 44 Vict, c. 35 (1880); 55 Vict, c. 8 (1892); 57 & 58 Vict, c. 24 (1894); 62 Vict, c. 1 (1899).

reduced the legal mesh size of sea-nets. Under an act of 1848, the country was divided into fisheries districts, and a licence system for inland fishermen instituted, with summary penalties for failure to hold. Later acts (1865, 1881 and 1886) revised these fundamental statutes in certain respects.[88]

Larceny

The trial and punishment of the offences of grand and petty larceny (of articles above or below 12 pence in value, respectively) was largely restricted to quarter sessions and assizes until the later 1840s. A consolidation act of 1828 explained the exceptions to this rule. These consisted of stealing deer from a paddock, or being found in possession of venison; stealing dogs or birds ordinarily confined; stealing growing trees or saplings to the value of one shilling, or any 'live or dead' fence, or being found in possession of wood, and stealing fruit or vegetables from gardens or unenclosed areas. Being found in possession, or receiving such property, was punishable in the same way as conviction for the original offences. Two justices were empowered to try each of these offences, and to convict in fines of up to £30 (thefts of deer being most severely fined) or in prison terms of up to 12 months for second offences. In 1845 the penalty for stealing dogs was made an indictable misdemeanour. Influenced by evidence that a large proportion of reported crimes of larceny were committed by children and youths (particularly during the Great Famine), legislation was introduced in 1847 for the 'more speedy trial and punishment of young offenders'. Under this act, persons under 14 convicted of the offence of simple larceny, became punishable before two justices in fines of up to £3 or terms up to three months, with the option of a private whipping for male offenders (under an act of 1862, whipping, by birch rod, was to be kept to a maximum of 12 strokes). The suspect initially received a choice of whether to submit to summary or jury trial. Justices at petty sessions were empowered in 1849 to issue warrants to search the houses of those credibly suspected of unlawful possession of stolen mutton, and to convict for the offence, in fines up to £5 or prison terms up to three months. An act of 1850 set out to further reduce 'expense and delay' sustained in the prosecution of petty thefts, by bringing those under 16 within the terms of the act of 1847. In 1856 the summary jurisdiction in cases of larceny was enlarged decisively. Two or more justices at petty sessions were enabled to try cases of the theft of articles of up to five shillings in value, on the consent of the suspect, and were empowered to

---

88   Fisheries: 2 Geo I, c. 21 (1716); 12 Geo I, c. 7 (1726); 3 Geo III, c. 24 (1763); 3 Geo III, c. 35 (1763); 17 & 18 Geo III, c.19 (1777–8); 23 & 24 Geo III, c. 40 (1783–4); 5 & 6 Vict, c. 106 (1842); 8 & 9 Vict, c. 108 (1845); 11 & 12 Vict, c. 92 (1848); 26 & 27 Vict, c. 12 (1863); 26 & 27 Vict, c. 114 (1863); 28 & 29 Vict, c. 121 (1865); 44 & 45 Vict, c. 66 (1881); 49 & 50 Vict, c. 39 (1886); 51 & 52 Vict, c. 30 (1888); 54 & 55 Vict, c. 20 (1891).

sentence in certain cases involving theft of articles of higher value, at discretion, provided a plea of guilty was returned. Suspects retained the right to trial at quarter sessions but were entitled to receive the advantages of summary trial if desired. Convictions for thefts under five shillings were punishable in terms up to three months, and sentences for thefts over five shillings could rise to six months. The Larceny Act 1861 consolidated and amended previous legislation: those committing simple larceny after having been twice summarily convicted of any offence under the larceny acts were made liable to conviction of felony and sentence of penal servitude. The scale of sentencing was altered with respect to certain larcenies. An act of 1884 brought the prosecution of young persons under 16 for indictable offences of all kinds (except homicide) within the ambit of summary jurisdiction, with the consent of the accused.[89]

Reformatories and industrial schools

Legislation to promote the development of reformatories and industrial schools, designed to rehabilitate young offenders, was enacted during the 1850s and 1860s, as summary prosecution expanded. An act of 1858 empowered justices to order young offenders (under 16), if sentenced to over 14 days' imprisonment, to reformatory school for terms of one to five years, on the expiry of their sentence. Industrial schools were established in Ireland on the basis of an act of 1868, to shelter and train destitute children, or those in the 'company of reputed thieves': children taken before justices at petty sessions were subject to summary order of removal. Misconduct at either reformatory or industrial school (including, poignantly, efforts to escape) was liable to summary prosecution.[90]

Assault and abuse

The introduction in 1829 of summary trial for the common assault strikingly accelerated popular use of petty sessions. Two justices of the peace were empowered to hear and determine cases of 'common assaults and batteries', not 'accompanied by any attempt to commit felony', nor in which a material question of title arose. The penalty was a fine of up to £2, with costs, or up to two months' imprisonment in default of payment. Administrative perception that the country was beset by chronic petty violence led, in 1839, to a further statute, permitting justices at petty sessions, for a period of five years subsequent to the act, to determine and fine (to a minimum amount of

---

89 Larceny: 9 Geo IV, c. 55 (1828); 8 & 9 Vict, c. 47 (1845); 11 & 12 Vict, c. 109 (1847–8); 12 & 13 Vict, c. 30 (1849); 13 & 14 Vict, c. 37 (1850); 14 & 15 Vict, c. 92 (1851); 18 & 19 Vict, c. 126 (1856); 24 & 25 Vict, c. 97 (1861); 25 & 26 Vict, c. 18 (1862); 47 & 48 Vict, c. 19 (1884).
90 Reformatories, etc: 21 & 22 Vict, c. 111 (1858); 31 Vict, c. 25 (1868); 31 & 32 Vict, c. 59 (1868).

ten shillings), assaults in which stones, loaded sticks, or loaded whips were employed. It was intended temporarily to speed up judicial process in the case of brutal assaults, but was renewed again in 1844 and 1849, lapsing in 1854. Special provision for assaults to deter from selling at market was made in an enactment of 1851. In 1861, persons convicted, before two justices, of aggravated assaults upon females, or boys under the age of 14, were made liable to fines of up to £20 or up to six months' imprisonment. The 'garrotting' act of 1863, induced by so-called 'moral panic' in metropolitan London, was not applied to Ireland.[91]

The neglect and abuse of children (boys under 14 and girls under 16) was made summarily triable at the discretion of two justices in 1889 and made punishable in fines of up to £25 or up to three months' imprisonment. The petty sessions bench was also given the power to remove a child from the custody of convicted adults. This and later acts (1892, 1894) categorised the use of children as beggars, street singers or contortionists (circus acts) as 'abuse' within the act of 1889, and raised the age of a male child in law to 16. Irish law, as distinct from English law, failed to give summary remedies to unmarried mothers seeking support from putative fathers at any time during the nineteenth century: any powers in this regard were reserved to poor law guardians. In effect, the clerk of each union was enabled under poor law legislation (1838), to sue summarily for maintenance expenses on admittance of mother and child to the workhouse.[92]

Public health

It is not proposed to pore over the *minutiae* of the sanitary and public health legislation of the 1840s to the 1890s, though such regulations were invariably enforceable at summary level. The Nuisances Removal and Disease Prevention Act 1848, and successive amending acts (1855, 1860, 1863, 1865, 1866) and the sanitary acts (1866, 1869, 1873) dealt with the consequences of modern urbanisation, defining a wide range of nuisances liable to summary order and prosecution by citizen or officer of a sanitary authority. The risk of infectious disease was one of the guiding priorities of this formidable mass of legislation, which focused on pollution of wells and pumps; waste deposits in urban spaces; fumigation of houses; drainage and sewerage; the debris of offensive trades such as blood, bone or soap boiling; cess pits; animals in dwellings; chemical pollution, or, in short, urban squalor. The majority of offences attracted fines on conviction of up to £5 or up to one month

---

91 Assault etc: 10 Geo IV, c. 34 (1829); 2 & 3 Vict, c. 77 (1839); 7 & 8 Vict, c. 23 (1844); 12 & 13 Vict, c. 38 (1849); 14 & 15 Vict, c. 92 (1851); 24 & 25 Vict, c. 100 (1861); 26 & 27 Vict, c. 44 (1863).
92 Cruelty to children: 52 & 53 Vict, c. 44 (1889); 55 Vict, c. 4 (1892); 57 & 58 Vict, c. 27 (1894); 57 & 58 Vict, c. 41 (1894); 1 & 2 Vict, c. 56 (1838).

imprisonment. Occasionally, in cases such as the corruption of water by gas, fines could reach £200.[93]

As a particular illustration of the stages in law of increased state intervention into social life, it is worth looking at legislation with regard to vaccination. From 1840, poor law guardians were required to make vaccination available in each union, and inoculation of 'variolous matters' by unauthorised persons was made summarily punishable by imprisonment for up to one month (raised to six months in 1863). Under acts of 1841, 1851 and 1858, poor law medical officers were required to vaccinate on request, free of charge, at set times and places. An act of 1863 finally made compulsory the vaccination of children, under pain of fines of up to ten shillings (raised to 20 shillings in 1879).[94]

A serious attempt has been made in this section to deal exhaustively (though with great concision) with most aspects of nineteenth-century summary legislation. (It is admitted that coverage of game and fishery laws passed in the eighteenth century or earlier and operational during the early nineteenth century, has been tentative.) Constraints of space regrettably also mean that summary jurisdiction under the peace preservation acts, combination acts, and lesser acts such as the Lodging House Act, Railway Act, Postal Service Act, and bye-laws (mainly, one suspects, regulating local markets) cannot be examined here. At the cost of 'a great stretching of the constitution',[95] in the view of certain Victorian legal commentators, the scope of summary law inexorably broadened during the century. In parallel, the older mechanisms for the administration of customary or statutory summary law, such as the manor court and the borough courts of conscience, were phased out. During the century, the justice of the peace was stripped of a great deal of local administrative authority while taking on increased judicial responsibility.

STATISTICAL ANALYSIS

The absence of a uniform and continuous series of statistical data on Irish petty sessions for the nineteenth century represents a serious stumbling-block to the evaluation of long-term trends in court usage under summary

93 Disease: 11 & 12 Vict, c. 123 (1848); 12 & 13 Vict, c. 111 (1849); 18 & 19 Vict, c. 115 (1855); 18 & 19 Vict, c. 116 (1855); 23 & 24 Vict, c. 77 (1860); 26 & 27 Vict, c. 124 (1863); 28 & 29 Vict, c. 75 (1865); 29 & 30 Vict, c. 41 (1866); 29 & 30 Vict, c. 90 (1866); 32 & 33 Vict, c. 108 (1869); 36 & 37 Vict, c. 78 (1873).

94 Vaccination: 3 & 4 Vict, c. 29 (1840); 4 & 5 Vict, c. 32 (1841); 16 & 17 Vict, c. 100 (1851); 21 & 22 Vict, c. 64 (1858); 26 & 27 Vict, c. 52 (1863); 31 & 32 Vict, c. 87 (1868); 33 & 34 Vict, c. 70 (1879). See also R.D. Cassell, *Medical charities, medical politics: the Irish dispensary system and the poor law, 1836–1872* (Woodbridge, Suffolk, 1997).

95 H. Humphries, *The justice of the peace for Ireland* (Dublin, 1881), p. 191.

jurisdiction, civil and criminal. Four main statistical series have been compiled from official data for this paper. From the later 1830s, an unpublished series (here called 'series A'; recovered sporadically for the years 1839 to 1847) described 'all offences committed or alleged to have been committed' each month and in each county and city, except for the city of Dublin, by offence, broken down into numbers of cases dismissed, sent to trial, or where conviction was obtained.[96] A printed series (series B) in the Irish Crimes Records gives global figures for cases at petty sessions in Ireland in the period from 1839 to 1850,[97] but unfortunately numbers reported cannot be made to correspond precisely with figures in the unpublished series (which was more comprehensive). Though published statistical returns of persons indicted to trial at quarter sessions and assizes record 'cases before magistrates and petty sessions' between 1838 and 1862 (series C),[98] these somewhat mysterious figures amount to no more than a small fraction of total cases (possibly indictable cases dealt with summarily). A continuous return of 'persons proceeded against for offences determined summarily' becomes available from 1863 (series D).[99] No adequate series bridges the gap between 1850 and 1862. Practically speaking, reports of the number of cases/offences administered at petty sessions (in series A and B) can be equated with reports of persons proceeded against at petty sessions (series D): different tables in the *Judicial Statistics* (series D) treat figures described in both ways interchangeably. The number of cases sent for trial in series A and B must be deleted from the total reported, for accurate comparison. Discrepancies between reported totals in series A and B (of the order of one or two per cent: see Table 3) are small but not yet explicable: it is unlikely that the omission of returns for the city of Dublin in series B can account for the difference – cases taken in the city regularly amounted to 20 per cent of the Irish total later in the century. More disturbing are differences in the reported range of offences/persons prosecuted in series B and series D. The unpublished figures (and by implication, series B also) give no account of cases of breach of the peace, cruelty to animals, cases under the factory, mutiny, poor law, police, or carriage acts, or of pawnbroking offences, revenue offences, master and servant disputes, prostitution and vagrancy offences – which together added up to 11 or 12 per cent of yearly totals in the 1860s.

---

96 NAI, VII–1–67/106, Home Office papers 100, vols. 248–56; monthly summaries of offences, 1840–47.

97 NAI, CSO Registered papers, Irish crime records, vol. 1, p. 8: Return of the total number of minor offences (of which no special reports were made) brought before the magistrates at petty sessions, in each month from January 1838 to December 1850.

98 See *Reports of the inspectors general on the state of prisons in Ireland*, H.C. 1839 (91) xx, 403; H.C. 1840 (240) xxvi, 165; H.C. 1841 (299) xi, 759; H.C. 1842 (377) xxii, 117; H.C. !843 (462) xvii, 83; H.C. 1844 (535) xxviii, 329; H.C. 1845 (620) xxv, 231, for reports of such cases in those years.

Broadly then, analysis of the figures reproduced in Table 3 must allow for understatement by perhaps as much as 30 per cent in figures for the period from 1839 to 1850.

Documentary evidence suggests that the flow of cases dealt with summarily rose steadily after the establishment of petty sessions in 1823. The introduction of summary jurisdiction for common assaults, in particular, accelerated from 1829 the growth of popular use of petty sessions, and usage may have doubled between 1823 and the late 1830s.[100] Having due regard for difficulties in correlating the statistical series of the 1840s with that of the 1860s and later, it would appear from Table 3, that the number of cases at petty sessions doubled proportionately, from an average of 2,220 per 100,000 in the period 1841–45, to 4,242 per 100,000 on average in the period 1863 to 1870. This high level of usage was maintained or exceeded in the decades from 1870 to 1910.[101]

Prosecutions fell to a minimum of 119,000 (or 1,627 per 100,000) during the most critical year of the Famine. It is not clear whether this indicated a diminution in the number of private prosecutions or of police prosecutions for road nuisances and the like. Unsurprisingly, there are signs that magisterial attendance at sessions was exceptionally poor during the Famine.[102] The number of cases sent up from petty sessions during the Famine increased from a pre-Famine average of about five per cent of cases taken, to nearly 12 per cent of cases taken, in 1847 and 1848, a reflection of magisterial desperation in the face of the overwhelming number of larcenies being carried out. A surge in prosecutions undertaken occurred in 1867 (a rise of 9.6 per cent). This registered a sudden rise in 'unclassified' offences dealt with at petty sessions that year, and coincided with, but was probably unrelated to, the Fenian rising in February. Movements in the petty sessions figures during the 1870s principally reflected fluctuations in numbers prosecuted for intoxication and offences against the highway acts.

99 *Judicial Statistics, Ireland*, H.C. 1864 (C.3418) lvii, 653; H.C. 1865 (C. 3563) lii, 657; H.C. 1866 (C. 3705) lxviii, 697; H.C. 1867 (C. 3930) lxvi, 735 : H.C. 1870 (C. 227) lxiii, 753; H.C. 1871 (C. 443) lxiv, 231; H.C. 1872 (C. 674) lxv, 235; H.C. 1873 (C. 851) lxx, 247; H.C. 1874 (C. 1034) lxxi, 251; H.C. 1875 (C. 1295) lxxxi, 259; H.C. 1876 (C. 1563) lxxix, 273; H.C. 1877 (C. 1822) lxxxvi, 261; H.C. 1878 (C. 2152) lxxix, 205; H.C. 1878–9 (C.2389) lxxvi, 279; H.C. 1880 (C. 2698) lxxvii, 251; H.C. 1881 (C. 3028) xcv, 243; H.C. 1882 (C. 3355) lxxv, 243; H.C. 1883 (C.3808) lxxvii, 243; H.C. 1884 (C. 4181) lxxxvi, 243; H.C. 1884–5 (C. 4554) lxxxvi, 243; H.C. 1886 (C. 4796) lxxii, 233; H.C. 1887 (C. 5177) xc, 241; H.C. 1888 (C. 5495) cviii, 241; H.C. 1889 (C. 5795) lxxxv, 241; H.C. 1890 (C. 6122) lxxx, 253. The series concluded in 1922, having undergone various changes in format.
100 McCabe, 'Law, conflict and social order', ch.6.
101 Annual figures have been compiled, but, for reasons of space, are not included here.
102 McCabe, 'Law, conflict and social order', ch.6.

Table 3: Cases brought before magistrates/persons proceeded against summarily,
Ireland, 1839–1895 (totals/rates per 100,000)

Cases at petty sessions, Ireland, 1845: series A		
	Totals	*Rates*
Common assault	34,067	420
Intoxication	31,159	384
Road nuisances	53,315	658
Sabbath breach	952	12
Weights and measures	734	9
Trespass and injury to property	29,266	361
Total	173,344	2,139

Series B	*Cases before magistrates*	*Less cases sent up*	*Rates per 100,000*
1839	225,576		
1840	203,342		
1841	194,068	183,377	2,370
1842	191,817	181,172	2,330
1843	166,497	156,550	2,003
1844	179,137	170,023	2,164
1845	184,564	176,152	2,232
1846	159,934	151,130	1,990
1847	134,242	118,746	1,627
1848	152,697	134,902	1,928
1849	198,630	154,897	2,313
1850	211,883	164,805	2,576

Series D	*Number persons*	*Rates per 100,000*	*Civil cases*	*Series D*	*Number persons*	*Rates per 100,000*	*Civil cases*
1863	237,522	4,237		1880	239,826	4,531	63,542
1864	232,363	4,145		1881	206,193	4,175	59,056
1865	233,879	4,173		1882	217,551	4,405	62,903
1866	236,835	4,225		1883	225,518	4,566	64,256
1867	259,691	4,633		1884	233,188	4,721	66,199
1868	238,302	4,251		1885	224,352	4,542	63,195
1869	239,390	4,271		1886	215,887	4,371	58,239
1870	234,005	4,175		1887	219,663	4,447	61,169
1871	220,179	4,160		1888	230,099	4,659	
1872	211,470	3,995		1889	233,060	4,719	46,704
1873	223,843	4,229	57,740	1890	235,680	4,772	51,569
1874	228,501	4,317	50,141	1891	230,057	4,890	
1875	243,145	4,594	53,900	1892	223,711	4,755	
1876	256,312	4,842	58,914	1893	215,118	4,572	
1877	266,298	5,031	57,630	1894	216,597	4,604	
1878	268,559	5,074	59,293	1895	183,827	3,908	
1879	255,670	4,830	64,963				

Table 4: Offences at petty sessions, Ireland, 1863–90, England and Wales, 1863–70 (Period averages: rates per 100,000)

	Ireland				England & Wales
	1863–70	1871–78	1879–82	1883–90	1863–70
Assaults on women and children	7.5	8	9	19	13
Assaults on peace officers	59	69	73	64	60
Common assaults	562	607	610	557	355
Breaches of the peace	61	54	42	47.5	60
Cruelty to animals	17	23.5	28	37	21
Drunkenness	1,448	1,892	1,706	1,796	511
Fisheries acts	21.5	12.5	10	9	2.5
Game acts	13	17	17	17.5	52
Beershop acts	38.5	49	108	185	35
Victualler acts	3.5	4			19
Lord's Day act	12	5	2.5	1	3
Malicious damage and trespass	166	138	114	124	97
Mutiny acts	11	18.5	14	15	15
Public health acts	6	7	24	78	3.5
Nuisances	70	96	64	12	10
Lodging house acts	4	0.6	0.4	0.4	4
Sanitary offences	12.5	11	11	5	10
Pawnbroking offences	4	2.5	2	3	5.5
Unlawful possession of goods	21.5	20	21	21	20
Constable: neglect of duty	0.2	0.3	0.3	0.2	0.4
Other police acts	29.5	36	35.5	13	74
Desertion of family	6.5	6	4	5	21
Workhouse disorder	7	7	6	5.5	15
Excise acts	13	16	16	15	8
Salmon fishery acts	10.5	8	7.5	7.5	3
Master/servant offences	47.5	38.5		10	44
Larceny under 16	8.5	8	8	7	38.5
Larceny under 5s.	34	27	32	30	74
Larceny over 5s.		17	21	21	38
Attempted larceny	41.5	12	12.5	10	38
Other larceny	16	14	15	13	26
Prostitutes	70	40	27	37	34
Begging	32	23.5	32	36	60
No visible means	3	8.5	10	13	22
General vagrancy acts	4.5	9.5	18	21	46.5
Carriage acts	106	60	71	63	34
Highway acts	744	576	434	331	62
Railway act	4.5	7	6	5	
Weights and measures	71	62	51	42	26.5
Bye-laws	50	103.5	278	365	
Total	4,242	4,530	4,441	4,599	2,241
Total (n)	237,748	239,788	229,810	227,181	479,244

Figures for intoxication were liable to rise and fall by 10,000–12,000 annually. The decline in petty sessions figures of about ten per cent, during the period of the land war from 1879 to 1882, was mainly in consequence of a severe fall in numbers prosecuted for intoxication and road nuisances (the bulk of highway offences), coupled with a slight falling off in the number of assault prosecutions. Though the absolute numbers of persons prosecuted were continually reduced during the 1880s and 1890s, rates of prosecution vary little between the 1860s and the 1900s.

The rate of civil prosecutions exhibited a tendency gradually to rise between the 1860s and the 1890s (see Table 4). Earlier series give no inkling as to the number of civil cases previously taken. A considerable increase took place in the number of summonses issued, decrees made and warrants taken out during the land war, directly contrary to the trend in summary criminal prosecutions at the time. It is not, unfortunately, possible to isolate fluctuations in particular categories of complaint from the information in the printed returns, which is a hindrance to analysis of the behaviour of debtors and creditors at the time. Summonses issued reached a maximum between 1882 and 1885, while the number of levy warrants taken out peaked in 1879.[103]

The causes of fluctuations in the number of criminal proceedings taken at petty sessions resolve primarily into variations in the number of police prosecutions taken for minor offences such as drunkenness, road nuisances and carriage offences. There is a strong correlation between police density and rates of prosecution to petty sessions. The number of policemen per head of population increased from one constable to 982 persons in 1840 to one constable to 420 persons in 1864 – it is revealing that the scale of increase almost exactly matches the rise in the rate of summary prosecution over the same period.[104] Police densities and prosecution rates were greatest in urban areas. Parallels are less definite in comparisons county by county, though counties in Ulster tended to be policed less thoroughly and to show relatively low levels of petty sessions prosecution (apart from Londonderry).[105] There

---

103 The figures have been extracted from the *Judicial Statistics*. The figure for total summonses issued includes summonses in respect of tenancy proceedings, reported separately in the returns. Figures tabulated are yearly averages for the different periods.

	Summonses issued	Complaints heard	Decrees made	Warrants issued	Total summonses
1873–8	96,234	56,269	40,696	8,990	
1879–82	110,756	62,616	48,734	14,001	135,045
1883–90	105,230	58,761	43,043	11,613	132,713

104 Hoppen, *Elections, politics and society*, p. 410; *Judicial Statistics, Ireland*, H.C. 1865 (C. 3563) lii, viii–ix.

105 In the later 1880s, Westmeath was the most intensively policed Irish county, with 41 constables per 100,000 of population. By contrast, Down, Antrim, Armagh, and Derry made do with 10–13 constables per 100,000: *Judicial Statistics, Ireland*, 1863–90, see note 99 above.

Desmond McCabe

Table 5: Persons proceeded against summarily, per city and county, Ireland, 1863–90 (Period averages: rates per 100,000)

	1863–79	1871–78	1879–82	1883–90
Carlow	3,184	3,619	3,264	3,283
Co. Dublin	1,865	1,632	1,520	1,597
Dublin city	18,593	16,939	18,400	22,138
Kildare	5,477	6,134	5,707	4,991
Kilkenny	3,628	4,106	4,042	3,673
King's County	3,865	4,042	4,354	3,831
Longford	3,937	4,291	3,952	3,565
Louth	4,403	4,044	3,998	3,720
Drogheda	5,064	6,271	7,262	6,308
Meath	3,883	4,249	3,995	3,385
Queen's County	4,603	4,497	3,782	4,002
Westmeath	4,146	5,132	4,470	4,466
Wexford	2,937	3,210	2,528	2,680
Wicklow	4,641	4,625	4,021	3,862
Clare	3,811	4,612	3,690	4,004
Cork	3,971	3,872	3,668	3,556
Cork city	10,879	10,551	10,273	9,413
Kerry	3,677	4,465	4,974	4,957
Limerick	4,765	4,678	3,471	3,761
Limerick city	6,247	8,907	5,745	8,415
Tipperary	5,206	4,941	4,059	3,948
Waterford	3,026	3,009	2,961	3,160
Waterford city	9,697	10,035	8,205	10,995
Antrim	2,279	2,658	2,184	1,943
Belfast	8,971	7,177	8,236	6,629
Armagh	2,783	2,866	3,119	3,530
Cavan	2,719	3,780	2,900	3,504
Donegal	2,300	2,463	2,105	2,078
Down	2,474	2,572	2,778	2,588
Fermanagh	2,300	2,837	2,848	2,975
Londonderry	2,442	3,829	3,837	3,842
Monaghan	2,711	3,114	3,537	3,295
Tyrone	2,556	3,133	3,210	3,280
Galway	3,064	3,774	3,601	3,030
Leitrim	3,168	3,479	3,143	3,189
Mayo	2,367	2,906	2,263	2,501
Roscommon	3,013	3,494	3,214	3,213
Sligo	2,862	3,284	3,877	3,622
Total	4,242	4,530	4,441	4,599
Total (n)	237,748	239,788	229,810	227,181

was no clear long-term relationship between changes in the incidence of serious (indictable) crime and annual changes in the national total of summary prosecutions, though a marginal fall in petty sessions usage accompanied the agrarian disorder of 1879–80.[106] The ramifying growth of civil legislation, invariably with provision for summary penalties, in areas such as public health, lodging houses, railways, postal service and others, produced no more than one to two per cent of offences taken annually to petty sessions. Individual acts could cause significant minor increases or decreases in summary prosecutions. The number of charges against publicans rose markedly after the Beerhouse Act 1864. The passing of the Employers and Workmen Act 1875 prompted a proportionately dramatic collapse in the number of prosecutions of this nature.[107] However the recurrent factor in changes of any scale was the intensity of police enforcement. For instance, the transfer of responsibility for the inspection of weights and measures, in 1850, from the grand jury inspectorate to the constabulary, boosted prosecutions from rates of nine to 71 per 100,000, between the 1840s and the 1860s.[108] Shifts in the intensity of enforcement of particular laws, which were visible, within and between counties, as well as from year to year, or decade to decade, manifest as yet unrecognised processes of change in police administration and in the climate of establishment/educated opinion (intoxication prosecutions may be a sensitive guide to such change). Differences in the make-up of petty sessions prosecutions between the 1840s and the 1860s underline the relationship between patterns of enforcement and the nature of developments in usage. Making a distinction between voluntary or private prosecutions and prosecutions by agents of official authority, such as the constabulary, it is clear that the proportion of private prosecutions fell from 48 per cent of cases in the 1840s to 21 per cent in the 1860s, and to 17 per cent in the 1880s. Though rates of private prosecution did decline (from 1,020 per 100,000 in the 1840s to about 800 per 100,000 in the 1880s) the impetus for change lay in the extraordinary rise in the rate of official prosecutions, from 1,099 per 100,000 in the 1840s to 3,808 per 100,000 in the 1880s. During the 1820s it is likely that private prosecutions took up the bulk of sessions business. By the 1890s business was monopolised by constabulary prosecutions. Popular usage of the petty sessions actually receded after the Famine.[109]

106 *Judicial Statistics, Ireland*, 1863–90. Movements in the rates of reported and indicted crime are really too slight for fruitful comparison with annual changes in the rate of summary proceedings.

107 It is not yet clear why this took place.   108 See Tables 4 and 5.

109 Offences classified for this purpose as 'official prosecutions' include assaults on peace officers, breaches of the peace, drunkenness, nuisances, offences under legislation relating to lodging houses, beershops, victuallers, Lord's Day, mutiny, public health, sanitary offences, unlawful possession of goods, neglect of duty by constable, other offences under police acts, excise acts, vagrancy acts, carriage acts, highway acts, railway acts, bye-laws, workhouse

Desmond McCabe

The *Judicial Statistics* disclose marked differences between rural and urban patterns of usage. Though most petty sessions business transacted was rural, and rural areas therefore dictated national patterns, rates of prosecution in the cities were in fact far higher than in the country (see Table 5): rural rates were on average 25 per cent of urban rates through the 1860s to the 1880s. Interestingly, the proportion of private prosecutions was twice as high in the country than in the city, being 18 to 19 per cent compared to nine per cent in the 1860s. For all that, there tended to be close resemblances between fluctuations in urban and rural business, with the significant exception of the land war, in which the modest rural decline of 1880–81 occurred as a curious delayed reaction in the cities, where a slightly steeper decline occurred in 1882–83. Looking at particular categories of offence, it is evident that urban rates of prosecution for common assault exceeded rural rates by about two to one, rates of prosecution for intoxication by about four to one, and rates for larceny by about three to one.[110] There are plausible correspondences between those counties with the highest rates of petty sessions business, and those with the greatest population and police densities, and with potent traditions of agrarian disturbance.

Table 6 illustrates the results of trial and the structure of sentences handed out by magistrates at petty sessions in Ireland. The total national rate of conviction varied from 73 to 82 per cent between 1863 and 1890.[111] But there were considerable variations within and between provinces. While magistrates in Leinster showed a propensity to convict in 85 to 90 per cent of cases, rates of conviction in Ulster were typically between 70 and 78 per cent. About 78 to 81 per cent of those convicted were fined.[112] From the 1860s to the 1880s the proportion imprisoned on conviction fell steadily from ten to 7.6 per cent, while magistrates became a little more inclined to make use of other modes of sentence, such as compensation orders. The majority of prison terms meted out ranged from one to four weeks: magistrates did not use the rigours of summary law to the full. Numbers sent to reformatory and industrial school (essentially children convicted of larceny or vagrancy) climbed from the 1860s.[113] For most of the period, the preference for

disorder, desertion of families, weights and measures offences, prostitution, begging, having no visible means. Prosecutions under the headings of, assaults on women and children, common assaults, breaches of the fishery or game laws, malicious damage and trespass, master/servant offences, larceny of all sorts, are considered to have been taken privately.

110 *Judicial Statistics, Ireland*, 1863–90. See D. McCabe, 'Crime and the urban economy in nineteenth century Ireland and England: Cork, Manchester and the Black Country', in D. McCabe (ed.), *European urbanisation: social structure and problems between the eighteenth and twentieth centuries* (Leicester, 1995), pp. 121–59.

111 Annual figures have been compiled but are not tabulated here.

112 *Judicial Statistics, Ireland*, 1863–90, see note 99 above.

113 See *Judicial Statistics, Ireland*, pp. 12, 40, H.C. 1866 (C.3705) lxviii, 697, 708, 736; and *Judicial Statistics, Ireland*, pp. 43–8, H.C. 1871 (C.443) lxiv, 231, 273–8.

imprisonment was greatest among Ulster magistrates (who also seem to have had a certain attachment to the unusual punishment of whipping), while it was least common among Connacht magistrates: the different proportions were about 20 per cent in Ulster and six per cent in Connacht. Convictions were proportionately highest in the case of official prosecutions, such as drunkenness or highway offences (at 90 to 95 per cent), and lowest in cases of common assault, master/servant disputes, and larceny from the person (at 50 to 55 per cent).[114]

Table 6: Results of trial, petty sessions, Ireland 1863–90 (percentages)

Sentences	1863–70	1871–78	1879–82	1883–90
Over 6 months	0.01	0.01	0.03	0.02
3–6 months	0.12	0.2	0.26	0.22
2–3 months	0.39	0.38	0.42	0.47
1–2 months	0.78	0.92	0.82	0.91
1 month–14 days	1.82	2.77	3.02	3.11
Under 14 days	6.88	5.03	3.59	2.89
Reformatory	0.08	0.12	0.12	0.1
Industrial school		0.32	0.51	0.59
Fined	78.12	80	80.6	77.66
Whipping	0.003	0.001	0.006	0.005
Sureties	2.58	1.94	1.89	1.87
Army/navy	0.17	0.28	0.21	0.26
Other	9.21	8.03	8.53	11.9
	100	100	100	100
Convicted	194,673	174,657	187,733	173,125
Dismissed	43,075	65,131	42,077	54,056
Total	237,748	239,788	229,810	227,181

CONCLUSION

This has been a highly condensed survey of the mechanics of the system of petty sessions in nineteenth-century Ireland. Priority was necessarily given to the problem of figuring out how things worked under summary jurisdiction,

114 *Judicial Statistics, Ireland*, 1863–90.

before much time could be spent on the impact of the petty sessions on contemporary social relations, as borne out in statistical data. Certain general points do emerge however, now that a little ground has been cleared. Despite the strictures frequently levelled at Irish magistrates for their slipshod ways up to this date, county benches lost little time in setting up an extensive petty sessions network in 1823–24. Popular use of the sessions also took firm root without delay. A first look at summary legislation as it unfolded over the century disconcerts by revealing how little the volume of new laws was reflected in petty sessions prosecution. Though rates of summary prosecution soared after the Famine, this was essentially due to an increased density of policing, and, as a consequence, to higher levels of enforcement with regard to many mundane matters which had been offences in law in one form or another for a long time. Rates of police density per capita in England and Wales in the 1860s were half those in Ireland at the time, accounting largely for 'the greater tendency [in Ireland] to enforce statutes which are more matter for discipline than crime':[115] rates of petty sessions usage as a whole were twice as high in Ireland as in England and Wales. The Irish petty sessions was, however, less of a forum for the adjudication of private disputes in 1900 than in the 1830s, in spite of the increase in the number of magistrates, improved magisterial attendance, and the more democratic composition of the bench. The nature of court usage was different in city and country, both in terms of rate and type of prosecution. The fascinations of reported petty sessions cases have been resisted in this paper in favour of an attempt to elucidate technical developments in summary jurisdiction and procedure during the nineteenth century. But the delicate statistical blooms of the last few pages offer some suggestive evidence as to changes in the nature of social relationships between governors and governed during the century, and frame questions for future analysis in depth.

---

115 *Judicial Statistics, Ireland*, p. 17, H.C. 1871 (C. 443) lxiv, 231, 273–8.

A security against illegality? The reservation of crown cases in nineteenth-century Ireland

DESMOND GREER*

There are two principles of law upon this subject which may sometimes conflict, or appear to do so. The one principle is, that there should be every opportunity given for deliberation, and for correction, before a sentence is carried into execution; that is one principle. The other principle is, that it is expedient for public purposes, especially in criminal cases, that execution should not be delayed, or the sentence, whatever it may be, unnecessarily deferred.[1]

INTRODUCTION

THE ADMINISTRATION OF CRIMINAL justice in Ireland during the nineteenth century was fraught with controversy, but amongst almost constant polemic about the quality of the 'justice' administered by the police, the prosecution, the judges and juries – and all the more surprising because of this – comparatively little is heard about procedures (or the lack of them) for dealing with alleged miscarriages of justice. This comparative silence may be contrasted with the position in England, where the struggle to create a 'proper' court of criminal appeal continued unabated for almost seventy years. When the movement for reform finally met with success in 1907, the legislation did not apply to Ireland and it was not until 1924 and 1930 respectively that persons convicted of offences following trial on indictment in the Irish Free State or in Northern Ireland became entitled to appeal against that conviction and/or sentence. The purpose of this paper is to encourage further discussion as to why the limited procedures for avoiding miscarriages of justice failed to become the focus for the level of debate which attended most aspects of the criminal justice process in nineteenth-century Ireland.

* [Editor's note: this paper was submitted to the Society in the 1990s for inclusion in a volume, planned but not completed, on the theme of criminal justice in Ireland in the nineteenth century.]
1 *William Smith O'Brien v. R.* (1849) 3 Cox CC 360, at pp. 416–17, *per* Crampton J.

Such an inquiry should ideally be conducted in the context of a general study of criminal trials on indictment such as those which have recently appeared in England.[2] In the absence of such a study, we may note simply that in the first part of the nineteenth century, the outcome of criminal proceedings on indictment in Ireland was somewhat unpredictable. In general terms, only three-quarters of those charged with serious offences each year were actually tried, and of those who were tried a further quarter (or more) were acquitted.[3] In other words, no more than one-half of those charged with serious offences were convicted. We know also that most of those who were convicted received short prison sentences;[4] approximately one in seven was transported (usually for seven years), while capital punishment was imposed in only a small percentage of cases, particularly after 1841.[5]

This broad picture conceals many important issues as yet unexplored in detail. In the present context, for example, we know that there were, at least in theory, a number of ways in which a defendant could challenge the process of trial or a verdict of guilty. At the trial itself, he or she could raise a demurrer, plea of abatement or enter a motion in arrest of judgment;[6] if successful, the defendant was not formally acquitted, but the prosecutor might be deterred from bringing fresh proceedings. These procedures were highly formal, and usually had little or nothing to do with the merits of the case. It seems unlikely that they were successfully invoked in many cases, particularly after the Criminal Procedure Act 1851 gave the criminal courts extensive powers to 'cure' verdicts which might previously have been set aside on purely technical grounds. On conviction, a defendant could in certain cases bring a writ of error or a motion for a new trial, but the conditions attaching to these procedures probably meant that they were available to few defendants. Finally, a convicted defendant could seek a full

2 See especially J.H. Langbein, *The origins of the adversary criminal trial* (Oxford, 2003), ch. 5; D.J. Bentley, *English criminal justice in the nineteenth century* (London, 1998), and D.J.A. Cairns, *Advocacy and the making of the adversarial criminal trial, 1800–1865* (Oxford, 1998).

3 See e.g. the 'comparative statement' of criminal proceedings for 1823–1829 in *Report of the select committee on the state of the poor in Ireland*, H.C. 1830 (667) vii, 137, and *Table showing the number of criminal offenders committed for trial or bailed for appearance at the assizes and sessions in each county in the year 1850*, H.C. 1851 [1386] xlvi, 97.

4 Sentences of imprisonment were imposed in roughly 80 per cent of convictions in the 1820s, and in roughly 70 per cent of cases during the 1840s; in both periods the sentence was usually for six months or less.

5 See S.J. Connolly, 'Unnatural death in four nations: contrasts and comparisons' in S.J. Connolly (ed.), *Kingdoms united? Great Britain and Ireland since 1500: integration and diversity* (Dublin, 1999), p. 200, suggesting that persons convicted in Ireland were *less* likely to the sentenced to death, but that those sentenced to death were *more* likely to be executed than in England and Wales. From the 1840s, sentence of death was normally imposed only for murder or related offences and represented less than 0.2% of all convictions.

6 See especially T.A. Purcell, *A summary of the general principles of pleading and evidence in criminal cases in Ireland* (Dublin, 1849).

pardon or at least commutation of the sentence under the prerogative of mercy which in Ireland was vested in the lord lieutenant. Without further analysis of the petitions to the lord lieutenant it is impossible to assess the efficacy or otherwise of pardons as providing a method of 'appeal' against conviction or sentence. Some cases, such as *R. v. Hargedom*,[7] suggest that there was an element of political expediency involved in the decision whether to extend 'mercy'; others, such as *R. v. Rochfort*,[8] suggest that a certain amount of 'influence' or social status could be helpful. But there do appear to be some cases at least where the procedure operated genuinely to prevent a miscarriage of justice.[9] Further research, however, is required before it can be accepted – as was to be contended for much of the nineteenth century – that *all* those who had been wrongly convicted were pardoned, thus making judicial reform unnecessary.

CASES RESERVED FOR THE CONSIDERATION OF THE TWELVE JUDGES

When a point of law arose at a criminal trial, whether by way of one of the procedures described above or otherwise, the trial judge could deal with it in various ways. First, he could simply decide the issue then and there.[10] If he was doubtful, he could either take time to think about the point, or discuss it with any judge who was close by – on assizes, for example, a trial judge frequently went to consult the other assize judge, and then announced his decision on the point.[11] Occasionally, an assize judge might even defer legal

---

7 See W. Ridgeway, *A report of the proceedings under a special commission ... for the counties of Sligo, Mayo, etc. 1806* (Dublin, 1807), p. 193 (decision whether to accept jury recommendation to mercy dependent on 'the state of the country').

8 See Anon, *A report of the trial of Richard Rochfort, esq, upon an indictment for the murder of Richard Castles in a duel* (Dublin, 1805).

9 See e.g. *Papers relating to the reprieve of Walter Hall, after having been convicted of murder at Dublin*, H.C. 1812 (309) v, 1015 and *R. v. McIlhone* (1819) 1 Cr & Dix 156 (below, note 11).

10 See e.g. *R. v. Garvey* (1844) 1 Cox CC 111 (Brady LCB held the indictment defective and directed the acquittal of the prisoner) and *R. v. Bodell* (1838) 1 Cr & Dix 1 (the defendant challenged the grand jury panel and the trial judge 'pro forma' gave judgment so that the crown, if necessary, could raise the issue by writ of error; this apparently was not done, because the defendant was acquitted).

11 See e.g. *R. v. Bryan* (1834) Jebb Rep 157. 'Jebb Rep' (or 'Jebb's Reports') refers to R. Jebb (ed.), *Cases, chiefly relating to the criminal and presentment law, reserved for consideration, and decided by the twelve judges of Ireland* (Dublin, 1841). Where a date is given before 'Jebb Rep', this is the date of the case in question, as reported in Jebb's one-volume work. In *Bryan*, Johnson J 'communicated with' Joy CB (the other assize judge) as to the admissibility of a confession; they agreed that the confession should be received, but that if the defendant was found guilty, sentence should be respited so that the opinion of the judges could be obtained. In *McIlhone*, Mayne J after the trial had doubts about the adequacy of his

argument on the point until his return to Dublin.¹² Finally, the trial judge could more formally 'reserve' the point for the consideration of the twelve common law judges.

In 1848, Parke B stated that there was no authority for reserving questions for the consideration of the judges 'except what is given by usage … [which] prevails back as far as our knowledge of law goes'.¹³ According to Professor Baker, however, '[t]here is no clear evidence that the reserved case was used before the sixteenth century'.¹⁴ In any event, the practice appears to have been well established in England when the first collection of reported cases was published in 1789.¹⁵ It seems very likely that the Irish judges adopted a similar practice from an early date,¹⁶ but there is as yet no clear evidence of

direction to the jury; he consulted the other assize judge and 'so satisfied … immediately on his return to Dublin, recommended the prisoner for a free pardon'. In *R. v. Lynch and others* (1844) 1 Cox CC 81, Jackson J, faced with a novel point, wrote to Cresswell J for advice as to the position in England; he then tried to obtain the collective opinion of the Irish judges, but they refused to give an *a priori* opinion. Jackson J then formally reserved the point and proceeded with the trial; the prisoner was found guilty – but the opinion of the judges does not appear to be reported.

12 In *R. v. Madden* (1843) Ir Cir Rep 731, Burton J considered this to be 'the cheapest and most expeditious course' of dealing with a difficult question of marriage law which arose in a bigamy case on assize. He added that if, after such argument he felt any doubt about the case, or if either counsel should desire it, he would bring the question before the twelve judges. This course 'was acceded to by all the parties'. The trial proceeded and the defendant was found guilty. But after legal argument in Dublin, Burton J was satisfied that the defendant was not legally guilty of bigamy. Madden was pardoned on Burton J's recommendation.

13 *Select committee of the house of lords on the bill entituled an act for the further amendment of the administration of the criminal law: Minutes of evidence*, p. 3, H.L. 1847–48 (523) xvi, 429 (hereafter, *Select committee evidence 1847–48*).

14 J.H. Baker, 'The refinement of English criminal jurisprudence 1500–1848' in L.A. Knafla (ed.), *Crime and criminal justice in Europe and Canada* (Waterloo, ON, 1981), p. 18: 'though it is possible that the King's Council had exercised some kind of supervision over the administration of criminal justice'. The earliest 'case stated' found by Professor Baker is *R. v. Gore* (1611) 9 Co Rep 81. Professor Baker gives further details of the early history of the practice in England in 'Criminal courts and procedure at common law, 1550–1800' in J.S.Cockburn (ed.), *Crime in England, 1550–1800* (London, 1977), pp. 15 and 299, and in 'Criminal justice at Newgate, 1616–1627' in *Ir Jur*, viii (1973), 307. All three articles are reprinted in J.H. Baker, *The legal profession and the common law* (London, 1986).

15 T. Leach, *Cases in crown law* (1st ed., London, 1789). See e.g. *R. v. Hodgson and others* (1730) 1 Leach 6, 168 Eng Rep 105. See generally D.R. Bentley, *Select cases from the twelve judges' notebooks* (London, 1997).

16 J. Alcock, *Observations concerning the nature and origin of the meetings of the twelve judges for the consideration of cases reserved from the circuits* (Dublin, 1838) (hereafter Alcock, *Observations*), p. 8 states that 'this meeting of the judges has existed, as a court, beyond the time of legal memory'. According to Brady CB in *R. v. Larkin* (1826) Jebb Rep 59, 'these meetings were not confined to deliberations on cases which had arisen and waited for judgment; they were frequently occupied in settling the course of intended trials, and resolving beforehand how such and such points should be ruled if raised thereon.'

the procedure in operation before the last decade of the eighteenth century, when a number of cases appear which suggest that the practice of reserving points of law was not regarded at that time as being novel in any way.[17] What is novel is that the practice of reserving cases in Ireland was *not* restricted to crown (i.e. criminal) cases, but extended to three other types of case which only in Ireland came before judges of assize, namely:

(i) Civil bill cases. When the jurisdiction to hear and determine small claims was transferred from the judges of assize to assistant barristers at quarter sessions in 1796, an appeal still lay to the next going judge of assize.[18] Although no evidence of this practice has yet been found from the eighteenth century, it would appear that a judge of assize, both before and after 1796, could reserve a question of 'civil bill' law for the consideration of the judges. Such a practice was, in any event, well established by the 1820s[19] and continued until it was superseded in practice by a statutory case stated procedure.[20]

(ii) Grand jury presentment cases. In nineteenth-century Ireland, local public expenditure was determined by the grand jury, as approved by the judge of assize; a person aggrieved by the grand jury's decision could 'traverse' the presentment before the judge of assize. Such cases (which included claims made under the Irish criminal injuries and malicious damage compensation codes) often raised technical issues, which the judge could, and often did, refer for the consideration of all the judges.[21] Indeed, such cases

---

17 See *R. v. Weldon (James)* (1795) 26 How St Tr 225, at p. 242; *R. v. Wasson* (1796) 1 Cr & Dix 197; *R. v. Greene and Lacy* (1797–98) 1 Cr & Dix 198; *R. v. Haly* (1798) 1 Cr & Dix 199; *R. v. Bigley* (1799) 1 Cr & Dix 202: *R. v. Finney* (1798) 26 How St Tr 1019, at pp. 1036–7. It seems that the judges met at the home of the chief justice of the king's bench or in the hall of King's Inns – see 'A Barrister', *A letter to the Rt Hon Lord John Russell upon the judicial obligation of opinions expressed by the majority of the Irish judges, in their meetings for the consideration of questions upon the registry law of Ireland* (Dublin, 1841), p. 7 (hereafter, Barrister, *Letter to Lord John Russell*).

18 Civil Bill Courts (Ire.) Act 1796 (36 Geo III, c. 25), s. 29. See D.S. Greer, 'The development of civil bill procedure in Ireland' in J.F. McEldowney and P. O'Higgins (eds), *The common law tradition* (Blackrock, Co. Dublin, 1990), p. 27.

19 According to *Napier's Practice of the civil bill courts and courts of appeal*, 2nd ed., by R. Longfield (Dublin, 1841), pp. 87–8: 'the judges often reserve questions for the opinion of their brethren'. See e.g. *Orr v. Lavery* (1837) Jebb Rep 280 and *Murphy v. Butler* (1840) Jebb Rep 320. Assize judges also heard appeals from the manor courts before their abolition in 1859; such appeals could also give rise to reserved cases: see e.g. *Carter v. Reid* (1843) 3 Cr & Dix 69.

20 See J.W. Carleton, *The jurisdiction and procedure of the county courts in Ireland*, (1st ed., Dublin, 1878), p. 771 *et seq*. It is suggested (on p. 774) that the statutory provisions did not entirely supersede the earlier practice; in *Doyle v. Hanks* (1871) IR 6 CL 83, Deasy B reserved a question for the opinion of the judges 'in the old way'.

21 See e.g. *In re presentment by the grand jury of the county of Down* (1822) Jebb Rep 20 (traverse of presentment to raise cost of building new county gaol); *In re presentments for… the repair of roads in the County Roscommon* (1835) Jebb Rep 172 (legality of presentment of sum to cover cost of repairing certain roads); *Ex parte Drainage Comm'rs* (1853) 3 ICLR 140; *In re*

represented a substantial percentage of reserved cases until the establishment of county councils in 1899.[22]

(iii) Parliamentary registry cases. Under the Parliamentary Elections (Ire.) Act 1829, a dispute as to whether a person qualified as a £10 freeholder fell to be determined by an assistant barrister, with a right of appeal to the judge of assize. These cases, too, could give rise to difficult legal questions, in respect of which the judge might wish to have the opinion of his colleagues.[23] As we shall see shortly, one such difficulty gave rise in the late 1830s to considerable controversy – and heated argument – as to the 'true' nature of 'reserved' cases. It appears that this aspect of the work of the twelve judges came to an end with the reform of the parliamentary franchise in Ireland in 1850.[24]

In short, during the period under discussion, and for many years thereafter, the twelve judges in Ireland (unlike their counterparts in England) did not deal solely with criminal cases. Indeed, it would appear that during the first part of the nineteenth century, they acted just as much as a 'court' for *civil* cases reserved.[25] However, although we cannot entirely ignore these 'civil' cases, our attention here will be focused primarily on the practice and procedure as it developed in relation to criminal cases.

The reserved case operated in various ways. In some instances – perhaps even in most – the reservation was 'conditional'. The trial judge, having acknowledged a point of difficulty or uncertainty, nonetheless made his ruling thereon and proceeded with the trial on the basis that if the jury convicted the prisoner, he would reserve the point in question.[26] Occasionally, he

---

presentment for expenses for the conveyance of prisoners (1883) 17 ILTR 46; *In re Carew's Presentment* (1890) 24 ILTR 22.

22 By the Local Government (Ire.) Act 1898 the grand jury's 'presentment' powers were, with the exception of malicious injury compensation claims, transferred to the new county councils. Jurisdiction to determine malicious injury claims was transferred to the county court; an appeal still lay to the judge of assize, but by s. 5(4) of the act, questions of law arising on such appeals were thereafter dealt with by way of case stated to the court of appeal. The last reported case under the old procedure appears to have been *In re Lalor's Presentment* (1899) 33 ILTR 81.

23 See generally J. Alcock, *Registry cases reserved for consideration and decided by the twelve judges of Ireland*, parts 1 (1832–37), 2 (1837–39) and 3 (1839–41), (Dublin and London, 1838, 1839 and 1841), (hereafter, Alcock Registry Cases).

24 Representation of the People (Ire.) Act 1850 (13 & 14 Vict, c. 69), ss. 58 and 74 substituted an appeal on a point of law to the court of exchequer chamber: see e.g. *In re Alexander* (1855) 8 Ir Jur Rep 71.

25 An analysis of the cases included in Jebb's Reports (see note 11 above) for the period 1822–40 produces an annual average of just over three crown cases, and a similar number of presentment and registry cases. In addition to the kinds of cases mentioned in the text, the twelve judges were occasionally used to ensure administrative consistency, both in civil and criminal contexts: see e.g. *In re judges' orders for support of deserted children* (1836) Jebb Rep 184 (statutory liability of grand jury for support of deserted children) and *In re prosecutors' expenses* (1825) Jebb Rep 41 (practice relating to expenses of prosecutors and witnesses).

26 See e.g. *R. v. Cahill* (1824) Jebb Rep 36; *R. v. Moran and others* (1828) Jebb Rep 91.

would indicate that he would reserve the point if counsel (and presumably in particular if counsel for the defence) were willing to argue the point before the twelve judges;[27] if they did not undertake to do so, no reservation was made. In other cases, particularly where the judge was obviously in doubt, he would refer the point without consulting counsel.[28] It seems more likely, however, that a point would be reserved at the behest of counsel for the defence – and that a point would seldom be reserved if the prisoner was not legally represented, as must often have been the case, particularly before 1836.[29] Occasionally, however, one comes across a case where the prisoner is not represented and a question is raised, essentially on his behalf, by counsel for the prosecution or by the judge himself. Thus it is reported in *R. (Governors of the Royal Hospital) v. Keefe*[30] that 'the prisoner was found guilty, and the learned serjeant [as trial judge], at the request of counsel for the crown (the prisoner being undefended), reserved [a question] for the consideration of the judges', who held unanimously that the conviction was bad. Where the defendant was legally represented, his or her counsel might have to struggle to persuade the judge to reserve a point. In *R. v. Gaynor*,[31] for instance, Torrens J appears to have reserved a point only because the prisoner's counsel 'continued to entertain a strong opinion upon the case'; but he was right to do so – the majority of the judges (Torrens J dissenting) ruled in the prisoner's favour.

Having decided to make a reservation the trial judge might nonetheless, on conviction of the prisoner by the jury, impose the appropriate sentence; if the twelve judges then decided the point in the prisoner's favour, he or she would be recommended for a pardon. Alternatively, the trial judge could respite sentence in order to obtain the opinion of the judges;[32] in such cases the prisoner might be bound over to appear at the next assizes (i.e. released on bail)[33] or he or she might be remanded in custody.

---

27 See e.g. *R. v. Collins* (1841) 2 Cr & Dix 138.

28 This appears to have occurred in *R. v. Beard* (1822) Jebb Rep 9, where the defendant was convicted of theft; after 'a very particular communication' with the jury, the trial judge was unsure whether the defendant was legally guilty. He referred the case to the judges, who held unanimously that the conviction was right. In *R. v. Noonan* (1830) Jebb Rep 108, one assize judge conferred with the other before deciding to reserve a case.

29 Prisoners' Counsel Act 1836 (6 & 7 Will IV, c. 114). In almost all of the printed memoranda of eighteenth and early nineteenth-century trials and in the cases reported in Jebb's Reports, the prisoner is represented by at least one counsel but these cases are probably unrepresentative.

30 (1822) Jebb Rep 6. Crown counsel might also request a reservation in order to obtain a clear and authoritative ruling on a disputed or unclear point: see e.g. *R. v. M'Dermod and M'Gann* (1831) Jebb Rep 118 (where the conviction was held to be wrong).

31 (1839) Jebb Rep 262.

32 As in *R. v. Moran and others* (1828) Jebb Rep 91, at p. 92: '[t]he learned judge did not pronounce any sentence, but entered *curia advisari vult* in the Crown book'.

33 See e.g. *R. v. Charleton* (1839) Jebb Rep 267, where a prisoner convicted of bigamy: 'on his

It was generally accepted that it was entirely a matter for the discretion of the judge whether he reserved a question, and if so, which question.[34] No reliable statistics for the period before 1848 are available in Ireland, but the evidence suggests that on average only two or three crown cases were reserved annually from 9,000 to 14,000 or so convictions on indictment – as compared with the 13 or 14 cases (out of some 14,000 to 20,000 convictions) which were reserved in England in the first part of the nineteenth century.[35] In 1847, Alderson B stated that 'a prisoner, as the law now stands, is not bound by the refusal or omission of the judge to reserve a point in his favour'. He gave two examples. In *R. v. Wait*[36] the prisoner was convicted of forgery and sentenced to death. During the trial, his counsel had objected to the admissibility of certain prosecution evidence, but the objection was overruled by the trial judges, who apparently refused to reserve the question. Following his conviction, the prisoner petitioned the king, 'soliciting a pardon in consideration of the doubt'. The report of the case continues: '[b]y direction of the Chancellor (to whom the petition was sent by command of his majesty) the points of law which had been raised [in the petition] were referred to the judges, and [were] argued by counsel on both sides in the exchequer chamber'. To no avail; the judges decided against the prisoner, who 'was ultimately ordered for execution'. In *R. v. Fauntleroy*,[37] another forgery case, the jury convicted the prisoner and his counsel immediately moved an objection in arrest of judgment; the objection was overruled, and the prisoner was condemned to death. The prisoner thereupon 'petitioned the Crown, on the ground that the objection taken by his counsel had been improperly overruled'. The question was once again referred to the judges, who, having agreed with the trial judges, 'reported their opinions to the King in Council, and the prisoner was subsequently executed'. Something similar occurred in the Irish case of *R. v. Robinson and Robinson*.[38] At a trial on a

application, and on the consent of the Crown ... entered into security to appear at the next assizes, and surrender himself to abide judgment'. The judges found against him, and the prisoner duly presented himself for sentence: see (1839) 1 Cr & Dix 315, 2 Ir LR 50.

34 The latter point was made very clear in the English case of *R. v. Brown* (1848) 3 Cox CC 127, where defence counsel attempted to raise a point which had not been reserved, and was immediately ruled out of order.

35 The number of cases reserved is derived from Jebb Rep; the average number of convictions per annum following trial on indictment during 1823–9 was in the region of 9,000 and during 1845–9 was 14,000: see above note 3. In England and Wales, the number of persons convicted following trial on indictment in 1845–9 was in the region of 20,000: see e.g. *Tables showing the number of criminal offenders committed for trial or bailed for appearance ... in the year 1849*, H.C. 1850 [1227] xlv, 455.

36 (1823) 11 Pr 518, 147 Eng Rep 551.

37 (1824) 1 Moo CC 52, 168 Eng Rep 1182.

38 (1839) Jebb Rep 286. See also *R. v. Hartnett and Casey* (1840) Jebb Rep 302 where the prisoners were convicted of murder and sentenced to death. However, the trial judge failed

charge of burglary and robbery, counsel for the prisoners objected to the reception of some evidence; Johnson J overruled the objection and the prisoners were ultimately convicted. It appears that the learned judge was unwilling to reserve the point, for the prisoners then presented a memorial to the lord lieutenant, claiming that their conviction was bad in law. Following the normal practice, the memorial was referred to the trial judge, Johnson J, who at this stage recommended that the sentence be respited so that the opinion of the judges could be obtained. The judges held unanimously that the conviction was wrong, and Johnson J accordingly recommended that the prisoners be pardoned.

The English cases led Alderson B to conclude that 'the prisoner, therefore, is not without remedy if a judge improperly omits or refuses to reserve a point. The crown, through the lord chancellor, will, on a proper case made, direct the body of the judges to hear the point argued.'[39] The cases cited do appear to support this proposition, but it is suggested that they are best regarded as exemplifying the flexibility applicable to the exercise of the prerogative of mercy rather than as a limitation upon the trial judge's discretion whether or not to reserve a case.[40]

The trial judge could only reserve a question of law; there was no 'appeal' on questions of fact.[41] There are occasional suggestions, however, of an attempt to obtain a more general review of the trial. Thus, in *R. v. Casey and M'Cue*[42] Burton J reserved a question relating to the need for corroboration of accomplice evidence and added that the case should go to the judges to find out whether 'under all the circumstances the conviction was not so satisfactory as that the prisoners ought to undergo their sentence, [in which

to direct that their bodies should be buried within the precincts of the gaol. When he tried to correct the omission, counsel for the prisoners objected and the trial judge 'communicated' with the attorney general, who suggested that he lay the facts before the twelve judges for their opinion. Following argument, the judges (by a majority of 6–4) ruled that the sentence was illegal and the prisoners were thereupon pardoned and discharged.

39 *Select committee evidence 1847–48*, p. 60.

40 A convicted defendant might have the alternative of suing out a writ of error in the court of queen's bench; this alternative was sometimes preferred even where the trial judge had intimated his willingness to reserve a point: see e.g. *Conway and Lynch v. R.* (1845) 1 Cox CC 210.

41 'It is remarkable ... that whilst so much is done, and so usefully done by the whole body of Judges in correcting errors or mistakes in point of law, they have no means of revising or rectifying any verdict for any mistake or error on the part of the jury, in point of fact, although it be manifest that if the facts be mistaken, the whole foundation of any legal judgment altogether fails': *Eighth report from her majesty's commissioners on criminal law*, p. 23, H.C. 1845 (656) xiv, 183 (hereafter, *Criminal law comm'rs eighth report 1845*).

42 (1837) Jebb Rep 203. See also *R. v. Ryan* (1822) Jebb Rep 5, where the judges held that certain evidence should not have been admitted and 'further declared their opinion that the prisoners should not be indicted again for this crime, their lives having being once in jeopardy'. The report does not say if this recommendation was followed.

case] he might recommend them to government for a pardon'. But the judges were unanimously of opinion that the conviction was right. An attempt to obtain a more wide-ranging review of a trial was rejected in the well-known English case of *R. v. Serva*,[43] where counsel for the prisoner tried to take exception to the way in which the trial judge had stated the case and sought to present it in his own way. Lord Denman CJ quickly stopped him: '[a]ny alteration in the case is a matter of private application to the [trial] judge, of the propriety of which we have no means now of forming an opinion. We have met here expressly for the purpose of considering the case as it stands, and to that our attention must be confined.'[44]

The procedure for dealing with reserved cases was set out in some detail by Bushe CJ in 1838 as follows:

> ... in the following term each judge who has done so [i.e. reserved a case] sends to each other judge, with a view of obtaining the advice and assistance of his brethren, a written statement of the facts of the cases, and the questions arising from them; and the Chief Justice, by notice, assembles the judges for the purpose of taking such references into consideration, at which meeting, if the judges consider it proper, or if the parties require it, a day is fixed for the argument of the case by counsel at both sides, and such argument is heard in public; and after the argument, the judges, among themselves and not in public, either on the same day, or on a subsequent day fixed for the purpose, discuss the case; and if there be a difference of opinion, each judge, beginning with the junior, states the reasons for his opinion; and according to what appears to be the opinion of the majority, the conviction if in a criminal case is held to be good or bad ...[45]

Prior to 1826, it appears that the twelve judges considered the reserved case without hearing counsel for either party.[46] However, at a meeting of the

---

43 (1845) 1 Denison CC 104, 169 Eng Rep 169.

44 But the outcome of the case led Lord Denman to criticise the whole procedure in such cases. Eight members of the royal navy had been killed on board a Brazilian slave ship on the high seas; the master of the ship was tried for murder, and the question arose as to whether the English courts had jurisdiction. The 'overwhelming' majority of the judges thought not, but Lord Denman vigorously disagreed, and later informed the home secretary that 'the result appears to destroy all reasonable hope of suppressing the slave trade': see J. Arnould, *Memoir of Thomas, first Lord Denman*, 2 vols (London, 1873), ii, p. 200 *et seq* and appendix VII (where the full text of Lord Denman's paper on the need for reform of 'the court of all the judges' is reproduced).

45 Letter to Lord Denman CJ, 8 Feb. 1838, as noted in 2 Alcock Registry Cases 343.

46 Day J is said to have written that 'it is to be lamented that the Irish judges do not hear arguments from counsel upon the criminal cases referred to them – opinions, however maturely formed, without the aid of argument, bind not even the judges themselves who

twelve judges in that year, it was resolved that the English practice should be adopted, namely, 'if the judge who reserved the case thinks it of such a nature that counsel should argue it, it generally is argued by one counsel on each side;[47] the argument is in open court, but the judges do not deliver any opinion in court; the opinion is made known by the judge who presides at the next assizes or sessions, as in cases where counsel are not heard.'[48]

The necessity for argument by counsel was underlined by the case of *R. v. Doolin and others*[49] in 1832, where the prisoners were charged with burglary (then a capital offence). The owner of the house in question gave evidence-in-chief for the crown, but shortly after the start of the cross-examination by defence counsel, he collapsed and died. Could the jury nevertheless take his evidence into account? Foster B held that they could, but stated that if the prisoners were convicted, he would reserve the point. The prisoners were convicted, and the learned judge thereupon named 'a distant day' for their execution, 'in order that the opinion of the judges might first be taken'. The case duly came before ten of the judges, who (apparently without hearing counsel) were of opinion (by a majority of 7–3)[50] that the conviction was good (on the grounds that the witness's evidence should be treated as a dying declaration). This opinion was apparently transmitted to the authorities, for 'on a subsequent day' the lord chancellor, Lord Plunket, 'came into the king's bench chamber, and stated to the judges there assembled that he had great difficulty in advising or deciding whether an execution should take place in this case'.[51] It emerged that he had 'strong doubts' as to the opinion of the majority of the judges, and it was finally agreed that the judges should reconsider the case, this time hearing counsel for both sides. On this second occasion, the case was heard by all twelve judges, but once again, seven judges took the view that the trial judge had acted properly.[52] This division of judicial opinion was, however, apparently

deliver them, and carry not the force and weight of authority': Barrister, *Letter to Lord Russell*, pp. 53–4. Much the same point was made by Jebb J in *Ranken v. Newsom* (1827) 1 Hudson & Brooke Rep 70, at p. 77. It may be that counsel could present a written case to the judges, as was done by defence counsel in *R. v. Larkin* (1826) Jebb Rep 60, but this case was determined after the judges' resolution about hearing counsel and may just have been one of the first cases under the new dispensation.

47 It seems that there was no *right* to representation by counsel: see Barrister, *Letter to Lord John Russell*, p. 7. In England, 'counsel were but *amici curiae* to the judges assembled': *R. v. Williams and Jones* (1840) 2 Moo CC 143, at p. 145n, 169 Eng Rep 57, 58n, *per* Tindal CJ and Gurney B.

48 *Resolution of the twelve judges of Ireland as to hearing counsel on reserved crown cases, Hilary term 1826*, reproduced in Jebb Rep, p. 1.

49 (1832) Jebb Rep 123.

50 In accordance with the usual practice, the trial judge participated fully in the judges' deliberations; in this case Foster B remained satisfied that he had acted correctly.

51 (1832) Jebb Rep 123, at p. 127.

52 Only one judge (Johnson J) appears to have changed his mind as a result of counsel's

enough to convince the government that the prisoners should not be executed; instead, they were transported.

Doolin also gives us some evidence of the speed with which reserved cases were despatched. The trial took place at Kilkenny spring assizes in 1832 (precise date unknown); the 'distant day' for the execution was 28 April 1832; the judges first determined the reserved case on 18 April; the lord chancellor's intervention must have been before 28 April (and it must have resulted in further deferral of the execution); the case was argued by counsel on 30 April and the judges gave their opinions on 2 May 1832.[53]

The reports show that some cases after 1826 were still dealt with in the absence of counsel; in others, one party only might be represented.[54] Some cases gave rise to prolonged argument, with counsel being extensively questioned by one or more of the judges; in such cases the prosecution might be represented by the attorney general and/or the solicitor general. In other cases, the judges obviously concluded fairly quickly that there was nothing in the points reserved and did not even call on counsel for the prosecution. A reserved case was usually dealt with at one hearing; indeed two or three cases might be dealt with on the same day. Occasionally the hearing was adjourned; the judges might be so divided in opinion even after argument that they asked for the case to be reargued at a later date.[55] Another reason for adjournment was to obtain clarification of, or evidence pertaining to, the case.[56]

It was normal practice for the judge who had reserved a point to sit with the other judges and to be fully involved in their deliberations. This could be

arguments; having first taken the view that Foster B had acted correctly, he subsequently decided that the evidence should not have been considered by the jury, because of 'the possible injury that might accrue to a prisoner, if evidence should be used against him, when there was no opportunity of cross-examining': ibid., pp. 129–30.

53 Most reserved cases appear to have been dealt with within three or four months of the trial, but occasionally it took longer. In *R. v. Sheehan* (1826) Jebb Rep 54, for example, the trial took place at the spring assizes in 1825; the determination of the twelve judges was given on 15 Feb. 1826, following a 'long discussion' on the need for corroboration of accomplice evidence. See also *R. v. Flannery* (1839) Jebb Rep 243 (trial at summer assizes 1837; judges' determination in favour of the defendant on 16 Jan. 1839).

54 There appears to have been a custom in England that if the prosecution was represented by counsel, but not the prisoner, the judges would 'decline to hear counsel for the crown': see e.g. *R. v. Cant* (1842) 2 Moo CC 271, at p. 274n, 169 Eng Rep 108, 109n and *R. v. Wallace* (1841) 2 Moo CC 200, at p. 204n, 169 Eng Rep 79, 80n.

55 See e.g. *In re presentments for dispensaries in the Queen's Co.* (1832) Jebb Rep 130, at p. 131n, referring to a presentment decision of the majority of the judges 'which was the result of a long discussion, at two several meetings', and which led to a previous decision of eleven judges being 'overruled'.

56 E.g. *R. v. Stonage* (1832) Jebb Rep 121, where the hearing of the reserved case was adjourned so that a document which had been given in evidence could be produced to the judges. It appears that the document was not produced, but the judges nonetheless held the conviction good.

useful to clarify the issues: '[w]hen a judge now reserves a case from the assizes, he can explain or amend it as often as is necessary, and can give any explanations which the other judges may require'.[57] The trial judge might also take the opportunity to explain why he had reserved the question – sometimes in terms which were singularly unhelpful to the prisoner.[58] Not all the other judges might be present; illness or absence from Dublin could mean that reserved cases were often decided by nine or ten judges.[59] Absence, however, was not necessarily a reason for withholding an opinion! In *R. v. Carroll*[60] the trial judge (Torrens J) was 'absent' when the judges met; but he 'sent his opinion that it [i.e. his ruling at the trial] was right'. Smith B was also 'absent', but he, too, 'sent his opinion' that part of Torrens J's ruling was wrong. Seven of the judges who were present held that the conviction was right.

The practice in the first part of the nineteenth century was for the twelve judges not to give reasons in public, but to say simply: '[u]pon consideration, the judges [or a majority of the judges] held the conviction to be right [or wrong]'. Reasons were nevertheless given in private, and were apparently written down and recorded.[61] There was no public announcement of the judges' opinion, which was delivered by the trial judge or by another judge at the next assizes.[62]

Where judgment had been respited pending the consideration of the case by the twelve judges, the trial judge subsequently entered judgment according to their opinion; but where judgment had been entered against a prisoner, subject in effect to the judges' opinion, that opinion was transmitted to the government. Normally, if the judges were of opinion that the conviction was good, the sentence was duly carried out; occasionally, this did not occur, either because the government relented for some reason or because the judges themselves suggested clemency on grounds that they were divided in their opinion or because there were other 'extraordinary' circumstances.[63]

57 *Select committee evidence 1847–48*, p. 60 (Rolfe B). See e.g. *R. v. Brown* (1848) 3 Cox CC 127 (Eng.).
58 See e.g. *R. v. Bowen* (1844) 1 Cox CC 88 (Eng.), where Tindal CJ explained that he had reserved a question 'because it was the first case ... under this [Act]'; he then added: 'but I certainly thought that there was nothing in the objection at the time, and I think the same now'. The judges found against the prisoner!
59 Only eight judges sat in *R. v. Beard* (1822) Jebb Rep 9 and *R. v. Jones* (1827) Jebb Rep 72.
60 (1827) Jebb Rep 78.
61 See e.g. *R. v. Sheehan* (1826) Jebb Rep 54, at pp. 57–8.
62 See e.g. *R. v. Ryan* (1822) Jebb Rep 5 where Johnson J reserved a case at the spring assizes and Jebb J delivered the judges' opinion at the ensuing summer assizes.
63 See e.g. *R. v. Gibney* (1822) Jebb Rep 15, at p. 19 (the judges found that a confession had been properly received, but recommended mercy 'on account of the extraordinary circumstances of the case'; the defendant was not executed). In *R. v. Fitzmaurice* (1824) Jebb Rep 29, the majority of the judges were in favour of conviction 'on each point'; but 'as

The right to reserve questions of law for the consideration of the judges was restricted to judges of assize, judges sitting on special commissions[64] and the recorder of Dublin. The practice did not extend to trials on indictment at quarter sessions, where 'by far the greatest portion of criminal offenders is tried'.[65] One reason for this presumably was that quarter sessions were not presided over by one of the judges; it was also thought that the comparatively minor cases tried at quarter sessions would not give rise to difficult questions of law. A chairman of quarter sessions, faced with a question of law on which he was doubtful, could apply to the lord lieutenant for advice; alternatively, the convicted prisoner could present a memorial to the lord lieutenant.

R. v. Houlton[66] shows that the difference between quarter sessions and the higher criminal courts was not as clearcut as might be thought. Houlton, a catholic parish priest, was charged with assault and riot arising out of a *fracas* which resulted when he administered the last rites to Jane Moffatt, a dangerously ill woman, contrary to the wishes of her protestant husband. He was tried at quarter sessions and, on conviction, 'the outrage being very great', was sentenced to twelve months' imprisonment and a fine of £40. He presented a memorial to the lord lieutenant complaining of injustice in the trial; his particular complaint was that Jane Moffatt was not allowed to give evidence on his behalf. The under-secretary of state (Gregory) wrote to Bushe CJ, 'conveying the desire of the Lord Lieutenant, that he should take the opinion of all the judges, whether the conviction was legal and proper'. For this purpose, Houlton's memorial and the assistant barrister's report of the trial were laid before the judges. Bushe CJ reported that the judges were unanimously of opinion that Mrs Moffatt's evidence should have been received, and that it was impossible to say whether, if it had been, Houlton might have been acquitted. They were therefore of opinion that Houlton ought to receive a free pardon. Consequently, 'the prisoner, together with others convicted on the same indictment, was accordingly pardoned'.

By 1845, it was widely accepted that the exclusion of quarter sessions was no longer justifiable:

> Although these courts are restrained … from proceeding to adjudication in matters of difficulty … the legal difficulties which may occur in such courts are not to be distinguished from those which occur in the higher criminal courts. Such difficulties frequently arise on new and unforeseen combinations of circumstances wholly unconnected

there was such a diversity of opinion and as they were equally divided on the whole, it was agreed that the prisoner should be recommended [for mercy]'.

64 E.g. *R. v. Heffernan* (1822) Jebb Rep 2 (special commission in Cork).

65 *Criminal law comm'rs eighth report 1845*, p. 23.

66 (1823) Jebb Rep 24.

with the gravity of the particular offence ... [I]t is impossible to suppose that frequent failures in justice do not occur in the proceedings in this extensive class of courts which are thus left without any means of correction at all adequate to the evil.[67]

THE 'REGISTRY' DISPUTE, 1832–1850[68]

As we have already seen, questions of law relating to the registration of parliamentary voters could be reserved for the consideration of the twelve judges. In 1837 the judges, by a majority of 10–2, gave their opinion on a question relating to the precise qualification required of a person claiming to be registered as a £10 freeholder or leaseholder.[69] Richards B, one of the dissenting judges,[70] promptly refused to follow the majority opinion, and gave his reasons for doing so at length.[71] Bushe CJ thereupon summoned a meeting of the twelve judges. He also ascertained from Lord Denman CJ that 'each of [the judges of England] does hold himself ... bound [by the opinion of the whole body of the judges on crown cases reserved], whether or not his own opinion may have agreed with that of the majority, and whether or not the case may have been argued by counsel.'[72] In April 1838 the Irish judges resolved, by a majority of 10–2 (Perrin J and Richards B again dissenting), that 'the judges of Ireland ought to hold themselves bound by the opinion of the majority of the judges, on cases reserved from circuit, whether their own opinion agreed with that of the majority or not'.[73]

---

67 *Criminal law comm'rs eighth report 1845*, p. 23.

68 See further D.S. Greer, 'Lawyers or politicians? The Irish judges and the right to vote, 1832–1850' in C. Costello (ed.), *The Four Courts: 200 years* (Dublin, 1996), p. 126.

69 *Glennon's Case* (1837) 1 Alcock Registry Cases 55. An apparent conflict between the requirements of the Parliamentary Elections (Ire.) Act 1829 and those of the Representation of the People (Ire.) Act 1832, which could mean that a person *not* qualified to register under the former might nevertheless qualify under the latter, did not escape the notice of the political factions in Ireland, with the result that the issue had arisen in a number of cases from 1832 onwards, with differing results. See e.g. editorials in *Freeman's Journal*, 2 and 3 June 1837.

70 The other was Perrin J. The interpretation which these two judges favoured would have led to more persons qualifying to be registered as voters.

71 See T. Welsh, *A report of the case of James Feighny ... at the summer assizes 1837 for the county of Sligo* (Dublin 1837), (hereafter, Welsh, *Feighny*). The learned baron repeated his opinion in *In re Richard Alcock*: see T. Welsh, *Registry cases argued and decided at Sligo during the spring assizes 1838* (Dublin, 1838), p. 1 (hereafter, Welsh, *Registry cases*).

72 Bushe CJ's letter and Lord Denman's reply are published in a note following *William Smith's Case* (1841) 3 Alcock Registry Cases 343.

73 See *Connellan's Case* (1841) 3 Alcock Registry Cases 208, at p. 215 n2, *per* Crampton J, and Jebb Rep, pp. 234–35.

It appears that the majority of the judges accepted and acted on this resolution,[74] but not Richards B or Perrin J, who were subsequently joined by several other judges.[75] The issue continued to generate controversy for a number of years[76] and does not appear ever to have been formally resolved, but the particular question which gave rise to it disappeared when Irish electoral law was radically revised in 1850.[77] The authority of opinions expressed by the twelve judges in Ireland appears to have been contested mainly in registry cases, and then solely with reference to an opinion given in a case other than that in which the reservation was made.[78] It is, therefore, entirely possible that these events were motivated simply by political considerations,[79] but many of the legal points made in the course of the controversy were equally applicable to criminal cases, and therefore require some consideration in this context.

74 In *William Smith's Case*, Crampton J, having stated that Bushe CJ felt himself bound by the majority opinion of the twelve judges in *Glennon*, added (at p. 319): '[m]y brother Burton and I have ever since followed the same course, as have the judges generally.' In *Connellan's Case*, Crampton J again stated (at pp. 214–15): 'I hold with the fifteen judges of England, and according to the resolution of the Irish judges ... that each individual judge ought to hold himself bound by the opinion of the majority of the judges on cases reserved from circuit, whether his own opinion agreed with that of the majority or not.'

75 Brady CB (see *In re Flood* (1840) 1 Cr & Dix 627, at p. 631 and *In re Larkin* (1841) 4 Ir LR 46, at p. 70) and Ball J (according to Brady CB in *Flood* at p. 631, and Crampton J in *William Smith's Case* at p. 319). The minority view was said to have been 'sustained' by the opinions of Lord Plunket LC, Sir Michael O'Loghlin MR and the late Woulfe CB: see Barrister, *Letter to Lord John Russell*, p. 7. Richards B apparently consulted Lord Plunket LC (whether before or after the meeting in April 1838 is not clear), and was advised that he committed no 'judicial indiscretion' in acting on his own opinion: Welsh, *Feighny*, p. 29. *Cf.* in *William Smith's Case* (at p. 331) Crampton J noted that Lord Plunket's opinion was given extrajudicially, and 'probably without any reference to authority'.

76 See e.g. *William Smith's Case*, p. 309, where Crampton J, hitherto one of the 'loyal' judges, was disinclined to follow 'my uniform course of conduct' and refer a *vexata questio* to the judges, since such a reservation would no longer 'ensure a final determination of the question'. See also *In re Waddy* (1841) Ir Cir Rep 218, at p. 220, *per* Pennefather B.

77 Representation of the People (Ire.) Act 1850 (13 & 14 Vict, c. 69), ss. 58 and 74 provided that an appeal from an assistant barrister sitting as a court of revision of the register lay to the court of exchequer chamber.

78 'I am not contending ... that in the particular case submitted, the judge who desires the advice of his brethren ought not, against his own opinion, to abide by the advice given': *In re Larkin* (1841) 4 Ir LR 46, at p. 64, *per* Brady CB. At p. 70 the chief baron says that Lord Denman's letter to Bushe CJ 'declares no more than this'.

79 The decision by Richards B in *Feighny* was 'hailed with great triumph' by O'Connell and his supporters. But 'the constitutional party' saw it as 'opening a door for the unlimited admission of fictitious votes': see Anon, 'Baron Richards and the twelve judges' in *Dublin University Magazine*, 11 (1838), 453. In this article (which supports the majority position for essentially political reasons), Perrin J and Richards B are castigated as '*new judges ...* whose extreme political opinions are well known' (original emphasis).

The majority view[80] was that the twelve judges constituted a court whose determinations were as binding as those of any other court, and whose authority had never before been controverted. Crampton J, for example, cited Blackstone and Coke and a number of cases 'to shew the character of this court'.[81] He relied in particular on *Smith v. Richardson*[82] as showing not only 'the common law existence of this ancient court of the twelve judges, but its high authority [and] ... also its precise limits and nature of its jurisdiction, and the manner in which it was set in motion ... to rule for the public benefit, cases of weight and difficulty.' It appears, however, that these references do *not* deal specifically with the status of the twelve judges when dealing with cases reserved from judges of assize. Crampton J would seem to be on stronger ground when he asks: '[c]an any reasoning mind be satisfied with the subtle distinction between the opinion of the twelve judges assembled in the court of error, which is admitted to bind each individual judge, and between the opinion of the same judges, assembled in their chamber, upon summons to deliberate upon and decide some grave question referred to them by the court, or by a judge?'[83] In criminal cases in particular, 'the opinion of the majority ... has ever been held binding on the minority'.[84]

The 'dissenting' judges denied that the meeting of the twelve judges, in the cases under consideration, constituted a 'court', since 'it wants every quality attached to the idea of a court by every legal authority'.[85] The twelve judges sat rather as assessors or advisers to the trial judge and their opinions, which did, of course, have 'mighty influence', were not conclusive, even in criminal cases, 'in swaying his decision as a judge against his reason'.[86] This latter view seems to have been shared even by some of the English judges,[87]

---

80 See e.g. Alcock, *Observations*, and *William Smith's Case*, p. 321, *per* Crampton J.

81 *William Smith's Case*, pp. 326–32.

82 (1737) Willes 20, 125 Eng Rep 1034.

83 *William Smith's Case*, pp. 334–5. Alcock, *Observations*, p. 6 even suggests that the 'court' of the twelve judges was an emanation of the court of exchequer chamber.

84 See note following *In re Flood* (1840) 1 Cr & Dix 627, at p. 631, referring to *R. v. Logan* (1837) 1 Cr & Dix 188n, where Bushe CJ 'felt himself bound by the decision of the twelve judges in *R. v. Campbell*'.

85 Barrister, *Letter to Lord John Russell*, p. 63. In *In re Larkin* (1841) 4 Ir LR 46, at p. 48 *et seq*, Brady CB set out to show that 'the ancient court of exchequer chamber ... resembled in nothing these modern chamber assemblies of the judges, except that it was composed of the same judicial personages'.

86 Barrister, *Letter to Lord John Russell*, p. 34. In *R. v. Lea and others* (1837) 2 Moo CC 9, at p. 11, 169 Eng Rep 4, 5, for example, Lord Abinger CB interjected during argument: '[w]e do not sit here as a court of appeal; we are merely assembled to advise the judge who presided at the trial'. *Archbold's Pleading and evidence in criminal cases* (16th ed., London, 1867) p. 169 states that 'the judgment ultimately pronounced was considered in law as [the trial judge's] judgment, the reasons on which it was founded not being publicly declared by the judges.'

87 See e.g. *R. v. Crow* (1823) 1 Lewin 88, at p. 89, 168 Eng Rep 970 (where Parke J declined to

and it subsequently appeared to receive support from Pigot CB in *R. v. Johnston*.[88] Referring to the opinion of the English judges in *R. v. Thornton*,[89] the learned chief baron stated:

> Undoubtedly, the resolution of a majority of the judges upon a question so reserved ... was and is entitled to the greatest respect. It ought to be followed by individual judges ... But the very circumstance that the judges, in considering points reserved in criminal cases, did not usually sit as an open court of law, hearing the questions argued with the assistance of counsel, and delivering their judgments, with their reasons, in the face of the profession and the public, constituted an objection to such a tribunal, which deprived it of much of the authority that would otherwise have attached to it ...[90]

Pigot CB then referred to *Ranken v. Newsom*,[91] where Jebb J had this to say about an earlier decision of the twelve judges on a civil bill 'appeal': '[w]ith respect to [*Hogan v. Fitzgerald*[92]], there certainly was a difference of opinion among the judges. It was not argued by counsel, and I have no hesitation in saying that I do not consider myself bound by it.'[93] Pigot CB went on to say that he had 'always thought that there was great force in [that] observation' and that a reserved civil bill case 'was exactly analogous to that of the judges determining upon a point reserved at a criminal trial'.[94] However, when Jebb J repeated his opinion of *Hogan v. Fitzgerald* in *Pluck v. Digges*,[95] O'Grady CB

---

follow *R. v. Smith* (1823) 1 Lewin 86 and directed the acquittal of the prisoner) and *R. v. Godfrey* (1838) 8 Car & P 563, at p. 564, 173 Eng Rep 619 (where Lord Abinger CB reportedly 'cannot accede to' the decision in *R. v. Cabbage* (1815) Russ & Ry 292, 168 Eng Rep 809). But the precise import of these statements is not clear and they are difficult to reconcile with the unequivocal view stated by Lord Denman CJ (see above note 72), and *R. v. Williams and Jones* (1840) 2 Moo CC 143, at p. 171n, 169 Eng Rep 57, 68, where it is stated that 'the judge reserving the case [is] always bound by the opinion of the majority'. Alcock, *Observations*, p. 26 says that *Crow* and *Godfrey* are either wrongly decided or wrongly reported.

88 (1864) 15 ICLR 60.

89 (1824) 1 Moo CC 27, 168 Eng Rep 1171.

90 (1864) 15 ICLR 60, at p. 117. Pigot CB had earlier (p. 115) suggested that *R. v. Gibney* (1822) Jebb Rep 15 had been incorrectly reported and that 'the point now before us was not at all intended to be determined by the judges'.

91 (1827) 1 Hud & Br 70.

92 (1825) unreported, but noted at (1827) 1 Hud & Br 77.

93 (1827) 1 Hud & Br 70, at p. 77. The case was heard by the court of king's bench.

94 (1864) 15 ICLR 60, at p. 117. *Cf.* Molloy QC *arguendo* referred explicitly to the judges' resolution of 1838 as laying down that 'the opinion of the majority of the judges *upon reserved crown cases* is binding upon the individual judges, whatever their own opinion may be': ibid., p. 69 (emphasis added).

95 (1828) 2 Hud & Br 1, at p. 11.

retorted that 'such resolutions of the judges, in criminal cases, have always been considered as of authority, and it would be strange if the same rule did not apply in civil cases'.[96]

Sensing, perhaps, that they might have been on weak ground with respect to criminal cases, the dissenting judges fell back on confession and avoidance. Crown reserved cases, they suggested, were distinct from other reserved cases, with the result that a trial judge might be bound by the opinion of the twelve judges in the former, but not the latter.[97] One basis for this argument was that in registry cases, but not in crown cases, the 'reserving' judge was 'a court of appeal, uncontrolled by any other legally constituted court'.[98] Alternatively:

> ... the practice, with respect to crown cases reserved, cannot be held applicable to [registry] cases ... because that practice has been resorted to in substitution of the more regular, but perhaps less satisfactory, course of suing out a writ of error. But the judge presiding at registry appeals appears, as regards the present question, to be in the situation of the judge in a court of equity, who may send a case for the opinion of a court of law, but is not bound by such opinion where it differs from his own ...[99]

Crampton J responded that if it was once accepted that the 'reserving' judge was bound in crown cases, then 'surely such cases [i.e. crown cases] are not merely *a fortiori*, but a *fortissimo* cases. For if the judgment of the tribunal of all the judges is to rule the judgments of the courts below, in cases of liberty, and in cases of life and death, can it be unreasonable to suppose, that it may, and must exercise, an equal authority in matters, merely, of private property and of civil franchise?'[100]

Those who considered that individual judges were bound by the opinion of the twelve judges further relied on policy considerations:

96 Ibid. But Jebb J failed to repent and castigated *Hogan* once more during the argument on a reserved case in *Fawcett v. Hall* (1833) Alcock & Napier Rep 248, at p. 253. It may be noted, however, that in none of these cases was he sitting alone as a trial judge. It may also be that his view of *Hogan* was peculiar to that case, especially in view of the fact (as Alcock, *Observations*, p. 26 argues) that it was not argued by counsel.

97 Richards B in Welsh, *Registry cases*, pp. 40–1. Thus, Ball J, who agreed with Richards B in relation to registry cases, appears in *R. v. Leary* (1844) 3 Cr & Dix 212, at p. 213, to have accepted that he was bound by a decision of the twelve judges in a crown case.

98 Brady CB in *In re Flood* (1840) 1 Cr & Dix 627, at p. 630.

99 Moore (solicitor general), *arguendo*, in *In re Flood* (1840), referring to *Lansdowne v. Lansdowne* (1820) 2 Bligh PC 60, 4 Eng Rep 250.

100 *William Smith's Case*, p. 333.

... does not public convenience ... impose a solemn duty upon every individual judge, not to set up his private, fallible opinion, against that of the assembled judges of the land? ... By subordinating the opinion of each judge to that of the body, certainty, uniformity of decision, decency, and gravity in the administration of the law is secured; and suspicion of partizanship is wholly excluded. But remove this restraint, and let every judge act upon his private opinion, and what is the result? All certainty as to the law, all uniformity as to decision, is abandoned.[101]

The minority also dealt with this argument by confession and avoidance. It would, of course, lead to some inconvenience if the opinion of 'the assembled judges' was not binding; but 'there are [also] manifest dangers and inconveniences in establishing ... a rule ... that opinions [arrived at under the 'secret' practice of the twelve judges] would be obligatory, for it would prevent the proper sifting of legal questions, the due investigation of them, would open a door to judicial negligence and would leave the public and the parliament in entire ignorance of the reason or principle upon which the law was expounded by the judges.'[102]

In view of all this uncertainty, the time was obviously ripe for reform.

THE COURT FOR CROWN CASES RESERVED

The 'registry' dispute does not appear to have given rise to discussion of the status of reserved cases in England and Wales,[103] but it is evident that there was growing judicial concern there with the way in which reserved cases were being dealt with. In 1845, Lord Denman, dissatisfied with the outcome in *R. v. Serva*,[104] wrote to the home secretary, summarising the strengths and weaknesses of the reserved case procedure as follows:

101 Ibid., pp. 334–5, *per* Crampton J. Alcock, *Observations*, p. 5 referred to the 'inconvenience which must necessarily result from a contrariety of opinion upon the construction of a statute, to be administered by ... 33 courts of original jurisdiction [i.e. the assistant barristers] and 12 co-ordinate courts of appeal [i.e. the judges of assize]'; certainty and uniformity could only be achieved if the judges 'should enter into a conventional arrangement to confer together upon all questions of doubt or difficulty as they arose, and to abide the decision of the majority.'

102 Barrister, *Letter to Lord John Russell*, p. 64. Warming to his theme, the author continued: '[t]he great and plain danger of committing to judges, by their mere will, to say such is the law, without any exposition of why it is the law [is] a principle never advanced save in times when power endeavoured to prop up tyranny and by corrupting the bench to extinguish our liberty.' *Cf.* Brady CB in *In re Larkin* (1841) 4 Ir LR 46, at pp. 70–1: '[i]f that inconvenience shall prove a serious evil, it is open to the legislature ... to provide a fitting remedy'.

103 The legislation which was ultimately enacted in 1848 contains no provision dealing with the issue.

104 Above, notes 43 and 44.

The benefits were great and obvious – security against illegality in the execution of a severe criminal code, and uniformity in the administration of the law. But some evils resulted. The judge on circuit, feeling the comfort of this relief from individual responsibility, was perhaps too ready to encourage or even suggest a doubt where none ought to have arisen, at least, none which he was not fully competent to annihilate by his own single authority. From this hesitation some want of confidence in the law would be felt by the bystanders and the public; the delay of passing sentence diminished its effect as a lesson and example.

The judge on circuit might also be induced, by the laudable wish to save the public time, to reserve the point when once started without any argument, and thus the case would be disposed of without all public discussion. Or if there was an argument at the assizes, *that* would go forth to the public as plausible and apparently reasonable, while the answer which satisfied the learned judges in consultation might be known to themselves only. Nor can it be denied or disguised that the sense of responsibility operates in a much less perfect manner among a number of functionaries assembled in secret conclave than on the minds of those who, after hearing an argument in open court, give their decision also in public. If the result is conviction, still a doubt may hang over the grounds and principles on which it rests; if it is acquittal, that doubt is unavoidable, the law is left uncertain, and the legislature is at a loss to know whether it ought to be amended, of, if amended, in what direction and in what particulars.[105]

Much the same analysis of the reserved case procedure (which is redolent of that presented by the minority in the Irish 'registry' dispute) had been made by Sir Fitzroy Kelly,[106] when he presented 'a bill to provide an appeal in criminal cases'[107] to the house of commons in 1844.[108] Furthermore the need for some reform appears to have been accepted by most of the judges who

---

105 'The court of all the judges', reproduced in Arnould, *Memoir of Lord Denman*, ii, pp. 442, 444. Lord Denman repeated many of these points in *Select committee evidence 1847–48*, p. 43.

106 Then MP for Cambridge, later attorney general and lord chief baron of the court of exchequer.

107 H.C. 1844 (367) i, 13. For a general discussion of the movement for reform, see e.g. R. Pattenden, *English criminal appeals 1844–1994: appeals against conviction and sentence in England and Wales* (Oxford, 1996), ch. 1, and L. Radzinowicz and R. Hood, *A history of English criminal law* (London, 1986), v, 758.

108 *Hansard's Parl. Deb., 3rd ser.*, vol. lxxv, col. 11 (30 May 1844). Kelly contended that the reserved case procedure was 'highly objectionable' because the case was decided 'privately' and not in open court, no reasons were given, and the prisoner had no right to counsel; in his view, the proceedings were altogether too informal.

gave evidence to the house of lords in 1848.[109] But there was a sharp difference of view on the question whether (English) judges could be trusted to reserve points in appropriate cases. According to Kelly, judges often refused to reserve good points, and there was considerable variation in judicial practice: '[o]ne judge would peremptorily refuse to reserve the same objection which another judge would reserve'.[110] The judges denied this: 'I consider the judges never do practically refuse to reserve a point that really deserves consideration; ... the error is, if at all the other way, in reserving questions ... in which their advice was hardly required.'[111] With the noteworthy exception of Lord Denman,[112] the judges stated that reservation should continue to be at the judge's discretion: 'I think it would be productive of great inconvenience if it were left to the uncontrolled will of the prisoner's counsel whether the point should be reserved or not, because in all cases where the punishment would be serious, they would necessarily insist upon the point being reserved, to take the chance of the result of an argument, and thus at all events delay the punishment justly due'.[113]

In due course, the government – and parliament – accepted the judges' analysis. The 'Act for the further amendment of the administration of the criminal law', enacted in August 1848,[114] for the first time gave *statutory* authority for the practice of reserving 'any difficult question of law which

---

109 *Select committee evidence 1847–48*, passim. No Irish judge gave evidence to this committee; but since the 1848 act applied to Ireland they were presumably consulted in some way and agreed that the act should so apply. Clause 7 of the original bill stated that the act was not to apply to Ireland or Scotland: see H.C. 1847–48 (585) ii, 223, but s. 7 of the act states only that it does not apply to Scotland.

110 *Hansard's Parl. Deb., 3rd ser.*, vol. lxxv, cols. 15–18 (30 May 1844). Kelly later stated: 'I have myself, within my own experience, known some ... fearful instances of injustice in the refusal by judges ... to reserve points which have afterwards been determined to be fatal to the conviction which has taken place that I think the people of this country are entitled to demand that an appeal should be a matter of right': *Select committee evidence 1847–48*, p. 32.

111 *Select committee evidence 1847–48*, p. 6 (Parke B). In 1853 James Napier, attorney general for Ireland, stated that 'he had for a great many years had a considerable practical acquaintance with the administration of criminal justice, and he never knew an instance in which, ultimately, any point that counsel thought to be favourable to his client was not reserved by the judges': *Hansard's Parl. Deb., 3rd ser.*, vol. cxxvii, col. 986 (1 June 1853).

112 'Supposing the judge has made a mistake, it is against all principle to leave it in his breast to have it revised or not': *Select committee evidence 1847–48*, p. 45. Alderson B could see 'theoretical objections' to having reservation at the discretion of the judge, but he could see no practical alternative: ibid., p. 10.

113 Ibid., p. 6 (Parke B). It was to take the case of Adolf Beck to convince the authorities that 'sometimes judges ... are a little jealous of their decision being made the subject of inquiry, and it has sometimes happened that a judge has refused to reserve a point': *Hansard's Parl. Deb., 4th ser.*, (lords), vol. cxlv, cols. 1297–98 (9 May 1905) (Lord Halsbury LC).

114 11 & 12 Vict., c. 78.

may arise in criminal trials',[115] and amended the procedure for doing so, both in England and Ireland, in four respects:

(i) Although the act did not, *eo nomine*, establish a court for crown cases reserved, it did provide (in section 3) that reserved cases were now to be heard by the justices of either bench and barons of the exchequer 'or five of them at the least, of whom the lord chief justice of the court of queen's bench, the lord chief justice of the court of common pleas, and the lord chief baron of the court of exchequer, or one of such chiefs at least, shall be part'.[116]

(ii) By the same section, the 'court' was to meet 'in the exchequer chamber or other convenient place', and to deliver its judgments 'in open court, after hearing counsel or the parties, in case the prosecutor or the person convicted shall think it fit that the case shall be argued, in like manner as the judgments of the superior courts of common law at Westminster or Dublin ... are now delivered'.

(iii) The power to reserve a case for the consideration of the new court was extended (by section 1) to courts of quarter sessions.

(iv) The court was (by section 2) given 'full power and authority to hear and finally determine the ... question or questions, and thereupon to reverse, affirm, or amend any judgment which shall have been given ... on the trial whereof such question or questions have arisen, or to avoid such judgment[117] ... or to arrest the judgment, or order judgment to be given thereon at some other [assizes or quarter sessions] ... or to make such other order as justice may require'.[118]

Such changes undoubtedly met some of the criticisms that had been made of the reserved case procedure, but as we shall see, they did not result (in England or in Ireland) in any significant increase in the number of reserved cases. More importantly, the 1848 act, by making 'only minor and largely cosmetic changes in the law',[119] represented a total defeat for those who had

115 In other words, the act did not apply to *civil* cases reserved by judges of assize in Ireland; in practice, however, these were treated after 1848 in the same way as cases which did come within the act.

116 The judges had accepted that having the case heard by all fifteen judges (in England and Wales) was unwieldy and unsatisfactory: see e.g. *Select committee evidence 1847–48*, p. 46 (Lord Denman): 'I think the court of the 15 judges ... is too numerous ... There is a great scattering of the sense of responsibility, and some want of decorum.' But the formula adopted in the 1848 act left the way open for a 15– (or in Ireland, a 12–) judge court in exceptional cases.

117 In which case the court could (for the first time) 'order an entry to be made on the record, that in the judgment of the [court] the party convicted ought not to have been convicted'.

118 Such powers could only be exercised if there had been a conviction. This meant that the court could not consider a question raised on a demurrer (*R. v. Faderman* (1850) 4 Cox CC 359 (Eng.)) or (possibly) a motion to quash an indictment (*R. v. Freeman* (1875) IR 9 CL 527; *R. v. Pierce* (1887) 16 Cox CC 213 (Eng.) (issue raised but not decided in either case). Nor did s. 2 empower the new court, when quashing a conviction, to order a new trial.

119 Bentley, *English criminal justice*, p. 287.

pressed for more radical reform. Calls for an appeal on questions of fact had begun in 1836 (if not earlier),[120] and the principal aim of the bill introduced by Sir Fitzroy Kelly in 1844 had been to provide a person convicted of a felony or misdemeanour at assizes or quarter sessions with the same right of appeal on a question of fact as was available to the unsuccessful party in civil proceedings – and which was in effect also available to a prisoner fortunate enough to be tried for a misdemeanour in the court of queen's bench.[121] By clause 1 of the bill, any of the common law courts was empowered 'upon motion to be made by appeal for or on behalf of such defendant ... to order that the verdict of guilty ... shall be set aside, and that a new trial shall be had, or that a verdict of not guilty shall be entered ... or that the judgment shall be arrested.'[122] Such a provision was necessary because, as a result of 'the fallibility of human judgment', many innocent persons were being wrongfully convicted, and (in spite of the prerogative of mercy) frequently had no effective means of challenging the conviction.[123]

Kelly's bill failed to obtain the support of the government and was withdrawn,[124] but the thinking that lay behind it received powerful support from the reasoning which led the criminal law commissioners in 1845 to conclude that 'the law of England is at present very defective as regards the means afforded for the correction or errors in criminal proceedings':

> A new trial in civil proceedings is now allowed on the plain and simple ground that the practice is essential to justice, for the purpose of

---

120 Pattenden, *English criminal appeals*, p. 3.

121 In roughly one-sixth of the cases in which the prisoner had moved for a new trial, a 'wrong conclusion in point of fact' had led to the verdict being set aside: *A return of the number ... [of] informations and indictments for misdemeanors preferred in the court of queen's bench ... since January 1824*, H.C. 1844 (408) xxxviii, 681. *Cf.* Parke B pointed out that 'generally speaking, indictments for misdemeanours are for matters [such as conspiracy and perjury] which involve more doubtful questions of law [and much greater complication of fact] than indictments for felony and there is [therefore] more occasion for motions for new trials in charges of this description': *Select committee evidence 1847–48*, p. 7.

122 H.C. 1844 (367) i, 13.

123 The prerogative of mercy was too dependent on the trial judge's opinion and the home secretary had no proper means of evaluating new evidence, with the result that 'however merciful a judge might be, or however desirous to do justice he might be, such a system was one that was calculated in some cases to permit the escape of the guilty whilst it allowed the innocent to suffer punishment': *Hansard's Parl. Deb.*, 3rd ser., vol. lxxv, col. 19 (30 May 1844) (Kelly).

124 The home secretary stated that, if pushed to a vote, the government would oppose the bill on the grounds that they had had insufficient time to consider 'a principle of the greatest importance in our law'; if the bill was withdrawn, however, 'the government would give the subject their utmost attention with a view to bringing forward their own bill in the next session': Kelly thereupon agreed to withdraw his bill: *Hansard's Parl. Deb.*, 3rd ser., vol. lxxvi, col. 1337 (24 July 1844).

correcting errors and miscarriages in its administration, which cannot be excluded ... These, however, are not peculiar to civil proceedings; some of them are even more likely to occur in criminal ... proceedings. Questions of civil right are for the most part dependent on facts, the effect rather than the existence of which is disputed. Criminal questions, on the contrary, frequently depend on transactions of a hidden and secret nature, the truth of which it is oftentimes difficult to unravel, and in consequence resort must often be had to a chain of presumptive or circumstantial evidence ... As regards the consequences of error in the one case and the other, it cannot be denied that a failure of justice in a criminal case ... is of much more serious importance than in a civil case ... These positions and their consequences are too obvious to be dwelt upon; yet, admitting them to be true, the conclusion must necessarily be that the precautions necessary to exclude error in the one case are, *a fortiori*, necessary in the other.[125]

The issue was once more put before parliament in February 1848 – and rejected.[126] Both government and the judiciary were wholly opposed to the idea, on grounds of both practice and principle.[127] In practice, appeals on questions of fact were not necessary because, criminal trials being more straightforward than civil trials, few innocent prisoners were convicted and those that were invariably received a free pardon; under the proposed reform all prisoners would appeal, however hopeless the case, causing unnecessary delay and expense and opening the door to fraud and perjury.[128] A right of appeal could not be restricted to prisoners, but would also have to be granted to prosecutors, thus undermining the principle of the finality of an acquittal. In principle also, allowing appeals would necessarily result in delays which would

---

125 *Criminal law comm'rs eighth report 1845*, p. 20.

126 A bill to establish a power of appeal in criminal cases, H.C. 1847–48 (128) i, 193, sponsored by Mr Ewart. On 29 March, Ewart gave way to the (limited) government bill which had been introduced in the house of lords by Lord Campbell CJ: see *Hansard's Parl. Deb., 3rd ser.*, vol. xcvi, col. 1300 (24 Feb. 1848) and vol. xcvii, col. 1101 (24 March 1848).

127 The government appears to have accepted – and largely agreed with – the views expressed by the leading judges in evidence to the house of lords, especially the hostile opinions expressed by Parke B, Alderson B and Lord Denman CJ, see *Select committee evidence 1847–48*. But notable reformers such as Lord Brougham and Lord Lyndhurst were also opposed to this particular reform.

128 The government and the judges insisted that there was no practical way to distinguish between frivolous and real appeals. *Cf.* Kelly suggested a rule *nisi* procedure and giving the trial judge a discretion in order to frustrate 'a frivolous attempt ... to delay the sentence of the law': *Hansard's Parl. Deb., 3rd ser.*, vol. lxxv, cols. 21 and 28 (30 May 1844).

129 A good summary of this debate is given in Radzinowicz and Hood, *History of English criminal law*, p. 758.

undermine the salutory effect of prompt conviction: 'the speedy punishment of guilt renders the law more effectual for the repression of crime'.

This summary does not do justice to the richness of the first round of a debate which was to last in England for a further sixty years.[129] We should not, however, leave this section without noting that the opposing views on criminal appeals reflect contrasting concepts of the criminal trial. To the judges, the criminal trial was a simple, straightforward business, seldom giving rise to difficult questions either of law or of fact; judges and juries could be trusted to see that the right verdict was reached, and the strength of the system derived from the speed and certainty of punishment.[130] The reformers had an altogether different view. They saw a criminal trial as a much more protracted and 'deliberate' inquiry, possibly involving a 'public' prosecutor and a prisoner legally represented at public expense.[131] Such a trial – and a 'proper' right of appeal – might well involve additional delay and expense, but 'the expenditure of labour and cost in criminal investigations can scarcely be placed in competition with the evils which must inevitably result from want of due caution.'[132]

The judges' view prevailed for some sixty years: indeed such conceptual disagreements, albeit at a more refined level, may still be seen today.

THE KIRWAN CASE[133] AND ITS AFTERMATH

The debates preceding the enactment of the 1848 act appear to have benefited from little or no Irish contribution,[134] but it was not long before

130 A typical judicial view is that expressed by Parke B: 'I consider that there are very few cases indeed of criminal charges in which the task either of the judge or the jury is difficult': *Select committee evidence 1847–48*, p. 6.

131 The case for a public prosecutor was put in *Criminal law comm'rs eighth report 1845*, p. 24 and by Sir Fitzroy Kelly in *Select committee evidence 1847–48*, p. 30. C.S. Greaves (p. 18) was in favour of the cost of defence counsel being met from public funds, as was John Pitt Taylor (p. 39). Parke B (rightly) foresaw (p. 4) that if a prisoner was permitted to appeal 'at public cost', it would soon follow that prisoners must also have the means afforded them by the public of preparing their defence.

132 *Criminal law comm'rs eighth report 1845*, p. 12.

133 The case attracted a great deal of literature, both immediately after the trial and since; the most important references are J.S. Armstrong, *Report of the trial of William Burke Kirwan for the murder of Maria Louisa Kirwan, his wife* (Dublin, 1853); J.K. Boswell, *Defence of William Burke Kirwan* (Dublin, 1853); Anon, *The Kirwan case, illustrating the danger of conviction on circumstantial evidence and the necessity of granting new trials in criminal cases* (Dublin, 1853); T.G. Geoghegan, *An examination of the medical facts in the case of The Queen v. W.B. Kirwan* (Dublin, 1853); R.S. Lambert, *When justice faltered: a study of nine peculiar murder trials* (London, 1935), ch. vii; M.McD. Bodkin, *Famous Irish trials* (Dublin, 1918), p. 106.

134 But as we shall see shortly, when the issue did arise in Ireland in the 1850s and 1860s, the

Irish legal interest in criminal appeals was stimulated by one of the most famous criminal trials of the century. On 6 September 1852 William Burke Kirwan and his wife Maria went over to Ireland's Eye island from Howth. They spent the day on the island – and (crucially, as it turned out) were alone on the island from 4.00 p.m. onwards. When the boatman came to collect them at 8.00 p.m., William was ready and waiting, but Maria had disappeared. After a search, the boatman found her body on a rock in an inlet known locally as the Long Hole. In spite of local gossip that Maria's death was not accidental, no post mortem was held. But at the inquest on the following day, the jury, after hearing evidence from various witnesses, including William, returned a verdict of accidental death. Maria's body was buried on 11 September.

That might have been that had allegations that William had in fact murdered Maria not begun to be made almost immediately after the inquest. It transpired that several witnesses in Howth claimed to have heard screams from the island; suspicious marks had been observed on Maria's body; the Kirwans had been on bad terms with each other; William was discovered to have had a relationship with another woman, Teresa Kenny, who had borne him eight children in twelve years, and so on. The case attracted wide public interest, and the allegations became such that the police were obliged to conduct further inquiries – and to exhume Maria's body. On 7 October William Kirwan was arrested and charged with Maria's murder.

The case came on for trial at Dublin commission court before Crampton J and Greene B on 8 December 1852. The prosecution case, that William had held his wife under the water until she drowned, consisted entirely of circumstantial evidence, and relied heavily on medical evidence relating to the condition of Maria's body. The defence, that Maria, while bathing, had had a fit which caused her to drown, was led by Isaac Butt QC, and it seems generally agreed that this was not one of his more outstanding performances.[135] The jury retired at 7.00 p.m. on the second day of the trial, and just

reformers used all the same arguments as those adduced in England in the previous decade. *Cf.* in a debate in the house of lords in 1845, Lord Campbell, anticipating a later controversy, argued that if extra judges were needed in England, they could be brought over from Ireland, where 'consolidation' of the circuits from six to five would leave 'two spare judges': *Hansard's Parl. Deb., 3rd ser.*, vol. lxxxii, col. 66 (7 July 1845).

135 For example, the defence failed to point out discrepancies between evidence given at the inquest and evidence given by the same witnesses at the trial, and they did not apparently investigate Maria's medical history, despite knowing of suggestions that she suffered from epilepsy. Lambert, *When justice faltered*, p. xii, is damning: '[w]as there ever a case in which a man's defenders, eminent counsel briefed by respectable solicitors, more nearly abdicated from their functions and all but conspired with the prosecution to hang their client, than that of Kirwan?' Butt had been elected MP for Youghal in July 1852, and shortly afterwards 'transferred his residence to England': D. Thornley, *Isaac Butt and home rule* (London, 1964), p. 19.

over four hours later returned with a verdict of guilty.[136] When Kirwan was
brought up for sentencing the following morning, Butt requested Crampton
J to reserve three questions for the consideration of the court for crown cases
reserved, but he refused to do so.[137] Kirwan was then sentenced to be hanged
on 18 January 1853.

It is at this stage that our interest in the case really begins, for Kirwan's
conviction was followed by intense speculation as to whether there might
have been a miscarriage of justice. The case excited great interest in the
English press;[138] the foreman of the coroner's jury, appreciating what Butt
had overlooked, wrote immediately to the lord lieutenant pointing out discrepancies between the evidence presented to the coroner's jury and that
given to the trial jury. A Dublin solicitor, J. Bright Boswell, was employed by
'those who believed in Kirwan's innocence' to make the inquiries within ten
days 'which his legal defenders should have made before the trial took
place';[139] this evidence, too, was presented to the lord lieutenant. This was
enough to persuade the lord lieutenant to follow the usual course of consulting
Crampton J as trial judge. On 24 December 1852, Crampton J replied:

> I was not at the time dissatisfied with the verdict, nor was my learned
> colleague; nor should I have been dissatisfied with the verdict had it
> been the other way. The question was a fair jury question and entirely
> for a jury. But I own after reading the documents which came in your
> enclosure and *numerous* letters which I have had from medical and non-
> medical persons ... that my satisfaction with the verdict is not as strong

136   The jury did in fact return to court at 11.00 p.m., to say that they were unlikely to agree;
        they also asked if one of the medical witnesses had testified that the appearance of Maria's
        body was consistent with simple drowning, and were told that he had said this. Some
        observers naturally thought that this suggested that the jury were inclining towards
        acquittal. The verdict twenty minutes later therefore took them by surprise.
137   Two of these related to the admissibility of evidence, the third to the judge's refusal to
        allow a defence medical witness to answer a question put by the defence. Crampton J said
        that he had carefully considered these points with Greene B and they were 'clearly of
        opinion against the prisoner': Anon, *The Kirwan case*, p. 5.
138   Thus, 'An Observer' commented to *The Times* on 16 December 1853: '[i]f the evidence
        you report is all that can be brought forward against the wretched man, indeed I must say
        that I never knew of a man's life being taken on evidence so unsatisfactory or proof so
        inconclusive.' However, 'Irish public opinion, apart from the doctors and a few lawyers,
        remained steadily unsympathetic towards him': Lambert, *When justice faltered*, p. 216.
139   Boswell proved to be 'an energetic and enterprising agent' who 'amassed a formidable
        body of new evidence ... which substantially controverted the evidence on which Kirwan
        was convicted': Lambert, *When justice faltered*, pp. 215–16. This evidence, consisting of
        depositions of defence witnesses *not* called at the trial, the opinions of 'sundry physicians
        and surgeons' and the results of experiments designed to test whether screams on
        Ireland's Eye could actually be heard in Howth, is reproduced in Boswell, *Defence of
        William Burke Kirwan*.

as it was ... Though I therefore will admit that the verdict of the jury *upon the case as it appeared in evidence before them* was fully warranted by that evidence ... yet I cannot but *now entertain a doubt* whether under all the circumstances of this mysterious case full justice has been done to the wretched Prisoner ...[140]

Crampton J concluded by suggesting an 'extension' of the royal prerogative of mercy and recommending commutation to transportation for life.

That did not end matters, for after Christmas the lord lieutenant again wrote to Crampton J, apparently asking whether this was a case in which a free pardon might be warranted. On 31 December, Crampton J replied in the negative:

> ... the effect of the several statements and suggestions contained in *the papers laid before me* by his Excellency's order is not to demonstrate that the verdict was erroneous, but merely to shew the possibility that had they been submitted to the jury the result might have been different. It is difficult indeed to speculate upon that point ... If on the one hand the consideration of the matters put forward since the trial might have raised presumptions favourable to the Prisoner, on the other hand it is to be remembered that it would have been for the jury to determine how far they could credit the witnesses brought forward or what weight they could attach to their testimony if believed. We cannot now say what might have been the effect of a cross-examination of those witnesses or how far their statements might have been encountered [sic] by contrary evidence ...[141]

The learned judge stressed that his earlier recommendation for commutation was *not* based on doubts about the original verdict, but on doubts about the effect that the new evidence *might* have had on the jury: '[w]hether by mistake or otherwise, the prisoner has lost whatever benefit or chance he

140 NAI, Convict Reference File 1853 K 1 (emphasis added). I am most grateful to the late Dr Phil Connolly for having drawn this file to my attention.

141 Ibid. (emphasis added). 'Yet the foreman of the jury has stated unreservedly that if any one of the many facts mentioned to him [since the trial] had been submitted in evidence to the jury, he would not have quitted the box without pronouncing a verdict of acquittal': Anon, *The Kirwan case*, p. 10.

142 James Napier, attorney general for Ireland, admitted that he had doubts about commuting Kirwan's sentence; but 'one of the English Judges, after having examined the whole case, agreed in the propriety of [Crampton J's] recommendation': *Hansard's Parl. Deb., 3rd ser.*, vol. cxxvii, col. 989 (1 June 1853). Napier also reported that he had obtained evidence as to the height of the tide on the day of Maria's death: see S. Haughton, 'On the true height of the tide at Ireland's Eye on the evening of 6th September 1852' in *Proc RIA*, 7 (1857–61), 511.

might have derived from the new matters upon which he now relies.'[142] That same day, Kirwan's sentence was formally commuted to one of transportation for life.[143] Subsequent efforts to obtain a free pardon were unsuccessful.[144]

The Kirwan case inevitably provoked the comment that, had there been a court of criminal appeal able to review the evidence, Kirwan 'would almost certainly have gone free'.[145] No doubt it was in this spirit that Isaac Butt proceeded on 25 February 1853 to introduce in the house of commons the New Trials (Criminal Cases) Bill, which applied only to Ireland.[146] The purpose of this bill, as stated in the preamble, was to enable 'persons who may be erroneously found guilty of any criminal offence [to] have an opportunity of appealing against such finding in cases where such error does not appear on the record of the proceedings'. Like Kelly in 1844 and Ewart in 1848 – though in somewhat different terms – Butt proposed to give a prisoner an 'absolute' right of appeal (i.e. without having to ask for the consent of the trial judge, the attorney general or anyone else), and to give the appeal court the same power to set aside a criminal verdict and to order a new trial as it had in civil proceedings.[147] The arguments in favour of this reform were much the same as before, but Butt made particular reference to the 'unsatisfactory' outcome of the Kirwan case. Either Kirwan was guilty

143 Kirwan was apparently sent to Bermuda, where he spent nine years building naval fortifications; however, he was then returned to Ireland to serve the rest of his sentence. He was still in prison in 1876 (see *Hansard's Parl. Deb., 3rd ser.,* vol. ccxxxi, col. 424 (3 Aug. 1876)), but he was released in 1879 (when he would have been about 62), on condition that he left the United Kingdom and never returned: *Freeman's Journal,* 3 Feb. 1879.

144 The Boswell group gathered further evidence and held a public meeting in London on 12 January 1853. But there was also a strong anti-Kirwan feeling, reflected in press allegations that Kirwan had committed other offences; no evidence was adduced to substantiate these allegations, 'but ugly suspicion hung over his head, and refused to be banished': see J.K. Boswell, *Exposure of an attempt to impute the murder of Messrs Crowe and Bowyer to William Bourke Kirwan* (Dublin, 1853) and Lambert, *When justice faltered,* pp. 222–4.

145 Ibid., p. 224. It was, of course, also suggested that the same result would have been achieved if Kirwan had been able to give evidence in his own defence.

146 H.C. 1852–53 (164) v, 215 and *Hansard's Parl. Deb., 3rd ser.,* vol. cxxvii, col. 964 (1 June 1853). The bill did not extend to England because Butt was 'not sufficiently conversant with English law to be confident that the machinery he proposed would be practicable in England', whereas he felt that 'it would be easy of application in Ireland'. The bill was, however, seconded by Ewart. Viscount Palmerston (home secretary) argued (at col. 979) that if the measure was right in principle, 'it ought certainly to apply to the whole of the United Kingdom'.

147 Ibid., col. 969. Clauses 1 and 5 would enable a prisoner to apply to one of the common law courts or to a special commission appointed by the lord chancellor to set aside the verdict and order a new trial 'in the same manner as any person … found guilty … for a misdemeanor may now … apply …'. *Cf.* by clause 7 an appeal on the ground that the verdict was against the weight of the evidence required the trial judge's certificate. The bill was not to 'alter or affect' the writ of error or the trial judge's right to reserve a question of law under the 1848 act (clause 32).

(and should have been executed) or he was not (and should have been released), and he contended: '[w]ould it not have been infinitely better to have submitted all the facts which created the doubt to the ordeal of a second investigation in public …?'[148]

The bill was opposed by the government on much the same grounds as the earlier bills. Apart from the interesting observation that the bill would give 'the greatest encouragement to the lowest class of practitioners',[149] the government's response included an assertion which was to be repeated for the remainder of the century: '[i]f the judge and jury knew that their verdict was only a preliminary ceremony and that their sentence, whether right or wrong, would be subjected to a subsequent examination, why it would make, if not the judge, at least the jury far more indifferent than they at present are to the case before them, and would lead to great laxity of practice in the administration in the first instance of criminal justice in this country'.[150] Three arguments against the bill which were specific to Ireland were put by James Napier, attorney general for Ireland. First – and inevitably – 'all the judges in Ireland to whom he had spoken on the subject, were unfavourable to a second trial in criminal cases'.[151] Secondly, the bill would be 'singularly inapplicable' to Ireland, because 'there the attorney general acted as public prosecutor, and sifted the evidence in every criminal case, and the only object he had was to obtain truth and justice, and not make the crown, as it were, a litigant party acting against the accused.' As for the Kirwan case, '[i]f this bill had been law, Kirwan might have had another trial, and what the result of it might have been he would not pretend to say … [I]f a mistake was made [in commuting the death sentence], it was on the side of mercy … [But] he considered there was no case for the bill'.[152] In the face of such opposition,

148 Ibid., col. 975 (1 June 1853).
149 Ibid., col. 978 (J.G. Phillimore).
150 Ibid., col. 981 (Viscount Palmerston). In his view, 'the present state of the law does afford to an innocent man every possible security which human institutions can afford for freedom from unjust punishment.'
151 Ibid., cols. 986–7. Cf. the pointed retort of Mr McMahon (MP for Wexford) (at col. 989): '[j]udges … were fond of irresponsible authority, and if their authority had been always regarded as decisive, men could now be hanged for stealing to the value of 13*d*., pleadings would still be in Latin and not one of the great reforms in the law would ever have taken place.' But Napier explained (at col. 986) that: '[i]t had always been considered that a second trial would be attended with many circumstances unfavourable to the prisoner, owing to the chances there would be of a defectiveness of evidence, and also owing to the prejudice likely to arise from the certificate that was to be given by the judge who had presided at the former trial as to his being satisfied or not with the evidence adduced on that trial.' In his view, a free pardon from the lord lieutenant was preferable to 'the peril of a second trial'.
152 Ibid., col. 988. Earlier in his speech (col. 987) Napier had said that 'he had, in all his experience, never heard of more than one verdict which he believed wrong … and it was remedied the very next day'.

Butt had little alternative but to withdraw the bill, but he reserved the right to pursue the matter further.[153]

In 1854 another Irish trial resulted in a verdict 'almost universally regarded by professional men as contrary to the weight of evidence',[154] and led to a renewed call for reform by way of 'a legislative scheme ... common to both kingdoms'.[155] Revision of the substantive criminal law, however, occupied most of the time of would-be reformers during the 1850s,[156] and there was no immediate support for radical reform of the system of criminal appeals.[157] But in 1858 another Irish lawyer (Mr P. McMahon, MP for Wexford), with Butt's support, introduced another New Trial in Criminal Cases Bill.[158] This met the same fate as the 1853 bill – as indeed did at least seven other bills introduced or supported by Butt and McMahon (and by Ewart and Kelly) over the next decade or so.[159]

153 Palmerston had suggested that the question could be considered by the committee appointed in March 1853 to revise the criminal law statutes and to produce a 'Code Victoria' – see *Hansard's Parl. Deb., 3rd ser.*, vol. cxxv, col. 294 (17 March 1853).

154 Editorial in *Ir Jur*, 7 (1854), 25, referring to *R. v. Jebb*, another case tried at Dublin commission court, which did not, however, attract great public interest.

155 Ibid., p. 26. The editor was rather wary of the dangers of 'abstract' justice, but he thought it 'inconsistent' to allow new trials in some criminal cases and not in others and he was in favour of empowering a 'competent court of criminal appeal' to review the evidence on which any conviction was founded, in proceedings 'where the merits of the case would be the principal element involved'.

156 The committee appointed in 1853 (above, note 153) was superseded by a 'statute law commission' appointed in 1854 to consolidate the criminal law statutes; it was their work which led to the great consolidation acts of the early 1860s: see especially *Hansard's Parl. Deb., 3rd ser.*, vol. cliv, cols. 483 (Whiteside) and 497 (Sir Fitzroy Kelly) (30 June 1859).

157 In 1856, C.S. Greaves, in his *Report to the lord chancellor on criminal procedure*, p. 49, H.C. 1856 (456) l, 128, recommended only that the court for crown cases reserved should be given power to order a new trial.

158 H.C.1857–58 (137) iii, 587; *Hansard's Parl. Deb., 3rd ser.*, vol. cli, col. 1051 (7 July 1858). The bill, supported by Sir Fitzroy Kelly (now attorney general) in principle but not in its details (see col. 1062), was accepted by the house of commons on second reading, but no further action was taken.

159 See Appeal in Criminal Cases Bill 1859, H.C.1859 (51, sess. 1, not delivered) i, 21; Appeal in Criminal Cases Bill 1859, H.C. 1859 (15, sess. 2) i, 17; Appeal in Criminal Cases Bill 1860, H.C. 1860 (1) i, 211; New Trials in Criminal Cases Bill 1861, H.C. 1861 (61) iii, 613; Appeal in Criminal Cases Amendment Bill 1864, H.C. 1864 (14) i, 39; New Trials in Criminal Cases Bill 1869, H.C. 1869 (1) i, 211, and New Trials in Criminal Cases Bill 1872, H.C. 1872 (94) iii, 467. The debate on the 1860 bill produced a lengthy rebuttal of the case for reform by the home secretary, Sir George Lewis (*Hansard's Parl. Deb., 3rd ser.*, vol. clvi, col. 408 (1 Feb. 1860)), who added a new argument against allowing new trials in Ireland: 'I ask any hon. Gentleman who is aware of the necessity of protecting witnesses before the trial, of removing them to a colony or some other place of safety after the trial, and of the difficulty altogether which there is in administering a system of trial by jury for a particular class of offences in Ireland ... what would be the effect of the changes which [this bill would] introduce?'

The 1848 act had little effect on the number of 'reserved' criminal cases. During the 1860s, assize judges reserved on average no more than two cases each year, and it was rare for a chairman of quarter sessions to do so. By the late 1880s, the court for crown cases reserved in Ireland was dealing with not more than one criminal case annually. Most of these cases concerned fairly routine issues of criminal law, evidence or procedure, but on at least four occasions the court made a noteworthy contribution to common law jurisprudence. In *R. v. Johnston*[160] and *R. v. Gillis*[161] the court dealt at length with the admissibility of confessions by accused persons, and thereby firmly established the 'voluntariness' test in Irish law.[162] In *R. v. Fanning*,[163] the court, by a majority of 7–4, held that a person was *not* guilty of bigamy under section 57 of the Offences against the Person Act 1861 if the second 'marriage' was otherwise invalid; on this issue, however, it was the dissenting judges who took what is now regarded as the better view.[164] The question in *R. v. Dee*[165] was whether a man, who had obtained a married woman's consent to sexual intercourse by impersonating her husband, was guilty of rape. This was a question which had long perplexed the English courts and, in what may be regarded as their finest hour, the court affirmed the conviction of the prisoner. In so doing the Irish judges declared their independence:

> The decisions of the Court for Crown Cases Reserved in England are most valuable to us as authorities. We pay them (as we are bound to do) the highest respect, and give them the most careful consideration. Were they in reference to the question in controversy uniform and

---

160 (1864) 15 ICLR 60. See J.D. Jackson, 'In defence of a voluntariness doctrine for confessions: *The Queen v. Johnston* revisited' in *Ir Jur*, xxi (1986), 208, who concludes (at p. 215) that '*Johnston* ... finally settled Irish law along the lines adopted in England that the true test of exclusion was whether a confession had been obtained by a threat or promises held out or excited by a person in authority', and notes (at p. 222) that '*Johnston* still continues to form the basis for the admission of confessions in Irish law'.

161 (1866) 17 ICLR 69.

162 Another interesting evidence case is *R. v. Burke* (1858) 8 Cox CC 44, where the court applied the 'collateral issue' rule to deny the crown's right to call a witness to prove that a defence witness, who had given evidence in Irish, could speak English. Less defensible is the court's decision in *R. v. Cavendish* (1874) IR 8 CL 178 to ignore the 'golden thread' of the common law and hold (by a majority of 6–1) that a prisoner charged with manslaughter had the burden of disproving that he had been negligent.

163 (1866) 17 ICLR 289.

164 The decision in *Fanning* was disapproved in *R. v. Allen* (1872) LR 1 CCR 367, where the English court (consisting of 16 judges) unanimously agreed with the minority in *Fanning* that the second marriage did not have to be valid, provided it was a form of marriage recognised by the law. *Allen* was followed in *R. v. Wright* (1894) 28 ILTR 131, and is still law: see *Halsbury's Laws online* (Criminal law, evidence and procedure – offences against the government and public – bigamy – para. 352.)

165 (1884) 14 LR Ir 468.

consistent, we should be slow to depart from them in a proceeding like the present, in which the question is raised in a form in which the decision will not be capable of being brought to the Court of ultimate Appeal. Nevertheless, they do not bind us in law, nor where they are, as here, varying and inconsistent, can they relieve us from the responsibility of deciding according to our own views of the law.[166]

The court was vindicated when parliament, the following year, enacted the Criminal Law Amendment Act, section 4 of which confirmed the view taken in *Dee*.[167]

Finally, reference should, perhaps, be made to *R. v. Hehir*,[168] where the court tackled the thorny question of the liability for larceny of a person who acquires property by mistake and later decides to appropriate it. In *R. v. Ashwell*[169] the English court had been equally divided on the issue, with the result that the prisoner's conviction was affirmed. While observing that it was desirable that the law should be the same in the two jurisdictions, Madden J once more took the view that 'it is still more important that the criminal law in Ireland should be administered in accordance with the judgment of this court, ... [which] was not absolved ... from the duty of forming an independent judgment upon the question'.[170] On this occasion also, albeit by the narrowest of margins (5–4), the Irish court took what may be regarded as the better decision and quashed the prisoner's conviction.

THE FINAL CHAPTER

In view of the failure by Butt and other Irish lawyers to achieve any degree of reform during the 1850s and 1860s, it may at first seem somewhat ironic that the first court of criminal appeal with power to hear appeals on questions of fact as well as law was created in Ireland in 1882, at a time when parliament was once again rejecting proposals for reform in England and Wales. The murder of Lord Frederick Cavendish and T.H. Burke by 'the

---

166 Ibid., p. 479, *per* Palles CB. See to the same effect May CJ (p. 478) and O'Brien J (p. 492), who distinguished criminal cases from civil cases on the grounds that the 'Court of Criminal Appeal' is 'the final tribunal in each country for cases reserved, and ... therefore each has a right to act independently of the other.' In *R. v. Middleton* (1873) LR 2 CCR 38, at p. 70, however, Bovill CJ stated that a 'divergence of opinion' between the two jurisdictions was 'undesirable'.
167 48 & 49 Vict, c. 69, s. 4 (1885).
168 [1895] 2 IR 709.
169 (1885) 16 QBD 190.
170 [1895] 2 IR 709, at p. 715. See also Gibson J at pp. 722–3: 'the weight of authority is not adverse, and we are free to decide in accordance with principle and reason, looking at the reality of things.'

Invincibles' in May 1882 was quickly followed by the Prevention of Crime (Ireland) Bill which, in spite of vehement opposition from Irish nationalist MPs, became law on 12 July 1882.[171] The preamble to the act recited that 'by reason of the action of secret societies and combinations for illegal purposes in Ireland the operation of the ordinary law has become insufficient for the repression and prevention of crime'. There followed a number of special provisions relating to criminal procedure, police powers and new criminal offences. In particular, section 1 created a special commission court for the trial, by three judges sitting without a jury,[172] of certain 'scheduled' offences 'whenever it appears to the Lord Lieutenant that ... a just and impartial trial cannot be had according to the ordinary course of law'. Section 2(1) then provided:

> Any person convicted by a Special Commission Court ... may, subject to the provisions of this Act, appeal either against the conviction and sentence of the court, or against the sentence alone, to the Court of Criminal Appeal hereinafter mentioned, on any ground, whether of law or of fact; and the Court of Criminal Appeal shall ... have power after hearing the appeal to confirm the conviction and sentence, or to enter an acquittal, or to vary the conviction or sentence ...[173]

This court was to consist of an uneven number, 'not less than five', of the judges of the supreme court,[174] selected according to a rota 'to be determined by [a ballot] held at the prescribed time and in the prescribed manner', but a judge who had sat in the special commission court 'shall not sit in the Court of Criminal Appeal on any appeal against a conviction or sentence ... to which he was a party'.[175]

171 45 & 46 Vict, c. 25. See in general F.S.L. Lyons, *Ireland since the Famine* (rev. ed., London, 1973), p. 176 and C. Townshend, *Political violence in Ireland: government and resistance since 1848* (Oxford, 1983), pp. 166–80. For our purposes, the most important debate is that in committee: see especially *Hansard's Parl. Deb., 3rd ser.*, vol. cclxx, cols. 197 (5 June 1882) and 237 (6 June 1882). For a (limited) legal commentary on the act, see H. Humphreys, *The Prevention of Crime (Ireland) Act 1882* (Dublin, 1882).

172 The act made special provision for change of venue and the use of special juries in an attempt to avoid resort to the special commission court. *Cf.* the Irish judges had agreed unanimously to a resolution that enactment of s. 1 would injure the administration of the law in Ireland and impair the respect entertained for the bench: *Hansard's Parl. Deb., 3rd ser.*, vol. cclxix, col. 1107 (19 May 1882). According to Cherry LJ, writing in 1911, Fitzgerald B informed the government that if this part of the bill became law, he would resign; it did – and he did: see *ILT & SJ*, 45 (1911), 282.

173 But note that the court had no power to order a new trial, on the grounds that a new trial would be impracticable (too few judges) and unnecessary (given trial by three judges and a rehearing before at least five judges): *Hansard's Parl. Deb., 3rd ser.*, vol. cclxx, col. 199 (5 June 1882).

174 With the exception of the lord chancellor and the judicial commissioner of the Irish land commission: ss. 3, 27(11) and 35.

175 Ss. 26(1) and 3(1) respectively.

The appeal, which had normally to be heard within fourteen days 'after the day on which the appellant was sentenced', was to be heard in open court in the presence of the appellant, who might appear by counsel or solicitor.[176] Section 1(3) had stipulated that the evidence given on a trial in the special commission court 'and the reasons, if any, given by the judges in delivering judgment' would be taken down by a shorthand writer; an appellant was entitled to a copy of the shorthand writer's notes, free of charge.[177] When the appeal came on for hearing, the court of criminal appeal 'may re-hear the case by the reading of the evidence as contained in the short-hand writer's notes, and may permit to be called or call any new witness, and recall any witness who gave evidence at the trial, and may either examine such witness or let him be examined and cross-examined by or on behalf of the appellant and the prosecutor.'[178] The appeal would then be determined by 'a majority of the judges who heard the appeal'.[179]

The government's reason for providing such an 'unusual' appeal from conviction or sentence by a special commission court was one that has a familiar ring: '[t]he Government felt that that was a desirable thing to do, because the [special commission court] was a new and extraordinary [tribunal], and because they thought it ought to be fenced round with reasonable provisions of this character.'[180] In other words, the extended right of appeal was an additional 'security' to offset the loss of trial by jury. No reference was made to the wider debates that had been taking place in parliament in connection with the proposed criminal code (which made provision for an 'ordinary' court of criminal appeal). This acceptance of a basic principle which had been officially rejected since 1844 seems to have been restricted to trial by judge alone; in the case of 'ordinary' crimes tried by judge and jury, it did not come to be accepted in England and Wales for another 25 years.

The 1882 act, however, proved to be an academic exercise; no cases were referred to the special commission court,[181] with the result that the court of criminal appeal never sat.

---

176 Sched. 1, rules (5) and (6).

177 Ibid., rule (10).

178 Ibid., rule (7).

179 S. 3(3). This was the provision which gave rise to the greatest dispute during the committee stage of the bill: see e.g. *Hansard's Parl. Deb., 3rd ser.*, vol. cclxx, col. 237 (6 June 1882). The Irish nationalist MPs argued long and hard that an appeal should be allowed unless the court of criminal appeal was unanimous in rejecting it; unanimity was required in the special commission court; most appeals would turn on questions of fact, where the established principle, in the case of juries, was unanimity; lack of judicial unanimity would mean that there was a reasonable doubt as to the prisoner's guilt, and no decision from which two judges dissented would command the respect or confidence of the public. But Sir William Harcourt, the home secretary, rejected all efforts to amend the 'majority' provision.

180 Ibid., col. 295 (Sir William Harcourt).

181 See e.g. Townshend, *Political violence in Ireland*, p. 179. The crown appear to have relied instead on other 'special' provisions, such as s. 4, which authorised the attorney general

In terms of the more general debate, it still appeared during the 1880s and 1890s to be agreed policy that any reform of the 'ordinary' machinery for reviewing convictions on indictment should apply equally to the two jurisdictions.[182] Nevertheless, when a court of criminal appeal was finally created in 1907, the legislation applied only to England, and it was not until after 1920 that similar provision was made in what had by then become the two jurisdictions in Ireland. It appears that the explanation for this development lies in the equally tortured history of legislative attempts to make a prisoner a competent witness in his or her own defence. By the 1880s, it had come to be generally accepted that the right to give evidence could be beneficial to prisoners, and as a result, parliament appeared ready by 1883 to enact legislation to this effect – and, as a matter of principle, in both England and Ireland. The government had, however, failed to take into account the opposition of the Irish nationalist members to this proposal. As Dr Jackson has explained,[183] their opposition was based on legal objections and political considerations. From a legal point of view, the administration of criminal justice in Ireland differed from that in England: '[t]he basis of the Nationalist [legal] argument for the exclusion of Ireland was that owing to political and agrarian conditions there the administration of justice was not impartial and inspired little public confidence ... [H]owever desirable it might be as an abstract principle to admit the accused to give evidence in his own defence,[184] to do so in Ireland could only heighten the sense of injustice felt.'[185] But 'of much greater importance' was the

to order trial by special jury: see e.g. *R. v. Poole* (1883) 15 Cox CC 368 and *Nally v. R.* (1884) 15 Cox CC 638.

182   E.g. the Court of Criminal Appeal Bill introduced by the government in 1883 applied to Ireland, with the exception of cases coming within the Prevention of Crime (Ire.) Act 1882: H.C. 1883 (9) ii, 211 (clause 29).

183   C. Jackson, 'Irish political opposition to the passage of criminal evidence reform at Westminster, 1883–1898' in J.F. McEldowney and P. O'Higgins (eds), *The common law tradition* (Dublin, 1990), pp. 185–201.

184   There was considerable legal opposition in Ireland, as in England, to the 'abstract principle' on the grounds that giving a prisoner the right to testify undermined the presumption of innocence and offered the prisoner 'a most illusory choice': see 'Prisoners as witnesses' in *ILT & SJ*, 31 (1897), 198 and 328.

185   Jackson, 'Irish political opposition', p. 186, who later (p. 197) states that the Conservatives 'consistently repudiated' such allegations and insisted, as a matter of principle, that the law in the two jurisdictions should be the same. But at least two leading Liberal lawyers – Sir Charles Russell (later Lord Russell LCJ) and Sir Henry James (attorney general, 1873–74 and 1880–85) – 'recognise[d] some merit in the Nationalist contention', given 'the tendency of prosecutors in Ireland to be more anxious than prosecutors in England to secure convictions'. But they also suggested that the 'hostility' of the nationalist MPs would mislead Irish prisoners into regarding reform not as beneficent, but as imposing 'a tyrannical inquisitorial power'. When experience in England confirmed the beneficial effect of the reform, 'a desire for its extension to Ireland would no doubt soon arise in that country': see *Hansard's Parl. Deb., 3rd ser.*, vol. cccxxiv, col. 71 (22 March 1888) and *Hansard's Parl. Deb., 4th ser.*, vol. iv, col. 305 (6 May 1892).

nationalists' use of attempts to reform the law of criminal evidence to further their political objective of home rule by obstructionist tactics in the house of commons. So effective were these tactics that after 1892 'no serious move was made by either the Liberal or Conservative administrations to extend the reform to Ireland,'[186] with the result that the Criminal Evidence Act 1898 reformed only the law in England and Wales.

One plank in the nationalists' *legal* opposition to criminal evidence reform was the lack of a proper court of criminal appeal in Ireland. During the debates on the Prevention of Crime (Ireland) Bill 1882, Joseph Biggar referred to 'a principle of great importance, and one which, sooner or later must become a common principle of English jurisprudence – namely, the right of appeal in criminal cases'.[187] The following year, nationalist MPs supported the latest Court of Criminal Appeal Bill,[188] and in 1888, T.M. Healy proposed, as an amendment to the Criminal Evidence Bill, 'that it is inexpedient to make any further change in the Criminal Law until a Court of Appeal in criminal cases is established'.[189] Ten years later (and in the very year that the Criminal Evidence Act was passed), Healy was one of the sponsors of yet another Court of Criminal Appeal Bill.[190] The nationalists, therefore, do not seem to have been opposed to *this* reform, but, having got their way in relation to the criminal evidence proposals, they did not actively campaign for the creation of a court of criminal appeal in Ireland.[191]

Be that as it may, until 1904 or thereabouts most of the subsequent attempts to create a court of criminal appeal extended to Ireland.[192] Support

---

186 Jackson, 'Irish political opposition', p. 195. As Jackson goes on to explain (p. 198), the decision by the government, in the face of unionist objections (from Carson in particular), to exclude Ireland from the Criminal Evidence Act 1898 exposed 'a fundamental divergence of opinion about the basic tenets of Unionism'.

187 *Hansard's Parl. Deb., 3rd ser.,* vol. cclxx, col. 296 (6 June 1882).

188 See e.g. *Hansard's Parl. Deb., 3rd ser.,* vol. cclxxvii, col. 1208 (2 April 1883): 'if [the bill] were passed, even in its present shape, it would do more towards introducing justice and equity into the trial of criminal cases in Ireland than any Bill, with the single exception of Lord O'Hagan's Act, which had ever been passed for Ireland since its connection with the British Crown' (Mr O'Donnell). Parnell also welcomed the bill, but was disposed to suggest 'that persons convicted of offences in Ireland should be permitted to appeal to the English Court of Appeal and not be compelled to go before the Irish Judges': ibid., col. 1244.

189 *Hansard's Parl. Deb., 3rd ser.,* vol. cccxxiv, col. 76 (22 March 1888). Healy's amendment was defeated by 173–119.

190 H.C. 1898 (3) i, 413. The bill was similar to that introduced in 1883 and (by clause 23) extended to Ireland. Healy had also spoken in favour of yet another bill in 1895: '[e]very lawyer knew it was most desirable that something should be done in the direction contemplated by this bill, not only in the interests of justice, but of the masses of the people': *Hansard's Parl. Deb., 4th ser.,* vol. xxxii, col. 876 (4 April 1895).

191 Healy and other nationalist MPs did introduce a Criminal Appeals (Ire.) Bill in 1889: see H.C. 1889 (375) i, 493, but their primary objective appears to have been to provide more extensive rights of appeal from magistrates' courts: see *Hansard's Parl. Deb., 3rd ser.,* vol. cccxxxix, col. 1145 (13 Aug. 1889). The bill did not proceed beyond a first reading.

192 See e.g. Criminal Cases Appeals Bill 1890, clause 22, H.C. 1890 (83) i, 535, and Court of

for reform was, indeed, forthcoming from other quarters,[193] although it is somewhat muted. It therefore comes as something of a surprise to find that, from 1904, the principal[194] reform bills no longer extend to Ireland – and that section 19 of the Criminal Appeal Act 1907 expressly so provides. The debates on the 1907 Act reveal no explanation for this development.[195] Four years later, however, Serjeant Moriarty suggested that Redmond was convinced that if the 1907 act applied to Ireland, 'the Act of 1898 ... would have to be extended to Ireland likewise'.[196] Given the nationalists' strong opposition to the Criminal Evidence Act for the reasons given above, this may well be the true explanation for what happened in 1907. Although the issue was not allowed to disappear after 1907,[197] there appears to have been no serious attempt to reform the appellate system in Ireland before 1920. In fact, the court for crown cases reserved sat very infrequently during the period 1900–20,[198] and this also may have contributed to the lack of interest in reform.

The partition of the island in 1920, however, required that the matter be given further consideration. By section 43(1) of the Government of Ireland Act 1920, '[a]ll questions which under the Crown Cases Act 1848 would be reserved for the decision of the Judges of the High Court shall be reserved for the decision of the High Court of Appeal for Ireland, whose decision shall, except as hereinafter provided, be final'. Although rules for hearing reserved cases were made, it does not appear that the high court of appeal

Criminal Appeal Bill 1895, clause 30, H.C. 1895 (53 – sess. 1) i, 493. *Cf.* the Criminal Appeals Bill 1888, H.C. 1888 (377) ii, 391, which did *not* extend to Ireland.

193 See e.g. G.D. Clancy, 'A criminal equity court' in *New Ir Rev*, 3 (1895), 99; Letter from 'Jurist' in *ILT & SJ*, xxix (1895), 241 and 266; Editorial in *ILT & SJ*, xxvi (1892), 579. A letter from 'X' in *ILT & SJ*, xxviii (1894), 607 made the novel suggestion that the judges themselves could introduce a power to order a new trial in criminal cases 'by merely framing a general rule to that effect'. The main impetus for these proposals appears to have come, not from Ireland, but by way of reaction to the *Maybrick* case, which had given rise to considerable controversy in England.

194 *Cf.* a bill introduced in 1905 with the limited objective of amending the 1848 act did extend to Ireland: see Crown Cases Act Amendment Bill, clause 8, H.C. 1905 (261) i, 387.

195 Clause 23 of the 1907 bill (H.C. 1907 (61) i, 557), which provided that it did not extend to Ireland (or Scotland), was agreed in committee without discussion. *Cf.* in 1906, an article in the *Irish Daily Independent* in favour of extending the criminal appeal bill to Ireland, principally as a remedy for the 'glaring inequality' in sentencing in Ireland, was republished in *ILT & SJ*, xl (1906), 141. A letter from 'BL' also argued for a court of criminal appeal on the more general ground of the need to avoid miscarriages of justice: ibid., p. 166.

196 *ILT & SJ*, xlv (1911), 282.

197 Although a review of A.C.F. Boulton, *Criminal appeals* (London, 1908) in *ILT & SJ*, xlii (1908), 125 suggested that the most defendants 'perhaps have no reason to be dissatisfied with the difference between the two countries', the *Journal* managed in most years to find some method of referring to the issue: see e.g. *ILT & SJ*, xlv (1911), 65.

198 In 1929, Hanna J observed simply that '[t]his Court seldom sat': *The statute law of the Irish Free State* (Dublin, 1929), p. 18.

ever dealt with any criminal cases; the further constitutional arrangements entered into in 1922 led to its abolition less than a year after its first sitting. Thereupon, there seems to have been something of a hiatus in the Irish Free State until the establishment of a court of criminal appeal under the Courts of Justice Act 1924. After the legal and political controversies of the previous eighty years or so, this was a very low key affair; a court with power to hear appeals on questions of law and of fact was finally introduced with little or no debate. As Jackson has noted with respect to the Criminal Justice (Evidence) Act of the same year,[199] there is a nice irony that the formal assent to the bill setting up the court of criminal appeal was given by none other that T.M. Healy, now governor-general of the Irish Free State.

The enactment of the Courts of Justice Act 1924 did not, however, bring the Irish court for crown cases reserved to an end. For some unexplained reason,[200] it survived for another six years in Northern Ireland. When the high court of appeal was abolished, its jurisdiction to hear reserved criminal cases was in Northern Ireland transferred to the court of appeal,[201] and from 1922 until 1930 the three judges of that court continued to act as the court for crown cases reserved in Northern Ireland.[202] However, controversy over the conviction of James Strannix in 1928[203] finally prompted the government of Northern Ireland to make a formal request for 'imperial' legislation, and this was forthcoming in the form of the Criminal Appeal (Northern Ireland) Act 1930.[204] With the establishment of the court of criminal appeal for Northern Ireland on 1 April 1931,[205] the last vestiges of the court for crown cases reserved in Ireland finally disappeared.

199 Jackson, 'Irish political opposition', p. 201.
200 In 1930 Lord Carson reported that 'the home secretary [of Northern Ireland] ... has found on various occasions that it would have conduced ... to the interests of justice if there had been a Court of Criminal Appeal': *Hansard's Parl. Deb., 5th ser., (lords)*, vol. lxxviii, col. 263 (3 July 1930).
201 Irish Free State (Consequential Provisions) Act 1922, s. 6.
202 See e.g. *R. v. McQuillan* [1923] 2 IR 93; *R. v. Nuttall* (1924) 58 ILTR 3.
203 Strannix was convicted of robbery and sentenced to three years' penal servitude. He was released under the royal prerogative after having served some three months of the sentence, but he was not granted a free pardon and there was 'no question' of compensation: *NI Hansard (commons)*, vol. 10, col. 1704 (11 April 1929). The attorney general observed that 'the sooner a Court of Criminal Appeal is set up in this Province the better for the administration of justice and for the confidence of the public that that administration is not only fair and pure, but that it is absolutely above suspicion': ibid., col. 1747.
204 'We are assured that all parties in the Parliament of Northern Ireland desire this Bill and it has been drafted in consultation with the authorities there and with the Chief Justice of Northern Ireland': *Hansard's Parl. Deb., 5th ser., (lords)*, vol. lxxviii, col. 261 (3 July 1930) (Lord Sankey LC). As Lord Sankey and Lord Carson both pointed out, Northern Ireland was the last jurisdiction in the United Kingdom (and the last jurisdiction in these islands) to obtain such a court, similar legislation having been enacted for Scotland in 1926.
205 By s. 19(1), the act applied to 'all persons convicted on indictment ... after 31 March 1931'.

Irish crime without the outrage: the statistics of criminal justice in the later nineteenth century

MARK FINNANE[*]

SINCE THIS ARTICLE WAS FIRST drafted in the early 1990s there has been a significant increase in scholarly interest in the history of crime and criminal justice in Ireland between the eighteenth and twentieth centuries. Much of it tends to confirm the views taken in this short overview of some themes in what one might characterise as the secular rather than sectarian history of modern Ireland. At the same time, the significant demands made by the disturbed condition of Ireland under the Union on the organisation of policing, courts and prisons, remain a crucial dimension of this history and continue to spawn rich fare. Peter Hart's *The IRA and its enemies*[1] is an outstanding work on the way in which violence impacted on both community and state; while Sean McConville's enormous treatment of the challenge posed to prisons administration by political prisoners, in *Irish political prisoners: theatres of war*,[2] speaks to the recent as well as the distant past.

But interest in what was happening in Ireland outside the public arena of contest between nationalist and unionist has accelerated in recent historiography. The most expansive examination so far of the social history of crime and its prosecution for the period covered in this article is by Carolyn Conley in *Melancholy accidents: the meaning of violence in post-Famine Ireland*.[3] To complement McConville's treatment of political prisoners it is necessary also to consider the regimes in place for common convicts, a topic examined by Patrick Carroll-Burke in *Colonial discipline: the making of the Irish convict system*.[4] A recent collection of essays edited by Ian O'Donnell and Finbarr McAuley, *Criminal justice history: themes and controversies* includes a number dealing with the nineteenth century.[5] The history of the Irish constabulary still awaits its major historian, though it has been the subject of a number of

---

[*] [Editor's note: this paper was submitted to the Society in the 1990s for inclusion in a volume, planned but not completed, on the theme of criminal justice in Ireland in the nineteenth century. The author has written a foreword noting significant scholarly contributions published since the paper was first submitted.]

1 Oxford, 1998.　　　　2 London, 2003.　　　　3 Lanham, MD, 1999.
4 Dublin, 2000.　　　　5 Dublin, 2003.

theses, monographs and occasional articles, for example, Brian Griffin's *The Bulkies: police and crime in Belfast, 1800–1865*,[6] and the anticipated social history of Irish policing by Elizabeth Malcolm, whose recent work includes 'Investigating the "machinery of murder": Irish detectives and agrarian outrages, 1847–70'.[7]

I have developed some of the themes in this paper, particularly relating to the statistics of crime, in work that is now published.[8] Sean Connolly has more recently explored some issues in the comparative statistics of violent death in an article in his edited volume, *Kingdoms united?*[9] A further important contribution to the treatment of nineteenth-century crime statistics, dealing with England but relevant to the Irish official data is Howard Taylor's 'Rationing crime: the political economy of criminal statistics since the 1850s'.[10]

In the perennial debate over the proper foundations of Irish historiography, the history of crime and policing has generally been approached from only one direction. The dominance of the national question has constrained the possibilities of exploring some of those aspects of Irish social and economic history which place it more on a par with its neighbours in the British Isles or elsewhere in the European or north Atlantic world. In brief my argument is that in spite of the frequent political and social turmoil of Ireland in the nineteenth century, there is much evidence of Ireland's 'normality' as a society in the post-Famine period. This is especially the case, I argue, with respect to the criminal law and criminal justice system, in spite of some important differences from conditions prevailing in England. This paper pursues such an argument not to its exhaustive conclusion but through at least some of the territory which would need to be explored in order to satisfy the case. I examine first some of the themes which have preoccupied the few commentators on this aspect of Irish history. Second, I outline some of the fundamental features of the criminal justice institutions in Ireland. Third, the chapter examines some statistical data about the incidence of crime and forms of its punishment in the later nineteenth and early twentieth centuries. Finally I draw attention to some of the sources which would repay detailed study in the future.

Let me start conventionally by justifying the claim that there has been little attention paid to the history of crime and policing. The glaring

---

6   Dublin, 1997.   7   In *New Hibernia Review*, 6:3 (2002), 73–91.

8   M. Finnane, 'A decline of violence in Ireland? Crime, policing and social relations' in *Crime, History and Societies*, 1:1 (1997), 57–70.

9   S. Connolly, 'Unnatural death in four nations: contrasts and comparisons' in idem (ed.), *Kingdoms united? Great Britain and Ireland since 1500: integration and diversity* (Dublin, 1998), pp. 200–14.

10 In *Econ Hist Rev*, 51 (1998), 569–90.

exception to this claim is the recent attention to the history of agrarian unrest in its various phases from the eighteenth century. This history has now been approached from a number of angles: in a 1985 article surveying the various contributions, David Fitzpatrick has identified the strengths and weaknesses of many of these contributions.[11] The major addition to the literature since then, Stanley Palmer's *Police and protest in England and Ireland*, remarkably exhaustive as it is, affirms the bias in this area of study towards seeing the history of crime and policing in Ireland as one which lies largely within the boundaries of the social and political conflict centred on the land and national questions. It is true that there is some indication in Palmer's book of an interest in the non-political dimensions of crime, but this receives, perhaps justifiably for the period he is concerned with, limited attention.[12]

Fitzpatrick's work itself has touched on the broader areas of the social history of crime. In his study of Co. Clare in the independence period, he attended to the incidence of ordinary crime as an indicator of some of the social (especially class) tensions in the pre-war era. In a characteristically revisionist essay on 'class, family and rural unrest' in 1982, he sought to contextualise 'agrarian crime' in the changing social relations of rural Ireland between the Famine and partition. It is a pity that others do not appear to have accepted the challenge to develop the insights into violence and conflict which were offered there, through micro-historical studies of particular localities.

Some other recent writing has taken regard of the historical significance of crime and its policing in the social history of nineteenth-century Ireland. Reviewing the state of Ireland in 1870 for the relevant volume of the *New history of Ireland*, W.E. Vaughan has considered the importance of the part played by the Royal Irish Constabulary (RIC) in the government of Ireland. The same theme is taken up in a paper by Richard Hawkins in a collection of articles on 'policing the empire'.[13] More directly related to the concerns of this paper, Vaughan goes on to draw some comparisons between the incidence of crime in Ireland and that in Great Britain. On an international scale of crimes of violence, Ireland, suggests Vaughan, was relatively peaceful. It is a point which has also been persuasively put by Sean Connolly in reviewing Palmer's work and critiquing his statistical inference about comparative homicide rates.[14]

11 D. Fitzpatrick, 'Unrest in rural Ireland' in *IESH*, xii (1985), 98–105.

12 S.H. Palmer, *Police and protest in England and Ireland, 1780–1850* (Cambridge, 1988).

13 W.E. Vaughan (ed.), *A new history of Ireland, vol. v: Ireland under the Union, 1801–70* (Oxford, 1989), pp. 765–73; R. Hawkins, 'The "Irish model" and the empire: a case for reassessment' in D.M. Anderson and D. Killingray (eds), *Policing the empire: government authority and control, 1830–1940* (Manchester, 1991), and W.J. Lowe and E.L. Malcolm, 'The domestication of the Royal Irish Constabulary, 1836–1922' in *IEHS*, 19 (1992), 27–48.

14 S.J. Connolly, review of Palmer, *Police and protest*, in *IHS*, xxvi (1989), 307–9.

Other social histories have occasionally taken note of the incidence of policing to help chart the dimensions of some particular aspect of Irish society in the nineteenth century. Hence Maria Luddy has drawn on the policing of prostitution in the context of exploring the history of female philanthropy in Ireland, while Colm Kerrigan has drawn tentatively on statistics of crime in the 1840s in an endeavour to assess the social impact of Fr Mathew's temperance movement.[15] As Elizabeth Malcolm suggests in her history of temperance in Ireland, police statistics in the nineteenth century were often part of the very substance of debate over desirable social and political objectives, hence the generation of such remarkable Irish statistical series as the annual police return of arrests for drunkenness made on Sundays in various cities of Ireland, a series which runs from the late 1870s into the twentieth century.[16] These various contributions, however, have been undertaken in something of a historical void. In spite of the richness of the Irish criminal statistics, particularly valuable for charting regional differences, there has been no systematic treatment of the broad outlines of the operations of the criminal justice system in the nineteenth century. It is my limited objective here to provide a basic outline of the structure of that system in the later nineteenth century and then to describe statistically its social reach and the disposition of persons who came within its view.

CRIME WITHOUT THE OUTRAGE

My title alludes to the most familiar treatment of crime in nineteenth-century Ireland, that is, as part of the struggle over land and resources in rural Ireland. Such a theme deserves the attention of historians, but it has a particular historiographic context – one which is concerned with charting the momentous changes of Irish economy and polity leading to the eventual demise of the Union. Seen from such a perspective, the modes of policing, prosecution and punishment are essentially of secondary concern. Only one study dealing with this theme, I think it is fair to say, addresses it with substantial attention to the framework of policy and practice in response to the phenomenon of agrarian crime and political rebellion, that is, Charles Townshend's study of political violence in Ireland, with its theme of government and resistance to it.[17] Others take up the issue with more interest

15 M. Luddy, *Women and philanthropy in nineteenth-century Ireland* (Cambridge, 1995); C. Kerrigan, 'The social impact of the Irish temperance movement, 1839–45' in *IESH*, xiv (1987), 20–38.

16 E. Malcolm, *Ireland sober, Ireland free! Drink and temperance in nineteenth-century Ireland* (Dublin, 1987); *Return of number of arrests for drunkenness in police districts of Dublin, Cork, Limerick, Waterford and Belfast, on Sundays*, H.C. annually between 1877–9 and 1900.

17 C. Townshend, *Political violence in Ireland: government and resistance since 1848* (Oxford,

in how it might be used to explicate some thesis about the nature of Irish society and economy. The history of government in Ireland itself of course encourages such attention to the phenomenon of agrarian crime. The frequency of legislative or administrative states of emergency in nineteenth-century Ireland was accompanied by a flood of statistical documentation of the incidence of disorder, hence the availability of much-used police returns of agrarian outrages in the various counties of Ireland from the early decades of the century. The need to treat such data with the usual caution was persuasively put by none other than the chief secretary for Ireland, A.J. Balfour, in 1887. Prior to the 1880s, noted Balfour, the agrarian crime returns provided by the police had been liberally constructed with respect to the categorisation of an incident as an outrage. After that period, however, there had been a gradual tightening of the definition of an agrarian outrage, so that by the 1880s inclusion was limited to what Balfour claimed was quite a narrow band of offences.

Nevertheless, I want to put aside here the issue of the meaning of the agrarian outrage returns. My starting point instead is the need to right the balance in studies of Irish crime and criminal justice. Agrarian crime does not need justification in the canon of historical concerns: its political significance is undoubted, whatever the debates we might want to engage in explaining its incidence and patterns. Beyond the sphere of 'agrarian outrage', it is true, the category of 'outrage' became by the end of the nineteenth century coterminous with the legal concept of 'indictable offences'. Nevertheless, it is the focus on agrarian outrage which has tended to preoccupy historians of Irish criminality in the nineteenth century. The result is a loss of perspective on the ordinariness of much Irish offending, a failure to recognise the degree to which Irish society, at least in certain regions for prolonged periods, was not endemically or abnormally violent.[18]

My proposition is a simple one: taking the volume of arrests, prosecutions and punishments in Ireland, agrarian unrest, even at its height, was never of major significance in the working of the criminal justice system. At its height, it is true, in the early 1880s for example, the influx of prisoners associated with the land war was considerably disruptive to the prison system. But the disruption was short-lived and had no serious impact on the functioning of the system in the longer term. On this basis then I want now to look at the framework of criminal justice which was the origin of the criminal and judicial statistics examined later.

1983), pp. 150–2, dealing specifically with violent crime which was 'agrarian'; but see also K.T. Hoppen, *Elections, politics and society in Ireland, 1832–1885* (Oxford, 1984), especially part v, 'Violence and its modes', and D. Fitzpatrick, *Politics and Irish life, 1913–1921* (Dublin, 1977), for accounts which extend from a consideration of political and agrarian violence to the broader social and administrative dimensions of the response to it.

18 Fitzpatrick, 'Unrest in rural Ireland', p.100.

THE FRAMEWORK OF CRIMINAL JUSTICE

The framework of criminal justice in modern Ireland was a nineteenth-century creation. By 1900, its essential institutions were the police, courts, public prosecution system, and prison. Only the court system was recognisably in place a century before, and even that was subject to major change during the nineteenth century. For the rest, the systems of police, public prosecution and punishment through imprisonment were substantially organised through the innovations of nineteenth-century government. These institutions owed only a part of their rationale and inspiration to the specific context of Irish society and law. Their establishment was contingent on changes in the form of government in Europe and north America during this period. Specific circumstances in Ireland however, affected their form and impact. The dimensions of the Irish criminal justice system can be identified in relief by comparing them with those of Britain during this period.

To take police first, the fundamental feature of Irish policing was its centralisation. Conventionally, appeal is made to the paramilitary character of Irish policing, but many of the functions of the Irish police required no resort to arms. By the eve of the First World War the carrying of arms by most police was an infrequent occurrence,[19] and the everyday duties of most police were, as elsewhere, mundane and non-violent. Centralisation and bureaucratisation were the *sine qua non* of Irish policing. This was of course in some contrast to the situation in England and Wales where police were only compulsory in the counties and boroughs after 1856, and where centralisation of policing has taken a century and more since then. Centralisation of policing may have more than mere administrative historical interest. Nineteenth-century statisticians, commenting on English crime, emphasised the difficulty of comparing regions because of differences in organisation and policies between various police forces. Their caution has been echoed in more recent historical comment.[20] A corollary is the possibility that regional variations in crime and prosecution rates in Ireland owe less to police personnel and policies than in England; that is, the policing factor, so important in the estimation of crime rates, is perhaps more constant than in states where police forces are organised on a local basis. However, such an implication about the significance of centralisation needs to be treated with caution. There is behind it an assumption that policies and priorities determined at Dublin Castle were unerringly implemented throughout the

19 See *Report of the committee of inquiry into the Royal Irish Constabulary and Dublin Metropolitan Police*, H.C. 1914 [Cd. 7421] xliv, 247, especially the reservation to report by M.F. Headlam, at pp. 281–3.
20 V.A.C. Gatrell and T.B. Hadden, 'Criminal statistics and their interpretation' in E.A. Wrigley (ed.), *Nineteenth century society: essays in the use of quantitative methods for the study of social data* (Cambridge, 1972).

land, an assumption that historians would regard sceptically. A better approach is to consider the possibility that policing arrangements determined at the centre were inevitably refracted through a prism of local differences.

The system of public prosecution has been the subject of some historical study through the work of John McEldowney.[21] Unlike England where prosecution of crime was still very much the business of private persons and agents, Ireland had moved during the nineteenth century to the use of public law officers for most indictable offences. This innovation has its context in some of the difficulties faced by private prosecutors in a society where communitarian norms and antagonisms were so strong as to impede the willingness of private persons to prosecute. The system of public prosecution, however, cannot be assessed solely in the context of coercion. Its impact on and contribution to the efficient maintenance of criminal justice was the subject of frequent comment by William Neilson Hancock, the political economist and statistician who was responsible for producing the Irish judicial statistics for nearly two decades. Hancock pointed to its advantages by way of reducing costs, through limiting the number of vexatious prosecutions. Further, by subjecting cases to more substantial pre-trial scrutiny, the number of cases likely to fail in the courts was reduced. Both factors bear on the interpretation of criminal arrest and prosecution statistics in any comparative context.

The prison as place of punishment was subject to more debate than any other element of the criminal justice system in the nineteenth century. Although the summary courts handled far and away more cases than ever got near a prison, and the police came into contact with a much greater proportion of the population than ever saw the inside of prison gate, the prison as an object of public debate was undoubtedly the focus of public discourse on law and order in the nineteenth century. Ireland was the location of one of the most important of nineteenth-century prison innovations: the marks system of Captain Walter Crofton, director of convicts in Ireland from the early 1850s. Crofton also prefigured twentieth-century practice in emphasising the need to oversee the course of the prisoner's release into the community: hence the intermediate prison at Lusk, where convicts served their last months before release. Hence also his plans for surveillance of released prisoners, which bore legislative fruit in the Habitual Criminals Act 1869, giving rise to the system of police surveillance of released criminals in the subsequent decades.[22]

21 J.F. McEldowney, 'Crown prosecution in Ireland' in D. Hay and F. Snyder, *Policing and prosecution in Britain, 1750–1850* (Oxford, 1989), and 'Policing and the administration of justice in nineteenth-century Ireland' in C. Emsley and B. Weinberger (eds), *Policing western Europe: politics, professionalism and public order, 1850–1940* (New York, 1991).
22 Habitual Criminals Act 1869, 32 & 33 Vict, c. 99.

The refinement of prison was not, however, limited to these ideas and initiatives of Crofton. Administrative efficiency and the forces of centralisation led to the reorganisation of Irish prisons after the consolidation of the General Prisons Board in 1877. The great number of local prisons was gradually reduced, making possible more control over the conditions of containment and classification. The need for a large number of prison places was in any case gradually being reduced by the changing structure of penalties and arrangements for paying fines. The prison system in 1900 was immensely more varied than it had been a century earlier. With the decline of transportation and capital punishment, the exact calculation of differences in the forms of punishment involved the separation of local, short-term prisoners from convicts serving penal servitude. The gap between ideal and practice was epitomised by Crofton's use of Spike Island, constantly criticised for its poor situation and infrastructure, and eventually closed in 1883.[23] The difference between ordinary and convict prisoners was not the only distinction refined in this era. Important additions to the spectrum of institutions were above all the women's prison at Mountjoy under female supervision and control, and the various reformatories and industrial schools appended to the penal system. A notable Irish dimension in the latter context was the prominent role of church bodies in running such institutions, an extension of the churches' important functions in philanthropy and education.[24]

At the centre of all of these institutional innovations of the nineteenth century were the courts. In the area we are dealing with here, the criminal law and its offshoots, two levels of jurisdiction operated. The assizes, held in various towns and cities before judges on circuit, heard the most serious trials, while the quarter sessions of the various counties dealt with offences of a less serious nature. A proportion of indictable offences, however – an increasing proportion as the century wore on and legislative changes took effect – became triable under summary jurisdiction. Courts of summary jurisdiction also heard the greater part of the police business, the hundreds of thousands of minor charges arising from offences of public order or against towns' statutes and other regulations.

The post-Famine history of all of these institutions, which remains largely to be written, would account for the internal development of each institution. A different task for social history, however, is to account for the interrelations of the different parts of the criminal justice system. In the remainder of this paper, it is proposed to sketch a statistical outline as a starting point for understanding this dimension of post-Famine Ireland.

---

23 *Royal commission on administration, discipline and condition of prisons in Ireland*, H.C. 1884–5
   [C. 4233] xxxviii, 1–44 (see preliminary report, 1883, ibid., p. 9).
24 See Luddy, *Women and philanthropy*.

THE STATISTICAL PICTURE

In their influential account of the nineteenth-century criminal statistics of England and Wales, Gatrell and Hadden avoided the task of documenting the Irish and Scottish judicial statistics.[25] They did so claiming that these series were constructed on quite a different basis to those of England and Wales. In fact, however, the Irish judicial statistics were consciously modelled to conform with the definitions and calculations of the English statistics. This is evident both in offence definition and in the underlying rationale of the tables. Like the English statistics, for example, the early years of the Irish series exclude from the count of indictable crime, offences of larceny involving a value less than five shillings. Similarly in conformity with English developments, the statistics were completely reformulated in 1895, following a report of a parliamentary committee on judicial statistics.[26] One result of this history is the familiar story of discontinuities in series, together with some uncertainty of definition of offences. Most serious appears the disruption to the series in 1895. For the assiduous researcher this may not be as critical as first appears. The scrupulous compiler of the statistics by this stage documented carefully in that year the relations between the new and the old series, with the result that reconstruction of some series is possible. In fact the statistician himself reconstructed some series going back to 1876, in order to develop a basis for estimating change over time. To some degree this paper relies on these reconstructed series. Even more importantly, and rarely for judicial statistics in any country, the statistician provided a schedule of offences and their statutory authority in that year.[27]

Acknowledging that there is a break in continuity, what can we learn from Irish judicial statistics? There are basically three kinds of returns making up the series from 1863. First, for the years from 1863 on, there are institutional returns for prisons, and later reformatories and industrial schools, documenting receptions and the nature of offences leading to committal and providing much social profile data on those incarcerated. Second, there are the police returns which form the basis for the first three decades of the judicial statistics. They make it possible to estimate the incidence of crimes reported, arrests and prosecutions for indictable and summary offences. This information is available for the whole of Ireland by offence, and by county or city for both sexes, though unfortunately county information is not available by offence, a severe limitation for social historians of crime in this period. An

25 Gatrell and Hadden, 'Criminal statistics', p. 427 n. 1.
26 The new format was introduced for England and Wales in 1893, for Ireland in 1895 and for Scotland in 1897. Closer attention was to be given to highlighting change over time and linking the incidence of reported crime and justice process to changes in criminal law.
27 *Judicial Statistics, Ireland, 1895*, pp. 33–5, H.C. 1897 [C. 8617] c, 761.

ancillary set of tables for the period from 1863 to 1895 provides details of the processes at assizes and quarter sessions, though not for summary courts, which were served only by the police returns. Third, after 1895, the tables provide a much greater range of information. In fact two complete series were now returned, one from the courts, another from the police. For both indictable and summary offences it was now possible to describe the processes of the courts as applied to particular offences. The returns provide information on charges and outcomes, including the range of penalties, and reason for failure of prosecutions brought. The police returns were somewhat altered after 1895, but still provide continuity with the earlier period. One advantage over the court returns is that they are more concerned with the social profile of offenders. It is not possible for example to consider sex-based differences in court processes from the judicial tables, but the police returns provide information in many categories by sex, and in some cases by age. The police returns also enable investigation of county differences.

Besides the tables it is also worth remarking on the commentaries which accompanied the annual tables. These are notable for the quality of their analysis in many respects. Like the English reports, they demonstrate a much greater appreciation of the interrelation of statistics and criminal justice processes than was usually evident in public discourse in the nineteenth century. That is, the temptation to reduce the message of the data to crude social, racial or cultural determinates was actively combated in many of these reports. To read William Neilson Hancock's painstaking explorations of the comparative criminal statistics of England and Ireland, or even more specifically, his comparison of Ulster and Scottish criminal data is to become aware of the nineteenth-century foundations of sociological analysis.[28] Note, for example, Hancock's explanation of the sex differentials in sentencing patterns in the early 1870s. In 1872 the summary offences tables showed that 20.7 per cent of women convicted were imprisoned, compared with 7.5 per cent of males so convicted. A typical judgment of the Victorian period, one to which Hancock himself was not altogether averse, would attribute this statistical disparity to the fact that the women brought before the courts were perceived to have a more degraded or immoral character. The appropriate explanation was at once simple and more elusive, since it required appreciation of the nature of charging and penalties and of the social status and condition of the sexes. As Hancock noted, many of the offences appearing in the police returns were charged under the roads, hackney and other regulatory acts, and were, in his view:

28 Hancock's commentary can be found in his introduction to the *Judicial Statistics, Ireland, 1872*, pp. 13–106, H.C. 1873 [C. 851] lxx, 247, 259–488.

... matters of mere discipline which men from their employment are more likely to commit than women, and for which fines are either the only or the suitable punishment. Again ... men are generally better able to pay fines than women, and so more likely to escape imprisonment.[29]

Moreover, reflecting on his own comments in which he had attributed certain features of recidivism and imprisonment patterns for indictable offences to the prostitute and habitual criminal status of many of the women in prison, Hancock warned against rushing to such a judgment in explaining the high rate of imprisonment of women in the summary court process. The figures showed a high rate of fines as penalty in prostitution cases, suggesting again that the foundations of the statistical picture were more complex than any crude reductionism might imply.[30]

As I imply, much might be done to explore the dimensions of Irish crime and prosecution on the basis of reading the statistician's commentaries alone. What follows, however, are some comments on selected aspects of the system of arrest, prosecution and punishment. Partly for reasons of comparability and accessibility, the data selected are from the last decades of the century.[31]

Patterns of prosecution and punishment

The outstanding feature of the criminal justice scene by the end of the century was the declining significance of the prison. This paradox, at a time when there was still so much concern over the problems and possibilities of incarceration, springs from two sources. One was the evident decrease in serious crime in the later nineteenth century, a phenomenon which Ireland shared with England. The other was the changing nature of penalties imposed by the courts. The limited use of imprisonment may be identified through various indicators. Long-term change in the proportion of the population in prison is one; the other is the outcome of charges in the various courts. The data on sentencing outcomes for summary offences are really quite limited before 1895, but around the turn of the century the proportion of those charged who were sentenced to imprisonment is quite stable at around six per cent. The vast majority of cases were punished on conviction with a fine, the outcome of over 93 per cent of convictions by the 1890s. We can calculate that in relation to summary offences by the turn of the century, of more than 200,000 cases being processed each year, about 85 per cent would result in conviction. Of those convicted, less than one per cent by 1900 were benefiting from probation, instituted as an alternative to imprisonment

29 Ibid., p. 287.
30 Ibid.
31 The following discussion draws on the evidence available in the statistical appendices and graphs at the end of this chapter.

of first offenders in 1887. More than 93 per cent were being fined, and just over six per cent imprisoned.

This is not the end of the story, however, in understanding the rate of imprisonment, even for summary offences, for a high proportion of admissions to prison resulted from default in fine payments. In spite of an early enthusiastic claim by the clerk of fines and penalties that there was an increasing rate of payment of fines during the 1850s,[32] the rate of payment after that time was remarkably stable. About two-thirds of the amount of fines was paid from the 1850s to the end of the century. While a large proportion of the convicted thereby avoided gaol, there remained a supplement which through non-payment of fines became vulnerable to incarceration. Hence in spite of a general decline in indictable offences, the contribution of fine default admissions resulting from the processes of courts of summary jurisdiction (including some indictable matters, such as petty larceny, which had become triable in summary jurisdiction) ensured that average daily populations in Irish prisons remained at about the same rate into the 1900s. Historically of course the question raised by such a phenomenon is the relation between offending and poverty, with a stable one-third of the convicted population failing to pay their fines in any year. Only at the end of the century did it become possible through the Fine or Imprisonment (Scotland and Ireland) Act 1899 for fine defaulters to remit a portion of their prison sentence through part payment of fines.[33]

The importance of fine default as a cause of imprisonment cannot be underestimated. To take just one year's figures, in 1907, even in spite of the various remedies available to provide time for payment, two-thirds of male imprisonment and an even higher proportion of female imprisonment resulted from fine default. At a time when many forces were leading towards a reduced emphasis on the use of imprisonment, there continued to be many thousands of people committed to prison each year for their incapacity to pay fines. Undoubtedly many of these were repeat offenders, but the sex differences point to the broader social impact of this phenomenon in other ways. Hancock's recognition of the inequalities of women in the criminal justice system in the early 1870s still applied three decades later.

The sheer volume of summary court business ensured that even a small use in those courts of imprisonment as a penalty would crowd the gaols. But how important was imprisonment as an outcome of trial for indictable offences? By the later nineteenth century up to one-third of cases brought to trial failed to lead to conviction, mostly through acquittal, but a significant number resulting from no bills or from the prosecution offering no evidence. Of the two-thirds convicted, about 70 per cent were imprisoned for periods

---

32 *Letter of Clerk of Fines and Penalties, 26 July 1858*, H.C. 1857–8 (503) xlvii, 501.
33 62 & 63 Vict, c. 11.

of up to two years, another six per cent for penal servitude of three years or more, while most of the remainder were required to enter into a recognisance of one kind or another, including probation. A fine was a very rare outcome for an indictable offence, owing to the prescribed penalties attached to such offences. Predictably then, imprisonment was still the major punishment outcome for indictable offences brought to trial. The total numbers of persons thus committed to prison in any year was of course very much less than those committed by courts of summary jurisdiction or gaoled in default of fine payment, but the longer sentences of offenders imprisoned following trial on indictment made their presence in the prisons of somewhat greater consequence.

The disposition of offenders described here appears consistent for the 1880s, 1890s and 1900s. Comparison of this period with the earlier decades will be necessary in the future to trace any changes in the structure of penalties in the Irish criminal justice system. What is notable, however, is how insignificant appear the effects of the agrarian agitation in the broader spectrum of prosecution and punishment. While more detailed investigation of the periods of greatest agitation might require some qualification of this judgment, it is consistent with what we would predict anyway: the ordinary business of daily life, with its quota of offending, was only briefly disturbed in its social course by the phenomenon of agrarian crime. The patterns traced here, especially the relatively low impact of imprisonment viewed in the wider spectrum of punishment, suggest nevertheless where some of the stresses of agitation were most likely to be felt. It was the prisons which had to make room for the thousand and more extra persons incarcerated during the land war.

But was this the only effect? The difficulty with the analysis pursued so far is that it is global. We know that agrarian agitation was localised, affecting particular counties in different ways.[34] Adequate understanding of the patterns of crime and prosecution needs to move beyond these global patterns of indictable and summary offences and their fate in the courts. We need to know more about what offences were charged, as much as possible about who was charged, and in particular in this context, where they were charged. Not all these questions can be satisfactorily addressed through published sources, but two further levels of analysis are made possible by the judicial statistics. Time series of offences charged can tell us whether or not there were significant changes over time in the incidence, perhaps of offending, certainly of arrest and prosecution. Regional analysis of persons tried can tell us how consistent is the global picture, or how necessary it

---

34 J. Lee, 'Patterns of rural unrest in nineteenth-century Ireland: a preliminary survey' in L. Cullen and F. Furet (eds), *Ireland and France: 17th–20th centuries* (Paris, 1980), pp. 223–37.

might be to undertake studies at a local or county level. Some information is also available on the sex and age of offenders, though not as comprehensively as one would wish. In concluding the paper I want to suggest how analysis at this level might raise questions about the function and role of the criminal justice system in Irish society in the later nineteenth century.

Taking the time series for offences first, it is evident that for most offences there is a gradual decline in rates of arrest and prosecution during the late Victorian period. This is consistent too with the experience of many other jurisdictions at this time.[35] Nevertheless there are differences between offences which bear further inquiry. In spite of the general decline in a major category of indictable offences such as common assault, there was no such trend for larceny offences, indictable in definition but mostly tried summarily owing to the small value of most thefts prosecuted (Graph 1). These continued at much the same level through the 1880s and 1890s, and showed an upwards trend in the early years of the twentieth century.

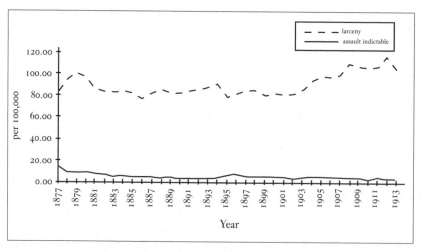

Graph 1: Assault and larceny, Ireland, 1877–1913

Interpersonal offences, as indicated by rates of prosecution for assault at both higher and lower courts, showed a downwards trend, as did those for assaults on the police, an offence sometimes taken by historians as an indication of the legitimacy of the police in society. Yet no such clarity of trend is evident for another category of offence, that of aggravated assault. In the judicial statistics this charge was as defined in section 43 of the Offences against the Person Act 1861, which limited the charge to assaults against females, and

35 See Gatrell and Hadden, 'Criminal statistics'.

boys under 14 years. Unfortunately the series is badly disrupted by the inclusion from 1895–99 of an unspecified number of arrests for assault made by Dublin police under the Dublin Police Act 1842: under this act, the offence does not appear to have been specifically limited to assaults against women and children.[36] For what it may be worth prior to further investigation, the trend for assaults under the category involving women and children was upwards during 1880s and 1890s, against the trend for other categories of assault (Graph 2). One may be tempted to investigate this as a further dimension to the literature on the ill-treatment of women in Ireland in the nineteenth century and later. However, clarification of the exact nature of the offences would be needed: for it is clear that some of the offenders charged under this head are women themselves, presumably involved in offences against children.

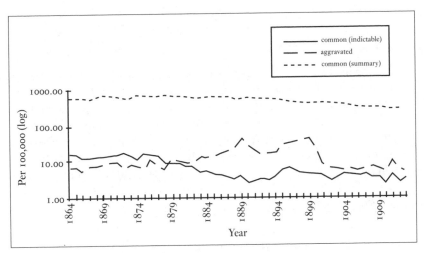

Graph 2: Assault charges, Ireland, 1864–1913

One cannot pass over the evidence relating to the major category of summary offences, that of drunkenness. Although arrests for this may have declined since mid-century, there was little improvement in the last decades of the century. Against the generally declining trend for many offences, the rates of arrests for drunkenness were well sustained through the end of the century and into the twentieth century (Graph 3). Understanding the variations and trends in this offence, however, will demand more sustained investigation at the regional level.

36 5 & 6 Vict, c. 24, s. 28.

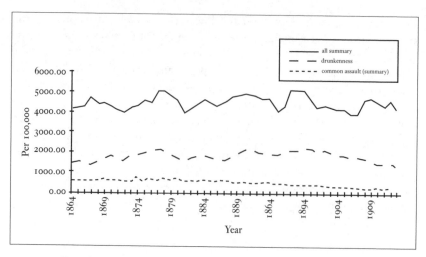

Graph 3: Summary offences charged, Ireland, 1864–1913

By looking at the county and city rates we can see how much is lost by the attention to global statistics. Taking just four court districts it is evident that there was a very large variation in arrest (Table 1). In 1879 the rates of indictable offence arrests of males in Dublin city exceeded those in Belfast, Kerry and Westmeath by factors of five and more: for females the disparity was even greater. Twenty years later, by which time Belfast was a city the size of Dublin, the rates were far more comparable. In 1899 the male arrest rate was the same in both cities, while the female arrest rate in Belfast was more akin to that in Dublin than in the rural counties.

Table 1: Offences charged, by region and sex

	Indictable		Summary	
1899*	*Male*	*Female*	*Male*	*Female*
Dublin	61	27	1,812	716
Belfast	60	17	732	356
Kerry	13	4	934	98
Westmeath	18	4	1,032	165
1879**				
Dublin	84	40	2,895	1,052
Belfast	16	3	1,510	496
Kerry	14	3	996	99
Westmeath	13	2	851	127

Source: *Judicial Statistics, Ireland*
[* Rate per 100,000 of 1901 population. ** Rate per 100,000 of 1881 population]

For summary offences, however, the comparisons are somewhat different. While Dublin exceeded the rates in the other selected areas, the position in Belfast was less stable. Population growth and urban expansion notwithstanding, by 1899 the rate of male summary arrests in Belfast was about half that in Dublin, and less than the rate in Kerry and Westmeath. The female arrest rate in both cities well exceeded that in these rural regions, although again there was a halving of the rate of female arrest in Belfast between 1879 and the end of the century. For specific offences, information on which is not available for summary offences in the counties and cities until after 1895, the data by sex is not available in the returns of police arrests, but the inter-regional differences have their own interest. Hence while in 1899, Dublin again topped the table of summary offence proceedings, rates of arrests there for drunkenness were below those in Kerry and Westmeath. In this sample Westmeath far exceeded the others in arrests for drunkenness, but its rate of arrest for summary assault offences was a quarter of that prevailing in Kerry. In one area, however, the rural counties remained distinct from the cities, namely, arrest for simple larcenies. This was overwhelmingly an urban offence, for which Belfast had a rate approaching that of Dublin.

What can be said of this confusion of statistics about regional differences, short of conceding that a good deal more calculation of the same kind for more years and districts needs to be carried out? The first is that a common source of appeal in explaining arrest rates, namely the ratio of police to population is unlikely to be very satisfactory in this case, at least on my speculation based on the reports of police ratios in the judicial statistics. Similarly, the tendency in the judicial statistics reports to highlight the high rates of offending in the cities of Ireland, to think of crime as primarily an urban phenomenon, is somewhat confounded by the perennial evidence of high rates of arrests for minor offences in some of the rural counties. Accounting for the different demographies of the various regions is likely to be more important. Adjustment for the disparate male/female population in

Table 2: Summary offences, by region and charge, and adjusted by sex ratio

1899	Rate			Adjusted		
	Drunk	*Assault*	*Larceny*	*Drunk*	*Assault*	*Larceny*
Dublin	2,296	691	152	2,457	739	163
Belfast	1,667	483	143	1,947	561	166
Kerry	2,308	645	48	2,223	621	46
Westmeath	2,965	229	61	2,611	202	54

Source: *Judicial Statistics, Ireland*
[Note: first three columns are rate per 100,000 population; the fourth to sixth columns are adjusted by the factor of the male : female ratio in each region at the 1901 census (Dublin = 0.93; Belfast = 0.86; Kerry = 1.04; Westmeath = 1.14)]

each of these four regions for example removes some of the difference in rates of arrest for assault in Dublin, Belfast and Kerry (Table 2). A similar effect is likely to obtain in the case of another county, Kildare, with a great excess of males over females, and which had very high rates of arrest in the 1900s. The other demographic variable which is crucial is that of age, since it affects the sample of those most likely to be policed.

Beyond these variables, which can be taken into account in further statistical analysis, the explanation of county differences of the magnitude evident in the judicial and police returns will undoubtedly require much more detailed local study. That is the proper task of social history, which might discover, for example, in the very high rates of assault arrests occurring in Kerry at the turn of the century the symptom of other patterns of social order, or the peculiar effect of a certain style of policing.

Conclusion

My conclusion is brief. This chapter started from the premise that there is a good deal more to the history of crime and punishment in nineteenth-century Ireland than the incidence of agrarian outrage. Neither should the history of crime, policing and punishment in Ireland stop at mid-century, or in the 1880s. A review of the institutions of criminal justice in the nineteenth century which touches only briefly on the significance of these as new forms of government suggests that their mundane, as much as their occasionally sensational, functions, deserve continued and sustained historical scrutiny.

Finally, I have tried to indicate briefly, with the crudest of statistical impressions, some of the dominant features of the criminal justice landscape in the later nineteenth century. A more through inquiry developing these themes is likely to shed light on many aspects of Irish social history during a most important period of change, perhaps in passing also providing a new context from which to view the phenomenon of agrarian crime.

ARCHIVAL NOTE

This chapter has drawn almost entirely on the official statistics, though my comments are informed in part by my previous study of the social history of lunacy administration in Ireland,[37] a subject which has some important overlaps with the history of summary jurisdiction and its human subjects. As I have indicated there is much to be done by way of detailed comparative study of the official statistics, with attention to those regional differentials that have repaid study in so many other areas of modern Irish social history.

37 M. Finnane, *Insanity and the insane in post-Famine Ireland* (London, 1981).

To understand the process of decision-making in the criminal process, however, we need to go beyond the official statistics. The future of historical investigation in this field in Ireland is bedevilled by the archival losses which were sustained in the Four Courts fire in 1922, losses which included a great part of the judicial records of the nineteenth century. Nevertheless the situation is far from hopeless, given the occasional survival of data for particular courts and places, especially for the later nineteenth century. My comments here are confined to the major repositories, the National Archives of Ireland in Dublin (NAI) and the Public Record Office of Northern Ireland in Belfast (PRONI).[38]

The major difficulty in an archival study of policing, prosecution and punishment in nineteenth-century Ireland is obtaining continuity of records for one place. Yet from the patchwork of records which might be used over time it seems quite feasible to build up a detailed account of the process of criminal law and its social uses in the post-Famine period. In order to describe the prosecution process one would need two kinds of record. The first is a register of prosecutions and their outcomes, to enable a qualitative judgment to be made about patterns over time or in a particular place. The second is the case files themselves, including depositions and a record of the trial process. The former is available in the form of 'crown books' for both assizes and the quarter sessions for selected counties and intermittent periods. The second comes in the form of 'crown files', the prosecutor's briefing papers, which help detail the social character of the defendant and other parties as well as the context of the offence. For Queen's Co. (Co. Offaly) for example, the crown book for the county assizes for 1874–1897 survives: from this source, one can obtain charge, verdict and sentence for the period covered. For Co. Clare, the crown books for quarter sessions survive for the period from 1873 on, and the crown files for quarter sessions are available (though incomplete) from the 1850s. For Waterford city, crown books for quarter sessions are available for 1877–1901, and crown files from the 1890s. For most counties there are some records, with the chances of useful runs of material increasing markedly from the 1890s.

These generalisations apply to the higher courts for the trial of indictable offences. In pursuing one of the objectives of this paper, namely the policing of 'ordinary' offending, an important source is the local or petty sessions court. The 'order books' for these courts recorded the results of police charges for a range of summary offences. Such records are now available for extended periods for some petty sessions districts, in NAI. Detailed study of them will eventually produce an account of local justice in Ireland to put beside the colourful fictional portrait of Somerville and Ross. Records for the

---

38 They should now be supplemented by a guide to the archival sources: B. Griffin, *Sources for the study of crime in nineteenth-century Ireland, 1801–1921* (Dublin, 2005).

counties of what is now Northern Ireland are in much the same condition, in PRONI. Crown books and files for both assizes and quarter sessions are available for most counties and for the cities of Belfast and Derry from the late 1880s, earlier in selected cases. For Belfast, the recorder's court crown books and files survive from 1888 and 1891 onwards respectively. A register of summary convictions at petty sessions is available for Co. Fermanagh for 1861–79 and the same county has a return of offenders (evidently indictable offenders) from 1850 to 1876. For Co. Tyrone, there is, in addition to the usual run of crown books and files for assizes and quarter sessions, a book of 'fines and estreats' for the period 1877–1912. Selected records at assizes and quarter sessions also appear to be available for Co. Armagh, Co. Antrim and Co. Londonderry for some years before the 1880s, including as early as 1797 (Armagh) and the 1820s (Antrim). PRONI also has available some long series of petty sessions order books (e.g. Forkhill, 1851–88, and Dromara, 1851–86). A drawback for criminal justice research in Northern Ireland as in Great Britain is the formal 100–year closure on court records regarding individual cases, an impediment which is always worth testing by application for access for research purposes having regard to the preservation of confidentiality.

The broader administrative picture can be filled in through a number of other archival sources as well as published papers (official inquiries including select committees, law reports and magistrate publications). The Chief Secretary's Office Registered Papers (NAI) are an indispensable source, with extensive correspondences relating to the administration of police and of the crown prosecutors. A proper knowledge of the administrative constraints is necessary to understand both policing priorities and critical areas such as prosecutorial discretion and decision-making generally. In this respect two important sources which will repay future analysis are the letter books to police and to magistrates, containing directives from Dublin Castle.

Analysis of the *Judicial Statistics*, on the lines outlined above, can be pursued at national, regional (county) and local level. Future research in the area of violent crime will need to compare such analysis with the data which is recorded in the RIC outrage returns, four volumes of which are available in NAI, covering the period 1848–93, with data on murder and manslaughter cases, including information to point of trial and outcome.

Capital punishment in Ireland, 1922–1964

GERARD O'BRIEN*

BY THE TIME THE IRISH FREE STATE came into existence in 1922 the question of whether to retain, amend or abolish capital punishment had already had a long life as an English political and social issue.[1] Among the Irish it was a political issue also, though one of a rather different hue. In the eighteenth and nineteenth centuries the popular meaning of capital punishment in Ireland was highly political in the sense that Irishmen were seen as being hanged by British authority. In the race-memory of the Victorian and Edwardian catholic Irishman, the English had hanged his forebears for their religion in the early modern period and for their politics ever since then. It was a selective memory, one which held in its spotlight the relatively few 'political' executions and gave no consideration to the parallel social phenomenon of 'ordinary' criminals hanged for their crimes. Had Ireland been granted some form of self-government during the nineteenth century Irish society might have been compelled to confront capital punishment as a social and moral issue, as had been the case in England. But the Victorians' failure to find a satisfactory political solution to the Irish question meant that the social aspects of capital punishment would remain firmly subordinate to its supposed political 'meaning'. Traditional Irish ballads telling of lost battles or failed insurrections were not infrequently rounded off with a depiction of heroic rebels dying on the scaffold at the hands of the English.[2]

An enduring effect of this 'politicisation' of capital punishment was the uncritical acceptance by nationalists that hanging was nothing more than a manifestation of English tyranny. The continuance of this 'mind-set' literally until the crucial amendment of death-sentence criteria in Ireland during the 1960s was demonstrated by the fact that Irish-born executioners were virtually non-existent. From the 1860s onwards, a period from which more

---

* The edited text of an address given to the Society at the premises of the Royal Irish Academy, Dublin, on 12 March 2004.
1 The beginnings of opposition to capital punishment are outlined in H. Potter, *Hanging in judgment: religion and the death penalty in England* (New York, 1993), chs. 1–3.
2 A fairly representative selection, produced by the Christian Brothers and used fairly widely in Irish primary schools, was *Amhranleabhar ogra Eireann* (Dublin, 1950, and reprinted many times.)

extreme forms of nationalism remained at least a permanent undercurrent in Irish life, it evidently became necessary to employ English hangmen to conduct executions in Ireland, a practice which continued until 1954 in Dublin and 1961 in Belfast.[3] Even during the 1940s and 1950s, by which time hanging had become an increasingly controversial issue, the British government was receiving several unsolicited applications each week from would-be executioners. In Ireland, however, Portadown-based George Murphy's offer in 1898 to hang Irish criminals and thereby save the 'useless waste of the Public Funds consequent on ... importing a foreigner' may have been unusual.[4] It also appears to have been unsuccessful. When the Irish administration in 1902 sought advice on 'competent' hangmen, the home office responded with a list of six men, all from Bolton, Rochdale or Manchester. During the final years of the British regime in Ireland executions were financed 'under a uniform scale applicable to Gt. Britain and Ireland'. The executioner's fee of £10, his second-class rail ticket, and his refreshment allowance of ten shillings (50 pence) were paid for out of the law charges vote. His maintenance whilst inside the prison was met out of the prisons vote, and the necessary printed forms connected with executions were paid for out of the stationery office vote.[5]

The upsurge of nationalist violence in 1919 and after, and the establishment's increasingly aggressive response, copperfastened the Irish tendency to make the hangman the focus of their displeasure. By 1921 the government had been compelled to raise its fees for Irish 'political' executions by 50 per cent in order to secure the attendance of the necessary English executioner. John Ellis, an experienced though neurotic executioner, hanged many Irish rebels from Roger Casement in 1916 onwards. When the authorities for some unknown reason short-changed him in 1921 by paying him merely the usual £10 fee, he complained bitterly that the £15 normally allowed him 'for single executions of Sinn Féiners' was 'little enough. The risk I have, the inconvenience I am put to, also the jeers and insulting remarks I have to put up with'.[6]

3 At Carrickfergus jail, no local man carried out executions after the 1840s. See S. Moore, *Behind the garden wall: a history of capital punishment in Belfast* (Antrim, 1995), p. 46.

4 PRO, Balfour papers, 30/60/23, George Murphy, Portadown, to Sir Matthew Ridley, 13 Dec. 1898.

5 PRO, HO 351/135, Charles S. Murdoch, Home Office, to under-secretary, Dublin Castle, 29 March 1902; memo to under-secretary, Dublin Castle, 25 Aug. 1917.

6 Ibid., John Ellis to [under-secretary], Dublin Castle, 27 April 1921. The man executed was Thomas Traynor. Ellis enclosed a cutting from the *Irish Independent* which identified him as Traynor's executioner. Ellis's problems did not end at Dublin Castle. Special arrangements had to be made for his safety in London in 1922 when he claimed that he had been threatened by the IRA in connection with the executions in August of the assassins of Sir Henry Wilson: PRO, HO 144/3689, Ellis to Sir Kyneston Metcalfe, under sheriff of the City of London, 24 July 1922, and the related minutes of 25 July and 4 Aug. 1922. For a broader view of Ellis, see J. Ellis, *Diary of a hangman* (London, 1996), and J. Doughty, *The Rochdale hangman and his victims* (Oldham, 1998).

The evidence which survives to us from the last generation of crown rule, that is, from the early 1890s until 1921, indicates that executions were few throughout this period and, in the last years before the outbreak of violence, virtually all death sentences were commuted. It is plain that, political 'crimes' apart, the crown administration's urge to reprieve far outweighed the urge to hang. When the early Free State administration was confronted with such dilemmas a short few years later, continuity rather than innovation was the watchword. The prison authorities, even as late as 1932, kept the basic record of state executions in the same ledger as had been in use since 1852.[7]

The Irish Free State came into being in political circumstances which effectively precluded any reasoned discussion of the desirability (or lack of it) of capital punishment in the new society. Of critical moment was the establishment of a committee to draft the new state's constitution. Virtually until the day of the publication of its final draft in June 1922 the public was kept in ignorance of the constitution's content and of the tortuous processes by which it was devised. The document which would outline the form and substance of civil society in the new state was in fact drawn up in conditions which stifled debate and subordinated constitutional issues to party divisions and political manoeuvres. In the aftermath of the rejection of the Anglo-Irish Treaty of 1921 by a very large minority of the Dáil, the head of the new provisional government, Michael Collins, intended that the proposed constitution should be drafted in a way which would paper over as many as possible of the differences between the two sides and help to isolate the republican extremists.

The end result of the formation of a drafting committee of 'politically neutral' men was the eventual splitting of the committee into three factions, each of which produced a draft constitution. Interestingly, one of these (known as 'draft B') included in its guarantee of trial by jury the provision that 'the penalty of death shall not be attached to any offence'. This draft was produced by James Douglas, a Dublin businessman and close associate of Collins; C.J. France, an American lawyer; and Hugh Kennedy, a prominent barrister who was then acting as legal adviser to the provisional government. Douglas was a member of the Society of Friends and both he and France had worked with the Irish White Cross, a humanitarian organisation formed to relieve the sufferings of civilians during the Anglo-Irish war. Their provision to exclude the death sentence, however, was dropped from the final draft of the constitution on the advice of a consultant (Professor George O'Brien) that it was 'a matter which should be left to legislation in the Oireachtas'. The drafts by other members of the committee which omitted all mention of the death penalty were composed respectively by Darrel Figgis, James

7   These conclusions are based on an examination of both the *Annual reports of the General Prisons Board (Ireland)* for the period 1891–1921, and NAI, GPB, CN5: 'The death book'.

MacNeill, and John O'Byrne ('draft A'); and by Alfred O'Rahilly and James Murnaghan ('draft C'). Figgis was an author and journalist; MacNeill a former colonial administrator; O'Byrne a barrister, and O'Rahilly and Murnaghan prominent academics. Both O'Byrne and Murnaghan were to become distinguished judges.

In the meantime, however, Michael Collins produced from the three documents a single draft constitution to be presented to the British government for approval. The negotiations with the British which followed and which led to the substantial revision of Collins' draft constitution centred more on bringing it into line with the 1921 treaty; the matter of the death sentence was not raised again as a constitutional issue.[8] By the autumn of 1922 capital punishment as it had been practised in Ireland by the British was adopted by the Free State because time, politics, and the outbreak of civil war had prevented ministers and public opinion from giving it any attention.

Ever since the leaders of the Irish separatist movement had first adjudged it legitimate to make war on the British establishment in pursuit of Irish independence, the practices of killing the enemy and 'executing' collaborators, spies and informers had never caused republicans any serious moral qualms. The death sentence, as applied by republicans to their enemies right up until 1921, was part and parcel of a military response to a perceived military situation. The military situation continued, however, beyond the period of British rule, and the much-needed opportunity for the new government to consider whether the death penalty was any longer a desirable deterrent was not forthcoming. As the shadow of disbandment fell on the Royal Irish Constabulary (RIC) and an effective new police force could not be brought to full strength instantaneously, crime and political disorder flourished and merged into one another in a way which made it all but impossible to distinguish between the two: '[h]omes and farms are burned in a wages dispute; haggards are burned in a land dispute; trains are attacked; Post Offices robbed; Banks raided, individuals robbed without any patriotic pretences in the name of the Republic, men are murdered for personal reasons in the name of the Republic and so on'.[9]

As the violence continued into the autumn of 1922, the government 'as a matter of military necessity' brought into being the Army Emergency Powers Resolution. This included a provision which allowed military courts or 'committees' to sentence civilians to death. The military courts' first victims

---

8 Information regarding the 1922 constitution has been taken from D.H. Akenson and J.F. Fallin, 'The Irish civil war and the drafting of the Free State constitution' in *Éire-Ireland*, 5:1 (1970), 10–26, 5:2 (1970), 42–93, and 5:4 (1970), 28–70; B. Farrell, 'The drafting of the Irish Free State constitution' in *Ir Jur*, v (1970), 115–40, 343–56 and vi (1971), 111–35 and 345–59; J.A. Gaughan (ed.), *Memoirs of Senator James G. Douglas* (Dublin, 1998), pp. 86–8; Trinity College Dublin, Edward M. Stephens papers, box 3, file 2, documents 53 and 56.

9 Quoted in T. Garvin, *1922: the birth of Irish democracy* (Dublin, 1996), pp. 102–3.

were executed for unauthorised possession of arms, on 17 November 1922. All four men, however, had claimed membership of the Irish Republican Army (IRA) and that they were belligerents. More interesting and less well-documented were the joined cases of Luke Burke (*alias* Michael Keenan) and Michael Greery (or Grealy), two 'non-politically motivated bank robbers', who were tried by military 'committee' and executed on 14 March 1923. They were the only persons listed as 'civilian' on the list of 81 persons (later mythologised as 'the 77') officially executed by the Free State army between 19 November 1922 and 11 April 1924.[10] On 7 December 1922, one day after the new constitution became effective, legality was temporarily abandoned altogether. The government, as an official reprisal for the killing of one member of the Dáil and the wounding of another, ordered the summary execution of four republicans who had been in custody since before the adoption of the Army Emergency Powers Resolution. Military executions and unofficial reprisals (the latter without number) were to continue; but the execution of Mellows, McKelvey, O'Connor and Barrett on 8 December was the nadir of official departure from civilised norms. However, in the history of capital punishment thereafter in Ireland the event formed an ugly precedent and had long-term effects on the attitudes of men on both sides of the civil war divide, men who would govern the country almost until the 1970s. The December reprisal had been undertaken in response to a direct threat to the state's public representatives from their political enemies: '[i]t was at once punitive and deterrent', said Kevin O'Higgins (the second-last member of the government to agree to it) addressing a shocked Dáil; '[t]he members of the Parliament of Ireland must be kept free and safe to perform their duties ... When one strikes at a representative man the crime is particularly horrid'.[11] The official reprisal was not repeated, but a certain ruthlessness had entered into the psyche of civil war participants which would surface again in later years when they were faced with the semblance of a similar threat.

On the day before the reprisal was decided upon, the first step had been taken towards the re-institution of capital punishment in non-military circumstances. The previous summer, after negotiations with the British government, it was agreed to recognise the judicial superiority of the privy council to the Irish supreme court; this meant, amongst other things, that the right of condemned Irishmen to appeal as a last resort to the king was

---

10 C. Campbell, *Emergency law in Ireland, 1918–1925* (Oxford, 1994), pp. 163–4, 247–50, 361–71. The first four executed, on 17 November 1922, were Peter Cassidy, James Fisher, John Gaffney and Richard Twohig.

11 See U. O'Connor, *Executions* (Dingle, 1992), esp. 'Introduction'; T. de Vere White, *Kevin O'Higgins* (London, 1948; Tralee 1966 edn.), pp. 131–4. A point of importance is that the reprisal was called for by Richard Mulcahy, minister for defence in 1922 and holder of cabinet office in 1948–51 and 1954–7.

preserved. In practice this appeal would be made to the governor-general, the king's representative in Ireland. The written instructions to the governor-general directed him not to 'pardon or reprieve any such offender without first receiving in capital cases the advice of the Executive Council [i.e. the Irish government] for the said State, and in other cases the advice of one, at least, of his Ministers'.[12]

Under the new regime the governor-general occupied roughly the same position in Ireland as had the lord lieutenant. But the critical innovation was the executive council, with a minister for home affairs (renamed 'justice' in 1924), in respect of which there had been no counterpart in the days of British rule.[13] In England for many generations a 'hanging' cabinet had passed advice on executions or reprieves to British monarchs who had considerable personal power in the matter. During the nineteenth century the practice developed whereby the home secretary reached a personal decision on whether to reprieve a condemned person and so advised the monarch who would be guided by that advice.[14] In the Free State the home secretary's counterpart in 1922 was the minister for home affairs. There had of course been no administrative experience in Ireland which mirrored the 'rise' of the home office in England. Also, on the first occasion when the executive council had had to decide on an execution, the reprisal of December 1922, the decision was not taken by any individual minister but by the entire cabinet. Extraordinary as the circumstances had been, they appear to have acted as a precedent in the administrative sense. It seems probable also that the executive council, like the new government in Northern Ireland (which had received identical governor-general's 'instructions'), interpreted the 6 December 'instructions' literally and assumed that each reprieve-applicant had to be considered collectively by ministers. A further year was to pass before the Irish government came to grips with the issue of the death sentence in criminal cases. But when in November 1923 it came to consider the case of William Downes, who had killed a policeman while fleeing the scene of a robbery, the decision to hang him was made by the full cabinet; the role of the minister for home affairs was confined to presenting his cabinet colleagues with the information necessary for them to arrive at a decision.[15]

---

12 NAI, Department of the Taoiseach [hereafter DT], S.7788A, 'Extract from instructions passed under the royal sign manual and signet to the governor-general of the Irish Free State', 6 Dec. 1922.

13 For the rather passive role of the Irish privy council under British rule, see R.B. McDowell, *The Irish administration, 1801–1914* (London and Toronto, 1964), pp. 106–7.

14 For these developments see F. Bresler, *Reprieve: a study of a system* (London, 1965), esp. chs. 4–8.

15 Downes, a veteran of the 1916 rebellion, had been a despatch rider in the Free State's National Army. For his crime, trial and execution, see *Irish Times*, 20, 30 Oct., 28, 30 Nov. 1923. It is believed that to some extent also the cabinet adopted the procedures used by the Castle before 1922: I am grateful to Tim Carey for this information.

The minutes of Irish cabinet meetings were (and, it seems, still are) terse, with virtually no indication of the character of discussions on this or any other issue. However, the content of each successive home affairs/justice 'memorandum for the government' on death sentence issues suggests at least some of the criteria which were then taken into account by ministers. A tabular statement drawn up some years later of death sentence 'decisions' by the government included details, often *verbatim*, of recommendations to mercy made, or not made, by the jury, and also of observations made by the trial judge. This seems to have mirrored the process in England where it had long been the practice to take judge and jury recommendations into account. In the Free State, as in England, these jury recommendations did not necessarily have to be followed. Out of 35 cases of persons sentenced to death under the Cumann na nGaedheal government, 1922–32, the government ignored the jury's recommendation to mercy in 15 instances. Significantly, in each of these cases the judge disagreed with the jury's recommendation. In deciding whether or not to reprieve, the government clearly took its 'cue' from the judge and not from the jury.[16]

Downes was the first 'criminal' executed by the Irish authorities, and other necessary procedures were put in place. Responsibility for an execution remained with the sheriff or sub-sheriff of the county in which the crime had taken place (in Downes' case this was Dublin), but it was decided that executions henceforth would take place in Dublin's Mountjoy prison.[17] Although there had been 'several applicants for the post of executioner' (it is unclear whether the applicants were Irish), the government decided to retain the services of experienced home office-listed executioners such as Thomas Pierrepoint.[18] Probably at his own insistence the identity of Downes' executioner was not disclosed to the public. While no public petition seems to have been organised for a reprieve in Downes' case, there may have been some popular unrest. When the official notice of his execution was posted on the gate of Mountjoy it was immediately torn down by a young woman 'shouting angrily: "[s]candalous, scandalous"'. At the inquest Downes' brother demanded to know under what statute his brother had been hanged.[19] As in

16 For English practice, see Bresler, *Reprieve*, pp. 55–6. The tabular statement referred to is in NAI, DT S.7788A. In the case of James Murray, a captain in the National Army, convicted of murder in 1925, neither the judge nor the jury seems to have made any recommendations, and the government on its own initiative commuted the sentence. Murray died in prison: see NAI, DT S.3415.

17 T. Carey, *Mountjoy: the story of a prison* (Cork, 2000), p. 208.

18 It should be noted that there was no official connection between the home office and the Free State in the matter of employing the executioner. The Free State 'made a separate private contract' with Pierrepoint, 'and they left the choice of his assistant to the executioner himself': A. Pierrepoint, *Executioner: Pierrepoint* (London, 1974), p. 99.

19 *Irish Times*, 30 Nov. 1923. The protest by Downes's brother doubtless was intended to highlight the fact that Downes, a 1916 veteran and member of the Free State's own army,

England the Irish authorities did not consider themselves under an obligation to explain their reasons for granting or withholding a reprieve. An occasion almost certainly never repeated was the granting by Kevin O'Higgins of a request for an interview by the condemned man's parents. O'Higgins, minister for justice at the time (the mid-1920s), was adamant to his colleagues that he had no intention of recommending a reprieve to the cabinet; he had agreed to the interview 'so that afterwards they [the parents] may feel assured that they had taken every step to secure their son's pardon. If I had refused to see them they might think afterwards that if they had seen me their son would have got off'.[20] Apart from its virtual uniqueness, the occasion was notable in that it suggested a clear belief in the public mind that the minister for justice was the counterpart of the home secretary when it came to deciding on reprieves.[21]

Of the 35 persons executed in Ireland between 1923 and 1954 (including six executed under emergency powers legislation during World War II), 16 died under the Cumann na nGaedheal administration of 1922–32. This disproportion may have reflected the stricter attitudes of senior judges who had served their time in late Victorian days; we have noted the many instances in which trial judges rejected the jury's recommendations to mercy. But it is suggestive also of the violent atmosphere of the post–civil war years. Of the first six persons executed by the Free State four were serving or former members of the National Army. One of the earliest cases, Lieutenant Jeremiah Gaffney, had murdered a youth as a personal reprisal for the killing of a local policeman. Another (former) officer killed a policeman in the course of a bank robbery in circumstances similar to those of the Downes case. Thomas MacDonagh, a farmer who killed one of his neighbours in a quarrel in May 1922, preferred to surrender initially to the local IRA rather than to the newly-formed Civic Guards.[22] The juries in some instances were

had been hanged on the authority of an Irish government in accordance with a British law. As with other 'non-political' murderers up to 1964, Downes was probably convicted under the Offences against the Person Act 1861. Nobody was executed under section 5 of the Public Safety (Emergency Powers) Act 1923. The inclusion of the death sentence in this measure for acts of 'armed revolt' attracted half-hearted attempts at amendment from two concerned senators; see *Seanad Deb.*, vol. 1, cols. 1648–54 (30 July 1923). The measure, true to its 'emergency' status, expired six months after its enactment.

20 De Vere White, *Kevin O'Higgins*, p. 137. The condemned man in this case was 'a soldier in the army', but it is unclear whether it was Downes.

21 The justice minister's 'Memorandum for the government', which would give the substance of a case for the Irish cabinet upon each application for a reprieve, could contain the department's recommendation as well as a paragraph indicating the minister's personal view, but the cabinet was not bound to accept the recommendation.

22 *Irish Times*, 8, 14 Dec. 1923 (Gaffney); 29, 30 Jan., 11 April, 2 Aug. 1924 (Felix McMullen); 13 Nov., 12 Dec. 1923 (Thomas MacDonagh). An ex-Free State soldier, Thomas Delaney, killed a shopkeeper during a robbery (dates as for MacDonagh). For McMullen, see also *State v. McMullen* [1925] 2 IR 9.

mindful of the disturbed national context. When Charles Molloy was finally convicted in 1926 for a murder committed three years earlier, the jury recommended mercy partly in view of 'the unsettled state of the country at the time the crime was committed'; the trial judge agreed. In the same year Patrick Fagan and James Myles received similar mercy from the jury (though in Myles' case the judge demurred).[23] In a startling demonstration of the continuance of civil war tensions, Kevin O'Higgins, the minister perhaps most closely associated in the public mind with reprisals and executions, was himself murdered in July 1927 and his killers never apprehended.

The political circumstances which had overshadowed many of the Cumann na nGaedheal government's decisions in capital cases during the formative years of the state would continue to haunt successive administrations and eventually bedevil decision-making when it came to the issue of reforming, retaining or abolishing the death penalty. But during the 1920s and 1930s public opinion seemed indifferent on the matter, at least between executions. One of the documents basic to an appeal to the government for clemency was the formal petition prepared by the condemned person's solicitor and laid before the cabinet along with the justice department's 'memorandum' and related papers. This could be reinforced, though with dubious effect, by a public petition organised by the condemned person's family and/or friends. Several petitions were put in hand in respect of Felix McMullen (the ex-officer who had killed a guard during a bank robbery, referred to above); among the signatories were a number of jurors from his trial who felt that the charge ought to have been reduced to manslaughter.[24] In the high-profile case of Henry McCabe, who had slaughtered and incinerated a Malahide household of six 'with the object of plunder', two members of the Dáil added their names to a 2,000-strong petition for his reprieve. Three days before Peter Hynes was hanged for murdering an ex-British soldier, an anonymous correspondent asserted that the condemned man and one of his parents were insane. Otherwise few persons appear to have put pen to paper on behalf of Hynes or almost anyone else who was executed between 1923 and 1932.[25]

23 Extrapolated from the tabular statement in NAI, DT S.7788A. For James Myles, a labourer who murdered two men he suspected were about to inform the police of his cattle-rustling activities, see *Irish Times*, 18, 19 June, 16 July 1926.

24 *Irish Times*, 1 Aug. 1924.

25 *Irish Times*, 8 Dec. 1926. Notably, however, the jury did not recommend mercy for McCabe. See the account of the case in K.R. Deale, *Beyond any reasonable doubt?* (Dublin, 1990), pp. 202–25. See also *Attorney General v. McCabe* [1927] IR 129. The exceptions were James McHugh, in respect of whom some 100 prominent citizens of New Ross, together with catholic and protestant clergymen, petitioned in vain in 1926, and Gerard Toal, on whose behalf the Women's International League for Peace and Mercy petitioned, also in vain, in 1928. See, respectively, NAI, DT S.5211 and S.5725.

The gathering of people at the prison gates on the morning of an execution may have betokened interest or curiosity but not necessarily concern. When James Myles was hanged it was noted that 'very few people were outside the prison'.[26] McCabe, perhaps less surprisingly, attracted 'a large crowd, composed mainly of women, including McCabe's wife'.[27] For William O'Neill, however, who was hanged for killing a pensioner for her savings, 'no public interest whatever was manifested'.[28] Even the high-profile case of Gerard Toal, who had murdered a priest's housekeeper with 'no motive save unfriendly feeling', brought forth only 'a small crowd of people'.[29] Toal was an orphan. For the execution of John Cox, however, who had bludgeoned to death his German foreman in order to rob him, some one hundred people turned out, 'women among them kneeling in prayer'.[30] Likewise for David O'Shea, the first person executed by the Free State for a sexually-motivated crime, 'about two hundred people – mostly women' assembled outside the prison.[31] The recommendation in 1930 of Britain's select committee on capital punishment that the death penalty should be abolished for an experimental period of five years fell on deaf ears in Ireland as it did in England.[32] In the Irish press it became commonplace for Pierrepoint to be named as the executioner and for executions to be reported as having taken place 'without a hitch'.

The years between the entry of Eamon de Valera's Fianna Fáil administration into office in 1932 and the establishment of the new constitution in 1937 saw few significant changes in the way in which decision-making on reprieves was conducted, but did witness the first organised attempt in the history of the state to publicly oppose the use of the death penalty. Initially

26 *Irish Times*, 16 July 1926.
27 Ibid., 10 Dec. 1926.
28 Ibid., 30 Dec. 1927. Mountjoy's medical officer, B.J. Hackett, observed that 'O'Neill realises his position, but exhibits neither anguish nor remorse'; NAI, DT S.5573.
29 *Irish Times*, 30 Aug. 1928. Curiously the newspaper recorded also that: '[t]here were no incidents of any kind, even when the notice of the execution had been posted up outside the gate by a warder'. It seems not unlikely that the minor disturbance in the wake of Downes' execution was not an isolated occurrence. For an analysis of the Toal case, see Deale, *Beyond any reasonable doubt*, pp. 29–51.
30 *Irish Times*, 26 April 1929.
31 Ibid., 5 Aug. 1931. The trial judge, in reply to a request for his views on a possible reprieve, wrote that 'there was no evidence to support the speculation of the jury as to the state of mind of the accused, except the appalling nature of the crime. We have never admitted the theory of brain storm or uncontrollable impulse in our law. The accused seemed a low degenerate with sex perversion ... I think the law should take its course': NAI, DT S.6176. See also *Attorney General v. O'Shea* [1931] IR 713.
32 *Report of the select committee on capital punishment*, H.C. 1930–1 (15) vi, 1. 'The Barr Report [as it was known] was criticised in many papers as being sentimental rhetoric, and a poetic apology for abolition. *The Times* disparaged the quality of the Committee's composition and doubted the worth of their conclusions': Potter, *Hanging in judgment*, pp. 135–6.

at least Fianna Fáil was presented with fewer problems than its predecessor in office, as the incidence of capital crime continued to fall. Of the fourteen persons convicted of capital offences in the years up to the outbreak of the IRA bombing campaign in 1939, only four were executed.

One of the earliest cases to come before the new cabinet, however, was the rare instance of a woman-applicant, who seemed to have little other than her sex to recommend her for a reprieve. Jane O'Brien had murdered her nephew, the Guards observed, in a cold-blooded and premeditated fashion. The governor of Mountjoy reported that she did not seem in any way mentally abnormal. In all other cases of women seeking reprieves, the justice department pointed out, the applications were granted due to:

> ... *some* doubt as to the women's guilt, or the youth of the offender herself, or the fact that the offender's mentality was not completely normal, or that she acted under the influence of a male accomplice. The Department cannot recollect any case in which there appears to have been so complete an absence of extenuating circumstances as in the present case.

It was clear that the prospect of executing a woman filled both officials and ministers with a peculiar horror. Only one woman, Annie Walsh, had been executed in Ireland since independence. Convicted with her nephew of the murder of her husband, both had been executed on the same day in 1925. It was the first time a woman had been hanged in Ireland since 1903, the crown regime having reprieved all six condemned women who had sought reprieves in the period thereafter to 1921. The Fianna Fáil ministers, plainly casting about for a pretext on which to reprieve Jane O'Brien, fastened on the private appeal to them by Archbishop Edward Byrne and on the routine (though rather hapless) petition from her solicitor both of which referred to the 'sinister shadow' such an execution would cast over the concurrent eucharistic congress. The ministers were mindful also of the facts that the jury had recommended mercy for Jane O'Brien and that their Cumann na nGaedheal predecessors had ignored the jury's recommendation of mercy for Annie Walsh. Jane O'Brien was reprieved.[33]

As before, under Fianna Fáil rule proper attention was paid to the recommendations of juries and trial judges, with, in 1937, an almost-unique demonstration of the importance attached to the judge's observations. Patrick Boylan had murdered his girlfriend in a drunken jealous rage and was sentenced to death. The jury had recommended mercy however, and the trial judge, John O'Byrne, emphasised in his 'confidential report' to the cabinet

---

33 For Jane O'Brien, see NAI, DT S.8653. If O'Brien had been a man it is almost certain that Archbishop Byrne's plea would have been in vain.

the unpremeditated nature of the crime and recommended a reprieve. In a striking demonstration that public opinion was not considered entirely irrelevant, the justice department officials drew attention to the fact that a petition was 'being extensively signed'. (The petition eventually contained 25,000 signatures). But the government for some unknown reason chose to reject the proffered advice and confirmed the sentence, only to reverse its decision a few days later. No document was added to the cabinet case file but it became known almost immediately that the trial judge had made renewed representations to the government. Had O'Byrne J simply accepted the government's original rejection of his advice it would have created a precedent and marked a serious departure from established procedure, one which might conceivably have seen the decision-making process with regard to reprieves pass from the professional hands of the judiciary into the relatively amateurish grasp of politicians.[34]

Boylan's crime had been a particularly brutal one (the girl had been killed with a razor blade), but an extraordinary number of people seemed concerned that he should not hang.[35] On Boylan's reprieve the president of the Dublin Working Men's Association (who may have organised the petition) thanked the *Irish Press* for its assistance in the campaign and expressed his 'great consolation ... to know and realise the growing horror of our people towards this barbaric system of hanging, and I sincerely hope we have seen the last visit of the English hangman to our shores, and I hope to see provision made in the Constitution for the abolition of the death penalty'.[36]

34 NAI, DT S.9849A (Boylan case-file): 'Confidential report' by Mr Justice John O'Byrne, 23 April 1937; S.A. Roche, dept. of justice, to secretary, executive council, 29 April 1937; L[iam] Trant-McCarthy, solicitor, to secretary, executive council, 29 April 1937; M[aurice] Moynihan, secretary, executive council, to private secretary, minister for justice, 1 May 1937; copy of cabinet minute 7/408, 30 April 1937, item 5; copy of cabinet minute 7/361, 5 May 1937, item 1. The *Irish Press*, 6 May 1937, believed that a decisive intervention had been made, but did not name the judge. When O'Byrne died in 1954, his *Irish Times* obituary, 15 Jan. 1954, without specifying the case suggested that it was he who had intervened. His intervention was confirmed in a note (in Irish) of 11 March 1953 by Maurice Moynihan on the capital punishment 'policy' file: NAI, DT S.7788B. See also the note of 30 May 1959 in NAI, DT S.7788C/94, which indicates that O'Byrne attended personally part of the cabinet meeting of 5 May 1937 to re-state his original recommendation. See also *Attorney General v. Boylan* [1937] IR 449.

35 As early as December 1932 in fact, 'thousands' of people had petitioned for a reprieve for Patrick McDermott who had murdered his brother in order to seize his land; *Irish Times*, 5 Sept., 18 Nov., 28, 29, 30 Dec. 1932. A year later, a petition for John Fleming, a particularly callous wife-murderer, was 'signed extensively'; *Irish Times*, 2 Jan. 1934. See the accounts of the Fleming case in Deale, *Beyond any reasonable doubt*, pp. 89–110, and in T. Reddy, *The murder file: an Irish detective's casebook* (Dublin, 1991), pp. 36–55.

36 *Irish Press*, 13 May 1937. The *Irish Press*, it should be remembered, was founded by de Valera and was staunchly pro-Fianna Fáil.

The evidence suggests, however, that public opinion could be mobilised on the issue only when an actual execution was imminent, and these occurred too infrequently in Ireland for any abolitionist campaign to achieve a sustained momentum. The National Council for the Abolition of the Death Penalty (NCADP), which in 1925 brought together representatives from some ten reformist and religious bodies, had enjoyed little success in England where its followers were described as 'few but dedicated'.[37] Its Dublin counterpart, the Society for the Abolition of the Death Penalty, had an experience no less dismal and a far shorter lifespan. It has left few traces behind but seems to have been founded by the historian and novelist Rosamund Jacob and the architect John Henry Webb, both Dublin-based Quakers, during 1937. Despite the formidable energy of the few principal members in organising petitions in respect of condemned persons, approaches to ministers, and public meetings to discuss the pros and cons of the issue, the Dublin branch never seems to have attracted an attendance of more than nine at its monthly meetings. At least one of Jacob's close friends thought the matter 'unimportant compared with the big issues facing people in all countries – war and revolutions and such'.[38] When they debated the issue at University College Dublin's law society they heard a catholic priest argue that 'mankind having always had c[apital] p[unishment] showed it was necessary'.[39] A church hall meeting in November 1938 attracted a 'tolerable audience all young of course … questions and arguing – usual stuff'.[40] At a similar, though notably male-dominated debate at a school hall later that month ('[n]one very much good …'), Jacob recognised the 'most blood-thirsty' of the pro-hanging speakers as one of de Valera's secretaries. When asked for their views of possible alternative punishments, the women in the audience said that they 'would have murderers set to dig turf', a reflection perhaps of the urban character of the attendance.[41] By October 1939 even the stalwarts of the society had begun to absent themselves and those remaining 'decided we c[oul]d do nothing at present – that the European war put civilised things into eclipse'.[42]

Meanwhile in the corridors of power the right of appeal to the British privy council and the office of governor-general, theoretical arbiters of executions and reprieves, had both preceded the Quakers' abolitionist society into eclipse. The governor-general's office had been replaced by that of the president of Ireland. It had been de Valera's policy to diminish the functions

37 Founded originally by Roy Calvert, a Quaker, it lasted 23 years and never numbered above 1,200 members: Potter, *Hanging in judgment*, p. 125.
38 NLI, Rosamund Jacob diaries, MS 32,582(83), pp. 69–70 (9 Dec. 1937).
39 Ibid., p. 71 (13 Dec. 1937).
40 Ibid., MS 32,582(85), p. 107 (8 Nov. 1938).
41 Ibid., pp. 116–7 (17 Nov. 1938).
42 Ibid., MS 32,582(89), p. 7 (24 Oct. 1939).

of the governor-general, thereby eroding the constitutional position of the crown in Irish affairs. In May 1935 the government decided that, since the governor-general was duty-bound to accept the advice of the executive council in the matter of reprieves, he was therefore 'not entitled to know the reasons which govern any action which he is advised ... to perform'. The practical result of this decision was to discontinue the practice of sending the department of justice file on each 'condemned' case to the governor-general: '[t]he communication to him will be confined ... to a formal advice in Irish addressed to him by this department [i.e. the department of the president of the executive council; from 1937, the department of the Taoiseach] on behalf of the Executive Council'. In a sense, the balance of dignity and status was being shifted in favour of de Valera, through whose department the critical file in each case would be transmitted to the executive council for consideration; the function of the governor-general in the matter became more than ever that of a rubber stamp.[43]

The transfer of 'the power to commute' to the president of Ireland as head of state was embodied formally in article 13.6 of the 1937 constitution. Within the department of the Taoiseach the existing procedure was confirmed whereby the question of a reprieve would be submitted to the cabinet by the department of justice together with a police report on the circumstances of the crime and (though not always) a copy of the trial judge's charge to the jury. As before, the 'confidential observations' of the trial judge would be recited at the cabinet meeting by the minister for justice.

With the introduction of the Offences against the State Act 1939, capital punishment at last became a matter of public concern. The ever-present threat of IRA terrorism to the stability and security of the state had taken on a new urgency with the imminence of European war and the initiation of a republican bombing campaign in England in 1939. De Valera overcame the opposition of at least some of his cabinet colleagues and brought forward a measure which included the death penalty for transgressors. Soon after the bill's passage through the Dáil, de Valera was approached by a senator of Fianna Fáil sympathies, David Robinson, who asked permission to introduce a bill in the senate to abolish capital punishment 'for a trial period of six years'. He felt that de Valera, speaking in the Dáil on the bill's second reading, was 'personally not very keen about the Death Penalty, and merely advocated its use for the crime of Treason since it was a recognized

43 NAI, DT S.7788A, memo by Michael McDunphy, president's department, 20 May 1935. This had the effect of creating a 'set' of case-files at the president's department to parallel the set held by the ministry of justice. But the administrative 'superiority' of the president's 'set' was clearly asserted in a further memo of the same date by McDunphy. See also the memo (in the same file) by Maurice Moynihan dated 29 Dec. 1938. The justice file prepared for the cabinet members would include also the judgment of the court of criminal appeal in cases where an appeal had been heard and rejected.

punishment'. Robinson had noticed also 'a tendency among Conservative people, not as a rule very favourable to Government to say that since the sentences in England are so very severe, it is a pity that we are introducing a Bill, which seems to be aimed at the IRA and which advocates the Death Penalty'. Moreover, the papal nuncio, according to Robinson, had 'advised me to do all I could to get it [capital punishment] abolished, at any rate for a Probationary period'. Robinson hoped that such a measure in the senate 'would convey to the Public that although what you said in the Dail still goes the Government would not object to an expression of opinion, [of] which you could make whatever use you liked afterwards'. De Valera and his advisers may have suspected that Robinson's proposal had originated with ministers who were less than enthusiastic about the 'Treason Bill'. P.J. Ruttledge, the minister for justice, was the principal of these. When consulted, however, he retreated behind an alternative and less confrontational proposal than Robinson's (one undoubtedly suggested by his officials) that consideration be given to 'amending the law and practice so as to ensure that sentence of death will not be imposed in any case where there are such strong circumstances of a mitigating kind as to make it certain that the penalty of death will not in fact be inflicted'.[44] To the outcome of this proposal we will turn presently.

Robinson's explicit suggestion that the Irish government was proposing to follow the English severity in sentencing, and his linking of that suggestion with a measure aimed at the IRA, was reflective of a perception of capital punishment then entertained perhaps quite generally by the Irish public and given a certain verisimilitude by the use of an English executioner. Albert Pierrepoint, who had acted as assistant to his uncle Tom during the 1930s and later took over from him as 'head' executioner, had grim recollections of his first execution in Dublin in 1932: '[t]he cul-de-sac outside Mountjoy Gaol was crammed with people. Many of them were holding banners. Some of them read: "British Hangman destroys Irishman. Abolish the system and abolish crime". "Pierrepoint the British Hangman hangs Irishman. Is this justice?"'[45] We have seen already how the president of the Dublin Working Men's Association, in giving thanks for Boylan's reprieve in 1937, linked the 'barbaric system of hanging' with the use of an English hangman. Jacob's and Webb's Society for the Abolition of the Death Penalty (SADP) made a written request that the government consider 'the general question' of capital punishment 'in a calmer and clearer atmosphere than was possible in connection with the Treason Bill'. They were sensitive to the possibility that the IRA 'might misconstrue a vote against the Treason Bill into approval of their activities'. They stated that an SADP member, also a member of the

---

44 NAI, DT S.7788A, David Robinson to de Valera, 30 March 1939; S.A. Roche, dept. of justice, to P. Ó Cinneide, dept. of the Taoiseach, 11 April 1939.
45 Pierrepoint, *Executioner*, p. 109. This was the execution of Patrick MacDermott.

Dáil, held this view and had voted accordingly for the bill, 'intending to oppose the death penalty when the general question of it could be raised without this difficulty of the moment'. They pointed out also that 'the unquestioning following of English law [since 1922] was the more unfortunate as the other civilised countries of the world ... were ... abandoning the death penalty as a proven failure'.[46] Robinson, in suggesting a senate measure, believed that it would pass unopposed, 'except from a small group of Fine Gael Senators who would think that they ought to justify their attitude in the past'. For many, it is clear, capital punishment, at least when aimed at the IRA, was a practice associated with the evils of British rule and the 'misguided' Cumann na nGaedheal policies of the civil war period.

In response to Robinson's proposal the department of justice established 'an informal committee' of judges 'to advise on possible reforms as regards trial of murder cases, with the general idea of not pronouncing the death sentence except in really bad cases'. The committee would meet in private, would not take evidence, 'and will *not* consider *total abolition* of capital punishment'. It was believed in official circles that 'neither the Taoiseach nor the Minister for Justice is in favour of total abolition'.[47] Despite regular reminders the four judges failed to produce their report for more than two years. When they finally did so it was 'short and clear' and so 'unduly cautious' that the department of justice greeted it with unconcealed disgust. Apart from minor recommendations on insanity and infanticide (and raising the age threshold on capital punishment from 16 to 18 years of age), the judges refused to countenance any interference with the system of death-sentencing as then practised.[48]

The department of justice secretary, Stephen Roche, produced instead a set of detailed recommendations of his own for the opinion of the attorney general. These included a proposed distinction between 'political' and 'private' murder. Roche thought '[p]olitical' murder by far the worse of the two, 'deadly and highly infectious disease ... too dangerous to be tolerated at all'; the guilty should be tried by special process and hanged speedily if convicted. He did not feel, however, that 'private' murder would in the foreseeable future constitute 'so grave a menace to the ordinary citizen that

46 NAI, DT S.7788A, R. Jacob to de Valera, 11 May 1939, together with a 'memorandum'.
47 Ibid., S.A. Roche, dept. of justice, to M. Ó Muimhneacháin [M. Moynihan], dept. of the Taoiseach, 1 May 1939 (original emphasis).
48 The judges were Timothy O'Sullivan, Conor A. Maguire, John O'Byrne and Henry Hanna. Ibid. S.A. Roche to M. Ó Muimhneacháin, 18 May 1939. A handwritten appendix to this sentence reads: 'I mean that both doubt the *prudence* of abolition'. See also Ruttledge to hon. Timothy Sullivan, chief justice, 26 April 1939, for his view that 'the time is not ripe for abolition'. It was emphasised to the committee members that they were being asked to suggest 'improvement' to the existing law 'subject to the understanding that *abolition* is not contemplated' (original emphasis). See the judges' *Report of the committee appointed to consider and report on the law and practice relating to capital punishment*, in the same file.

it is necessary to be Draconian about it'; death should continue to be an option, but 'the appropriate severity should be carefully measured in each case'. Roche thought that the practice of involving the cabinet in the reprieve process was 'clumsy' in that it was 'non-judicial'. He suggested that the attorney general be empowered to designate 'as manslaughter any case in which there appeared to him to be clear grounds for not imposing the death penalty'; also, that in cases where judge and jury agree unanimously to recommend mercy the judge be permitted to impose a sentence other than death, thus removing the cabinet from the process. He reiterated his department's view that total abolition was not advisable, particularly in view of the continued existence of 'violent' political crime. For Roche 'the question is largely one not of reducing the number of persons actually executed but rather of introducing an element of leniency at an earlier stage of the proceedings'. Or put differently, capital punishment was not so much a point of principle as a matter of improving the procedures.[49]

More conservative counsels prevailed, however, and the legislation eventually considered by the government in 1944 merely reflected the judges' recommendation as supported by the attorney general. The century-old 'McNaghten rules'[50] were to be updated so that mental afflictions other than simply 'insane delusions' were acknowledged as the mainsprings of some forms of criminal behaviour, including murder. The illogical verdict 'guilty but insane' was to be abolished and replaced by one of 'not guilty on grounds of insanity'. Also, the existing law on infanticide was to be replaced by fresh legislation along the lines of the British Infanticide Act 1938 which recognised the probable effects of the birth and lactation processes on a woman's state of mind.[51]

In the meantime de Valera's administration had executed six IRA men for the murder of policemen and other officials; these executions took place against a background of near-deafening public protest. In February 1940 two Irishmen, Peter Barnes and Frank McCormick, had been hanged in England for bombings which had resulted in death. In Northern Ireland an IRA man, Tom Williams, was hanged in September 1942 for murdering a policeman. The Irish public, fortified by memories of British misrule and by two decades

49 S.A. Roche, dept. of justice, to P.P. O'Donoghue, attorney general's office, 25 Aug. 1941.
50 *M'Naghten's case* (1843) 10 Cl & Fin 200.
51 The matter was first discussed by the cabinet on 10 August 1943. The legislation enacted was based on the department of justice's review of the judges' recommendations in January 1944, and the government agreed to proceed with the legislation on 18 April 1944. Because of a related provision of the Children Act 1941 it was decided to raise the age of the death-sentence imposition to 17 rather than 18 years. See NAI, DT S.7788A, 'Proposed legislation to amend the law relating to {1} insanity as a defence to criminal charges, and {2} infanticide', 4 Jan. 1944. I am grateful also to Ms Karen Brennan for a copy of her unpublished conference paper, 'The modern history of child killing legislation in these islands'.

of a nationalist educational system, reacted with particular outrage when de
Valera's government refused to tolerate renewed IRA activity. Kathleen
Clarke, widow of an executed 1916 leader, articulated the confusion of many:

> I could understand the British government, with a war on their hands,
> punishing the IRA for their action in England at such a time. What I
> could not understand was the action of the Irish government in
> punishing men for doing what they themselves had been doing in
> opposition to the Cosgrave [Cumann na nGaedheal] government.
> Military courts were again set up, followed by raiding, arresting,
> imprisoning and even executing men. It nearly drove me insane, as I
> was a member of the Fianna Fáil organisation. Of course the organisation
> was not consulted in the matter; appealing to ministers or the govern-
> ment was useless, it was appealing to deaf ears. It is extraordinary the
> change that comes over men ... when they get a little taste of power;
> they seem to become so intolerant.[52]

The supposedly 'intolerant' members of the cabinet were in fact united in
their belief that the executions were 'a disagreeable necessity'. All ministers
were concerned at the possible effect on Garda morale if the murderers of
policemen were not executed.[53] It is almost needless to add that the few less-
heroic figures who murdered their girlfriends, their brothers or their wives
for unpatriotic reasons during these years were executed to loud public
indifference.[54]

The post-war government in Britain found itself in an era in which efforts
to abolish capital punishment took on the façade (at least) of a popular

---

52 K. Clarke, *Revolutionary woman* (Dublin, 1991), p. 223. For the efforts of Mrs Clarke on
    behalf of Barnes and McCormick, see PRO, FO 371/24252. The case of Tom Williams is
    outlined in Moore, *Behind the garden wall*, pp. 165–78, and dealt with in more detail in J.
    McVeigh, *Executed: Tom Williams and the IRA* (Belfast, 1999). For general accounts of the
    IRA's wartime campaign, see T.P. Coogan, *The IRA* (London, 1970), pp. 116–96, and J.
    Bowyer Bell, *The secret army* (London, 1970), pp. 175–281; also U. MacEoin, *The IRA in
    the twilight years, 1923–1948* (Dublin, 1997).
53 T.P. Coogan, *De Valera: long fellow, long shadow* (London, 1993), pp. 525–6. For a stark
    example of public outrage and government determination during the war years, see NAI,
    DT S.13567: Charles Kerins, a young IRA man convicted of murdering a detective, was
    hanged in December 1944. Some 77,000 signatures were obtained for his reprieve.
    Hundreds of people bombarded the government with telegrams and letters pleading for
    leniency. The eve of his execution witnessed one of the most disorderly debates in the
    history of the Dáil: *Dáil Deb.*, vol. 95, cols. 1136–40, 1221–33, 1331–2, 1407–72 (29 Nov.–1
    Dec. 1944).
54 These included Daniel Doherty, Bernard Kirwan (later immortalised as *The quare fella*), the
    poisoner James Lehman, and Harry Gleeson (in support of whose reprieve application
    7,000 signatures were collected). For details see Reddy, *Murder file*, pp. 68–79, 92–111,
    112–27, and M. Bourke, *Murder at Marlhill: was Harry Gleeson innocent?* (Dublin, 1993).

movement. The movement was fuelled by the government's sharp reaction to a seemingly sudden rise in violent crime, and particularly through a series of high-profile cases which suggested that the judicial system respect of capital punishment was flawed.[55] Ireland suffered no parallel crime-wave and in 1945 the war-time justice minister, Gerald Boland, felt able to declare 'that the IRA was dead and that he had killed it'.[56] Only one person was executed in Ireland in each of the years 1947 and 1948 and none thereafter until 1954. That this was so is a little surprising, given the attitudes of some of the ill-matched members of the new inter-party government of 1948–51. A junior member of the cabinet, Noel Browne, recalled how he and another junior colleague, Sean MacBride, argued on several occasions (apparently with success) for reprieves against the opposition of elder ministers. One of these, Richard Mulcahy, had been a prime mover of the reprisals policy in 1922: '[i]n his usual style on such "simple issues", he was curt, brash and uncomplicated: "They must hang". The deeply religious Blowick's comment, in his high-pitched squeak, was "[h]ang them, hang them". There was no attempt to argue or rationalise their positions'.[57]

It was perhaps inevitable that Sean MacBride, minister for external affairs, who had defended with fatal lack of success a number of IRA men and others tried for their lives during the war, should have been the first Irish minister to confront the ethical aspects of capital punishment. Sharing a platform at a student debate with the *doyenne* of the British abolitionist campaign, Mrs Violet Van der Elst, he rehearsed many of the traditional anti-capital punishment arguments, illustrated with his own experiences of the manner in which accused persons' lives often hung on the fickleness of eccentric jurymen, obvious miscarriages of justice, and failure of police investigation procedures. His personal point, he said, was to establish that the abolition of wars 'must start under the premises that no human being had the right to take human life, be it on behalf of the State or on behalf of an individual'. He claimed also that 'he was not speaking as a member of the Government, but was hoping his views would help them to take a part in forming public opinion that would agitate for the abolition of capital punishment'. Mrs Van der Elst added a traditional note by observing that it was 'to the credit of Irishmen that none of them would act as public hangman'.[58]

---

55 The cases of Timothy Evans, Derek Bentley and Ruth Ellis have an extensive literature.
56 Bowyer Bell, *Secret army*, p. 279.
57 Noel Browne, *Against the tide* (Dublin, 1986), pp. 128–9. J. Blowick was minister for lands. Browne's recollection almost certainly relates to the cases of John Fanning and Edward O'Connor whose applications were considered by the cabinet on 19 October 1948. Both were reprieved.
58 *Irish Times, Irish Independent*, and *Sceala Éireann*, 25 Oct. 1948, all printed accounts of the debate, but reported MacBride and Mrs Van der Elst to the exclusion of all pro-capital

Mrs Van der Elst soon added to the government's difficulties by bragging falsely to the British press that she had been responsible for two reprieves in Ireland.[59] When gleeful Fianna Fáil deputies (now in opposition) had finished demanding the dismissal of MacBride for violating the collective responsibility of the cabinet, they called loudly for Mrs Van der Elst's boasts to be confirmed or refuted. In the midst of the political point-scoring, however, Peadar Cowan, an independent (though pro-Fianna Fáil) deputy, asked if the government had considered the possibility of abolishing the death penalty at least in respect of murder. He called also for a commission to enquire into the whole issue and make recommendations.[60] In England the period 1948–53 had seen the establishment and report of a royal commission on capital punishment. Its proceedings attracted little excitement in Ireland but a few independent-minded deputies raised the issue infrequently in the Dáil.[61]

During these same years the debate in England on the issue was fuelled even further by a series of apparent miscarriages of justice. The finality and irrevocability of the death sentence came under sharp and critical public scrutiny. No Timothy Evans or Derek Bentley arose to haunt the Irish establishment, but had the Irish public been made aware of some of the details of the reprieve 'process' as conducted by the cabinet ministers it might have identified a few points for concern. As outlined earlier, the procedure inherited from the old British regime in cases where the executive considered applications for reprieves included perusal of a police report on the crime and of the observations of the trial judge (specifically requested). A survey by the present author of a number of available case-files which were circulated to the cabinet in such instances gave rise to several disturbing conclusions.

For instance, basic procedures were not invariably followed in all cases. The Boylan case in 1937, in which the cabinet's dismissal of the judge's views led to personal interference by the judge and the reversal of the government's

---

punishment speakers. The motion that capital punishment was 'not necessary' was 'carried by a large majority'. Mrs Van der Elst lived rather unhappily at Sutton House near Dublin from 1948–50, much of her time being spent fighting lawsuits brought by her assaulted and libelled domestic staff; see C.N. Gattey, *The incredible Mrs Van der Elst* (London, 1972), pp. 197–8, 208–15, 217–18. For the Irish government's single unsuccessful attempt (in the 1940s) at training a competent hangman, see Pierrepoint, *Executioner*, pp. 158–60, and Carey, *Mountjoy*, pp. 209–11.

59 *Evening Mail*, 19 Nov. 1948. Mrs Van der Elst is said to have later denied making the boast: *Dáil Deb.*, vol. 113, col. 460 (25 Nov. 1948).

60 *Dáil Deb.*, vol. 113, cols. 459–60 (25 Nov. 1948), col. 1170 (9 Dec. 1948).

61 James Larkin in 1948: *Dáil Deb.*, vol. 111, cols. 1186–7 (5 May 1948); Sean MacBride in 1951: *Dáil Deb.*, vol. 127, cols. 1158–66 (21 Nov 1951); and Larkin again in 1953: *Dáil Deb.*, vol. 142, cols. 25–6 (20 Oct. 1953). See also *Report of the royal commission on capital punishment*, 1953 [Cmd. 8932].

decision, has been referred to earlier.[62] The possibility that John Fleming was hanged in 1934 less for murdering his wife than for outraging the sexual *mores* of his day might merit consideration. The cabinet was presented with Fleming's brief unsuccessful appeal to the court of criminal appeal but decided to make no further enquiries: '[t]he facts of the case are, doubtless, well known to the members of the Executive Council, and it has not been deemed necessary to call for reports from the trial judge or the Garda Siochana'.[63] In the case of John Hornick, executed in 1937, a Church of Ireland bishop (Dr Day) was allowed an interview with de Valera on the eve of the execution to plead for a reprieve.[64] The 'report of the trial judge' was in virtually all instances conveyed verbally to the cabinet in session by the minister for justice. In the case of Thomas Kelly, however, in 1937, copies were circulated to the ministers.[65] By the time of the Somerville case of 1938 it had become common (though not invariable) practice for ministers to consider also the *verbatim* summation made to the jury by the trial judge as well as the detail of the appeal to the court of criminal appeal, both often very lengthy documents.[66]

Aside from procedural inconsistencies, the cabinet's eventual attitude to the condemned person must have been formed partly, or at least strongly influenced, by the Garda and department of justice reports on the crime and its perpetrator. By the time each case reached the cabinet the guilt or innocence of the condemned person was of course no longer an issue; the ministers, in theory at least, were concerned purely with compassion,[67] but

---

62 NAI, DT S.6375, S.A. Roche, dept. of justice, to secretary, executive council, 15 Dec. 1932: '[t]he only factor in favour of a reprieve [in Patrick McDermott's case] ... is that the verdict was not unanimous; it was the verdict of nine out of the twelve jurors, the legal minimum for a conviction'. McDermott was the first person executed under the de Valera government, some five years before Boylan.

63 NAI, DT S.2343, D. de Brun, dept. of justice, to secretary, executive council, 29 Dec. 1933. See also *Attorney General v. Fleming* [1934] IR 166.

64 NAI, DT S.9862, M. Ó Muimhneacháin, secretary, executive council, to Messrs Peart and O'Hanrahan, solicitors, Dublin, 16 June 1937.

65 NAI, DT S.10370A. The judge was George Gavan Duffy. He made no personal recommendation in his report but observed that the jury's 'unanimous' recommendation to mercy 'may have been due to a doubt or it may have been prompted by the fact that the prisoner has undergone the ordeal three lengthy trials on a capital charge'. Having outlined the evidence of the principal witnesses he stated: 'I do not believe that the jury discredited these witnesses, but they must have thought them mistaken'. Kelly was reprieved. For Duffy's career, see G.M. Golding, *George Gavan Duffy 1882–1951: a legal biography* (Dublin, 1982).

66 NAI, DT S.11040: Mary Somerville, who killed her daughter's illegitimate newborn baby, was reprieved. NAI, DT S.7788B: a note dated 13 March 1953 records that a full transcript of the judge's charge to the jury was furnished in six cases between 1937 and 1940. A full transcript of the judge's charge to the jury was provided also in Michael Manning's case in 1954; see NAI, DT S.15641, notes dated 18–22 Feb. 1954. Likewise in the early (1929) case of Cox: NAI, DT S.5853.

67 Bresler, *Reprieve*, p. 68.

it was on this issue that the cabinet was in effect trying that person for a second time. In court, he or she had been tried in accordance with a detailed and rigidly applied set of rules on a level playing field. Before the cabinet the condemned person was at a severe disadvantage; in place of the rules of evidence there were administrative procedures orchestrated by civil servants who often had no training in the law, and presided over by politicians whose decision inevitably would be determined by their own, often untrained, perception of the complex legalities, their emotional responses to the crime and its perpetrator, and possibly even in response to public opinion on the crime nationally or in their respective constituencies.

In the great majority of cases the lengthy Garda reports (often more than one per case) were heavily slanted against the condemned person, some reports amounting to little more than character assassinations. The Gardaí felt that McDermott (1932) had committed 'one of the most savage murders' with 'cool deliberation' and that 'he appears to be the type that would be prepared to carry out a similar crime again under similar circumstances'.[68] The Gardaí, while prepared to concede that Mary Somerville (1938) 'was a very hard-working, industrious woman', described her also to be 'of loose moral character' and 'had little sympathy' for her. For no apparent reason they felt it necessary to point out that she was a protestant and to repeat local rumours that her husband had not been the father of her younger children.[69] Daniel Doherty, hanged in 1941 for the murder of his pregnant girlfriend, had been regarded always by the local Gardaí 'as a rather giddy individual' who neglected his wife in favour of 'lewd and immoral' pursuits. Unrestrained by rules of evidence which in court would have excluded records of past offences, the Gardaí reported that Doherty had 'committed a criminal assault on two local young women'.[70] Likewise when reporting on the case of Joseph McManus in 1947 the Gardaí balanced their admission that he had never been convicted of any crime by pointing out that in 1923 McManus had been 'detained on suspicion by the Royal Ulster Constabulary for 4 or 5 weeks following the finding in Fermanagh of the outraged and mangled body of a young girl'. Also in 1923, it was said, McManus 'was suspected of an indecent assault on a lady doctor at Swanlinbar … but the injured party failed to identify him'.[71] A feature of present-day murder trials, but missing

---

68 NAI, DT S.6375: reports by the Garda superintendent and chief superintendent, Roscommon, 19 Nov. 1932, and by the deputy commissioner, Crime Branch, Dublin, 22 Nov. 1932.

69 NAI, DT S.11040: report from chief superintendent's office, Monaghan, 17 Nov. 1938. NAI, DT S.9862: the Garda report on John Hornick (also a protestant), on the other hand, was a rare model of impartiality; see superintendent's report, Wexford, 21 April 1937.

70 NAI, DT S.12227: Report from superintendent's office, Buncrana, 5 Dec. 1940.

71 NAI, DT S.14009: 'Memorandum for the government', submitted by the department of justice (synopsising the Garda report), 18 March 1947. See also the early examples of this

from those of the past, is the formal attention given to the impact of the crime upon the victim's family. Their clear determination in former times that the convicted murderer should get his just deserts may have been rooted in the Gardaí's awareness (though there is no explicit evidence of this) that, during the cabinet meeting on the reprieve application, the victim's voice and that of his or her family could be heard only through the police reports. Such reports, however harsh their tone, formed a perhaps-necessary counter-balance in a situation where otherwise only the perpetrator's advocates would be heard.

Other more subtle factors were introduced also to influence a potentially indecisive cabinet. When William Gambon, soon after his marriage, bludgeoned to death his oldest male friend and financial support, the cabinet was told explicitly that the motive had been 'robbery'. The clear possibility raised by the circumstances of the crime of a homosexual motive had been abruptly dismissed by the judge who had insisted to the jury that 'there was no suggestion that the money received by Gambon each week [from his victim, over several years] was other than a friendly contribution'; this statement was repeated to the cabinet.[72] It was not the function of the government to retry a court case in which guilt had already been established. However, the case of Michael Manning, the last person to be executed in the Irish Republic, serves as a sharp reminder of the arbitrary nature of the cabinet's role in deciding a man's worthiness of mercy. Manning, a young married man of unblemished character whose wife was expecting a child, was convicted in 1954 of the rape and murder of an elderly nurse who had been a total stranger to him. He had been drinking and would later state before the Gardaí that '[d]rink was the cause of it'.[73] Manning's legal team tried to prove him insane but neglected to produce the necessary expert testimony to support this contention. (There was a history of mental illness in Manning's family). The jury, and eventually the cabinet also, were left with Manning's personal assertion that he had committed the crime in a state of drunkenness. But since 'drunkenness cannot negative an attempt to rape because rape cannot be committed unintentionally' (the judge's words), Manning was left without an effective defence and was convicted.[74] In the department of justice 'memorandum for

practice in the cases of Cox (1929) whose record included a 1914 larceny and the theft of a bicycle in 1926; and of Toal (1928) who had also once stolen a bicycle; NAI, DT S.5853 and S.5725 respectively.

72 NAI, DT S.14429, 'Memorandum for the government' submitted by the department of justice, 13 Nov. 1948. See also the account in Reddy, *Murder file*.

73 *Irish Times*, 17 Feb. 1954.

74 NAI, DT S.15641. The trial concluded with a lengthy exchange between the judge and the defence counsel regarding the judge's directions to the jury on the point of possible insanity. The judge eventually recalled the jury to clarify the issue. Later the jury returned at its own request to seek clarification of 'circumstances where the mind is affected by alcohol'. These incidents are detailed in the file copy of the judge's charge to the jury, dated 17 Feb. 1954.

the government' on the case, the cabinet was made aware of the evidence of witnesses that Manning was 'not drunk' and reported also that 'no evidence of insanity was tendered'.[75] Capital punishment ended in the Republic in the practical sense on 20 April 1954, attended only by 'a small group'. Again the women prayed and, for the last time, Pierrepoint was the executioner.[76]

Even as the abolitionist icon-cases of Evans and Bentley had no obvious Irish counterparts, neither did the Irish public demonstrate any strong reactions to the royal commission's 1953 report on capital punishment. The commission's vain efforts to seek some compromise solution 'had rendered the division between retention and outright abolition all the starker'.[77] The Irish government's inclination to emulate the British establishment's inactivity in the matter was rooted not in any ideological certainty but more probably in the declining incidence of capital crime. The number of persons convicted of murder in Ireland had always been extremely low; the highest in a single year (1929) was six, of whom only one was executed. In England the figures had climbed quite steeply since the end of the Second World War, a fact which both fuelled the death penalty debate and kept a steady stream of individual cases before the public. In the years between the executions in Ireland of Gambon in 1948 and Manning in 1954, less than half-a-dozen persons had been convicted of murder, and none of these were hanged. After Manning, three years were to elapse before another murder conviction and no more than six further convictions occurred between 1957 and 1962.[78] With such low numbers and the obvious fact that the circumstances of each case were unique, it is not difficult to see why capital punishment never became a political issue in 1950s Ireland. The low numbers had their effect also on public sentiment. The individual murders of the period were no less horrific than those committed in Britain, but in Ireland there was no post-war 'crime wave' to heighten public concern. The case-files of Irish condemned persons are littered with pleas for mercy from individual members of the public, but there was not a single example of a demand that they be executed. Even as few people seemed interested in saving the condemned, so nobody seemed to be demanding their blood. While Manning prepared for

See also the comments in T.F. O'Higgins, *A double life* (Dublin, 1996), pp. 182–3, that fees paid to counsels defending those without means 'were miserably low' and that murder cases were 'a truly exhausting experience' for lawyers.

75 NAI, DT S.15641. In fact Manning's case was considered by the cabinet *twice*. His application to the court of criminal appeal had been delayed until after the cabinet's initial discussion of his case. The ministers were obliged, therefore, to consider his reprieve application afresh following the court of criminal appeal judgment.

76 *Irish Press*, 21 April 1954.

77 Potter, *Hanging in judgment*, p. 159. See also *Report of the royal commission on capital punishment*, pp. 274–83.

78 Figures taken from *Report of the royal commission on capital punishment*, pp. 300–1, and from *Dáil Deb.*, vol. 205, cols. 323–4 (24 Oct. 1963).

his trial, an early book on the Evans and Bentley cases was reviewed in the Irish press as if such things were naturally a British phenomenon.[79]

Capital punishment as an issue had made its appearance in the Dáil some dozen times between 1936 and 1963 but was debated there only once, in 1951–52, all other occasions being merely brief question-and-answer exchanges.[80] The debate took place while the royal commission continued to gather evidence in Britain, and centred on a motion by Sean MacBride that a select committee of the Dáil should examine 'the desirability of capital punishment'. There is no sign amongst the official records that the government (now Fianna Fáil again) made any elaborate preparations for the debate. The government counter-arguments were led not by the minister for justice (Gerald Boland) but, rather oddly, by the minister for lands, Tom Derrig. The debate afforded a shameful insight into the ignorance, confusion, hypocrisy and political prejudice which had haunted the issue since the foundation of the state. MacBride, it emerged, was not himself a 'total' abolitionist; he merely wanted hanging confined 'to cases where it is essential for the preservation of society'. He was concerned in particular to redress the historical accidents which had compelled Ireland to accept without 'objective examination' the British penal code in 1922.[81] The fact that an early draft of the 1922 constitution had specifically excluded capital punishment was revealed publicly for the first time, along with the intriguing detail that Michael Collins had been 'opposed to the death penalty for treason and that he had an open mind as to whether it should be imposed for murder'. Reportedly Collins had believed abolition to be 'worth a trial' and had intended (or may even have tried) to persuade the provisional government to accept the idea.[82]

One deputy who favoured abolishing the death penalty in cases of treason nevertheless wanted it retained for poisoners: '[t]here is only one way of

---

79 *Irish Times*, 4 Jan. 1954; review by Patrick Morris of S. Silverman and P. Paget, *Hanged and innocent? A study of the Rowland, Bentley and Evans cases* (London, 1953). Brendan Behan's play, *The Quare Fella*, first staged in Dublin in 1954, appears to have been received by its Irish audience purely as an entertainment. The play's English audiences, however, interpreted its message as one of abolitionism; see U. O'Connor, *Brendan Behan* (London, 1970), pp. 166–70, 176–9, 182–4, 186–8.

80 *Dáil Deb.*, vol. 50, col. 781 (19 Feb. 1936); vol. 74, col. 7 (8 Feb. 1939); vol. 111, cols. 1186–7 (5 May 1948); vol. 113, cols. 459–60 (25 Nov. 1948); vol. 119, col. 314 (21 Feb. 1950); vol. 127, cols. 1158–66 (21 Nov. 1951); vol. 128, cols. 409–34 (5 Dec. 1951); vol.129, cols. 137–56 (30 Jan. 1952); vol. 142, cols. 25–6 (20 Oct. 1953); vol. 155, col. 462 (14 March 1956); vol. 173, cols. 18–19 (25 Feb. 1959); vol. 181, cols. 1257–8 (12 May 1960); vol. 193, cols. 696–7 (22 Feb. 1962); vol. 196, col. 337 (19 June 1962); vol. 198, cols. 41–2 (27 Nov, 1962); vol. 199, cols. 432–3 (24 Jan. 1963). I have excluded a question regarding an individual case in 1924, the Kerins debate of 1944 which was political in character, and out-of-context jibes about the 'English hangman' in 1945 and 1948.

81 *Dáil Deb.*, vol. 127, cols. 1158–66 (21 Nov. 1951).

82 Ibid., vol. 128, col. 409 (5 Dec. 1951).

dealing with a person of that kind and that is to treat that person the way you would treat a mad dog'. Against those who believed that life imprisonment was 'the harshest punishment that can be imposed on a human being' were those who felt that jail 'has now very little terrors ... Prisoners may smoke. They may have their radios. They may have their newspapers ... I see now in Belfast they propose letting them out for Christmas'.[83] In the course of a debate that quickly began to generate more heat than light, MacBride, having argued originally that Ireland had lagged behind progressive British developments in the penal code, was provoked by Derrig's responses into condemning slavish imitation of Westminster policies: '[a]re we to follow the House of Lords of the English Parliament in every step which we take? Is that what we have come to?' Derrig's replies were interrupted, almost inevitably, by the jibe that it was necessary to employ 'foreign people' as executioners.[84]

Derrig's responses, however, were important. They represented not only the attitude of the Fianna Fáil party whose leaders would govern Ireland for most of the 1950s and all of the 1960s, but also the attitude of the Fianna Fáil members of the 'revolutionary' generation, some of them now entering their third decade at the helm of government. While clearly he found it impossible to avoid all reference to the Westminster debates on the issue, Derrig played the green card with much force. Reforms in other 'so-called civilised countries ... are not such as are likely now, or at any time in the future, to commend themselves to the Irish people'. The Irish, he argued, cannot be accused of 'lagging behind in the march of civilisation ... when we fail to take the direction which those have taken of plain immorality in social life'. The 'primary consideration', Derrig felt, should be to have regard 'to our own circumstances, and to what we consider to be right and proper in the interests of our own community'. Any such proposed committee, he concluded, 'would create quite unnecessary fears in the public mind and that, with the death penalty abolished, would-be murderers would be given a certain licence to pursue their fell designs'.[85]

When the debate resumed following the Christmas recess of 1951, Derrig showed signs of more careful preparation and a closer familiarity with academic arguments on the issue. His favourite approach, however, tailored to fit the sympathies of Dáil and nation, concerned catholic church teaching on the subject, which was, he said, 'that punishment is primarily and essentially retributive in character'. MacBride reacted furiously but impotently to the government's removal of a debate on a 'civil' issue into the realm of

83 Ibid., cols. 421–3, 426 (5 Dec. 1951).
84 Ibid., col. 433 (5 Dec. 1951). For MacBride's original point, see ibid., vol. 127, col. 1160 (21 Nov. 1951).
85 Ibid., vol. 128, cols. 428–34 (5 Dec. 1951).

catholic orthodoxy. 'You cannot', concluded Derrig pompously, 'get away from moral teaching on these matters'.[86] In a sparsely-attended but often heated debate during which attention focused bizarrely at one stage on why the 1916 executions had not been a deterrent, Derrig's most important remarks – in effect a policy statement – went unappreciated:

> It is very noticeable that in some of the most progressive of the countries he [MacBride] mentioned the last execution took place very many years before capital punishment was abolished. There was no question of trying to antedate public opinion or the ordinary evolution in this respect which had taken place in the circumstances of these countries, and I think there is some real hope for the cessation of capital punishment from allowing it to fall into disuse and from that being the case for a period than through any premature efforts to abolish it by legislation in advance of public opinion.[87]

When the issue was debated again in 1956 a Fine Gael-dominated coalition government (though MacBride was not a member) was in power. A standard negative reply by the minister for justice (James Everitt) to a Dáil query on the prospects of abolition was followed by a motion for a full debate, proposed by five senators.[88] The standard of discourse was traditionally higher in the senate and debates were not invariably political in the 'party' sense. When the cabinet, in advance of the debate, discussed 'the line to be taken', Everitt admitted to being 'in general sympathy with the views of those who are opposed to capital punishment'. He would not, he said, 'be in favour of retaining it for its own sake'. He was, however, impressed by the need to retain the death penalty 'on security grounds'. The IRA border campaign of 1956–62 was not to begin until December, but half-a-dozen arms raids had taken place in Northern Ireland and England since 1951 and the Garda Special Branch was well aware of republican activities. The previous November the Taoiseach, John A. Costello, had publicly slated the re-arming and had undertaken 'to use if necessary all the powers and forces at our disposal to bring such activities effectively to an end'. At the cabinet discussion in April 1956, Everitt suggested following the existing line – as stated by Derrig four years earlier – by 'not formally abolishing (or suspending) capital punishment at all ever but letting it fall into disuse instead'. There had been, he noted, only one execution since 1948. The government's position, he emphasised, must be clear and unambiguous: 'there should be

86 Ibid., vol. 129, cols. 137–40, 151–2 (30 Jan. 1952).
87 Ibid., vol. 129, col. 139 (30 Jan. 1952). MacBride's motion was lost eventually by 63 votes to 24: see ibid., cols. 153–6.
88 Ibid., vol. 155, col. 462 (14 March 1956). The Dáil query was by deputy Finlay; the senators were Stanford, McHugh, Skeffington, Douglas and Bergin.

no shilly-shallying about it as nothing could be more detrimental to the public interest than any uncertainty about the death penalty'. The cabinet agreed, however, to consider formally the 'views' which would be expressed at the senate debate.[89]

The quality of that debate, on 30 May 1956, did not disappoint, and while the familiar 'Irish' elements of the argument were present, they were advanced with greater clarity and a noticeable lack of rancour. Professor Stanford, having spelled out that, historically, capital punishment was a British rather than an Irish institution, made the unusual point that Ireland might soon be the only 'unreformed' country as regards the death sentence, and that therefore 'the spotlights of the sensational newspapers will be turned on any executions in this country with tenfold strength'.[90] Dr McHugh, who joined Stanford in proposing the motion, did not believe that Irish murders were usually premeditated, but that they were attributable instead to 'passion, or ... drink'. He felt it to be significant that 'hangmen have to be imported – that no [Irish] citizen will take responsibility for it' [i.e. an execution]. He was moved also by the apparent probability that the Stormont government would retain the death penalty even if England decided to abolish it: 'we are often critical of the form of Government practised there [in Belfast], and we are to imitate its worst procedure at our peril?'[91] The greater opportunities for mayhem afforded to political traitors by advanced technology was a theme of the pro-retention lobby led by Professor Fearon. Uniquely he was in favour of setting up 'a small committee' to consider cleaner, less distasteful methods of execution.[92] The only trace of anglophobic tension arose when two pro-abolitionists fell out over the desirability of following Westminster's lead in the matter.[93] No vote was taken, as the motion sought merely an enquiry on the issue; and the motion was adopted by the senate.[94]

When the cabinet came to give its much-delayed consideration to the senate resolution in late October it displayed no explicit awareness of the

---

89 NAI, DT S.7788B, 'Memorandum for the government' relative to the 'senate motion on capital punishment', 12 April 1956. A 13-page appendix to this memorandum sets out the case for and against capital punishment as understood by dept. of justice officials; see also cabinet minutes, GC 7/115, 20 April 1956, item 5. For IRA developments during 1951–6, see Coogan, *The IRA*, pp. 266–308; Costello's 1955 statement is quoted at p. 300. On 10 November 1955 the British government had rejected all the recommendations of the royal commission.

90 *Seanad Deb.*, vol. 46, cols. 173–4, 180 (30 May 1956).

91 Ibid., vol. 46, cols. 184–5 (30 May 1956). The need to 'import hangmen' was referred to by Skeffington at col. 192.

92 Ibid., cols. 194–5 (30 May 1956).

93 Ibid., col. 198 (Kissane) and col. 200 (Hickey) (30 May 1956).

94 Ibid., col. 208 (30 May 1956). The instances of Evans, Bentley and Ellis as classic 'miscarriages of justice' were referred to by several speakers.

imminence of the British Homicide Bill, announced only a week later. As well as abolishing the concept of 'constructive malice' and introducing that of 'diminished responsibility', the British bill provided for 'degrees' of murder: '[c]apital murders were defined as those committed in an attempt to resist arrest or escape or during the course of theft, where a firearm or explosive was used, a policeman or prison officer killed on duty, or when the killer had previously been convicted of murder'.[95] The Irish ministers did, however, note that 'in England the opponents of the retributive theory of punishment have shifted the emphasis of their argument from a dogmatic assertion that retribution is barbarous to the no less dogmatic assertion that the notion of criminal responsibility is based on an illusion ...' The cabinet declined to act regarding the abolition or suspension of the death penalty and ignored the senate suggestion of an enquiry. The influence of events in London, however, was clearly discernible in the decision that Everitt 'should examine the question whether the law relating to the crime of murder requires to be amended'.[96]

Costello's government was replaced by another Fianna Fáil administration in 1957 and any emergent proposals for amending the law of murder appear to have withered on the vine. The death sentence remained on the statute-book, was imposed on half-a-dozen murderers between 1957 and 1962, but was never used. Noel Browne, from the opposition benches, pressed in vain for the law to be brought into line with the British Homicide Act 1957, but the matter of retention or abolition remained a minority interest.[97] Nevertheless, despite its apparently intentional state of discontinuance, the possibility of execution was seriously considered on each occasion when a reprieve application came before the cabinet; reprieves were never 'automatic'.[98]

---

95 Potter, *Hanging in judgment*, p. 178.

96 NAI, DT S.7788B, copy of cabinet minutes, GC 7/154, 30 Oct. 1956, item 2. See also the dept. of justice 'Memorandum ... on capital punishment', 11 Oct. 1956. By 1956 a new abolitionist group had appeared on the Irish scene. The 'Irish Association of Civil Liberty' was presided over by Sean O Faolain, with Edgar M. Deale and Mrs Le Brocquy acting as secretary and treasurer. Its vice-presidents included Mrs M.S. Kettle, Professor T.W. Moody, Dr Bethel Solomons, Professor W.B. Stanford, the earl of Wicklow, Professor Desmond Williams and Miss Dorothy Macardle. For their concern in the notorious case of 'Mame' Cadden, who was reprieved in 1956, see NAI, DT S.16116.

97 *Dáil Deb.*, vol. 173, cols. 18–19 (25 Feb. 1959), Noel Browne; vol. 181, cols. 1257–8 (12 May 1960), Frank Sherwin; vol. 193, cols. 696–7 (22 Feb. 1962), Noel Browne and Jack McQuillan; vol. 196, col. 337 (19 June 1962), Oliver J. Flanagan.

98 NAI, DT S.7788C/94: See the note dated 30 May 1959 recording the attendance of the president of the high court, Mr Justice Cahir Davitt, at part of a cabinet meeting to consider the reprieve application of William Wall. This had occurred on two previous occasions only: Patrick Boylan in 1937 and Patrick Heffernan in 1951, both of whom were reprieved.

Between 1922 and 1944 the minister for justice had been responsible for the release on licence after a suitable number of years of a number of reprieved persons whose sentences had been commuted to penal servitude for life. After 1944 he continued to issue such releases after consultation with the government in each case. It seemed unclear whether in law the president, the government, or the minister for justice, or all three, had such responsibility, and much paper and ink were expended on the matter over the years. When the matter surfaced again in July 1962, however, the justice secretary, Peter Berry, felt 'that it would be as well to leave the matter over until the overhaul of the penal code, a job which the Department of Justice hopes to tackle in the next twelve months'.[99]

The reconsideration of the death sentence may not originally have been part of the intended 'overhaul'. Less than a month later there was an unusual degree of press attention afforded to the reprieve of one James Kelly who had been under sentence of death since May. The *Irish Times* accused everyone (but, implicitly, the government) of 'hiding our heads in the sand, and conveniently avoiding the complex of ethical questions which are raised by capital punishment'. Referring to the lapse of over eight years since the last execution, the paper queried 'whether by retaining a penalty which seems to have passed its practical application, any useful purpose is served'.[100] Ten days later, it was 'informally arranged' that the minister for justice, now Charles J. Haughey, would prepare a memorandum for the cabinet 'on the general question of capital punishment'. This decision, it was stated, had arisen from the cabinet discussion on Kelly's reprieve and because of 'subsequent public comment' on that reprieve.[101]

Having spent some six months considering the matter, Haughey told the cabinet 'that there is no case for retaining capital punishment any longer except as a deterrent and that there is no reason to suppose that an increase in murder cases in this country would follow abolition contrary to the experience of other countries … which have abolished it'. He referred to the point made by the royal commission that, quite aside from the deterrent effect of capital punishment on potential murderers, the same 'deterrent force' acted also 'by building up in the community a deep feeling of peculiar abhorrence for the crime of murder'. That deterrent effect, however, 'is reduced when, as in this country from 1946 to the present day, only one in 24 of those charged with murder and only 1 in 6 of those sentenced to death for murder, were in fact executed, and when there has been no execution in the last eight years'. In other words the ritual solemn pronunciation of the death

---

99 NAI, DT 98/6/49, Berry to T. Ó Cearbhaill, dept. of the Taoiseach, 14 July 1962.

100 *Irish Times*, 11 Aug. 1962. A copy of this editorial was placed in the capital punishment 'policy' file, NAI, DT 98/6/49.

101 NAI, DT 98/6/49, note by Nioclas Ó Nualláin, dept. of the Taoiseach., 21 Aug. 1962.

sentence had become well recognised as an empty formula. The lapse of eight years since the last execution had placed Ireland 'in a better position than Britain or Northern Ireland to abolish capital punishment'. Because of 'the great variety of circumstances in which murders may be committed', Haughey was not in favour of the type of compromise represented by the controversial distinction made in the British Homicide Act between capital and non-capital murder. The IRA, however, was to be excepted from the new rule. Haughey retained Everitt's 1956 position and stated 'that only the death penalty is an adequate deterrent for those crimes [of murder and treason] and in his opinion it is essential in the public interest that it should be retained for them'. The death penalty had been retained in legislation of 1954 as regards 'mutiny with violence by persons subject to military law'; Haughey was in favour of retaining this provision.[102] In brief the minister was recommending abolition in peacetime except for treason, army mutiny, and murder tried before the special criminal court (i.e. IRA murders).[103] The cabinet discussed the memorandum on 15 January 1963, accepted abolition 'in principle', and asked Haughey to draw up 'detailed proposals'.[104]

While the arguments cited by Haughey before the cabinet were no doubt a faithful reflection of his own views and those of his officials at the department of justice, they do not fully explain the apparent *volte-face* in Irish governing and administrative circles between 1956 and 1963 over an issue on which change had been resisted since the foundation of the state. The political environment of the post-1959 period which almost certainly influenced the sea-change was reflected in the shift of government attitudes in areas such as economic policy and also in the beginnings of an effort to get to grips with some longstanding social problems. Much of the impetus stemmed from the retirement of de Valera as Taoiseach and his replacement by Sean Lemass, no less a man of the revolutionary generation but of somewhat broader vision than his predecessor. De Valera's last cabinet of 1957–59 had seen also the introduction of younger ministers, many of them too young to remember the civil war. Six of the seven new ministers of the 1957–59 government served also in the cabinets of 1959–61 and 1961–65.[105]

102 Defence Act 1954, s. 128.
103 NAI, DT 98/6/49, 'Memorandum for the government – proposed abolition of the death sentence in certain cases', 31 Dec. 1962. The matter of mutiny with violence by persons subject to military law was dealt with under section 128 of the Defence Act 1954.
104 NAI, DT 98/6/49, copy of cabinet minutes, GC 10/74, 15 Jan. 1963. item 2. The decision was revealed to the Dáil nine days later; see *Dáil Deb.*, vol. 199, cols. 432–3 (24 Jan. 1963). Despite its apparent role in the government's reconsideration of the issue, the press viewed the proposal 'as rather a surprise. The retention or abolition of the death penalty has not been passionately debated in Ireland … It is possible that there is no strong public opinion for or against, because the problem has not continually forced itself on the attention of the people'; see *Irish Independent*, 25 Jan. 1963.
105 These were: Kevin Boland, Neil Blaney, Jack Lynch, Micheal O Morain, and Art O

254 *Gerard O'Brien*

These were joined by three further 'young' ministers in the 1959–61 cabinet, all of whom went on to serve in the 1961–65 administration.[106] Haughey was the 'new' minister of the 1961–65 government, followed in 1964 by Brian Lenihan and, in 1965, by C. Condon (attorney general). The gap in terms of age and experience between 'old' and 'young' ministers when the abolition issue came before cabinet in January 1963 was considerable. Four ministers (Lemass, Frank Aiken, Sean MacEntee and James Ryan) had served in every Fianna Fáil government since 1932; one other, Paddy Smith, since 1944. Of the other ten, nine 'dated' from 1957; of the younger ministers only Erskine Childers had been in office when the last execution took place in 1954. Haughey (who had first entered the Dáil in 1957) had been influenced less by the echoing debates in Britain over Evans, Bentley and Ruth Ellis than by the transatlantic sensations of the Barbara Graham and Carl Chessman cases.[107] He had accepted the justice portfolio in October 1961 privately determined that nobody should be executed during his term of office.[108] Almost within days he was confronted with the issue in the form of one Daniel Galvin, sentenced to death on 25 October. In line with then-established practice the sentence was commuted and the issue did not arise again until the Kelly case in August 1962.[109] Between February and August 1962 Haughey fended off two Dáil questions on the prospects of abolition; one of these concerned a request for 'factual information' on capital punishment which had been made by the United Nations Economic and Social Council.[110] The two final executions in Northern Ireland, in July and December 1961, appear not to have impacted significantly on Haughey personally, but his officials could not have been unaware of the fierceness of the debate which surrounded those executions in Ulster circles.[111] The officials were also aware (as was their

Caoimh (attorney general). I have included also Erskine Childers, perhaps the oldest of the younger ministers, who had served in the cabinet of 1951–54. The seventh minister was J. Ormonde who served in the 1957–59 cabinet only.

106 Michael Hilliard, Gerald Bartley and Patrick J. Hillery.

107 Author's interview with Charles J. Haughey, 1 March 2000. The Graham story was made into a lurid but popular movie, *I want to live*, in 1958. Chessman popularised his own case in several books during the 1950s. Soon after his execution in 1960 Deputy Sherwin invoked his name in a Dáil appeal for abolition of the death penalty; see *Dáil Deb.*, vol. 181, cols. 1257–8 (12 May 1960).

108 Haughey interview.

109 NAI, DT 98/6/49, N. Ó Nuallain, secretary, dept. of the Taoiseach, to private secretary, dept. of justice, 9 Feb. 1962, formally advising that the president, on cabinet recommendation, had commuted Galvin's sentence.

110 *Dáil Deb.*, vol. 193, cols. 696–7 (22 Feb. 1962), Browne and McQuillan. The other (brief) Dáil query was by Oliver J. Flanagan; see *Dáil Deb.*, vol. 196, col. 337 (26 July 1962).

111 Haughey interview. Also NAI, DT 98/6/49: Haughey's 'Memorandum for the government', Dec. 1962, submitted a year after the execution of Robbie McGladdery in Belfast (20 Dec. 1961), indicates his awareness that motions in both houses of the

minister) of the apparent failure of the 1957 British distinction between capital and non-capital murder to show the desired results.[112] It seems not improbable that it was these various factors, in conjunction with the changes in ministerial personnel, and the tendency (referred to above) to re-evaluate older policy determinants, that made the autumn of 1962 an opportune time to re-examine the capital punishment issue.[113]

The 'informal agreement' in August 1962 to re-examine the matter did not, however, indicate that any decision, even in principle, had then been made. Haughey responded to a mundane Dáil query on abolition in November 1962 with a short negative and quelled a 'hangman' jibe by inviting the jibing deputy (Sherwin) to volunteer for the job himself.[114] When, in the aftermath of the January 1963 cabinet discussion, Haughey revealed to the Dáil the decision to abolish the death penalty 'in principle ... generally' but pointed out that 'it will be retained for specific types of murder', he could give no details to the querulous house.[115] As ever, no details of the cabinet discussion of 15 January 1963 were recorded, but in Haughey's recollection most of the older ministers were in favour of retaining the death penalty mainly on grounds of national security, while the younger ministers favoured abolition. The personal support of Sean Lemass was important in carrying the issue for Haughey.[116]

Having consulted the attorney general's office (A. Ó Caoimh, a 'young' minister) and the departments of defence (G. Bartley, also a 'young' minister) and external affairs (F. Aiken, an 'old' minister), Haughey prepared to lay his detailed proposals for legislation before the cabinet on 21 February 1963. Because of the controversy which still surrounded the British Homicide Act, Haughey had hoped that the murder of police officers in non-political instances could be included in the 'general abolition' of the death penalty, and the concurrence of the Garda commissioner had been obtained to this end. Aiken, however, took the view that murderers of policemen and prison officers and those who murder for political reasons whatever the circumstances ought to remain subject to the death penalty.[117] This disagreement

---

Stormont parliament earlier in 1962 for a review of capital punishment had been defeated. For the McGladdery case, see Moore, *Behind the garden wall*, pp. 185–90.

112 NAI, DT 98/6/49, 'Memorandum for the government', 31 Dec. 1962, 'Views of the minister for justice'.

113 The recruitment of a young minister for justice was paralleled in the administrative sense by the appointment of Peter Berry as the department's secretary on 23 Feb. 1961 at the relatively early age of 51. (Berry was born on 7 June 1909.)

114 *Dáil Deb.*, vol. 198, cols. 41–2 (27 Nov. 1962), Coughlan and Sherwin.

115 Ibid., vol. 199, cols. 432–3 (24 Jan. 1963). The opposition clearly feared that an Irish version of the British Homicide Act was in contemplation.

116 Haughey interview.

117 NAI, DT 98/6/49, 'Memorandum for the government: Bill to abolish the death penalty in certain cases', 21 Feb. 1963.

between Haughey and Aiken, explicit in the justice department's memorandum, became a matter for the cabinet to resolve. In the end, perhaps
acknowledging that some concession should be made to the experience or
apprehensions of the older ministers, Aiken's amendment was accepted and
it remained a capital offence to murder a police or prison officer. The death
penalty was also retained for those who would murder a foreign head of state
or a foreign diplomat in Ireland.[118]

The remaining passage of the measure into law as the Criminal Justice Act
1964 was relatively trouble-free. The principal amendment which appeared
in the 'white print' format of the bill before cabinet on 3 July 1963 had been
introduced by the department of justice. The cabinet was advised to abolish
the doctrine of 'constructive malice'. This originally was a concept whereby
a quite accidental killing in the course of committing a violent felony or
resisting arrest or escaping from custody had been regarded as murder and
punishable as such. The British had abolished it under the Homicide Act
1957. Irish justice officials felt that it would be 'anomalous' to retain such a
doctrine in a bill 'which abolishes the death penalty for many deliberate
killings'.[119] The cabinet approved the text of the bill and it became law on 25
March 1964.[120]

In two stages, at the beginning of the 1990s and in 2001, the Irish totally
abolished capital punishment.[121] During the same decade the Irish finally
confronted a number of long-neglected (and some even half-forgotten) social
problems which had flourished since the foundation of the state and many of
which had predated the state's existence. These included the endemic
brutality and abuse which had for generations prevailed in the state's

---

118 NAI, DT 98/6/49: The 'Memorandum' was revised at Peter Berry's instigation and
discussed at a cabinet meeting on 26 Feb. 1963. The revised version makes it clear that no
agreement could be reached between the depts. of justice and external affairs in advance
of the cabinet meeting; see the note headed 'Capital Punishment' dated 22 Feb. 1963, and
the revised 'Memorandum' dated 21 Feb. 1963 but with the critical paragraph 13 expanded
to highlight the disagreement. The file contains also a copy of the full cabinet decision,
cabinet minutes, GC 10/83, 26 Feb. 1963, item 1.

119 NAI, DT 98/6/49, 'Memorandum for the government: Criminal Justice Bill, 1963'. The
Seanad debate on the Bill was no less verbose and protracted than that which had taken
place in the same House in 1956 or in the Dáil in 1951–2. The previous debates, however,
had the potential to influence policy and even practice with regard to reprieve applications.
In 1964 the Seanad was debating a piece of legislation the central principle of which had
already been decided upon in cabinet. See *Seanad Debates*, vol. 57, cols. 463–525 (26 Feb.
1964); vol. 57, cols. 659–94 (4 March 1964); vol. 57, cols, 733–61 (18 March 1964).

120 NAI, DT 98/6/49, M. Slattery, secretary to the president, to secretary, government, 25
March 1964. See also the copy of cabinet minutes, GC, 10/110, 9 July 1963, item 10.

121 Criminal Justice Act 1990, s. 1 provided that '[n]o person shall suffer death for any offence'.
The Twenty-First Amendment of the Constitution Act 2001, s.1 and sched.1, pt. 2,
provided for a subsection to art. 15.5 of the 1937 constitution stating that '[t]he Oireachtas
shall not enact any law providing for the imposition of the death penalty'.

religious-run schools and children's institutions; the convent laundries staffed by so-called 'fallen women'; the widespread graft and corruption in public life; as well as the vacuity and hopelessness of the state's Ulster 'policy'. If the winding-up of the capital punishment issue could be included in this apparently general wave of national self-purgation, then the failure of the Irish people to 'deal' with capital punishment between 1922 and 1964 is fairly easily explained. But it is not so simple.

No condemned person ever bribed his or her way to a reprieve nor did any cabinet accept a backhander to hang a convicted murderer. Except for bland advice furnished to de Valera during the preparation of the 1937 constitution, the intrusive shadow of Archbishop McQuaid and that of the catholic church in general appear not to have influenced either established policy or individual decisions as regards the death sentence.[122] By Haughey's account the catholic hierarchy was not consulted at the time of the passing of the Criminal Justice Act 1964.[123] In a sense, capital punishment had more in common with the convent laundries in that both institutions predated the foundation of the state, and therein lay the reasons why both were tolerated so unquestioningly. The Irish failed to debate the issue of capital punishment because they had a perception of it quite different from that entertained by the British or American public. Like parliamentary procedures, like local government, and like the civil service, the practice of executing convicted murderers had been inherited in established form from the British in 1922. The political fact that it had been a British institution was ignored as easily as was the use of Westminster procedures in the Dáil, time-honoured practices in local government, and the fact that crown civil servants had effortlessly become Free State civil servants.

For the most part the Irish wanted a quiet life after the events of 1916–22. 'Transferred' institutions were subjected to scrutiny only if their role under the crown had been seen as 'political'; hence the disbandment of the RIC and its replacement by the Garda Síochána. The practice of hanging fellow-Irishmen had (as noted at the start of this paper) been politically tainted for centuries. It might have been expected that the Irish in 1922 would have sought its abandonment with the same self-righteousness with which the abolition of the RIC was insisted upon. But by 1922 the Irish had settled to a dual perception (or 'double-think') in regard to capital punishment. As a

---

122 John Cooney, *John Charles McQuaid, ruler of catholic Ireland* (Dublin, 1999), pp. 95, 103. I regard Derrig's citation of catholic doctrine during the 1952 Dáil debate as a tactic of the moment rather than as a sign of church influence on this area of policy. For McQuaid's advice to de Valera on the issue in 1937, see University College Dublin Archives, de Valera papers, P150/1091: 'For lawful death penalty on part of supreme authority, it is absolutely requisite to have moral certitude *in trial* concerning commission of very grave crime. Admission of guilt is not requisite for lawful execution'.
123 Haughey interview.

matter of social and moral concern it scarcely existed; only when it appeared in its 'political' guise was it seen to be an issue. Depending on the person and on the nature of the crime the Irish between 1922 and 1964 would feel sometimes more and sometimes less than sympathetic to the plight of a condemned killer; only when the condemned killer was a member of the IRA were the Irish outraged at his fate. To this extent capital punishment had been part and parcel of the long political struggle for Irish independence. Its periodic re-emergence after 1922 as a political issue every time the Irish government executed an IRA man (as in the 1939–45 period) reflected merely the extent to which the broader issue of Ulster was continuing to bedevil Irish political perceptions. The colossal irony that they were ignoring the ethical features of capital punishment, features which were increasingly moving the British (who had allegedly brought capital punishment to Ireland) to abolish it, evidently was lost on Irish public and politicians alike. Like the issue of the Irish language and the primacy of catholic doctrine in social matters, the 'national question' tended to hog the political limelight and divert the attention of public and politicians away from issues which, like capital punishment, like the convent laundries, like corruption in public life, like brutality and abuse in orphanages and schools, occasionally stood squarely in front of them in human form. In Ireland each reprieve represented at best a postponement and at worst a refusal to deal intelligently with the whole issue of capital punishment; each execution reflected yet another failure by the Irish people to face their own shortcomings.

In the improving conditions of the early 1960s the Irish finally began to confront the ethics of capital punishment, and dealt with the matter so decisively that they stole a temporary march both on Stormont and Westminster. The story of the death sentence in Irish history between 1964 and 1990, a period bedevilled by economic collapse, social stagnation, the unending predominance of the Ulster 'troubles', and for the first time since the 1940s, scarred by the murder of Gardaí, remains to be told.[124]

---

124 The post-1964 story has been told, insofar as is possible from published sources, in L. O'Callaghan, 'The history of the death penalty in Ireland since the civil war' (unpublished, M.Phil. thesis, University College, Cork, 2003), chs. v and vi. See also the useful discussions of the role of the judiciary in J. Grundy, 'The death penalty and the Irish state' (unpublished, M.Litt. thesis, University College, Dublin, 2000), ch. 5.

The making of law in eighteenth-century Ireland: the significance and import of Poynings' law

JAMES KELLY*

THE MOST MATERIAL STATUTORY influence on the making of law in Ireland was Poynings' law, or *An act that no parliament be holden in this land until the acts be certified into England* to give the measure its full title. Enacted by the Irish parliament convened at Drogheda in 1494, it directed that 'no parliament be holden' in Ireland without the prior communication of such 'causes and considerations and all such acts as ... seemeth should pass in the said parliament', and that were deemed 'good and expedient' by the king in council before they became law.[1] Despite some practical difficulties, notably in respect of the advancement of legislation that arose in the course of a parliamentary session, and to the relief of which it was determined in 1557 to permit the viceroy and council to communicate bills after the authorisation to convene parliament had been granted, the enactment achieved its purpose of curtailing the Irish executive.[2] This remained the position until 1634 when the lord deputy, Thomas Wentworth, whose loyalty to the crown was unimpeachable, appealed to the measure (in the words of Edwards and Moody) 'as a weapon against parliamentary self-assertion'.[3] He achieved this contentious end by asserting the sole authority under Poynings' law of the lord deputy and council in Ireland 'for the framing and drawing up any acts to pass in parliament'. He acknowledged in a statement to the house of lords that peers possessed the right 'to represent to the lord deputy and council ... such public considerations as they shall think fit and good for the common-wealth, and so to submit them to be drawn into acts and transmitted into England'. But his accompanying assertion that any proposal so submitted might be 'altered or rejected according as the lord deputy and [Irish] council in their wisdom shall judge and hold expedient', and that any measure that

---

* A revised version of an address given to the Society at the Mansion House, Dublin, on 27 February 2002. It anticipates a larger study of the impact of Poynings' law on the making of law in Ireland between 1660 and 1800.
1 10 Henry VII, c. 4. See D.B. Quinn, 'The early interpretation of Poynings' law, 1494–1534' in *IHS*, 2 (1940–41), 241–54.

had negotiated both councils that was amended by the Irish parliament was obliged to be transmitted to be scrutinised anew at the English privy council board, was manifestly intended to reduce the Irish parliament, in Aidan Clarke's words, 'to the subordinate status of a legislative agency obediently giving statutory effect to executive policy'.[4]

This was not acceptable to many (perhaps a majority) of the political communities of the Old and New English that dominated the Irish legislature. The observation of Charles, Lord Lambert, that 'if Poynings' law be so understood as that parliament can do nothing but pass bills, that is scarce a parliament', informed an attempt in 1641 to assert the right to transmit draft bills, but this was denied by Charles I.[5] This is not to suggest that Wentworth's conception of how Poynings' law should operate prevailed. The representatives of the protestant interest in Ireland in parliament were no less eager for the restoration of the monarchy in 1660 than the Old English were during the 1640s to possess an active role (rather than the passive role envisaged by Wentworth) in the making of law for Ireland. Significantly, they were to discover that Charles II and his successors were more willing to accommodate their wishes, but this did not make the identification of practical administrative arrangements that satisfied the respective requirements of the crown and Irish interests a straightforward or simple process. Indeed, despite steps in this direction in the 1660s when several bills that reached the statute-book took their rise in the Irish parliament as heads of bills, no clear mechanism was established until the mid-1690s. It was only then that heads of a bill, which resembled a bill in all respects save for the important opening formulary that read 'we pray that it be enacted' when the customary rubric read 'be it enacted', became the primary means by which law was initiated in Ireland. Significantly, though heads of bills could rise with either house of the Irish parliament, attempts in the 1690s and 1730s to give them added status by having them approved by both houses prior to their referral to the Irish privy council, were repulsed. More importantly, the Irish privy council retained the right to respite (i.e. to veto) and amend all heads of bills and to determine which were certified and forwarded as bills to the English (from 1707, British) privy council where they could also be amended, respited or postponed. This was the procedure required to satisfy Poynings' law that bills must receive the prior approval of the crown, which was indicated by their return to Ireland under the great seal of England. Bills so returned were submitted to the Irish parliament, but they were only eligible to receive the

2   3 & 4 Ph and Mary, c. 4; R.D. Edwards and T.W. Moody, 'The history of Poynings' law: part 1, 1494–1615' in *IHS*, 2 (1940–41), 418–9.
3   Edwards and Moody, 'The history of Poynings' law', p. 415.
4   A. Clarke, 'The history of Poynings' law, 1615–41' in *IHS*, 17 (1972–3), 214.
5   Clarke, 'The history of Poynings' law', pp. 219–21.

royal assent, whereby they achieved legal effect, if they proceeded unaltered through both houses of the Irish parliament. The heads of bills process was, as this suggests, an inherently restrictive arrangement, but from the perspective of the Irish parliament, which was eager to possess maximum legal initiative, it represented a considerable advance on the procedure that Wentworth sought to apply, and on what might have been the practice had certain officials in Ireland as well as England had their way in the 1660s and 1690s. Once the process became established, and it was firmly in place by the beginning of the eighteenth century, the way was clear for the Irish parliament to affirm its entitlement to originate the legislation approved for operation in Ireland. The fact that between 1703 and 1800 a grand total of 2,201 acts reached the Irish statute-book, in contrast to the number – just 138 – ratified between 1660 and 1699, certainly suggests that it was neither as procrustean nor as inhibiting as the rhetoric of eighteenth-century patriots has led generations of politicians and political commentators to conclude. It was limiting to be sure (as the crown and its officials desired), but it was not inflexible as the application and import of the law differed significantly over time.

In this paper Poynings' law will be examined during three time periods – 1660–99, 1703–82, and 1782–1800 – corresponding with what are, it is suggested, the main sub-phases in the application of the law during what may be termed its 'parliamentary' phase. Surprisingly, given the large volume of documentation generated by the application of Poynings' law at the English/British privy council board, its operation during this phase has attracted less notice than its earlier 'executive' phase, which has been the subject of the seminal articles by Quinn, Edwards and Moody, and Clarke cited earlier.[6] The later phase has not been neglected entirely. Both Beckett and O'Brien have offered useful perspectives on the implications of the achievement of legislative independence.[7] However, the rich archive of material generated by the English/British privy council remains remarkably under-explored. Recently, there have been indications of a welcome revival of interest in the operation and membership of parliament, symbolised by the devotion of a special issue of the journal, *Parliamentary History*, in 2001 to the Irish parliament in the eighteenth century and by the publication of the monumental *History of the Irish parliament, 1692–1800* by Johnston-Liik.[8] It is appropriate also to single out two essays, one a case study of the operation of Poynings' law during the 1760s published in *Parliamentary*

6 See notes 2, 3 and 5.

7 G. O'Brien, *Anglo-Irish politics in the age of Grattan and Pitt* (Dublin, 1987), pp. 20–1, 28–31; J.C. Beckett, 'Anglo-Irish constitutional relations in the later eighteenth century' in *IHS*, 14 (1964), 20–38.

8 D.W. Hayton (ed.), *The Irish parliament in the eighteenth century: the long apprenticeship*, special issue of *Parliamentary History*, 20:1 (2001); E.M. Johnston-Liik, *History of the Irish parliament, 1692–1800: commons, constituencies and statutes*, 6 vols, (Belfast, 2002).

History, the other an overview of the administrative application of the measure written by Bergin who is embarked on what promises to be a model close study of its operation during the 1690s and early eighteenth century.[9] What is apparent from both is that the impact of Poynings' law on the making of law in Ireland was, if anything, greater than generally assumed even by its many contemporary critics.

1660–99

1660–66

When it was decided towards the end of 1660 to convene a parliament in Ireland, the fact that the instructions to the lords justices who headed the Irish executive included an order to '[d]raft such bills as you, with the advice of the Council, think are for the good of our subjects there, and submit them for our consideration according to the text of Poynings' Law, in order to the calling of a Parliament there', demonstrated the intent of the restored monarchy to continue to employ Poynings' law to control the Irish parliament.[10] Five bills were duly transmitted to the English privy council board where they were referred to the crown's law officers (the attorney general and solicitor general) for a report. The return of four of the five (the oath of supremacy bill was 'suspend[ed] for the present') means that the requirement explicitly ordained in Poynings' law that due 'causes and considerations' were provided for calling a parliament in Ireland was observed.[11] This was not contentious. What was problematic was the method by which the houses of the Irish parliament could assert a right to initiate legislation. The establishment by the house of commons on 8 June 1661 of a 'grand committee to consider the manner and method of preparing and drawing of bills in order to [facilitate] the transmission of them into England according to Poynings' Law'[12] represented an expression of intent, but no report was forthcoming. Its absence, which suggests that executive disapproval of the proposition was not wanting for support among peers and MPs, ensured that the Irish parliament confined itself for a time to the preparation of 'declarations' on matters of concern that were given three readings in both houses before they were sent to be published.[13] Though this provided a

---

9 J. Kelly, 'Monitoring the constitution: the operation of Poynings' law in the 1760s' in Hayton (ed.), *Irish parliament in the eighteenth century*, pp. 87–106; J. Bergin, 'Poynings' law in the eighteenth century' in *Pages: postgraduate research in progress* (Faculty of Arts, University College Dublin), i (1994), 9–18.

10 Draft instructions for the lords justices, [Dec. 1661] in *Cal.S.P. Ire., 1660–2*, pp. 678–9.

11 *Cal. S. P. Ire., 1660–2*, pp. 224, 269, 272.

12 *Commons' jn. Ire.*, i, 401.

13 F. O'Donoghue, 'Parliament in Ireland in the reign of Charles II' (unpublished, M.A.

mechanism whereby both houses of parliament could express their opinions on matters of public or political moment, its limitations were highlighted by resistance from the lords to a suggestion by the commons to employ the term 'ordinance' in preference to 'declaration'.[14] The fact that the commons also professed that they alone possessed the authority to raise financial issues serves as a further illustration of the fact that the lower house was more active in asserting the legislative authority of the Irish parliament. Be that as it may, it was the proposal originating with the king, and presented to the house of commons on 10 June 1661, that MPs should prepare a bill of settlement for referral to the privy council that was crucial to the emergence of what we know as the heads of bill arrangement. Despite attempts, notably by Hayden, to trace the origins of the heads of bill process back to the 1615 parliament, this is not sustained by the frequency with which what we know as heads of bills (i.e. measures that took their rise in the legislature and were then referred to the Irish privy council) were described by officials in the early 1660s as bills.[15] The term 'heads of a bill', though not yet commonplace, nevertheless had achieved sufficient currency by the summer of 1662 for Lord Chancellor Eustace and Lord Orrery to employ it correctly in correspondence.[16]

While this was so, the close interrogation at the Irish privy council of the small number of heads of bills that arose with the Irish parliament, and of the resulting bills at the English privy council board, was not encouraging. The likelihood of a measure that took its rise as the heads of a bill proceeding to law was diminished further by the fact that the processing of Irish bills at the English council, whether they originated with the Irish privy council or as heads of bills in parliament, was neither systematic nor expeditious. As a consequence, the English council acted as a severe brake on the efficient making of law in Ireland.[17] During three sittings of parliament held over ten months in 1661–62, only seven bills, all of which originated with the Irish privy council, were enacted. This was in keeping with the pattern of lawmaking established in the sixteenth century, when one of the observed consequences of Poynings' law was that it 'limited the total amount of legislation considered and passed',[18] but increasingly this was not what was required in the 1660s.

thesis, University College Dublin, 1970), p. 57; Archbishop of Armagh to Nicholas, 1 June 1661 in *Cal. S.P. Ire., 1660–2*, p. 345.

14 O'Donoghue, 'Parliament in Ireland', pp. 57–9.

15 M.T. Hayden, 'The origins and development of heads of bills in the Irish parliament' in *J Royal Society of Antiquaries*, 55 (1925), 112–25.

16 Eustace and Orrery to Ormond, 20 June 1662 in *A collection of the state letters of the Rt Hon Roger Boyle, first earl of Orrery*, 2 vols, (Dublin, 1743) i, p. 123.

17 NA PC2/55, passim.

18 Quinn, 'The early interpretation', p. 253.

It may be that some changes introduced in the mid-1660s to the manner in which bills received from Ireland were managed (such as referring bills to the solicitor general alone, rather than to both law officers as was previously the practice, and setting deadlines for the submission of reports) reflected a desire for expedition as well as the obvious need to refine procedures.[19] Significantly, this was accompanied by a greater readiness on the part of privy councillors to intervene to order specific amendments (including the addition and deletion of clauses) to secure English interests, to protect petitioners and to rectify errors and omissions.[20] The proportion of bills that were subject to extensive amendment, in common with the proportion of bills forwarded unaltered, was modest. This set a pattern for the future, but the receipt of petitions and other papers appertaining to the bill of settlement and the complex rewriting required in respect of the proposed bill of explanation indicated that the English privy council (and one may assume the Irish privy council too though there is little evidence to illustrate directly how it conducted business) was secure both in its authority to do with Irish bills what it saw fit, and in its perception of its role as an impartial arbiter where there was disagreement or differences of opinion on a measure.[21] In tandem with the greater number of heads of bills that were presented, improvements in administrative practice at the English privy council helped to ensure that the fourth and fifth sessions of the 1661–66 parliament were strikingly more productive than their predecessors. A total of 24 acts received the royal assent during the fourth session and 23 during the fifth (1665–6). Significantly, among them were a number that originated as heads of bills.

As the management of legislation during the course of the five sessions of parliament held between 1661 and 1666 well illustrated, Poynings' law gave the English privy council enormous power in respect of the process of making law for Ireland. At the same time, procedural and administrative refinements combined with the adoption, albeit in a limited capacity, of the heads of bills process in 1665–66 ensured it was poorly equipped administratively to respond expeditiously to the task of processing Irish legislation. A grand total of 54 acts (eight of which may be deemed private, though the distinction between public and private acts was not strongly drawn at this time) were approved by the Irish parliament over the five sessions held between 8 May 1661 and 7 August 1666.[22] The destruction in 1711 of the records of the Irish privy council, procedural and organisational weaknesses at the English privy council board, and the inconsistent application by the Irish parliament of the terms 'bill' and 'heads of bill', make it difficult to

19 NA PC2/55, ff. 196, 233–4; PC2/56, ff. 9, 56, 76, 95.
20 NA PC2/55, ff. 187, 214, 233–4, 260, 442, 513.
21 NA PC2/55, ff. 188, 206, 230.
22 These and subsequent calculations of legislative output are based on *The statutes at large passed in the parliaments held in Ireland, 1310–1800*, 20 vols, (Dublin, 1789–1800).

establish with precision what proportion of legislative initiatives reached the statute-book, but a rough calculation suggests it may have been as little as one-third. While this is low, it is less noteworthy than the fact that perhaps as many as 70 per cent of initiatives rose with or took shape at the Irish council.

Despite their uneven legislative profile and low legislative average, the five sessions held between 1661 and 1666 were sufficiently productive to suggest that, had parliament met again during the lifetime of Charles II, it could have continued to operate in this manner. However, parliament was not convened for more than a quarter-century following its dissolution in 7 August 1666.[23] As a result, the Irish parliament of Charles II was unique in respect of some of the practices permitted and procedures employed. At the same time, during its comparatively short existence, it established some important principles that had a distinct bearing on the future operation of the Irish parliament, on the nature of the Anglo-Irish nexus and, not least, on the procedural implications and operation of Poynings' law. Most crucially, the interpretation of Poynings' law applied contrasted markedly with that favoured by Thomas Wentworth since it acknowledged that the role of parliament was not confined to approving legislation that took its rise in the privy council. Parliament was to be allowed to initiate legislation, although MPs (for it was emphatically the lower house that took the lead in this) were obliged for the most part to accept that theirs was a subordinate role. Thus, they sanctioned requests to the privy council to prepare bills and transmitted measures to the lords justices and lord lieutenant with the entreaty that he would bring them to the privy council for preparation for transmission to London.[24] More generally, they fully accepted that they would have to work within the parameters defined by Poynings' law.[25]

Parallel with this, there was an acceptance at executive and council level that parliament must be afforded a role in the making of law. In theory, heads of bills were merely developed requests for legislation rather than formal legislative proposals. However, they were treated in the house in which they arose as if they were full and proper bills, and the increasing frequency with which despatches from Dublin animadverted to what was acceptable to the commons when legislation was at issue emphasises that they were perceived officially as possessing greater substance than mere requests. Yet, there remained many outstanding jurisdictional issues. In particular, the assertion by the house of commons in March 1666 that additional financial legislation could not be introduced without their prior approval, which was not accepted, remained unresolved.[26]

23 Leigh to Williamson, 6 Aug. 1666, *Cal.S.P.Ire., 1666–9*, p. 175.
24 *Commons' jn. Ire.*, i, 403, 419; O'Donoghue, 'Parliament in Ireland', p. 214.
25 *Commons' jn. Ire.*, i, 401; Orrery to Bennet, 1 Dec. 1663 in *Cal. S.P. Ire., 1663–5*, p. 348.
26 O'Donoghue, 'Parliament in Ireland', pp. 246–7; P. McNally, *Parties, patriots and undertakers: parliamentary politics in early Hanoverian Ireland* (Dublin, 1997), p. 42.

This assertion was made, of course, within a framework that explicitly acknowledged the legislative roles of both the English and Irish privy councils. These roles were complementary but also differed in fundamentals. The most striking difference was that the Irish council initiated legislation. The English privy council did claim the right to draft bills in the winter of 1665–66, but criticism from Ireland that to do so would infringe upon Poynings' law indicated that such a claim was unsustainable. As a result, despite suggestions to the contrary in the 1690s, it contented itself with asserting its entitlement to respite, veto and amend prospective legislation referred to it from Ireland. Any statistical analysis of the percentage of bills so affected in the 1660s must be incomplete because of the inadequacy of the minutes taken at this time, but perhaps as many as 30 per cent of the bills referred to the English privy council from Ireland were not returned.

1692–95

Because there was such a long interval until the Irish parliament reconvened following the adjournment of the fifth session of the 1661–66 parliament, several critical procedural and constitutional matters that remained unclarified in the 1660s were lost sight of and were thus unresolved when parliament resumed in Ireland in 1692. The resistance of James II to the suggestion advanced during the Jacobite parliament to repeal Poynings' law underlined official inclination to do nothing that would diminish the powers vested in the English privy council to control the legislative deliberations of the Irish parliament.[27] The events of the 1660s had indicated unambiguously that the Irish parliament was the junior, the English privy council the senior, and the Irish privy council somewhere in-between in the hierarchy of bodies responsible for making law for Ireland. And this was how the post-revolutionary regime that was firmly in place in England by 1692 wanted things to continue. They signalled this intention in the late spring of 1692 when preparations commenced for a meeting of the Irish parliament later the same year by conveying lists bearing the titles of 14 bills they deemed it appropriate for the Irish privy council to prepare.[28] The implicit assumption that the Irish council was subordinate to that of England was reinforced some months later when, in response to the tardiness of the Irish council to respond to the request to transmit bills, three draft bills were conveyed from London to Dublin.[29] Significantly, these were restructured at the Irish privy council board before being returned engrossed for formal consideration by the English privy council. Furthermore, the Irish privy council asserted its

27 J.G. Simms, *The Jacobite parliament of 1689* (Dundalk, 1966), pp. 7–9.
28 Nottingham to lords justices, 9 March 1692 in *Cal. S. P. Dom., 1691–2*, p. 174; Nottingham to lords justices, 2 April 1692: NA SP67/1, ff. 159–60.
29 Nottingham to lords justices, 9 July 1692: NA SP67/1, ff. 169–70.

primacy in this respect – as ordained by Poynings' law – by preparing and transmitting a further 21 bills, three of which were money bills, thereafter. The inclusion of three money bills was at the request of the lord lieutenant, Lord Sydney, who was eager to lay the foundations of a financially secure system of administration in Ireland.[30] Matters seemed set fair when, following their close examination by the English attorney general, 13 bills (two of which were money bills) were forwarded with some 'not very materiall' amendments to pass under the great seal of England and, provided they proved acceptable to the Irish parliament, to receive the royal assent in Ireland. This meant, of course, that others, deemed 'irregular', were passed over. The manner in which this was done underlined where ultimate authority lay in respect of Irish legislation. In the instance of bills to punish mutiny and desertion, and to encourage protestant strangers, both were sent back to be revised and retransmitted in a more acceptable form, while a bill of indemnities was virtually totally rewritten.[31]

Though a substantial number of prospective bills shaped by the Irish privy council fell at the hurdle of the English privy council prior to the assembly of parliament in October 1692, the fact that the Irish administration had 13 bills with which to meet parliament was a positive outcome. The ready endorsement of one of these – *An act of recognition of their majesties undoubted right to the crown of Ireland* – certainly offered a dramatic contrast to the 'angry' sentiments articulated by MPs who began the session with 'talk of freeing themselves from the yoke of England [and] of taking away Poynings' Law'.[32] However, the latter sentiment proved enduring, and it took more tangible form on 24 October when the commons refused to accept two privy council money bills returned from England 'under the great seal there' on the ground that 'it has always been conceived the original right of the commons that mon[e]y bills should take their rise in their house'. The commons justified this action on the basis that it was in keeping with 'a standing order' of the house that 'no bill to tax the subject be brought into the House without leave of the House first obtained', but the Irish attorney general denied that this was so.[33] Convinced that the commons' claim to possess the 'sole right', as it was soon defined, to initiate financial legislation was an 'entirely new' and threatening doctrine that was in contravention of Poynings' law, the view of the Irish administration (expressed by Lord Sydney) was that it would have the effect of 'lessening the dependency of

30 Lords justices to Nottingham, 21 July, Sydney to Nottingham, 9, 13 Sept. 1692 in *Cal.S. P.Dom., 1695*, pp. 190–2, 198–9, 202.

31 NA PC2/75, ff. 3, 6–7, 9–10; Nottingham to Sydney, 8 Oct. 1692: NA SP67/1, f. 18.

32 4 Wm & Mary, c. 1; Sydney to Nottingham, 12, 17 Oct. 1692 in *Cal.S.P.Dom., 1695*, pp. 212, 213–4.

33 *An account of the sessions of parliament held in Ireland, 1692* (London, 1693), pp. 14–5.

this kingdom upon the crown of England'.[34] If this was reason enough for both the Irish and English executives to take a firm stand on the issue, they felt justified in so doing when the judiciary in both kingdoms concluded, in response to an instruction to adjudicate on the legal points at issue, that the commons did 'not' possess 'the sole and undoubted right ... to prepare heads of bills for raising money'.[35]

The implication of this was that Lord Sydney was quite justified in responding to the refusal of the Irish commons to accept a privy council money bill by ordering the prorogation of parliament. This was a legitimate conclusion in law, but it did nothing to revolve the political and legislative impasse. Moreover, it was an impasse that could not be allowed to endure, for unless a solution acceptable to the crown and to the Irish executive was identified and agreed, an alternative mode of making law for the kingdom of Ireland and, critically, of raising the revenue required to pay for the government, would be necessary. This was not something ministers or MPs were prepared to contemplate, though a solution was not readily forthcoming. Indeed, three years were to elapse before there was a real indication that a compromise was possible. An essential precondition for this was the emergence of Lord Capell – first as one of the three lords justices who took the reins of power in succession to Sydney, and, from May 1695, as lord deputy – as the dominant figure on the Irish executive. But of equal importance was the readiness of the most enthusiastic advocates of the 'sole right' to soften their position in return for Capell's agreement to allow the Irish parliament to forward legislation that provided for the settlement of Ireland along the lines favoured by the protestant interest.[36]

Put in these terms, what ensued may seem like an ordinary political bargain. What made it especial was the magnitude of the matters at issue for, as well as its implications for the pursuit of the 'sole right' and the management of government business in the Irish parliament, it shaped the operation of the Anglo-Irish nexus for many decades and the manner in which Poynings' law was applied. Ironically, given the controversy generated in

34 J. McGuire, 'The Irish parliament of 1692' in T. Bartlett and D.W. Hayton (eds.), *Penal era and golden age* (Belfast, 1979), pp. 1–32; Sydney to Nottingham, 6 Nov. 1692 in *Cal.S.P. Dom., 1695*, pp. 217–18.

35 *Opinion of Irish judges on sole right*, 14 Feb. 1693: BL., Harleian MS 6274, ff. 123–38; *Opinion of the judges of England*, 23 June 1693 in *Cal. S. P.Dom., 1693*, p. 191. The opinion of the Irish judges can also be consulted in City of Dublin Public Libraries, Pearse Street, Gilbert Collection, MS 39, pp 139–50, and the opinions of both Irish and English judges are printed in G.E. Howard, *Miscellaneous works*, 3 vols (Dublin, 1782), iii, pp. 193–204, 205–6. I wish to thank Professor Nial Osborough for these references.

36 C.I. McGrath, 'Securing the protestant interest: the origins and purpose of the penal laws of 1695' in *IHS*, 30 (1996), 25–46, and by the same author, *The making of the eighteenth-century Irish constitution: government, parliament and the revenue, 1692–1714* (Dublin, 2000), pp. 90–117.

1692, once Capell had established that the Irish parliament was likely to agree to vote the finance required to provide for the government of Ireland and such other legislation as he deemed necessary, and he, in return, undertook to accommodate the desire of Irish protestants for anti-catholic legislation, preparations for a meeting of parliament in 1695 proceeded smoothly. This was symbolised by the fact that all 14 bills transmitted from the Irish to the English privy council in preparation for the session were returned under the great seal of England.[37] Saliently, the money bill that was among their number was a minor measure, included in order to affirm the principle that money bills did not rise with the Irish parliament alone, without overtly challenging the Irish parliament's claim to the contrary.[38] Following the enactment of the bill, which proved non-contentious, the house of commons initiated a number of heads of supply bills that provided the Irish executive with the funds required to pay for the government of Ireland. In return, MPs were encouraged to advance a number of anti-catholic measures and to initiate other heads of bills. Matters did not proceed entirely without difficulty in that the English council intervened to ensure that bills referred to it were consistent with the Treaty of Limerick (which necessitated several major amendments), and it held back a significant number of others.[39] The Irish parliament likewise did not approve every bill that was presented for its approval having passed under the great seal of England, but these losses were and must be kept in perspective. In all, 31 acts were added to the statute-book in the course of the successful 1695 session. Moreover, a significant proportion of these took their rise with parliament as heads of bills.

Therein lies the significance of the 1695 parliament: it dispelled the spectre of failure that was the main legacy of 1692 by demonstrating that it was possible, even within the restrictive parameters of Poynings' law, for the Irish parliament to function as a law-making body. Furthermore, it did so in a manner that successfully accommodated the desire of the protestant interest in Ireland to play an active legislative part and the resolve of the crown to sustain its legal entitlement to give prior approval to the law that was being made. The positive and co-operative political mood thus generated was vividly displayed on 13 December when the commons agreed an address thanking William III for 'those inestimable laws given us by your majesty in this session of parliament ... whereby not only our religion and legal rights are confirmed to us, but this your majesty's Kingdom of Ireland is firmly secured to the Crown of England'.[40] The contrast with the acrimonious

37 Capell to lords justices, 28 May 1695 in *Cal. S.P.Dom., 1694–5*, p. 480; NA PC2/76, ff. 101–2, 103–5.
38 Capell to Shewsbury, 18 June 1695 in HMC, *Buccleuch and Queensbury*, ii, 193–4.
39 McGrath, 'Securing the protestant interest', pp. 36–8, 41–2; NA PC2/76, ff. 103–5, 126–7, 128.
40 *Commons' jn.Ire.*, ii, 815.

conclusion of the 1692 session could not have been sharper. The parliament of 1695 was not only the most legislatively productive in the history of the Irish parliament to date; it was a defining session for the future. In the course of approximately ten weeks, it had broken the impasse over the principle of 'sole right' with a compromise agreeable to all parties and established that parliament and executive could work effectively together in preparing and agreeing the law that would apply in Ireland. In return for the acceptance by MPs that they did not possess the 'sole right' to initiate financial legislation, parliament was accorded the authority effectively to determine the amount and the manner in which money was to be raised through bills of supply. All of this took place, moreover, within the parameters of Poynings' law. It was a considerable achievement, not least because it seemed to square the circle of the crown's determination to maintain its influence over the Irish parliament's law-making authority and that of the protestant interest in Ireland to possess an active say in the making of law for that kingdom.

1703–82

If the 1695 session can be seen, in retrospect at least, to have established the framework that was to shape the pattern of parliamentary management in Ireland for three-quarters of a century until Lord Townshend dispensed with the undertakers in 1769, and the pattern of law-making until legislative independence was conceded in 1782, this was not clear at the time. It took a number of sessions for the making of law to assume the pattern that students of the eighteenth-century Irish parliament will immediately recognise. This pattern involved the overwhelming bulk of legislation taking its rise as heads of bills in the house of commons, from where it was sent for scrutiny to the Irish and English privy councils where individual items could be 'respited' or returned, amended or unaltered. Part of the reason for its gradual embrace was unease at the English privy council board, arising out of liberties taken in the course of the 1697 and 1698–99 sessions by the Irish parliament and Irish executive, in respect of a number of measures. Agreement was reached in most instances, though not always in a manner that was equally agreeable to all parties.[41] As it happened, such differences soon became part of the natural political order in the eighteenth century, and it was unusual for a session to pass without some difference over one or more legislative proposals. Significantly, they occurred within a context in which the Irish parliament operated effectively and successfully as the law-making body of the kingdom of Ireland as an examination of the process between 1692 and the accession of George III in 1760 well reveals.

41 Discussed in detail in J. Kelly, *Monitoring the constitution: Poynings' law and the making of law in Ireland, 1660–1800* (forthcoming).

The most striking feature of the legislative output of the Irish parliament in the early 1690s was its modest character. With only four enactments in the course of the aborted 1692 session, the legislative return at that point bore close comparison to that of the early 1660s or successive Tudor parliaments. However, as a result of the *modus operandi* established by Capell, the three sessions that followed produced 31, 30 and 19 enactments respectively.[42] The fact that just over a quarter (27.5 per cent) were private bills and that 13 of the 30 statutes enacted in 1697 alone fit this category cautions against exaggerating the legislative productivity of these years, but it is worth more than passing notice that it set a pattern that was to endure for several decades and several crowned heads. Thus the seven sessions of parliament held during the reign of Queen Anne (1703–14) produced a total of 129 enactments, the reign of George I produced 131 enactments over six sessions, and during the longer reign of George II, 383 enactments were added to the statute-book in the course of 17 sessions, producing the comparable averages of 18.4, 21.8 and 22.53 enactments per session respectively (Table 1). As this suggests, as well as in frequency, duration (approximately six months every two years), and management (delegated by successive lords lieutenants to managers and undertakers), the content and the manner in which legislation was agreed by the Irish parliament during the first six decades of the eighteenth century followed an identifiable pattern.[43] That this was so was a vindication not alone of the political but also of the administrative processes in place. One must not, at the same time, overlook the subtle shifts in emphasis that such a statistical overview occludes. For instance, the number of private bills passed per session declined, though the effect of this is masked by the number of public bills that were approved which rose from an average of 14.3 per session during Anne's reign to 19.1 per session during the reign of George II (Table 1). This shift occurred independently of Poynings' law, and was not connected in any way with the administrative procedures required by the law.

This was not the case, of course, with privy council bills which, in the absence of agreement on the heads of bill process, may have accounted for as many as 70 per cent and 42 per cent of the legislative initiatives that were ventured in the 1660s and 1690s respectively. The 1698–9 session was a turning point in this respect in so far as the proportion of legislative initiatives that arose with the Irish privy council fell below a quarter (approximately 23 per cent) of the total. Significantly, it remained close to this level throughout the reign of Queen Anne. Some 73 of the 385 legislative measures proposed during her reign took their formal rise at the Irish privy council, and though the sessional percentage fluctuated between 17 and 27

42 *Irish statutes at large.*
43 McNally, *Parties, patriots and undertakers*, passim.

Table 1: Legislation of the Irish parliament, 1660–1800

Monarch	Public bills	Private bills	Total	Number of sessions	Average per session
Charles II (1661–66)*	46	8	54	5	10.8
William III and Mary II (1692–94)*	62	22	84	4	21
William III (1695–99)*					
Anne (1703–13)*	87	42	129	7	18.4
George I (1715–26)*	95	36	131	6	21.8
George II (1727–59)*	325	58	383	17	22.53
George III (1761–1782)*	415	73	488	13	37.53
George III (1783–1800)*	976	81	1057	18	58.7

Source: Irish Statutes.

* The dates cited in respect of each reign refer, not to regnal years, but to the span of years during which parliament sat.

per cent until the brief, difficult and anomalous 1713 session, when the percentage was no more than 10.5, it seemed as if the Irish privy council would continue to be a major force in the making of law when a further 11 bills (21.56 per cent of the legislative initiatives raised that session) took their rise with the Irish council in 1715–16. In fact, this was the last session in which the privy council was so active in initiating legislation. In all, a comparatively modest 21 bills originated with the Irish privy council during the 13-year reign of George I, and following the sensation caused by the decision of the Irish house of commons in the spring of 1730 to reject an otherwise unobjectionable riot bill simply because it took its rise at the Irish privy council, no more than one or two 'privy council bills' (and in some sessions none) were forwarded from the Irish privy council during each session of parliament held during George II's reign.[44] The Irish council continued to be responsible for preparing bills pursuant to the requirement of Poynings' law that due 'causes and considerations' were set before the king in council.[45] This was insisted upon by successive monarchs and their English ministers who deemed it sufficiently critical to the maintenance of the royal prerogative in respect of Ireland and the Irish parliament that they insisted on the inclusion of a money bill among the bills that were presented

44 Boulter to Newcastle, 19 May 1730 in *Letters written by Hugh Boulter, lord primate of all Ireland*, 2 vols (Dublin, 1770), i, p. 287.
45 10 Henry VII, c.4.

on such occasions.[46] Since prior to the ratification of the Octennial Act in 1768, this occurred on no more than four instances (1713, 1715, 1727, 1761) generally coinciding with the death of the monarch, this was an occasional rather than a regular responsibility. As a result, not alone was the issue of the 'sole right' pushed to the political margins, but the Irish privy council had effectively ceded responsibility for initiating law, other than as reason for calling a parliament, to peers and MPs long before the lords justices admitted as much in November 1760.[47]

Since the means favoured by MPs and peers to progress law was the heads of bill process, a massive 96 per cent of the 667 legislative proposals proffered during the 17 sessions of parliament held during the 33-year reign of George II arose with them. At the same time, the Irish council continued to perform a critical part in the process of making law for Ireland, as heads of bills arising in the Irish parliament which were referred to it for certification were scrutinised as a matter of course. The absence of records makes it difficult to establish how it acquitted itself of this duty, but by comparing the number of heads of bills referred to it with those received at the British privy council board, it is apparent that it took its responsibilities as seriously as the British privy council and that it did not shirk using its power to veto or decline to forward bills it deemed objectionable. During the reign of Queen Anne, 38 (21.2 per cent) of the 179 heads of bills referred to it were vetoed. This proportion fell significantly during the reign of George I to 12 per cent, and it eased further during the reign of George II to 10.3 per cent. This was an important trend, and its impact on the legislative aspirations of the Irish parliament was reinforced by the fact that the British privy council respited a further 40 (18.7 per cent) of the bills referred from the Irish privy council during the reign of Anne; 14.7 per cent of those received during George I's reign and 11.2 per cent (54 bills out of 482) during the longer reign of George II. Since over the reigns of George I and George II, only 13.5 per cent of bills referred to the British council were sent to pass under the great seal without amendment, it is apparent – the emergence of the heads of bill as a means of allowing the Irish parliament an active role in the initiating and making of law for Ireland notwithstanding – that the powers available to the English and Irish privy councils under Poynings' law to respite and to amend legislation arising with the Irish parliament were not just extensive, they were readily used to ensure it was acceptable to ministerial wishes, consonant with the legislation currently emanating from Westminster and properly drafted.[48]

46 This issue is discussed by C.I. McGrath, 'Central aspects of the eighteenth-century constitutional framework' in *Eighteenth-Century Ireland*, 15 (2001), 9–34.
47 Lords justices to [Bedford], 23 Nov. 1760: NAI, Irish Correspondence, 1697–1798, MS 2446.
48 The basis for the calculations provided in this and subsequent paragraphs will be described in the author's forthcoming study of the impact of Poynings' law on the making of law in Ireland.

Of course the dependent position in which the Irish legislature was placed by Poynings' law was not received with equanimity within Ireland. At the same time, the absence of significant protest and the comparative legislative quietude of much of the reign of George II suggest that, though MPs did not welcome the restrictions, they were broadly content to operate within these parameters. The political atmosphere changed palpably during the 1750s, climaxing with the prorogued 1753–54 session when only three acts were added to the statute-book, and this soon had a palpable impact on the way in which both the Irish parliament conducted its business and upon the way in which MPs and the increasingly politicised public regarded Poynings' law.[49]

One of the most tangible and pertinent indications of the animation of the parliamentary and political world that ensued is the striking increase in the amount of law being made. During the 13 sessions of the Irish parliament that were held between the accession of George III and the concession of legislative independence in 1782, a grand total of 488 laws were added to the statute-book. This averaged 37.5 per session which was double the sessional average registered during the early eighteenth century (Table 1). (If one excludes private bills, the sessional average of 32 also constitutes a dramatic increase on the outcome in respect of the category of public bills on three preceding reigns.) Interestingly, though the overall trend in the volume of law that was passed is upwards, it was not a steady progression. For the first time, as many as 50 (public and private) acts received the royal assent in 1773–74, but this rate of activity did not become commonplace until 1777–78. Moreover, this figure was eclipsed in turn by the fact that 71 bills reached the statute-book in 1781–82, the last session that Poynings' law had a major bearing on the pattern of law-making in eighteenth-century Ireland. Unsurprisingly, a modest two bills (2.2 per cent) from an unprecedented total of 89 received at the British privy council board were deemed inappropriate to progress in 1781–82 and a mere 25 were recommended to pass with amendment, compared with 62 that were sent to pass under the great seal without alteration. These are striking figures, not just because they contrast so vividly with the picture earlier in the century, but because they represent the culmination of an emerging pattern, traceable over several decades, of a steadily increasing preparedness by the Irish and British privy councils to cede more initiative in the making of law to the Irish legislature before they were obliged to do so by law as a result of the repeal in 1782 of the powers granted under Poynings' law to the Irish council to determine what heads

---

49 This context is fully described in R.E. Burns, *Irish parliamentary politics in the eighteenth century*, 2 vols (Washington, 1989–90); E. Magennis, *The Irish political system, 1740–65: the golden age of the undertakers* (Dublin, 2000).

referred from the Irish parliament should be certified for transmission to London and the British privy council to amend such laws.[50]

This is not to state that Poynings' law was resorted to with diminishing frequency, as the demand for the repeal of its most controversial provisions became increasingly clamorous during the 1770s. It remained a requirement that the heads of every bill that took its rise with either the Irish lords or commons (and the majority came from the lower house) were referred to the Irish and British privy councils, and a significant proportion continued to be vetoed or subject to amendment during the 1760s and 1770s despite the changing political atmosphere, which meant that MPs and public alike were now less accepting of the intervention of these bodies to amend and to respite heads of bills. Thus, 33 (12 per cent) of the heads of bills referred to the Irish privy council between 1761 and October 1771, and 17 (or 8.6 per cent) of the bills referred from there to the British privy council board were respited, while just over half (55.2 per cent) of the remainder which were deemed appropriate to proceed were ordered to be amended. The situation eased somewhat during the 1770s; between 1771 and 1782, 52 (nine per cent) of the total heads referred were lost at the Irish privy council and seven per cent of bills at the English privy council board while 53 per cent of bills that were deemed appropriate did so with amendments. Interestingly, these figures suggest that the British privy council was more responsive to the changed mood in Ireland in respect of Poynings' law than its Irish equivalent.

1782–1800

As these figures indicate, Poynings' law continued to affect the passage of the heads of every bill to emerge from the Irish legislature until the ratification in 1782 by the Irish parliament of Yelverton's Act explicitly deprived the Irish and British privy councils of the power to amend Irish legislation. Moreover, though there is evidence to suggest that Poynings' law was enforced with greater circumspection during the late 1770s than it had been at any point since the inauguration of the heads of bills process, the authorities were no more inclined then than they had been at any prior point to overlook contentious or badly drawn Irish law. At the same time, the rise in the number of heads of bills initiated during the 1760s and 1770s and the falling proportion deemed worthy of being respited indicated that the Irish parliament was developing rapidly as a body, and that it was well-placed to assume the responsibility for making law for the kingdom of Ireland unfettered by the requirements of Poynings' law. From 1782, both houses of

50 21 & 22 Geo III, c. 47; J. Kelly, *Henry Flood: patriots and politics in eighteenth-century Ireland* (Dublin, 1998), pp. 311–24.

the Irish parliament could introduce full bills. Such measures were required to proceed through all stages in the Irish parliament, following which they were transmitted to the lord lieutenant, who transferred them to the Irish privy council for certification prior to their conveyance to the British privy council for the attachment of the great seal so they could receive the royal assent in Ireland on their return. Though the withdrawal from both privy councils of the power to amend legislation deprived them of the power they had most commonly used, bills received from Ireland continued to be referred by the British privy council board to the crown law officers for a report. It remained open to the law officers to recommend that bills were not suitable to pass under the great seal of Great Britain, but this was a power they were reluctant to employ. Reservations were expressed with just over three per cent of the 1,061 bills received at the British privy council board between 1783 and 1800, but since only four objectionable Irish bills were laid aside (two in 1785, one in 1788 and one in 1792) arising out of criticisms expressed by the crown law officers, it was clearly not a power frequently resorted to.[51] Officials relied more generally on issuing warnings or on making appeals to the Irish executive to introduce supplementary legislation to redress a particular difficulty. The fact that they chose these options was indicative of just how politically risky it was to hold up any Irish bill since each instance could, had the Irish parliament chosen to make an issue of the matter, have provoked a constitutional crisis over the meaning and impli-cations of legislative independence. Matters never came to that for two reasons: Irish MPs did not monitor closely what legislation was returned, and the bills at issue were not deemed sufficiently important. Furthermore, they were few in number.

The Irish parliament added 1,057 items to the statute-book between 1783 and its abolition in 1800. The vast bulk of that law (92.3 per cent) comprised public bills, but the proportion of public to private statutes is less consequential than the overall number, which constitutes the most visible testament to the legislative dynamism of the Irish parliament following legislative independence. While it may be tempting to ascribe this to the constitutional changes made in 1782, it must be noted that the trend towards increased legislative activity antedated legislative independence. Be that as it may, the repeal of Poynings' law helped by both simplifying the process and by encouraging the Irish legislature to assume full responsibility for the making of law for the kingdom of Ireland.

It was certainly the case that, over the 122 years prior to the emasculation of Poynings' law in 1782, the provisions of this statute were used to particular effect to ensure that the legislative output of the Irish parliament

---

51 O'Brien, *Anglo-Irish politics in the age of Grattan and Pitt*, pp. 133–4.

did not collide with the legislative wishes of the king and his ministers. The manner in which the crown pursued this goal during the 1660s and early 1690s, if it had been maintained, would have entirely subordinated the Irish parliament to the Irish privy council in initiating law. The refusal of Irish MPs to acquiesce in this dependent situation enabled them to establish that they, rather than the privy council, took the lead in initiating legislation, though parliament remained palpably subordinate to both the Irish and English/British privy councils until 1782. As a result, MPs had to put up with the fact that a sizeable but declining proportion of legislation inaugurated in the Irish parliament was never enacted; they also had to endure a proliferation of alterations and amendments, both major and minor. This source of frustration provided the occasion for many political disagreements. At the same time, it was also the means by which deficiencies in Irish draft bills were remedied, and many problems as well as many questionable measures were sidelined to advantage.

Be that as it may, the procedures introduced to meet the requirements of Poynings' law were purposely designed and pursued to ensure that Ireland remained a dependent kingdom of Britain. Given the changing nature of the Anglo-Irish relationship during the long existence of Poynings' law, it was essential if that law was not to become fossilised or an anachronism that the manner in which it was interpreted and altered changed accordingly. It is this fact that makes its history more than ordinarily interesting, and important. It provides an unrivalled window both on the operation and on the changing nature of the Anglo-Irish nexus in respect of one of its key features – the making of law for Ireland – and underlines what is not always apparent from the many efforts to explain the nature of the Anglo-Irish connection in the eighteenth century – that this was no ordinary dependent colonial relationship.

'Middling hard on coin': truck in Donegal in the 1890s

DESMOND GREER[*]

SOME TIME AGO I AGREED to edit, for publication by the Society, a thesis by Dr James Nicolson on the operation of the factory acts in nineteenth-century Ireland.[1] One of the features of this thesis is a series of case studies, and I was so taken with one of these cases that I decided to try to find out a bit more about it. What should have been a simple and straightforward prosecution at petty sessions turned out to involve a cast of fascinating characters – gombeen men, middle-class lady undercover agents, partisan magistrates and profiteering industrialists – all allegedly engaged in petty corruption or jobbery of one kind or another. The case itself provides not just a revealing snapshot of the local administration of justice in Ireland at the end of the nineteenth century, but also illustrates the complex relationship which may exist between legal regulation and social and economic conditions. But let me begin by setting the case in context.

THE LEGAL CONTEXT

Classic economic theory has it that the state has no right to interfere in the level of wages paid to an employee, nor should it be concerned with the manner in which those wages are paid: '[i]f it should be more convenient or profitable for a workman to receive payment for his labour partly or wholly in goods, why should he be prevented from doing so? For if such a practice is inconvenient or injurious to any man, he will not work a second time for the master who pays him in that manner.'[2] Indeed, 'truck', or payment in kind as opposed to cash, was not necessarily 'inconvenient or injurious'; a

---

[*] An edited version of a presidential address given to the Society in Archbishop Marsh's Library, Dublin, on 3 November 2000.

[1] J.W. Nicolson, 'Factory legislation and inspection in Ireland, 1878–1914' (unpublished, Ph.D. thesis, University of Guelph, Ontario, 1984). See now D.S. Greer and J.W. Nicolson, *The factory acts in Ireland, 1802–1914* (Dublin, 2003).

[2] Joseph Hume MP, in *Hansard's Parl. Deb., 1st ser.*, vol. xxiii, cols. 1175–76 (21 July 1812). See also Ricardo's criticism of a later truck act as 'obnoxious' in *Hansard's Parl. Deb., 2nd ser.*, vol. vii, col. 1123 (17 June 1822).

benevolent employer such as Robert Owen could purchase goods in bulk and pass on the benefits to his employees. The problem, of course, was that many employers, especially when times were bad and profits hard to come by, used the company store (or 'tommy shop') to charge inflated prices and thus reduce the real level of wages, sometimes by as much as a quarter or even one third.[3]

Contrary to received economic wisdom, the state from an early age sought to restrict such practices. The first truck acts were passed in the fifteenth century and required certain workers to be paid 'the entire amount of their wages' in 'the current coin of the realm'.[4] But the motive for this intervention was the protection, not of workers, but of employers:

> … by far the commonest reason for the use of truck was that it enabled employers to undercut their competitors or to evade fixed or union-agreed wage rates. Frequently, it was the smaller and less reputable employers who resorted to these tactics, and it was their competitors who sought anti-truck legislation, or the enforcement of the existing legislation, as a means of restricting competition.[5]

Truck was practised in Ireland before the Famine,[6] but probably not just for these reasons. In 1831, the prospect of fresh anti-truck legislation in response to a strike by weavers in Gloucester produced an interesting response from O'Connell. This legislation, he said, would be 'destructive to Ireland', and he explained:

> The truck system was the result and the proof of the existence of poverty and distress in the country; and this was not the way to remedy such a state of things. The way to do that was to increase the market for labour, and to increase the competition amongst the masters … In the present state of Ireland [this bill] might do great evil, for although some inconvenience might arise from the truck system near Belfast, it was not to be compared to the injury which would be done in the South, by throwing many hands out of employment.[7]

---

3   *Cf.* G.W. Hilton, *The truck system* (Cambridge, 1960), p. 40, estimating that overcharging represented no more than 7–10 per cent of profits.

4   For a general history of this legislation in England and Wales, see Hilton, *Truck system*, passim. A brief history of truck in Ireland will be found in Greer and Nicolson, *The factory acts*, ch. 6.

5   P.S. Atiyah, *The rise and fall of freedom of contract* (Oxford, 1979), p. 534. See also Hilton, *Truck system*, pp. 40–45.

6   See e.g. *Hansard's Parl. Deb.*, 2nd ser., vol. xxiv, cols. 327–28 (3 May 1830); County Works (Ire.) Act 1846, s. 20; W.J. Davis and A.W. Waters, *Tickets and passes of Great Britain and Ireland* (Leamington Spa, 1922).

7   *Hansard's Parl. Deb.*, 2nd ser., vol. xxv, col. 947 (5 July 1830); *Hansard's Parl. Deb.*, 3rd ser., vol. iii, col. 1258 (12 April 1831) and vol. vi, col. 1359 (12 Sept. 1831).

Classical economists such as Torrens agreed: 'the abolition of truck would diminish the demand for labour, and throw operatives out of work'.[8] But such reasoning was rejected by the government, no doubt encouraged by the industrial establishment, and the bill duly became the Truck Act 1831. O'Connell's opposition meant, however, that the act did not apply to Ireland, where earlier truck legislation nevertheless remained theoretically in force.[9] But O'Connell need not have been so concerned, since the 1831 Act, like the earlier legislation, was largely ineffective.[10] The reason for this is not hard to find. Enforcement was a matter for the individual employee, and it would have been a brave worker who took an employer to court – in the virtual certainty of losing his or her job, and the distinct probability of being blacklisted by other employers.[11]

As the nineteenth century progressed, however, the problem of truck generally diminished, as 'the wage-relationship [between employer and employee] was transformed into a pure market relationship, a cash nexus ... thus making the market bargain more sensitive and flexible'.[12] That may have been true in urban areas, and in industries in which the workers were becoming increasingly unionised. But evidence of a continuation of truck practices in some parts of England[13] led to further legislation in the form of the Truck (Amendment) Act 1887, and this time the legislation (and by extension, the 1831 act also) did apply to Ireland. Indeed, the legislation was welcomed, T.M. Healy in particular categorising it as 'an excellent measure'.[14] Under the act, employers were not only bound to pay their workers in cash; section 6 provided that:

> No employer shall, directly or indirectly ... impose as a condition,
> express or implied, in or for the employment of any workman any

---

8 *Hansard's Parl. Deb., 3rd ser.*, vol. vi, cols. 1361–62 (12 Sept. 1831).
9 See especially Unlawful Combinations Act (Ire.) 1729: 3 Geo II, c. 14 (Irish).
10 According to Atiyah, *Rise and fall*, p. 535: 'despite a spate of prosecutions when the Act came into force, it was extensively violated and by 1838 it was said to be a dead letter, though this was certainly an exaggeration.'
11 Cf. the development of anti-truck societies in parts of England, which 'were an anti-competitive device ... to prevent concealed wage reductions in the form of truck, usually when depressions were forcing down prices': Atiyah, *Rise and fall*, p. 536.
12 E. Hobsbawm, *The age of capital, 1848–1875* (London, 1975), pp. 218–19.
13 And Ireland: see e.g. W.A. Seaby, 'Employers' truck tickets and food vouchers issued in Ulster during the latter half of the 19th century and the early part of the 20th century' in *Numismatic Society of Ireland occasional papers*, nos. 5–9 (1969), 11, where W.T. Boyd, manager of the Blackstaff Flax Spinning and Weaving Co., is quoted as saying that 'there is no doubt that prior to the Truck Act [1887] there were many abuses and workers were literally forced to take groceries, etc in lieu of wages ... [and] employers recovered a considerable percentage of their outgoings through profits made in the so-called "shops".'
14 *Hansard's Parl. Deb., 3rd ser.*, vol. ccxiv, col. 306 (28 April 1887).

terms as to the place at which, or the manner in which, or the person
with whom, any wages ... paid to the workman are ... to be expended,
and no employer shall ... dismiss any workman from his employment
for or on account of the place at which, or the manner in which, or the
person with whom, any wages ... paid by the employer to such
workman are ... expended or fail to be expended.

More importantly in the present context, the act extended the definition of
'workman' by incorporating section 10 of the Employers and Workmen Act
1875, so that these prohibitions now applied in the case of 'any person other
than a domestic or menial servant who, being a labourer, ... journeyman,
artificer, handicraftsman, miner or otherwise engaged in manual labour ...
has entered into or works under a contract with an employer, whether the
contract ... be a contract of service or a contract personally to execute any
work or labour'.

Section 13(2) of the 1887 act further provided that it was now to be the
duty of government officials – the home office factory inspectorate – to
enforce this legislation throughout the United Kingdom, with the same
powers and authority as they already had under the factory acts. This
innovation became even more significant for our purposes in 1893, when the
home secretary finally yielded to considerable pressure and appointed the
first lady factory inspectors.[15] It was not to be long before a number of these
remarkable women found themselves seeking to enforce the new truck act in
the wilds of Co. Donegal. But why Donegal?

HOME-WORKING IN DONEGAL

Economic conditions in the west of Ireland had not made much progress by
the 1890s. The relative density of the population, the poor quality of much
of the land and the absence of industrial development combined to keep
living standards at a low level. Those who were unable to emigrate eked out
a living as best they could. For many of the men this meant spending the
summer in England or Scotland; for women and girls, it meant engaging in
some form of 'home-work' to supplement the family income. By the 1890s,
the broad pattern of 'out-working' in the county had become fairly well
established.[16] In the small farms of Glenties and the Rosses in west Donegal,

---

15 For the background to this development, see M.D. McFeely, *Lady inspectors: the campaign
   for a better workplace, 1893–1921* (Oxford, 1988), chs. 2–4. The middle-class background of
   the six lady inspectors who had been appointed by the end of the 1890s is emphasised by
   H. Jones, 'Women health workers: the case of the first women factory inspectors in Britain'
   in *Social History of Medicine*, 1:2 (1988), 165.
16 The issue of truck is extensively examined in the *Report of the departmental committee on the*

the emphasis was on the knitting of woollen hosiery; in the southern part of
the county (from Ballyshannon to Ardara), the women engaged in 'sprigging'
– the embroidering of handkerchiefs, wearing apparel and household linens;
while in the northern part of the county, particularly the Inishowen
peninsula, button-holing, collar-hemming and other finishing work was
undertaken for the shirt and collar industry centred in Londonderry. Most
of this work was poorly paid: '[w]e found that 1s. was considered to be a good
day's wage; and we were informed that the usual wage was 9d. a day, and
many old women can earn only 3d. to 6d. a day.'[17] The goods which they
made, of course, retailed at a much higher price.[18]

Widespread poverty allied with irregular (as well as inadequate) sources
of income meant that many families were dependent on credit from their
local shopkeepers.[19] Often this was given on reasonably favourable terms,[20]
but in other cases, 'gombeen men' took advantage of the situation by charging
exorbitant rates of interest, while at the same time making sure that the debt

truck acts of 1908. The report was published in four volumes: vol. I: *Report and appendices*,
H.C. 1908 [Cd. 4442] lix, 1; vol. II: *Evidence (days 1–37)*, H.C. 1908 [Cd. 4443] lix, 147;
vol. III, *Evidence (days 38–66) and Index*, H.C. 1908 [Cd. 4444] lix, 533, and vol. IV: *Précis
and appendices*, H.C. 1909 [Cd. 4568] xlix, 177, (hereafter, *Departmental committee on the
truck acts*, followed by the report volume number, and the page number in that volume.) On
the particular aspect noted in the text, see Inspector Hilda Martindale, 'Truck and
gombeening in Ireland' in vol. III of the report at p. 247. Inspector Martindale thought
highly of the quality of the work: '[i]t is impossible not to be impressed by the complicated
patterns knitted [or sewn] and the large variety of them, as well as the skill and dexterity
exhibited': ibid., p. 248. See also E. Boyle, *The Irish flowerers* (Holywood, Co. Down, 1971)
and B. Collins, 'The organisation of sewing outwork in late nineteenth-century Ulster' in
M. Berg (ed.), *Markets and manufacture in early industrial Europe* (London, 1991), p. 139.

17 Martindale, 'Truck and gombeening in Ireland', p. 249. Given that most women and girls
    also had farm and other duties to perform, it was difficult to estimate the number of hours
    worked per day, but Martindale thought that 'work is seldom begun before 9 a.m., or
    carried on long after dusk, and intervals are taken during the day. Undoubtedly, the
    universal introduction of oil lamps has made embroidery on winter evenings easier than it
    was in the days when the girls had to crouch over a "bog" fire and do their sprigging by this
    flickering light, and accordingly the working day has been lengthened; but I have come to
    the conclusion that the hours worked in this industry are not so excessive, although fairly
    long': ibid.
18 For example, men's socks which were knitted for 1s. 6d. per dozen pairs were sold at 9d. per
    pair in the shops: *Departmental committee on the truck acts*, vol. II, p. 80 (Inspector Rose
    Squire).
19 'The scarcity of ready money during most of the year has brought about and encouraged a
    system of buying goods on credit, a system which in some districts has grown to an
    alarming extent': Martindale, 'Truck and gombeening in Donegal', p. 251. For a more
    general study, see e.g. *Report of the departmental committee on agricultural credit in Ireland*,
    H.C. 1914 [Cd. 7375] xiii, 1.
20 '[R]eal benefits [are] conferred by many traders in standing out of their funds for
    lengthened intervals, with little or no extra charge, in order to assist poor and deserving
    customers': *Departmental committee on agricultural credit*, p. 76.

was never fully redeemed. Continuing custom could then be ensured by threatening legal proceedings if the debtor took his or her business elsewhere.[21] Not surprisingly, many shopkeepers prospered financially – and socially: 'by their shops, their inns, their ownership of cars, they represented the wealth and carrying power of the local community; in their connections through marriage with the priests' and magistrates' families, and sometimes even their position as magistrates, they represented the order of the community.'[22]

A recent study based on data produced by the Congested Districts Board suggests that by the 1890s the worst excesses of 'gombeening' had abated and that shopkeepers in the 'congested' districts of the west of Ireland tended to make only a 'modest' charge of 10–15 per cent per annum for credit.[23] Indeed, the board itself reported in 1897 that 'credit dealing was almost universal some few years ago, but now, as far as I can judge, half of the purchases of the district are cash transactions, and both buyers and sellers are glad of the change.'[24] But that is not the picture which presented itself to the home office in the mid-1890s, as they received reports that a substantial number of Donegal shopkeepers[25] were extending their credit practices to

21 'I was informed that shopkeepers seldom take proceedings for debt. Provided the debtor has a growing family and provided he does not deal at another shop ... the debts are allowed to remain from year to year. The profits on the goods are so high that the shopkeeper can afford to obtain his money gradually; in fact, in many cases the customer is encouraged to remain in debt, because in this way the shopkeeper ensures his custom. The customer is afraid to deal at another shop, because he knows that if he does so, legal proceedings will swiftly follow': Martindale, 'Truck and gombeening in Donegal', p. 251.

22 A.M. Anderson, *Women in the factory: an administrative adventure, 1893 to 1921* (London, 1922), p. 83 and *Annual report of the chief inspector of factories for 1899*, p. 276, H.C. 1900 [Cd. 223] xi, 525. Miss Anderson was principal lady inspector from 1897 to 1921.

23 L. Kennedy, 'Retail markets in rural Ireland at the end of the 19th century' in *IESH*, 5 (1978), 46. *Cf.* C. Ó Gráda, *Ireland: a new economic history, 1780–1939* (Oxford, 1994), pp. 269–70 suggests that this is an underestimate, and that even at this time 'some degree of extortion seems likely in the remoter areas', even though 'competition from increasingly accessible shops in the bigger towns and cities' was forcing local shopkeepers to reduce the rate of interest charged on credit.

24 Congested Districts Board, *Reports on congested districts* (Dublin, 1892–1897), p. 132. According to L.M. Cullen, *An economic history of Ireland since 1660* (London, 1972), p. 152, as a result 'partly ... of higher prices generally, partly ... of higher earnings by migratory workers in England and Scotland, partly ... of quickened emigration from the region', cash incomes in the congested districts rose from the 1890s, 'a fact reflected in the replacement of credit dealings by cash dealings'.

25 While most agents were shopkeepers, others were publicans and hoteliers or both. '[I]n nineteenth-century rural Ireland the archetypal retailer was the grocer-publican, who combined general shopkeeping with the tasks of dispensing drink, moneylending, and the purchase and sale of farm produce such as eggs': Ó Gráda, *Ireland: new economic history*, p. 266. In some instances, the agent did not own a grocery store, but was a draper or dry goods proprietor; in such cases, the women were enticed or coerced into taking not necessities

the giving-out of home-work to local women and then maximising their profits by the use of truck – paying for the work not in cash but in goods from their shops.[26] There was nothing particularly new in this; the obvious connection between a system of credit and the practice of truck had often been used elsewhere as a method of tying a worker to his or her employer through debt.[27] But the home office was resolved to put an end at least to the practice of truck by enforcing the new act through the Irish courts.

Looking back at the situation, however, there are two factors which should perhaps have been taken into further account before the home office swung into action. First, the enforcement of the truck acts in a depressed area such as Donegal was not a straightforward matter. In an attempt to encourage economic development, the Congested Districts Board had been set up in 1891 to deal with the special problems of the west of Ireland.[28] The Board was empowered to purchase land for distribution to tenants, to improve the land and farming techniques and to increase opportunities for local employment by the development of fishing and home industries. Progress was slow and difficult and, as O'Connell had pointed out sixty years earlier, perhaps truck was a price worth paying for the opportunity to obtain work, however poorly paid. This kind of short-term view was rejected by the home office:

> The frequent evasions and infringement of these Acts ... certainly encourage the shiftlessness and the poverty which are so deplorable, and form a real obstacle to the efforts of those public-spirited persons who are endeavouring to ameliorate the lot of the peasantry in those parts. Self-respect and proper independence are almost impossible in the circumstances and under the conditions produced by a wide-spread disregard of the right of the worker to the free control of her own earnings unhampered by any condition as to where and how they should be spent.[29]

such as tea, corn meal and flour, but draperies or other goods 'in case you are in want': *Annual report of the chief inspector of factories for 1907*, p. 218, H.C. 1908 [Cd. 4166] xii, 585 (Martindale). Similarly, Inspector Lucy Deane had reported in 1897 that 'a pair of thin elastic-sided boots ... constituted the wages paid to a worker, who according to the practice of the countryside generally went barefoot': *Annual report of the chief inspector of factories for 1897*, p. 109, H.C. 1898 [C. 8965] xiv, 109.

26 *Annual report of the chief inspector of factories for 1885–86*, pp. 10–11, H.C. 1887 [C. 5002] xvii, 549–50; *Annual report of the chief inspector of factories for 1887–88*, pp. 146–47, H.C. 1889 [C. 5697] xviii, 505–06; R. Squire, *Thirty years in the public service: an industrial retrospect* (London, 1927), pp. 83–87. 'The truck masters are reputed in their district to have their fortunes entirely out of the truck system, and in many cases the chief house in a small town is the house occupied by the truck master': *Departmental committee on the truck acts*, vol. II, p. 81 (Squire).

27 See Hilton, *Truck system*, pp. 4–5, citing F.A. Walker, *The wages problem* (London, 1877), pp. 343–44.

28 See e.g. W.L. Micks, *History of the Congested Districts Board* (Dublin, 1925).

29 *Annual report of the chief inspector of factories for 1900*, p. 403, H.C. 1901 [Cd. 668] x, 403

Nevertheless, there may well have been a conflict of interest between the Congested District Board (and the Irish government generally) and the home office. The board were naturally anxious to do all that they could to increase employment opportunities in Co. Donegal; the home office, on the other hand, were naturally anxious to enforce the law, and not to condone working conditions which they regarded as wholly unsatisfactory.[30] The issue had already arisen in another context at Burtonport, where the Duke of Abercorn had been instrumental in setting up a fish-curing factory.[31] When inspected by a lady factory inspector, Mary Paterson, in December 1898, the factory was found to be in breach of various requirements of the factory acts. Negotiations having proved fruitless, Paterson instituted proceedings early in 1899. The owners of the factory were furious at this attempt 'to strangle a new industry in Ireland by putting restrictions on it',[32] and a sympathetic bench of magistrates[33] at Dungloe petty sessions dismissed the charges. An appeal by way of case stated failed in circumstances which suggest that it may well have been 'sabotaged' by an Irish government anxious to encourage such philanthropy.[34] In rather less than measured tones, T.M. Healy was later to

(Deane). Squire later explained the practical disadvantages of this system: '[t]he expenses which should be met by money extend beyond the cost of the tea and sugar and flour; there is rent, there are implements, there is help that the women need in getting in their crops when the men are away; there are seeds and necessaries for the ground and garden; there are the household goods to be renewed, and there is the clothing. The Truck masters prefer to give tea to any other thing, because I presume their profit upon it is greater, and the women drink a great deal more tea than is good for them': *Departmental committee on the truck acts*, vol. II, p. 80. To make matters worse, 'heavy deductions' were often made for work damaged or spoiled: ibid., p. 81.

30 The issues were neatly summarised in a parliamentary exchange in 1900. T.D. Sullivan, MP for Donegal West, criticised the factory inspectors for prosecuting 'employers in poor districts, where, until local industry was started, emigration was the only resource of the population'; Sir Matthew Ridley, the home secretary, replied that 'owing to the existence of grave abuses on the part of employers in some parts of Donegal, it has been found necessary to take proceedings for the protection of the women who work for them': *Hansard's Parl. Deb., 4th ser.*, vol. lxxxv, cols. 959–60 (9 July 1900).

31 *Annual report of the chief inspector of factories for 1898 (part II)*, p. 179, H.C. 1900 [Cd. 27] xi, 179; *Annual report of the chief inspector 1899*, p. 247.

32 *Annual report of the chief inspector 1898*, p. 248. See also *Freeman's Journal*, 29 July 1899.

33 *Annual report of the chief inspector 1899*, pp. 247–48; Anderson, *Women in the factory*, p. 214. The bench included James Sweeney (John's father) and three of the other justices who were later to sit in *Squire v. Sweeney*: see further below, p. 295. It appears that they 'overruled' the resident magistrate (Gaussen), who presided.

34 Notice of the case stated was not duly served on the respondents, and the case was struck out. The chief inspector of factories observed that 'this important case would seem to have been mismanaged from first to last': B.A. Whitelegge to K.E. Digby, under-secretary, home office, 3 July 1899: PRO HO 45/B29311. See also *Hansard's Parl. Deb., 4th ser.*, vol. lxxiv, cols. 29–30 (6 July 1899) and vol. lxxv, col. 675 (28 July 1899), where it is reported that the sessional crown solicitor had been 'reprimanded and cautioned'.

claim that as a result of the Donegal fish-curing case, 'there is now an army of [inspectors] squatted around Dungloe watching every little industry and striving to throttle them.'[35]

Secondly, it is by no means clear that the shopkeepers were primarily to blame for the situation. After all, they were simply agents for manufacturers and other large organisations in Belfast, Londonderry and other industrial centres in England and Scotland. There is conflicting evidence as to the general relationship between principals and agents and the terms on which they did business. Many of the principals no doubt acted with propriety.[36] But:

> It is a matter for incessant self-congratulations by certain of these firms that they have 'opened up' and 'given employment' to thousands of these peasant women in distant parts of the country, but where this process is carried out unaccompanied by a sense of responsibility, the result is but too often marred by the evils which invariably attend the irresponsible employment of cheap labour.[37]

In particular, the commission given to the agent was often small or even non-existent, with the result that 'if he is to make any profit at all, [he] must make it out of the unfortunate workers by paying them in cheap tea and sugar'.[38] Where commission was paid, it would seem that the normal rate was ten per cent, less the cost of transporting the finished goods back to the manufacturer. On the other hand, 'wholetime agents employed by the firm may cost 30 per cent or more if an attempt is made to distribute directly in the remote parts of the country'.[39] In other words, it was much more profitable to employ a part-time shopkeeper than a full-time agent. But it was the workers who suffered:

> It was very clearly proved that too often the ignorant little 'agents' for such firms, struggling with the difficulties of organisation and lack of proper carriage facilities, were obviously unable to do the work

---

35 *Donegal Vindicator*, 29 June 1900.
36 'The high-class firms refuse to give their agencies to shopkeepers, and it would be well if it were made illegal to do so': *Annual report of the chief inspector 1899*, p. 277 (Squire).
37 *Annual report of the chief inspector 1900*, p. 404 (Deane). Many of the firms also failed to supply sufficient 'particulars' of the payments to be made for each parcel of work, so that the outworkers often did not know how much they should be paid.
38 *Annual report of the chief inspector 1899*, p. 277.
39 *Departmental committee on the truck acts*, vol. II, p. 170 (Peter Ward, draper and publican in Dunkineely). See also *Annual report of the chief inspector of factories for 1913*, p. 106, H.C. 1914 [Cd. 7491] xxix, 647, where Inspector Emily Slocock added: '[t]he shopkeeper finds an agency a nice little addition to his income and a means of attracting customers, whereas a non-shopkeeping agent must have a very large and certain amount of work to make a living.'

required of them on the profits of the 'commission' alone, and 'the shop' and 'truck system' naturally followed. The head firms are in constant touch with these agents ... and it is impossible to hold [them] free from blame for conditions which were patent to all who chose to take an interest in the subject.[40]

From time to time, approaches were made to the principals,[41] but by and large they were left alone; indeed, on at least one occasion a lady inspector was instructed, in a tone 'which *smells* of Home Office', to prosecute the agents, but not to put pressure on the suppliers.[42]

THE INITIAL PROSECUTIONS

Thus it was that Adelaide Anderson, the principal lady inspector, came to Ardara in the summer of 1897. She quickly became convinced of two things – that truck was widespread in south Donegal, and that it would be very difficult to obtain sufficient evidence for a successful prosecution. She decided that the best approach would be to 'target' one of the leading truck-masters, Mrs Theresa Boyle,[43] and to that end she sent one of her colleagues, Lucy Deane, to south Donegal to get the necessary evidence.[44] Deane talked to a number of local women, and found that although they were vehemently opposed to truck practices, they also had a 'strong natural inclination ... to

40 *Annual report of the chief inspector 1900*, pp. 403–4 (Deane). 'There is ... no doubt that the head firms employing agents should give a reasonable commission; where it is so miserably low, the agent, if he is to make any profit at all, must make it out of the unfortunate workers ...': *Annual report of the chief inspector 1899*, p. 277 (Squire). Martindale later explained that 'owing to the weighty nature of the household items, the inaccessibility of many of the townlands, and the distance of Donegal from Belfast, the expense of carriage is often fairly heavy': 'Truck and gombeening in Donegal', p. 248.

41 'Special care was also directed to bringing prominently before the "head firms" in the large manufacturing towns in the north and west of Ireland, the grave responsibility which they had incurred in this matter': *Annual report of the chief inspector 1900*, p. 403 (Deane).

42 McFeely, *Lady inspectors*, p. 80 (quoting Deane)(original emphasis).

43 Boyle was a local shopkeeper who gave out sprigging work (embroidering handkerchiefs with decorative sprigs and flowers) to outworkers who were allegedly paid with 'little pieces of paper on which certain values were written', redeemable in goods from her shop. Deane explained that 'these "tickets" consisted ... only of a torn scrap of ordinary paper with the amount of its nominal value inscribed on it ... without either the date of issue or the signature of the "utterer" and were purposely arranged in this form to evade the risk of legal identification': *Annual report of the chief inspector 1897*, p. 109.

44 See McFeely, *Lady inspectors*, pp. 78–82, an account based on entries in Deane's diary, in the Deane Streatfield papers, Modern Records Centre, University of Warwick, MS 69. See also *Annual report of the chief inspector 1897*, pp. 90–6 and 108–09 and *Departmental committee on the truck acts*, vol. II, p. 103.

regard with suspicion and dislike any official attempt to enforce the law, even when it was for their own protection'.[45] They were also worried that if they gave evidence they would get no more work: 'when the result of giving such evidence is the dismissal from employment of the witnesses who give it, the cruel alternative of total loss of livelihood is too hard to be faced, and the necessary evidence on which to found a case is withheld.'[46] Nor were the local priests very helpful; although they too disapproved of truck, they were reluctant to offend an influential parishioner. Deane then resorted to the device of bringing in a second lady inspector, Mary Paterson, to work undercover 'dressed as a country girl'. Paterson mingled with the working women when they attended Mrs Boyle's shop and saw them being given tickets in return for embroidery.

Armed with this evidence, Deane felt able to launch a prosecution. As it turned out, some of the women did agree to testify[47] and Paterson was not required to give evidence. On 14 December 1897, Mrs Boyle was convicted at Ardara petty sessions on four charges and fined £40.[48] Deane was delighted: '[t]he magistrates unanimously held the cases to be of such gravity and affecting the country to such a serious extent that they did not feel justified in imposing anything less than the full penalty in each case. They hoped the prosecution would act as a warning to similar offenders'.[49] But it did not prevent the witnesses from being dismissed; fortunately, however, alternative arrangements were made for their benefit.[50]

---

45 *Annual report of the chief inspector 1897*, p. 109, adding '[m]y efforts to obtain evidence were constantly defeated by the fear [of a witness] ... that he or she would be held up to scorn and hatred by the local public opinion as "an informer" ...'

46 *Annual report of the chief inspector 1899*, p. 250 (Deane).

47 Deane admitted that during the hearing she had 'the absorbing fear lest the witnesses should at the last moment break down under the threat of their employer to deprive them of their only possible means of livelihood'; but they did not let her down: *Annual report of the chief inspector 1897*, p. 95.

48 Unreported, but see ibid., pp. 95–6 and 282n.

49 Ibid., p. 282n. The Congested Districts Board made no reference to this case when it later claimed the credit for the reduction of truck in this area: '[d]uring the past two or three years, we have had an agent at Ardara who, with funds chiefly supplied by us, pays cash for the drawn-work and embroidery produced in [the] district ... The "truck" system, which had previously been very prevalent, has now almost entirely disappeared. The presence of even one agent, who is always ready to pay cash, must have a very beneficial effect in any district': *Ninth annual report of the Congested Districts Board for Ireland*, p. 40, H.C. 1900 [Cd. 239] lxviii, 223. According to Deane 'the head firms in Belfast and Londonderry, whose contractors are in Donegal, took steps to see that the women workers were not treated in this way. They gave strict injunctions to their agents [not to pay in kind]': *Departmental committee on the truck acts*, vol. II, p. 103.

50 'The witnesses, on whose courage the case depended, have since been provided with work by the aid of persons interested in their unfortunate condition': *Annual report of the chief inspector 1897*, p. 96. Anderson explained that this 'aid' was initially provided by Deane and

Deane was given to understand that this prosecution 'has successfully checked the continuance of these practices in that special district'.[51] That may have been rather optimistic, even in south Donegal, but the case clearly went unheeded in the western part of the county. In the summer of 1899, Anderson, acting on information received, returned to Donegal and was able to 'ascertain with certainty' that truck was being systematically practised in and around Dungloe.[52] Accordingly, in September 1899 she despatched another lady inspector, Rose Squire, incognito to carry out another under-cover operation. For three weeks Squire moved around the area dressed as a tourist, talking to local women and establishing the basis for a series of prosecutions. She found direct evidence difficult to obtain; on only one occasion was she able, 'by a carefully planned stratagem', to witness a truck transaction.[53] As at Ardara, the evidence of the women themselves would be crucial. At the end of her visit, Squire returned to London, only to reappear a few weeks later in her official capacity, to institute proceedings.

Thus began a legal drama which lasted for almost a year, and became so intense that the mere enforcement of the truck acts:

> ... became almost lost sight of, [as the affair] developed gradually into a prolonged struggle for the vindication of law and order ... a struggle in which the whole neighbourhood and population took a keen and very personal interest ... enlivened for us by a perpetual element of absurdity which occasionally developed into incidents too extravagantly ludicrous or abnormal to be easily described in an official report.[54]

SQUIRE v. SWEENEY[55]

Squire was convinced that 'the chief offender' was the firm of Messrs Sweeney and Sons of Burtonport and Dungloe.[56] This firm functioned as grocer, draper, and hotelier/publican, but it also acted as hosiery contractors

---

her friends, 'but latterly this care has been taken from her by an Irish lady interested in their condition': ibid.

51 Ibid., p. 96.   52 *Annual report of the chief inspector 1899*, pp. 275–6.
53 Ibid., pp. 276–7.   54 Ibid., pp. 248–9.
55 The following account is based largely on the evidence of Squire in *Departmental committee on the truck acts*, vol. II, p. 79 and on the account given in her memoirs (*Thirty years*, pp. 80–96), the evidence of Sweeney in *Departmental committee on the truck acts*, vol. III, p. 18, and McFeely, *Lady inspectors*, pp. 83–90.
56 The firm apparently consisted of John Sweeney and his brother Morris. John Sweeney was a county councillor and clearly 'an influential citizen', as McFeely, *Lady inspectors*, p. 88, describes him. As already noted, his father, James Sweeney senior, was a justice of the peace; his son Joseph was to serve as a pro-Treaty TD for Donegal from 1921–1923, before joining the Irish Army and attaining the rank of major-general.

for wholesalers in Belfast and further afield. For reasons which will become obvious, it must be explained that the office from which the work was given out was located in a separate part of the Dungloe premises, and managed by an employee, Hugh Dunlevy. Squire's case was that a hosiery outworker, Mary McGeoghegan [or McGeehan or McGeoghan], had received wool from the firm to be knitted into socks.[57] According to Squire, Mrs McGeoghegan lived alone and did the knitting herself; according to Sweeney, she lived with her daughters who did most of the knitting. This detail, too, was to become relevant. In any event, when the work had been done, Mrs McGeoghegan returned to Sweeney's shop on 7 October 1899, handed over the socks and received in exchange a ticket with the sum of 2s. 3d. marked on it.[58] She then took the ticket into Sweeney's grocery shop, where it was exchanged for groceries (in particular, tea[59]) – an apparently open and shut case of payment otherwise than in current coin contrary to section 3 of the 1831 act.

Sweeney vehemently denied the charge,[60] and claimed that he always paid outworkers in cash.[61] His case basically was that the ticket was a voucher for cash, which Mrs McGeoghegan had voluntarily used to buy goods from his shop.[62] This was only fair: '[w]e expect that if we give employment to the poor people in the country ... [and since] the business [of giving out] ... is

---

57 Sweeney claimed that the socks were of mixed colours – even 'gaudy looking' – for working men 'when they go out on Sundays in their best clothes': *Departmental committee on the truck acts*, vol. III, p. 20. He claimed that the socks were not knitted by Mrs McGeoghegan ('as only young can do it') – a detail which became relevant to his defence that he had not committed any offence under the truck acts – see below, pp. 299–300.

58 According to Sweeney (ibid.), Mrs McGeoghegan received 4s. 6d. per dozen for these socks, which it would have taken her twelve days to knit: in other words, she earned 4½d. per day. But Squire said that the rate of payment was 1s. 6d. per dozen.

59 Squire claimed he sold tea at 3s. 6d. per pound; Sweeney said the price was 2s. Cf. *Irish Times*, 14 June 1900, Samuel Bewley & Co. advertised tea from 1s. 8d. per pound, and H. Williams & Co. Ltd., with 'agents in nearly every town in Ireland' sold tea with 'strength, flavour and richness combined' from 1s. 2d. per pound.

60 Although Sweeney obviously pleaded not guilty, there is no indication that he gave evidence; in 1908 he could only say that 'I do not think I gave evidence at all': *Departmental committee on the truck acts*, vol. III, p. 26. It seems that he could not lawfully have done so. Although special provision had been made in the Factory and Workshop Act 1895, s. 49, to enable a person charged with an offence under the factory acts to testify on his or her own behalf, this did not apply to truck offences – and, of course, the general provision recently made by the Criminal Evidence Act 1898 did not apply in Ireland. Sweeney was later to claim that Squire had told his solicitor that if he pleaded guilty, 'she would let him off with a 1s. fine', an offer which 'showed the weakness of the case and the groundwork on which it was based ...': *Departmental committee on the truck acts*, vol. III, p. 26.

61 Ibid., p. 20. Indeed, speaking as a county councillor seeking to uphold the reputation of the region, he asserted that 'there is no such thing in our country as gombeen men'.

62 His assistant Hugh Dunlevy, apparently told the court that Mrs McGeoghegan was given a ticket, but that it was marked 'cash'; she was given cash, and then voluntarily purchased goods from Sweeney: *Londonderry Sentinel*, 8 March 1900.

not one that would pay a very large profit ... we expect that our own customers will buy from us ...'[63] He insisted there was no compulsion; Mrs
McGeoghegan and others like her were free to go elsewhere, and if they did,
he would not refuse to give them further work. Any evidence to the contrary
was unreliable:

> Miss Squire was wrongly informed ... [She] went round there [to Mrs
> McGeoghegan's house] as a lady philanthropist and went among the
> people and sympathised with them ... and, of course, the people being
> poor, and she requiring to make up a case, and sympathising with them,
> got them to say more than they would say in the ordinary way. She took
> one side of the story.

The real problem was Squire's excessive zeal:

> People who are trying to formulate an industry to employ the people
> should not be harassed by over-anxiousness on the part of inspectors.
> We have always found that male inspectors went on and did their duty
> rigorously; but they did not go about it and were not guided by impulse
> as females are. They were guided by reason.[64]

But Sweeney's problem was that no-one in authority believed him.[65]

Squire was soon to find out that a prosecution might not be entirely
straightforward. Towards the end of October, she was in her room in
Hanlon's hotel in Dungloe when she was visited by Anthony O'Donnell, one
of the local magistrates. Having satisfied himself that the window blinds were
tightly drawn, he pleaded with her 'in impassioned tones' to drop the charges
against his relative and fellow-shopkeeper, because the evidence was so strong
that he was bound to be convicted. Squire protested that she had no power
to stay the proceedings, and managed to usher O'Donnell out of the room.
But shortly afterwards, when some of the witnesses came to see Squire,
O'Donnell followed them into her room, saying he wanted to hear what they
had to say. When he refused to leave, Squire sought the assistance of the
hotel proprietor, Mr S.B.P. Hanlon, who also happened to be the clerk of the
petty sessions. He managed to remove O'Donnell, but not before the
magistrate had so discomforted the women that they 'all took back their
promise to appear as witnesses and declared nothing would make them come

63 *Departmental committee on the truck acts*, vol. III, pp 20–21. He produced audited accounts
   (for 1906) to show how little profit he was making from the knitting business.
64 *Departmental committee on the truck acts*, vol. III, pp. 22, 25.
65 Having listened to the evidence of the factory inspectors and Sweeney, the departmental
   committee concluded that the position had been described 'with substantial accuracy' by
   the inspectors: *Departmental committee on the truck acts*, vol. I, pp. 11–12.

to the court'.[66] Squire saw to it that the home office protested to Dublin Castle, but in vain;[67] O'Donnell 'continued to sit on the bench and adjudicate during three successive prosecutions of his fellow tradesmen and friends'.[68]

Sweeney's case was one of three truck prosecutions brought by Squire which came before the Dungloe petty sessions on 14 November 1899. The first two cases proceeded quickly to a successful conclusion, as two other local shopkeepers were each convicted and fined.[69] But Sweeney had resolved to dispute the charge and appeared with his solicitor, Mr James Boyle of Stranorlar. It seems that the summons was addressed to 'John Sweeney and Sons', and that Sweeney's solicitor promptly contended that it should have been addressed to a particular individual.[70] The bench agreed, and refused to accept the summons.[71] Undaunted,[72] Squire, accompanied by Deane and

66 Squire, *Thirty years*, pp. 93–94. Note that it is not clear from Squire's account that this incident was directly linked to the *Sweeney case*.

67 O'Donnell was ordered by the lord chancellor to answer for his conduct. He duly submitted a report (in which he denied 'absolutely' the charges brought against him) which was sent to the home office: Sir David Harrel, under-secretary, chief secretary's office, to Sir Kenelm Digby, under-secretary, home office, 1 Dec. 1899: NAI CSO Letter Book no. 303, p. 728. Squire disagreed with many aspects of the report, and the lord chancellor was advised that 'Sir Matthew Ridley [home secretary] believes that entire reliance may be placed on the accuracy of Miss Squire's statements': Sir Kenelm Digby to Sir David Harrel, 9 Dec. 1899: PRO HO 152/2, p. 647. However, the lord chancellor 'felt himself unable to take further action in the matter': J.B. Dougherty, assistant under-secretary, chief secretary's office, to Sir Kenelm Digby, 27 Jan. 1900: NAI CSO Letter Book no. 303, p. 864.

68 Squire, *Thirty years*, p. 94. For a similar allegation in relation to magistrates in Connemara, see *Royal commission on congestion in Ireland, Appendix to the tenth report: Minutes of evidence taken in counties Galway and Roscommon*, pp. 16–17, H.C. 1908 [Cd. 4007] xlii, 114–15 (Fr Flatley): 'the magistrates utilise their position on the bench for the purpose of promoting their business. It is quite a common thing to see magistrates back out their own customers in the face of evidence. They do not look upon it as a thing to be ashamed of, although it is a most flagrant injustice, but as an advertisement for their business ... And not only is this so, but it is a well-known fact that magistrates go to the length of coaching witnesses as to the evidence they will give before the court ...'

69 Patrick O'Donnell, a hosiery agent of Doochery Bridge, was fined £5 (plus £1 costs) for one offence (a second charge was withdrawn when a witness failed to appear); Maurice Boyle, a shirt agent of Dungloe, was fined £5 (plus £1 costs) for one offence (six other cases were withdrawn 'in deference to the magistrates'): *Annual report of the chief inspector 1899*, p. 405.

70 This was Squire's recollection; Sweeney thought that the summons had been addressed to him, and should have been laid against the firm: *Departmental committee on the truck acts*, vol. III, p. 19. The nub of the problem was that the truck acts referred only to the actual 'employer', whereas the Factory and Workshop Act 1901, s. 146(3) expressly provided that 'it shall be sufficient to state the name of the *ostensible* occupier ...' (emphasis added).

71 Cf. Petty Sessions (Ire.) Act 1851, s. 39 provided that 'no objection shall be taken or allowed in any proceedings to any ... summons ... for any alleged defect therein in substance or in form ... [unless] any such ... defect shall appear to the justice or justices at the hearing to be such that the defendant has been thereby deceived or misled ...'

72 McFeely, *Lady inspectors*, p. 50 refers to Squire as 'perhaps the most spirited prosecutor of them [the lady inspectors] all'.

Constable McCaughey of the Royal Irish Constabulary, immediately went to Sweeney's premises to obtain further information with a view to issuing another, legally valid, summons. They found Sweeney in the drapery shop – that is, as already indicated, in a part of the premises separate from the office where the hosiery work was given out. Squire entered the shop to speak to Sweeney, but he refused to reply and instead ordered her 'in a violent manner' to leave his premises, and was generally abusive. Sweeney, of course, denied that he had used force against anyone, but he did admit that he had refused to answer questions, since 'I did not consider from the arrogant tone they took up that I was going to make them any wiser, and that they might find out for themselves.'[73] Nevertheless, as a result of this encounter, Sweeney was charged with obstructing a factory inspector in the exercise of her duty, and it was this charge which next came before the Dungloe justices on 12 December 1899.

Squire now knew what to expect from the local magistracy, and arranged for the home office to advise Dublin Castle that 'it is very desirable that ... the bench should be strengthened in any way that may be practicable'.[74] Accordingly, two of the resident magistrates for the county – G.B. Butler[75] (Letterkenny) and C.P. Crane[76] (Donegal) – were directed to attend the hearing. Squire was also represented by junior crown counsel (E. Morphy), who was briefed by the sessional crown solicitor (Mackey). Once again, the hearing began with the successful prosecution of another local shopkeeper.[77]

---

73 *Departmental committee on the truck acts*, vol. III, p. 19.

74 Sir Kenelm Digby to Sir David Harrel, 8 Dec. 1899: PRO HO 152/2, p. 643.

75 Butler had been appointed a resident magistrate in 1889 at the age of 32. Prior to his appointment he had been 'engaged in agricultural pursuits': see *Return of the resident magistrates in Ireland on 17th July 1911, showing their names, ages, when appointed, former vocation*, etc, p. 2, H.C. 1911 (277) lxv, 462.

76 '[A] Protestant, Yorkshire-born former RIC officer appointed RM in 1897 [and] ... a predictably "true-blue" Conservative-unionist who feared that Home Rule was a threat not merely to the United Kingdom but to the survival of the empire itself': P. Bonsall, *The Irish RMs: the resident magistrates in the British administration of Ireland* (Dublin, 1997), p. 60. In his *Memoirs of a resident magistrate, 1880–1920* (Edinburgh, 1938), p. 151, Crane commented: '[c]ases under the Truck Act were perhaps the most important [in the petty sessions court] ... The prosecutions by the Home Office under the Truck Act put a stop to this form of extortion and gave the producers a chance of making something by their work.'

77 Charles Kennedy, a hosiery agent, was fined £15 (plus £1 6s. 6d. costs) for two offences: *Annual report of the chief inspector 1899*, p. 405. Sweeney was later to claim that the three defendants convicted on 14 November and 12 December had pleaded guilty because 'they could not bear the law expenses that they would be put to if they fought it': *Departmental committee on the truck acts*, vol. III, p. 22. This seems unlikely, at least in Kennedy's case, since he gave notice of appeal to quarter sessions. However, he does not appear to have proceeded with the appeal: Sir Henry Cunynghame, legal assistant under-secretary, home office, to Sir David Harrel, under-secretary, chief secretary's office, 20 Dec. 1899: PRO HO 152/2, p. 669.

But then, in spite of all the precautions, Sweeney's solicitor was able to persuade the court to dismiss his case on the grounds that Squire's right of entry under section 68(4) of the Factory and Workshop Act 1878[78] was limited to the particular office where the work was given out, with the result that she had not entered the drapery shop upon her lawful duty, and Sweeney therefore could not be guilty of obstructing her.[79]

On appeal by way of case stated,[80] however, the queen's bench division held that the magistrates' interpretation of section 68(4) was erroneous.[81] Palles LCB for the court stated that there was nothing in the wording of the section which restricted its operation to the place where the work was actually given out, and that Squire therefore could have been acting lawfully. Accordingly, the case was remitted to the magistrates with an order not for conviction but for a redetermination in accordance with the opinion of the court.[82] The outcome of this rehearing is not entirely clear, but it seems that the obstruction charge was ultimately dismissed on the facts.[83]

Squire's attention now turned to the truck charge, only to find that 'every artifice which the Irishman's wit could devise was employed to prolong and complicate legal proceedings and to avoid conviction';[84] in all, the case was to come before the Dungloe bench on seven occasions.[85] The next problem was the non-attendance of witnesses. Women who had given Squire information

78 Section 13(2) of the 1887 Act gave factory inspectors 'the same powers and authorities' for enforcing the act as they had under the factory acts; s. 68(4) of the 1878 act gave an inspector power 'to make such examination and inquiry as may be necessary to ascertain whether [the factory acts] ... are complied with, so far as respects *the factory or workshop* [in question] ...' (emphasis added).

79 *Donegal Vindicator*, 29 June 1900, p. 3; *Annual report of the chief inspector 1900*, p. 29. The hearing of the truck charge was adjourned until 7 January 1900: Sir Henry Cunynghame to Sir David Harrel, 20 Dec. 1899: PRO HO 152/2, p. 670.

80 The Home Office tentatively suggested that the constitution of the bench might be put in issue, but appears to have accepted that this could not be raised by way of case stated: Sir Henry Cunynghame to Sir David Harrel, 20 Dec. 1899: PRO HO 152/2, pp. 669–70. But Mackey was instructed to prepare a draft case stated for approval by crown counsel (Morphy) in case the magistrates did not prepare the case themselves: Sir David Harrel to Sir Kenelm Digby, 29 Dec. 1899: NAI CSO Letter Book no. 303, p. 797.

81 *Squire v. Sweeney (No. 1)* (1900) 6 Ir WLR 30, 34 ILTR 26; *Annual report of the chief inspector 1900*, p. 29. The case was heard on 30 January 1900; Squire continued to be represented by Morphy, but Sweeney was now represented by Denis Henry QC and J. Gallagher.

82 In accordance with the Summary Jurisdiction Act 1857, s. 6. Palles LCB was of the opinion that 'under all the circumstances of the case ... it was not one in which he should make any order as to costs': ibid., p. 32.

83 At the hearing on 6 March 1900: C.S. Murdoch, assistant under-secretary, home office, to Sir David Harrel, 14 March 1900: PRO HO 152/3.

84 *Thirty years*, p. 89.

85 *Departmental committee on the truck acts*, vol. II, p. 90, pointing out that the other three cases heard at Dungloe had been similar, and yet had resulted in convictions without any complications.

in confidence were either afraid of being stigmatised as informers or intimidated by the threat of being refused further work or further credit.[86] When they failed to appear, Squire issued witness summonses, and even went with the summons server to assist him. They invariably found only deserted houses, 'the inhabitants hiding on our approach'.[87] Service was then effected by nailing the summons to the door, but not unexpectedly, a number of the witnesses ignored the summons. The hearing was therefore adjourned so that these witnesses could be arrested, only for the police to report that they were unable to execute the arrest warrants! The home office once again took the matter up with Dublin Castle; 'the police were severely reprimanded and the witnesses were arrested at a later date and produced in court'.[88]

Having solved the witness problem, Squire's attention turned to the matter of getting a fair hearing from the Dungloe magistrates, given that, as she herself acknowledged, 'local feeling had been deeply roused, the Truck system was a burning question, [and] all were personally involved on one side or the other'. Once again, the home office requested the lord lieutenant to make 'every effort possible ... to secure a proper hearing of the case ...'[89] The chief secretary's office again secured the attendance of two resident magistrates, and the services of the sessional crown solicitor and junior crown counsel.[90] But although the home secretary 'cannot but think that [Mr O'Donnell's] sitting to adjudicate on this case is a matter which calls for serious consideration',[91] there was apparently nothing which could be done to prevent this. Nor could anyone prevent the attendance of other local magistrates. Accordingly, when the case finally came to be heard on 6 March 1900, the court consisted of two resident magistrates (S.A. Gaussen,[92] who was in the chair, and G.B. Butler) and seven local justices.[93]

86 '[Miss Squire] finds that her witnesses are being intimidated' and the lord lieutenant was therefore requested to instruct the RIC 'to afford [her] any assistance and protection that may be necessary': Sir Kenelm Digby to Sir David Harrel, 9 Nov. 1899: PRO HO 152/2, p. 528A. The request was repeated on 19 Jan. 1900 (ibid., p. 740).
87 '[Witnesses] who beforehand seemed most staunch, when the time drew near managed to evade service of the summons, and disappeared from their homes in a wonderful manner and were with difficulty brought to the court. Every device is resorted to to escape appearing in court as a witness ...': Annual report of the chief inspector 1899, p. 277 (Squire).
88 Squire, Thirty years, pp. 89–92.
89 Sir Henry Cunynghame to Sir David Harrel, 20 Dec. 1899: PRO HO 152/2, p. 669; Sir Kenelm Digby to Sir David Harrel, 19 Jan. 1900: ibid., p. 740.
90 Sir David Harrel to Sir Kenelm Digby, 27 Jan. 1900: NAI CSO Letter Book no. 303, p. 864.
91 Sir Kenelm Digby to Sir David Harrel, 19 Jan. 1900: PRO HO 152/2, p. 740.
92 Stewart A. Gaussen had been appointed resident magistrate for the Dunfanaghy area in 1897. T.M. Healy, QC, MP, later referred to him as 'the removable magistrate' on the grounds that 'the Crown has shown what they think of him by removing him to Kerry': Donegal Vindicator, 29 June 1900. Gaussen was certainly moved to Kerry shortly after the Sweeney case, but this may have been part of the normal pattern for resident magistrates: '[t]here was no clear pattern to length of postings but in general newly appointed junior

Not unreasonably, Squire's counsel began by objecting to four of the justices on the ground that they were engaged in the same trade and occupation as the defendant, and to a fifth, on the ground that he was a nephew of the defendant.[94] But the five magistrates in question refused to withdraw, crown counsel did not press the issue and the hearing commenced. The proceedings quickly became chaotic:

> During the hearing ... the court was the scene of an indescribable tumult. The defending solicitor fiercely attacked the presiding stipendiary [i.e. resident] magistrate, and demanded his withdrawal from the bench. Encouraged by one of the local magistrates, he became more and more abusive and called the chairman 'a liar' ... [O]n the solicitor agreeing to withdraw his remark, the case proceeded, but not without difficulty, as the utmost confusion prevailed, several persons talking at once and each raising his voice louder to drown the other. The defendant insisted on so frequently interrupting his own solicitor that ... the exasperated lawyer sat upon his client, not metaphorically but physically ...[95]

After somehow hearing the evidence, which, according to Squire, 'was truthfully given [and] supported the case for the prosecution', the bench retired to consider their verdict. When they returned, Mr Gaussen, as chairman, announced that the case was, by a majority of six to three, dismissed on the merits.[96] Both

---

RMs tended to move more frequently than their senior colleagues. Some moved from place to place several times in a few years while others stayed on in the same district for twenty years or more': Bonsall, *The Irish RMs*, pp. 64–65.

93 According to the *Londonderry Sentinel*, 8 March 1900, the bench included Major Johnstone, J.A. Pomeroy, J.E. Boyle, J.M. Boyle, J.F. O'Donnell and Anthony D. O'Donnell; but it would seem that there was a seventh local magistrate who was not named. Healy asserted that the bench consisted of magistrates appointed by a conservative administration, and emphasised that it contained no 'Morley men': *Donegal Vindicator*, 29 June 1900. This was a reference to magistrates appointed between 1892 and 1895, when the Liberal John Morley was chief secretary for Ireland. Crane, *Memoirs*, pp. 191–92, explains that justices of the peace were normally appointed on the recommendation of the lieutenant of the county, but that in Morley's time, many men not so recommended had been appointed and they turned out to be weak, partial or unjust: 'They were, for the most part, men dependent on the people for their living – shopkeepers, farmers, publicans and the like – and independent action was well-nigh impossible for those with the shadow of boycotting hanging over them on the one hand, and the shadow of bribery and corruption on the other.'

94 *Departmental committee on the truck acts*, vol. II, p. 90 (Squire); *Londonderry Sentinel*, 8 March 1900. *Cf.* Truck (Amendment) Act 1887, s. 15 provided that '[a] person engaged in the same trade or occupation as an employer charged with an offence against the ... Act shall not act as a justice of the peace in hearing and determining such charge'.

95 Squire, *Thirty years*, p. 95.

96 The majority included the five magistrates (both Boyles and both O'Donnells, together with Major Johnstone) to whom objection had been taken.

resident magistrates and one of the justices dissociated themselves from this decision, 'with which they entirely disagreed'.[97]

The obvious response for Squire was to bring another case stated, but the court refused to accede to her application. This it was only entitled to do if of opinion that the application 'is merely frivolous'.[98] In such a case, the court was required, on Squire's request, to sign and deliver to her a certificate of such refusal. The court duly obliged,[99] and Squire promptly invoked section 5 of the Summary Jurisdiction Act 1857:

> Where the justice or justices shall refuse to state a case ..., it shall be lawful for the appellant to apply to the Court of Queen's Bench upon an affidavit of the facts for a rule calling upon such justice or justices, and also upon the respondent, to show cause why such case should not be stated; and the said court may make the same absolute or discharge it, with or without payment of costs, as to the court shall seem meet, and the justice or justices upon being served with such rule absolute shall state a case accordingly ...

Squire duly obtained an order of *mandamus* from the queen's bench division, and a meeting of the magistrates was arranged to discuss their response.[100] But they could not agree on the case to be stated.[101] Six justices therefore stated one case,[102] which the minority refused to sign on the grounds that it was 'grossly incorrect and misleading'. The minority stated the case as they saw it, and attached thereto the note of evidence taken at the hearing by the clerk and rejected by the majority justices as erroneous. Not surprisingly, the

---

97 Squire, *Thirty years,* p. 95.

98 Summary Jurisdiction Act 1857, s. 4.

99 C.S. Murdoch to Sir David Harrel, 14 March 1900: PRO HO 152/3.

100 According to J. O'Connor, *The Irish justice of the peace* (Dublin, 1911), p. 239, 'the statement of the case is the duty of the justices, and not of the parties; and there is no rule of law or practice to oblige them to show the case, or to prevent them from showing it, to the parties before it is signed: *Whelan v. Fisher* (1890) 26 LR Ir 340, 356. It is however, advisable to have the facts agreed to between the parties and, in case of dispute, settled by the justices: *R. (Byrne) v. Knox* (1888) 22 LR Ir 599, 603.'

101 Tempers became frayed on both sides. At one point, for example, Gaussen, who as chairman had been served with the original writ of *mandamus*, seized it and put it in his pocket, saying '[h]ow will you state your case now?' – and then went away 'to a distant part of the country': *R. v. Boyle and others* (1900) 6 Ir WLR 140, at p. 141. See also *Hansard's Parl. Deb., 4th ser.,* vol. lxxxv, cols. 959–60 (9 July 1900) and vol. lxxxvi, cols. 883–84 (23 July 1900), where this incident is repeated by T.D. Sullivan, MP for Donegal West, who also alleged that the sessional crown solicitor (Mackey) pretended to the queen's bench division that no case had been stated; he had then declined to accept the case which had been stated by the majority and instead lodged with the court a case signed by a minority of the justices 'as if it were a genuine case stated'. See also *Donegal Vindicator,* 29 June 1900, p. 3.

102 Apparently – and somewhat incredibly – on the basis of advice from Sweeney's solicitor.

queen's bench division took the view that there had not been a formal return
to the writ; in particular, no case had been signed by all nine justices.[103]

It appears that further efforts to have a single case stated by all the justices
were unsuccessful, and on 13 June 1900 the solicitor general applied for and
obtained a conditional order for attachment against the majority justices.
This gave the magistrates one week to show cause why they should not be
committed for contempt. Accordingly, they briefed counsel – T.M. Healy
QC, MP – and one week later the whole sorry matter came before Palles
LCB and his learned brethren to be sorted out.[104] This they did pragmati-
cally by declaring that the note of evidence taken by the clerk of petty
sessions was to be preferred to the 'recollection and belief' of the majority
justices;[105] attaching this note to the case stated by the majority could then
entitle the court to hold that there had been a sufficient return to the original
order of *mandamus*. The conditional order for attachment against the justices
was therefore discharged.[106]

But Palles LCB was clearly perturbed with the actions of all concerned:

> ... he was shocked when he read the statement in the affidavit that the
> solicitor for the Crown had charged these six justices with corruption,
> and he was equally astounded to hear it made, in argument, part of the
> case for the Crown. He had not, and could not come to any such
> conclusion; he, personally, acquitted these justices of any corruption.
> No doubt they had acted foolishly and unadvisedly in getting to act for
> them the solicitor for one of the parties. He [also] thought that there
> had been too much communication with the solicitors, and too much
> interference by the solicitors. If the Court had power to award costs to
> the justices, they would do so, were it only to completely vindicate
> them from the unproved charge of corruption.[107]

103 According to O'Connor, *Irish justice of the peace*, p. 239, '[i]t is now definitely settled that
     all the justices who took part in the decision must sign the case stated, even though some
     of their number may have dissented from the judgment of the court.' The authorities cited
     include *Fogarty v. G S & W Rly Co.*, unreported, KBD (Ire.), 26 April 1911, and *Kean v.
     Robinson* [1910] 2 IR 306.
104 This part of the case, which was heard on 22 June 1900, is reported as *R. v. Boyle and
     others* (1900) 6 Ir WLR 140.
105 The notes were made under the Petty Sessions (Ire.) Act 1851, s. 5, which Palles LCB (at
     p. 143) stated 'was intended to give a protection to the defendant in having the notes of
     evidence taken – much like though not as far as depositions ...' O'Connor, *Irish justice of
     the peace*, p. 239 cites *Boyle* as holding that '[t]he court may, where it sees fit to do so,
     disregard the facts as stated where they differ from the facts appearing in a note, taken at
     the hearing, by the justices or by a person directed by the justices to take such note.'
106 The fullest account of these proceedings appears to be in the *Donegal Vindicator*, 29 June
     1900. A brief report also appeared in the *Freeman's Journal*, 13 and 23 June 1900.
107 (1900) 6 Ir WLR 140 at pp. 143–44. Cf. on 23 July 1900, the attorney general stated that
     'the authorised shorthand notes of the judgment of the court ... do not contain any

After all this excitement, the substantive appeal by way of a case stated 'by certain of the justices' was heard by the queen's bench division on 27 June 1900.[108] Sweeney's contention now was that even on the case stated by the minority of the magistrates, the truck acts simply did not apply to Mrs McGeoghegan, since she was not a 'workman' as defined in section 10 of the Employers and Workmen Act 1875.[109] No doubt to Squire's consternation after all that had gone before, Palles LCB, for the queen's bench division, agreed with Sweeney, for two reasons.

First, Mrs McGeoghegan had not entered into a contract 'personally to execute any work or labour', since she was not bound to knit the socks herself. 'By the contract as disclosed upon the evidence, she was not bound to perform the work of knitting personally or any part of it. Her contract ... would have been performed had she had the work done either in whole or in part by others or wholly by herself.'[110] It made no difference that the work in question had in fact been performed wholly by Mrs McGeoghegan.[111] Nor was she employed under a contract of service, since the contract was not for a definite period of time. Accordingly, she was not a 'workman' to whom the truck acts applied. Was the learned chief baron right in so holding? The

censure on Mr Mackey or any other Crown official'. He accepted that Palles LCB had 'found some fault with the mode in which the case had been conducted by the counsel', but the attorney was prepared 'to justify in this House the action of the Crown in every particular'. He finished by saying that the crown did not see fit to recoup to the (majority) justices the expenses incurred by them in successfully defending themselves in the attachment proceedings: *Hansard's Parl. Deb.. 4th ser.*, vol. lxxxvi, cols. 883–84 (23 July 1900).

108 *Squire v. Sweeney (No. 2)*, unreported, QBD, 27 June 1900, but see *Departmental committee on the truck acts*, vol. I, p. 111 and *Donegal Vindicator*, 29 June 1900. The importance of the case is shown by the fact that Squire was represented by the solicitor general (Dunbar Barton QC) and Morphy, Sweeney by Serjeant Dodd QC and Gallagher. Although the justices were represented by T.M. Healy QC, for the earlier part of the proceedings (see above), it is unlikely that he participated at this stage. O'Connor, *Irish justice of the peace*, p. 244, citing *M'Gann v. Kelly* [1894] 2 IR 8, says that the justices cannot be heard; but he adds that cases have occurred in England in which counsel for the justices has been heard as *amicus curiae*: see e.g. *Stanton v. Brown* [1900] 1 QB 674n.

109 See above, p. 281. This definition had given rise to much litigation: see e.g. *Redgrave's Factory Acts* (14th ed. by J. Owner, London, 1931), pp. 359–61.

110 As Squire herself later explained: 'It was argued that the woman who took the work did not agree with the person who gave out the work that she would do it herself personally. It was said that the only verbal understanding with them was "here is certain material, bring it back in the form of knitted socks", and it was not asked or required that the work should be done only by the person to whom the wool was given ... I was not able to prove that either of these conditions existed in the case of the out-workers in Donegal': *Departmental committee on the truck acts*, vol. II, p. 90.

111 Squire knew that this might be a problem: '[w]e selected the case of a woman who herself did the work so that there might be no flaw', and had proved in court that the work had in fact been done by Mrs McGeoghegan: ibid., p. 91. Sweeney insisted that this was not so: *Departmental committee on the truck acts*, vol. III, p. 20.

definition in section 10 of the 1875 Act had been in use for some time before that date, and Palles LCB regarded himself as 'coerced' by two earlier English decisions as to its interpretation.[112] The limitations imposed by these earlier decisions had, indeed, been recognised in 1871, when a commission of inquiry recommended that outworkers should be included within the truck acts by drawing a distinction between 'contractors who engage to supply the result of other persons' labour on a large scale' and cases where 'it is consistent with the contract that the person should give his personal labour, and ... he has in fact done so to a substantial extent'.[113] But this distinction was not adopted in the 1887 act,[114] and the apparent explanation was that parliament had intended to retain the definition of 'workman' as then judicially understood. This may be an unduly legalistic interpretation, but in 1905 it was 'upheld' by the queen's bench division in England.[115]

Palles LCB then went on to hold in favour of Sweeney on a second ground – that Mrs McGeoghegan had not been engaged in 'manual labour', as that term had hitherto been judicially construed. Squire should have had some warning of this additional problem since, in June 1899, Palles LCB in *R. (Hollywood) v. Louth Justices*[116] had held that a barber was not covered by the 1875 act on the ground that his work did not require 'such expenditure of physical energy as is necessary to render it manual "labour" within the meaning of the section'. He now held that knitting socks also fell short of being manual 'labour', since it did not 'test the muscles and the sinews'.[117] This, too, seems a narrow legalistic interpretation and Squire is highly unlikely to have considered that this test would be invoked to exclude Mrs McGeoghegan from the protection of the truck acts.[118]

---

112 *Sleeman v. Barrett* (1864) 2 H & C 934, 159 Eng Rep 386 (Ct Exch) and *Ingram v. Barnes* (1857) 7 El & Bl 115, 119 Eng Rep 1190 (Ct Exch Ch).

113 *Report of the commissioners appointed by the Truck Commission Act 1870 for the purpose of inquiring into the operation of the [Truck Act 1831] and upon the operation of all other acts or provisions of acts prohibiting the truck system*, p. xlvii, H.C. 1871 [C. 326] xxxvi, 47.

114 'Why this was so, is not apparent': *Departmental committee on the truck acts*, vol. I, p. 10.

115 *Squire v. Midland Lace Co.* [1905] 2 KB 448 – see further below, p. 303.

116 See e.g. *Freeman's Journal*, 21 June 1900, and [1900] 2 IR 714 at p. 716. As can be seen e.g. from *Redgrave's Factory Acts*, pp. 360–1, the meaning of 'manual labour' had also come before the courts on numerous occasions before 1900.

117 The test laid down in *Yarmouth v. France* (1887) 19 QBD 647, at p. 651, per Lord Esher MR and followed by Palles LCB in the *Holywood* case.

118 The home secretary took the view that this interpretation of 'manual labour' was 'contrary to the view upon which the Truck Acts have hitherto been administered': *Hansard's Parl. Deb.*, 4th ser., vol. lxxxv, cols. 958–59 (9 July 1900). See also *Departmental committee on the truck acts*, vol. I, p. 19: '[k]nitting was included in the trades to which the Act of 1831 applied; it is one of the industries included in section 10 of the Act of 1887; and the decision is inconsistent with decisions of the English courts as to the meaning of the same phrase in the factory acts (compare *Hoare v. Robert Green Ltd.* [1907] 2 KB 315)'. However, the court in *Hoare* expressly stated that 'manual labour' for the purposes of determining

That should have been that. But it will come as no surprise to learn that the case came back to the queen's bench division yet one more time, since the parties could not agree on which of them should 'return' the case to the Dungloe magistrates. In *Squire v. Sweeney (No. 3)*,[119] Palles LCB finally bade farewell to the case by deciding that this was the duty of the solicitor having carriage of the case, namely, Squire's solicitor, Mr Mackey. The costs of this final hearing were awarded to Sweeney.

THE EFFECTS OF THE DECISION

The decision in *Squire v. Sweeney (No. 2)* may be said to have had four consequences.

The effect on the women who had given evidence

'Several of the poor girls on whose behalf proceedings were instituted at Dungloe, were ... deprived of the work upon which they depended, and the fear of a similar fate was always before the eyes of others in like circumstances.'[120] Fortunately, an indemnity fund had been organised by the Industrial Law Committee in 1898 at the instigation of Mrs Tennant[121] so that women and girls who had given testimony against their employers and had, as a result, lost their employment, were duly compensated. As Deane stated: '[i]t is not too much to say that the action of the Fund Committee which stepped in at this critical juncture, and after prompt and careful sifting of each separate case of distress, undertook to indemnify the witnesses, thus dismissed, against the actual loss of employment and to find work for them, alone made proceedings for the enforcement of the law possible.'[122]

The effect of the decision on other home-workers in Ireland

The application of the decision to other home-workers in Co. Donegal (and elsewhere in Ireland) was quickly confirmed. The attorney general (Atkinson) acknowledged that any person aggrieved by the decision could petition the

whether premises constituted a 'factory' under the factory acts did not necessarily have the same meaning as it had in the different context of the 1875 act.

119 (1900) 6 Ir WLR 210.

120 *Annual report of the chief inspector 1899*, p. 250 (Deane). 'The fact ... that the witnesses were unwilling [to testify] and only appeared under compulsion, did not prevent the employers refusing to give them any more work...': ibid., p. 277 (Squire).

121 May Abraham, the daughter of a Dublin solicitor, became active in women's labour politics in England and was one of the first two lady factory inspectors appointed in 1893. She became senior lady inspector in 1896, but resigned on marriage to H.J. Tennant in 1897. See generally V.R. Markham, *May Tennant: a portrait* (London, 1949).

122 *Annual report of the chief inspector 1899*, p. 250.

lord lieutenant for remission of a fine,[123] and the four defendants who had earlier been convicted at Ardara and Dungloe promptly did so. To the surprise of the home office,[124] the fines in all four cases were duly remitted in full.[125]

The effect of the decision on the practice of truck

Even though the queen's bench division had decided in Sweeney's favour, Squire was cautiously optimistic:

> [The court's] interpretation of the law created great dissatisfaction and proved a serious obstacle in the path of reform, which had steadily been gaining ground as a consequence of the convictions obtained in the earlier cases, and the similar campaigns carried out both by myself and other inspectors, notably Miss Lucy Deane, in other parts of Ireland. The Truck system had, however, received a serious check given from the publicity given to it, and workers, emboldened to ask for money payment, obtained it.[126]

Some years later she was to advise the departmental committee on the truck acts that 'most of the persons engaged [in truck] were impressed with the fact that there had been convictions, and they considered that it was illegal. ... The fact that the High Court decision had really put those workers outside [the 1887 act] did not seem to have impressed them so much as the convictions actually in their own neighbourhood.'[127] Perhaps more realistically she added that 'the practice was still going on, but it had been driven deeper in, so that it was difficult to get information'.[128]

But the committee received a much more pessimistic report from Martindale, who in 1907 had conducted a special enquiry on their behalf. Her assessment was that 'no real change' had taken place as to the existence of truck:

123 *Hansard's Parl. Deb.*, *4th ser.*, vol. lxxxvi, cols. 882–83 (23 July 1900).
124 The home office took the view that they had not been consulted, a departure from previous practice: '[t]he Secretary of State had already fully consulted the Law Officers for England and the Attorney General for Ireland ... and he thinks it is not impossible that, had he been been communicated with, a different course might have commended itself to the Irish Government': Sir Henry Cunynghame to Sir David Harrel, 22 May 1901: PRO HO 152/5, p. 813. See also *Hansard's Parl. Deb.*, *4th ser.*, vol. xciii, col. 429 (2 May 1901).
125 But the costs paid by the defendants were not remitted: see *Hansard's Parl. Deb.*, *4th ser.*, vol. xci, col. 1378 (26 March 1901), vol. xcii, cols. 1453–54 (26 April 1901), vol. xciii, col. 456 (2 May 1901), where Atkinson stated that the decision to remit the fines *had* been made after consultation with the home office, and vol. ic, cols. 933–4 (15 Aug.1901).
126 *Thirty years*, p. 97.
127 *Departmental committee on the truck acts*, vol. II, p. 95.
128 In 1908 Martindale reported a truck prosecution in the west of Ireland where a number of

The prices charged for the tea and other articles may be less exorbitant, but the evil still exists ... [T]he Truck Acts may be nominally observed by handing actual coin to the worker. But, as a general rule, no work is to be obtained, at any rate not the best work, unless the wages are left at the shop; or else the workers are allowed, or even induced, to get heavily into debt, to be wiped off subsequently by out work ...[129] [T]hough ... the workers [complain] as to the difficulty of obtaining coin, it seems to be almost instinctive with them that it would be an ungenerous act to take their wages from the shop'.[130]

The position of outworkers in England and Wales

When questioned by Sir Charles Dilke as to the position in England and Wales, the home secretary (Ridley) replied that the consequences of the decision in *Squire v. Sweeney (No. 2)* were being examined by the law officers.[131] In May 1901, however, the new home secretary (Ritchie) stated that he had been advised that the decision 'should not be taken as binding in England'.[132] Four years later, however, the matter was put beyond doubt by the English king's bench division in *Squire v. Midland Lace Co.*[133] Without any reference to *Sweeney*, this court also held itself bound by *Ingram v. Barnes* to hold that a Nottingham lace clipper was not a 'workman' for the purposes of the 1875 Act. But Kennedy J went on to state:

> We [dismiss this appeal] with some reluctance, having regard to ... the nature of the employment and the position of the women clippers, who, though they do sometimes employ assistants, are evidently, as a class, wage-earning manual labourers, and not 'contractors' in the

witnesses 'went back entirely' on their written statements and the case was dismissed – only for her to be told that 'Mr X had paid wages in goods from "time immemorial" and that everyone in the court knew it': *Annual report of the chief inspector of factories for 1908*, p. 159, H.C. 1909 [Cd. 4664] xxi, 696.

129 According to Martindale, '[t]he truck acts have been too carefully studied during the last ten years ... and methods have been adopted which are more indirect in character but prove just as efficacious ... We became accustomed to the remarks: "[o]ut of friendship we might be getting a little coin" ... He's middling hard on coin", etc': *Departmental committee on the truck acts*, vol. III, p. 250.

130 Ibid., vol. i, 11. Martindale had reported that truck was admitted by 106 out of the 154 outworkers she had interviewed: ibid., vol. iii, 250. A second inquiry by Martindale in 1911 produced much the same findings: see *Committee of inquiry into the conditions of employment in the linen and other making-up trades of the north of Ireland: Report and evidence*, p. xviii, H.C. 1912–13 [Cd. 6509] xxxiv, 383.

131 *Hansard's Parl. Deb.. 4th ser.*, vol. lxxxv, cols. 958–59 (9 July 1900) and vol. lxxxvi, col. 177 (31 July 1900).

132 *Hansard's Parl. Deb., 4th ser.*, vol. xciii, col. 429 (2 May 1901).

133 [1905] 2 KB 448.

ordinary and popular sense ... and we venture to express the hope that some amendment of the law may be made so as to extend the protection of the Truck Act to a class of workpeople practically indistinguishable from those already within its protection.[134]

This hope was ignored. Notwithstanding the widespread dissatisfaction which *Sweeney* and *Midland Lace* produced[135] and a strong recommendation from the departmental committee on the truck acts in 1908,[136] neither the 1875 act nor the 1887 act was amended.[137] As Anderson had explained:

Where outworkers hold a strong enough position to make clear in their contract express or implied with the giver-out of work that they are not ... in the position of sub-contractors employing for profit other workers, this decision would not injure their prospects of securing payment in current coin of the realm. But our reports abundantly show that the peasant women in congested districts of Ireland are not in the position to impose their will upon any would-be employer, and unless the long campaign on their behalf making clear, as it did, the injury they suffered, and thus enlisting the sympathies of the better section of public opinion, arouses some organised effort in their midst, they cannot hope for release in the meantime from the tyranny of uncontrolled payment in kind.[138]

134 Ibid., p. 455.
135 *Departmental committee on the truck acts*, vol. I, p. 10.
136 Outworkers should be included within the scope of the truck acts as 'the first step to the introduction of a better system [of payment]', although the committee accepted that 'it cannot be expected that [this] ... will immediately or entirely remedy the conditions prevailing in these remote districts'. They continued: '[m]oreover, the relation of persons so employed to the truck masters, who act as general merchants supplying from their shops to their workers most of their necessities, is such that the habits of the people, including chronic indebtedness as one of the conveniences of life, might be temporarily so disturbed by a sudden alteration of the present system that it would not be surprising if the change were for a short period distasteful both to employers and employed. The application, however, ... of the Acts ... will in itself be a substantial gain ...': *Departmental committee on the truck acts*, vol. I, p. 13. On the other hand, Deane did not think that requiring payment in cash would cost the women their work altogether, but it would result in even lower earnings; however, they could then buy at the cheapest shops and would probably be in much the same position in real terms: ibid., vol. II, pp. 109 and 111.
137 As late as July 1914 the home secretary (McKenna) was declaring that he hoped to introduce a bill 'very shortly' to give effect to the recommendations of the departmental committee: see *Hansard's Parl. Deb.*, 5th ser., vol. lxiv, cols. 2106–07 (16 July 1914). But nothing had been done by the time Squire published her memoirs in 1927: *Thirty years*, p. 98. Indeed, no relevant amendment appears to have been made to the 1831 or 1887 acts before they were finally repealed almost one hundred years later by the Wages (NI) Order 1988 and the Payment of Wages Act 1991.
138 *Annual report of the chief inspector 1900*, p. 359. In 1908 the evidence showed that the

No direct action was forthcoming. But, as Martindale pointed out, truck was only part of a larger problem:

> ... it will be impossible to stamp out the truck system until the credit system changes greatly for the better, because at the present time the two systems are working hand in hand. The effect of being always in debt, and never being encouraged to free themselves from it, the knowledge that proceedings will follow if any offence is given to the shopkeeper ... the want of thrift and foresight which is the result of this system, have a moral effect on the people, the seriousness of which can hardly be overestimated.[139]

Fortunately, three more general developments were by 1910 helping indirectly to improve the lot of outworkers in rural areas such as Co. Donegal. The growth of agricultural credit societies prepared to make small loans at low rates of interest, and the establishment of co-operative agricultural societies providing farm supplies at wholesale prices[140] reduced the level of dependence on shopkeeper credit, while the development of employment in local fisheries and creameries, which helped to bring in ready cash throughout the year, reduced the need for any kind of credit.[141] These developments may have had limited significance in the present context;[142] nevertheless, they encouraged Martindale to conclude:

> [The truck system] could be largely stamped out if the Belfast firms discontinued the practice of appointing shopkeepers as agents, and had their own stations in Donegal staffed by salaried men and women,[143]

practices in question 'prevail most largely in remote parts of the United Kingdom where little publicity attends them and where the workers have no trades unions or organisations to voice their grievances or promote any attempt at legislative remedy': *Departmental committee on the truck acts*, vol. I, pp. 10–11.

139 'Truck and gombeening in Donegal', p. 252.

140 See especially P. Bolger, *The Irish cooperative movement: its history and development* (Dublin, 1977), chs. 12 and 13, and by the same author, 'The Congested Districts Board and the co-operatives in Donegal' in W. Nolan, L. Ronayne and M. Dunlevy (eds), *Donegal: history and society: interdisciplinary essays on the history of an Irish county* (Dublin, 1995), ch. 22.

141 Martindale later commented that co-operative stores and the credit banks helped considerably by making workers more independent, and added: '[t]hat will touch the question probably better than [truck] legislation': *Committee of inquiry into the linen and other making-up trades*, p. 60. See also H. Martindale, *From one generation to another, 1839–1944: a book of memoirs* (London, 1944), pp. 134–35 and 137–38.

142 See e.g. Cullen, *Economic history of Ireland*, p. 155: '[b]ut in fact, with some exceptions, the cooperative movement proved successful only in the dairying districts, and apart from the cooperative creameries the bulk of cooperative ventures in selling or buying were themselves offshoots of creamery societies.'

143 As was then the practice with regard to shirt-making: Martindale, *Departmental committee*

who gave out the work ... [O]ut-workers should be shown that their
relationship to the employer is quite a separate relationship to that of
customer to shopkeeper, and that it is their right to receive ready
money regardless of debt. If workers received ready money for their
sprigging and knitting, much would be done to stop the injurious credit
system ...[144]

But as late as 1913, Inspector Slocock was still reporting that she could find
no evidence of concerted action on the part of employers to distribute work
through agents other than shopkeepers.[145] The incidence of truck in Co.
Donegal might have been reduced, and its effects mitigated by other
developments, but the practice itself was to continue well into the twentieth
century.

---

on the truck acts, vol. III, p. 255. She later told the 1912–13 committee that it would be a
   great benefit if it were made illegal for outwork to be given out by retail shops (q. 1149).
144 'Truck and gombeening in Donegal', p. 252.
145 *Annual report of the chief inspector 1913*, p. 106.

The 'one judgment rule' in the supreme court

RONAN KEANE*

I REMEMBER AS A LAW STUDENT COMING across a book in the King's Inns library, called *The dissenting opinions of Mr Justice Holmes.*[1] I was somewhat surprised that anyone had taken the trouble to collect a number of judgments which had only one feature in common, namely, that they were wrong. I felt a little sorry for the eminent justice who was, as I naïvely assumed, being immortalised solely on the basis that he had not only got the laws wrong, but had done so on so many occasions that it was possible to have a book solely devoted to these unfortunate aberrations. Of course, I know better now and like every sensible person acknowledge that today's dissent may very well be tomorrow's received wisdom, and that this is true of a number of Holmes J's dissents. In the area of freedom of speech, his principle that there should be freedom for the thought we hate ultimately prevailed over the opposite view with its tendency to uphold government policy. His acceptance that in a democracy the judges should defer to the will of the majority as reflected in legislation, and not seek to impose their own views on social and economic matters, in the end triumphed over those who invoked the constitution to strike down legislation in those areas.

The institution of the dissenting judgment has, it is beyond argument, an honourable place also in the legal tradition which we inherited. In areas of the law where there is uncertainty or where such certainty as there is might plausibly be seen as reflecting a view of the law seriously in need of reform, dissenting judgments clearly perform an important function. Their very existence, altogether apart from any intrinsic merits the judgments may possess, encourages those who believe the law to be in need of reform to persist with their efforts. This need not take the form of an invitation to the court in question to review its earlier judgment. That indeed may be a possible route, and one that may be particularly attractive if there has been a change in the composition of the court and, better still, some indication of judicial discomfort with the majority view. The dissenting judgments may

*   The edited text of an address given to the Society at the premises of Dublin City Public Libraries and Archive, Pearse Street, on 26 November 2004.

1   Ed. A. Lief (New York, 1929).

also encourage a legislature already disposed to change the law and can provide valuable material for those bodies concerned with bringing about changes in the law, notably the Law Reform Commission.

The incorporation in the Irish constitution of a prohibition on the publication of dissenting judgments in specified cases, extending even to a ban on the disclosure of the existence of a dissent, is a departure from the almost universal practice in the common law world, and voices have for some time now been raised advocating the removal of article 34.4.5 of the constitution which states:

> The decision of the Supreme Court on the question of the validity of a law having regard to the provisions of this Constitution shall be pronounced by such one of the judges of that Court as that Court shall direct and no other opinion on such question, whether assenting or dissenting, shall be pronounced nor shall the existence of any such other opinion be disclosed.

To the same effect is paragraph 2.2 of article 26 which deals with references by the president to the supreme court of a bill passed by both houses of the Oireachtas for a decision as to whether the measure or any particular provisions are constitutionally invalid. It says:

> The decision of the majority of the judges of the Supreme Court shall, for the purposes of this Article, be the decision of the Court and shall be pronounced by such one of those judges as the Court shall direct and no other opinion, whether assenting or dissenting, shall be pronounced nor shall the existence of any such other opinion be disclosed.

The relevant part of this sub-paragraph is in virtually the same terms as article 34.4.5. It also makes clear, however, that the fact that there is a division of opinion in the court does not prevent the majority view on the validity of the referred measure from having binding effect. It has been suggested that this simply reflects the fact that the article 26 reference procedure does not constitute the resolution of a justiciable issue and that it was accordingly thought advisable to make it clear that the normal rules of the common law allowing for the binding effect of a majority view were to apply.

It may be noted in passing that the reference procedure itself was not wholly without precedent on this island: section 51 of the Government of Ireland Act 1920 expressly provided for a reference procedure in the case of legislation passed by the parliament of Northern Ireland established under that act, in order to resolve any issue which might arise as to whether the provision in question was within the powers of that parliament. For that purpose, the judicial committee of the privy council was to be the adjudicating body. The same machinery has been availed of more recently by the Westminster parliament to resolve any issues as to the *vires* of legislation passed by the devolved assemblies of Scotland,[2] Wales[3] and indeed Northern Ireland itself.[4] The judicial committee of the privy council also enjoyed a general power under section 4 of the Judicial Committee Act 1833[5] to resolve disputed points of law, a procedure notably availed of to resolve the dilemma posed for the United Kingdom government by the refusal of the Northern Ireland parliament to nominate a representative to the Boundary Commission charged with determining the line of the boundary between Northern Ireland and the Irish Free State. In exercising their powers, however, in these areas, the judicial committee, while observing a 'one judgment' procedure under which the 'advice' of the committee was conveyed to the crown in a judgment of one of the law lords, permitted the expression of dissenting opinions.

There is, it would seem, no precise precedent for the immutable one judgment rule enshrined in articles 26 and 34. It was introduced into the constitution by the Second Amendment of the Constitution Act 1941, passed during the transitional period of three years when the constitution could be amended by an act of the Oireachtas without the need for a referendum. It appears to have been partly modelled on section 28 of the Courts of Justice Act 1924 which, in the case of the court of criminal appeal, permits the delivery of one judgment only, except where the president of the court allows the delivery of a dissenting judgment. There is no similar qualification in the case of the supreme court, and I know of no case in which a member of the court of criminal appeal has delivered a dissenting judgment having sought and obtained permission from the president of the court.

As to the other appellate courts in the common law world, they all without exception permit the delivery of dissenting judgments and (save in the case of the privy council) the delivery of more than one assenting judgment. A different tradition prevails in the civil law countries and it is presumably its existence that explains the one judgment rule in force in the court of first instance and the court of justice of the European Union. The fact that in contrast the European court of human rights permits the delivery of dissenting judgments may perhaps be explained by the significant part played by lawyers from the United Kingdom in the framing of the European Convention on Human Rights and the establishment of the European court of human rights.

The reasons for the amendment effected by the Second Amendment to the Constitution Act in relation to the delivery of judgments were made clear by the Taoiseach, Eamon de Valera, during the debates on the measure in the

2 Scotland Act 1998, s. 33.   3 Government of Wales Act 1998, sched. 8.
4 Northern Ireland Act 1998, sched. 9.   5 3 & 4 Will, c. 41.

Dáil. It was thought that the authority of the court's finding on the constitutionality of a law would be weakened if it was believed to be that of a majority only of the supreme court. He canvassed the possibility which could arise where a divisional court of three judges of the high court and the supreme court reached different conclusions where, as he suggested, it could be argued that the majority of judges in the superior courts were opposed to the conclusion reached by a majority in the supreme court.

What actually prompted the amendments, however, it is generally accepted, was the decision of the supreme court in the case of the first reference of a bill under the provisions of article 26. The measure in question was the Offences against the State (Amendment) Bill 1940. That bill in turn had been rendered necessary, in the view of the government, by the decision of the high court (Gavan Duffy J) to the effect that the provisions of the Offences of the State Act 1939 allowing for internment without trial on the certificate of a minister were repugnant to the then recently enacted constitution. The 1939 legislation had reached the statute-book only months before the outbreak of the Second World War at a time when the IRA had begun a bombing campaign in England, and extreme disquiet was felt by the de Valera government as to the security situation confronting them. The Taoiseach made no secret of the surprise, not to say dismay, with which he and his ministers received the news of Gavan Duffy J's decision in *The State (Burke) v. Lennon*, striking down the internment provisions of the new legislation within weeks of the outbreak of war.[6] Their anxieties were compounded by the fact that, when the attorney general sought to appeal the decision, the supreme court ruled that under the law, as it was then understood, no appeal lay from a decision of the high court to grant an order of *habeas corpus*, the form of relief sought in the actual case. The decision had as its immediate consequence the release of all the suspected members of the IRA. The final catastrophe for the beleagured government was a raid successfully carried out by the newly freed prisoners on the magazine fort in the Phoenix Park, resulting in the capture by them of large quantities of ammunition and the consequent depletion of the resources of the defence forces.

The government might have relied on the fact that a resolution had been passed under article 28.3.3 by both houses of the Oireachtas resolving that an emergency existed because it was a 'time of war' and that the constitution had been amended by the first act passed in the interim period to make it clear that the expression could apply to a war in which the country was not actually engaged. If the contentious legislation had been passed under that resolution it would have been immune from scrutiny in the courts. Legislation was in fact passed under its terms providing for the internment of Irish citizens, but the government, for whatever reason, wished the

6 [1940] IR 136.

Offences against the State Act, including the internment provisions, to remain an effective measure. An even more drastic option – to remove the power of judicial review entirely from the courts – was hinted at by the Taoiseach but not pursued.[7] Another course which may have been considered was to avail of the power to amend the constitution by ordinary legislation. However, the likelihood that the new bill, which differed only from the impugned measure in requiring the minister to be 'of opinion' rather than 'satisfied' that the person should be detained, would be referred by President Douglas Hyde to the supreme court, at least meant that the bar against an appeal to that court from Gavan Duffy's decision could be effectively circumvented.

The judgment of the court, upholding the constitutionality of the measure, was delivered by Sullivan CJ who announced at the outset that it was a judgment of 'the majority of the judges'.[8] That wording simply followed the wording of article 22.6 even in its unamended form but it was seized on by some as an indication that the court was divided in its view, and the possibility that there had been a minority in favour of condemning the bill was raised in the Dáil by James Dillon. It was also at one stage suggested that the government, alarmed by the possibility of a divided supreme court, had sought to 'pack' the court. This was based on nothing more substantial than the fact that one of the members of the court, Meredith J, was stated to be unavailable and that his place was taken by the president of the high court, Mr Justice Conor Maguire. In truth there was nothing surprising in the absence from the court in midwinter of an elderly member who died only two years later. His replacement by the president of the high court who was *ex officio* a member of the supreme court was inevitable: to have chosen any other member of the high court would have more plausibly attracted criticism. The suggestion that the chief justice selected Maguire P rather than another high court judge because he had been a Fianna Fail TD and attorney general in de Valera's government before being appointed a judge and might therefore be relied on to uphold the legislation was bizarre and appears to have been first put forward in the 1960s by an American writer, Professor Loren Beth, who later withdrew it.[9] It was, however, resurrected in a biography of Gavan Duffy by Graham Golding and trenchantly attacked by Brian Walsh (Walsh J) in a review of that work in the *Irish Jurist*.[10]

Dr Gerard Hogan's diligent researches which resulted in an illuminating article on the whole episode – to which I am indebted – failed, not

7 *Dáil Deb.*, vol. 78, col. 1353 (3 Jan. 1940).
8 *Re Offences against the State (Amendment) Bill* [1940] IR 470, at p. 475.
9 L.P. Beth, *Development of judicial review in Ireland, 1937–1966* (Dublin, 1967).
10 B. Walsh, Review of G.M. Golding, *George Gavan Duffy, 1882–1951: a legal biography* (1982) in *Ir Jur*, 17 (1982), 384, at p. 386.

surprisingly, to unearth any evidence for the existence of such a deliberate manoeuvre.[11] It is, however, the case that James Dillon in the Dáil, whose comments were mentioned earlier, said:

> ... as a matter of fact, did not Mr Justice Gavan Duffy, Mr Justice Murnaghan, and Mr Justice Geoghegan hold that it was unconstitutional and the Chief Justice, the President of the High Court and Mr Justice O'Byrne hold that it was not?

When the Taoiseach replied that he did not know where Deputy Dillon had got this information, the latter responded that it was 'public property', adding: '[w]as it not correctly stated that it was a majority of the supreme court?'[12] Dr Hogan, who correctly described Dillon as being a non-practising barrister who was well-connected in legal circles, adds:

> It seems unlikely that he would have made such a definite statement unless he was relatively sure of his facts. A further point which provides some further corroboration is that, as we have already seen, counsel for the State was closely questioned by both Murnaghan and Geoghegan JJ during the course of argument ... For present purposes, there seems little alternative but to assume that Deputy Dillon was correct.[13]

With all respect to Dr Hogan, I do not think that such an assumption is warranted. It is generally accepted that to draw inferences from the interventions of judges on the supreme court as to how they will ultimately decide the case is somewhat hazardous. It also has to be pointed out that it is one thing for a person to be well-connected in legal circles and quite another for him to be the repository of such indiscreet confidences on the part of members of the court. All I can say is that, in my experience, members of the court are extremely careful not to disclose their opinions even in private conversations. It is just as reasonable to assume that Dillon's surmise as to the voting patterns on the court was no more than speculation. He was also technically incorrect in his assembly of judges supposedly in favour of striking down the bill: Gavan Duffy J should not have been included since he did not have the opportunity of deciding on the results of the alteration effected in the amending legislation, although it is certainly safe to suppose that it would not have made any difference to his view.

One returns again to the actual phrase used by Sullivan CJ, namely that the judgment being delivered was that of the majority of the court. Could it

---

11 G. Hogan, 'The supreme court and the reference of the Offences against the State (Amendment) Bill 1940' in *Ir Jur*, 35 (2000), 238.
12 *Dáil Deb.*, vol. 78, cols. 1723–4 (21 Feb. 1940).
13 Hogan, 'The supreme court', p. 273.

be that this meticulous adherence to the actual wording of the article in the constitution was no more than that and was not intended to give any hint as to whether there were any dissentients? What is more puzzling is the decision not to permit the delivery of any dissenting judgments, if such there were, even though at that stage there was nothing in the language of the constitution to prohibit the delivery of a dissent. Was this because the court considered that the relatively novel nature of the jurisdiction conferred by article 26 rendered the delivery of more than one judgment, whether assenting or dissenting, inappropriate? Again we are reduced to speculation: all one can say with safety is that judges of a collegiate court would not normally take kindly to the proposition that they should be prevented from delivering dissenting judgments. It is fair to say, I think, that the only safe basis for the belief that there were one or more dissenting opinions in the case was the not unambiguous statement of Sullivan CJ that the judgment he was delivering was the judgment of 'the majority of the judges'.

One is on safer ground in concluding that Dillon's comments, whether wide of the mark or not, were present to de Valera's mind when he introduced the amending legislation providing for the one judgment rule. He said:

> From an educational point of view, the proposal [for separate judgments] would no doubt be valuable, but after all, what do we want? We want to get a decision. The more definite the position is the better, and from the point of view of definiteness, it is desirable that only one judgment be pronounced ... [and] that it should not be bandied about from mouth to mouth that, in fact, the decision was only come to by a majority of the Supreme Court. Then you would have added up perhaps the number of judges who dealt with the matter in the High Court before it came to the Supreme Court, as might happen in some cases. You would then have an adding up of judges and people saying: 'they have five on this side and three on the other and therefore the law is the other way.' That would be altogether undesirable.[14]

As we have seen, Dillon had attempted, with however slender a basis, an exercise of this nature. The Taoiseach was undoubtedly correct in envisaging that such judicial head-counting might have a more solid foundation where a divisional court of three or more judges had sat in the high court. I say three or more advisedly, since as McCarthy J pointed out in his reflections on the 'one judgment rule', there is in theory no limit to the number of high court judges who can sit in a divisional court, leading to the awesome possibility today of a bench of 33 judges sitting in judgment on the constitutionality of a statute.[15]

14 *Dáil Deb.*, vol. 86, col. 1861, (25 April 1941).
15 N. McCarthy, '*Una voce poco fa*' in J. O'Reilly (ed.), *Human rights and constitutional law: essays in honour of Brian Walsh* (Dublin, 1992), pp. 163–8.

The framers of the amendment either overlooked or were not concerned with two consequences which rendered it questionable. It did not address the difficulty that might arise where a majority of the judges in favour either of striking down a measure or upholding its constitutionality could not agree on the reasons for so holding. That has led in one case to the chief justice simply stating that the decision of the court was to affirm the high court judgment rejecting the challenge to the constitutionality of an act and declining to give any reasons, presumably because a majority of three could not be found to agree on those reasons.[16] That is a distinctly unsatisfactory posture for a court of final appeal to be required to adopt. The second difficulty was that, as judicially interpreted, the reach of the one judgment rule was confined to cases concerning the constitutionality of legislation enacted by the Oireachtas since the constitution came into force in 1937.[17] This has meant that in the case of legislation of the Westminster parliament prior to 1921, or legislation of the Oireachtas of the Irish Free State, or delegated legislation under either regime, the one judgment rule does not apply. A broad or purposive approach might have resulted in a finding that the words 'the validity of any law' extended to such legislation. Moreover, there have been major cases in which no specific item of legislation was under consideration and yet constitutional principles of the first importance were under consideration to which the one judgment rule did not apply. Thus, in *Attorney General v. X. and others*,[18] dealing with the extraordinarily sensitive area concerning the extent to which the constitution as amended in 1983 permitted abortion, all five members of the court gave judgments.

The number of judgments in that case reflects, not surprisingly, the tendency of judges of the court to deliver separate judgments in cases with far-reaching constitutional ramifications, including assenting judgments which contain different nuances. That has been a notable feature of judgments delivered by the court in such cases since its membership was expanded from five to eight in 1994. Thus in *Sinnott v. Minister for Education*,[19] *Maguire v. Ardagh and others*,[20] and *A.O. and O.J.O. v. Minister for Justice, Equality and Law Reform*,[21] in each of which cases seven judges sat, seven judgments were delivered, including dissenting judgments. These dealt respectively with such major issues as the constitutional entitlement of children to free primary school education and the separation of powers, the rights of committees of the Oireachtas to conduct inquiries, and the rights of non-national parents of children born in Ireland to reside in Ireland.

In cases dating from the enlargement of the court, one is also struck by the variety of judgments, again both assenting and dissenting, in constitutional

16 *The State (Hunt) v. O'Donovan* [1975] IR 39.
17 *The State (Sheerin) v. Kennedy* [1966] IR 379.
18 [1992] 1 IR 1.   19 [2001] 2 IR 545.   20 [2002] 1 IR 385.   21 [2003] 1 IR 1.

cases not affected by the one judgment rule. Notable examples are *Norris v. Attorney General*[22] concerning the criminalisation of homosexual behaviour; *Attorney General v. Hamilton (No. 2)*[23] upholding by a majority the constitutionality of cabinet confidentiality; *Re a Ward of Court (No. 2)*[24] in which the right to withdraw artificial nutrition from a patient in a near-persistent vegetative state was upheld by the majority, and *McKenna v. An Taoiseach*[25] where the expenditure of public funds by the government in support of a particular result in a referendum campaign was condemned as unconstitutional. The last two cases are particularly striking as they had far-reaching implications for the future and it was clearly of value for all those concerned at every level in giving effect to them to have the fullest possible statements of the reasons which led the judges to their conclusions. So too in *Crotty v. An Taoiseach*,[26] where the government was restrained by a majority of the court from implementing without a referendum the treaty provisions of the Single European Act of the European Communities, 1986.

If one turns to the cases in which only one judgment was possible, they consist of 14 which took the form of a reference by the president of the high court, and a much larger number where the issue arose by way of appeal from the high court – on my very rough computation somewhere over 70 in the period from 1937 to 2000. Contrasting them with the cases in which more than one judgment was possible, the conclusion is irresistible that, whatever may be the merits of the one judgment rule, its application has deprived us of a significant range of considered legal opinions which might have been of the greatest value to those concerned at every level with the development of the law.

Those concerned, despite the constitutional inhibition, to ascertain by legitimate means whether a judgment of the court was that of a divided court, might perhaps have turned in some hope to the requirement in the articles that the judgment be delivered by such one of the judges as the court should direct. This at least enabled the chief justice or the senior judge of the court to avoid delivering a judgment with which he disagreed, which would have been particularly unattractive in the days when the judgments of the court were read in court in full instead of being handed down in written form which is the present practice. But the identity of the judge delivering the judgment is clearly far too slender a basis on which to infer the existence of a dissent. Save in cases where the judges were unable to agree on reasons, of which there is only one instance, the public remains in the dark as to the existence of different opinions, as the framers of the constitution envisaged they should.

That, of course, does not preclude speculation – it can be no more than that – as to the form dissenting or even assenting judgments might have

---

22 [1984] IR 36.   23 [1993] 3 IR 227.   24 [1996] 2 IR 79.
25 [1995] 2 IR 10.   26 [1987] IR 713.

taken. It is, I think, instructive to conduct such an exercise in a case which considered the effect of the articles of the constitution which assign to the courts established under the constitution, with some qualifications, the exclusive role in the administration of justice or, it is sometimes put, the exercise of the judicial power of the state. Article 37.1 contains the following crucial proviso:

> Nothing in this Constitution shall operate to invalidate the exercise of limited functions and powers of a judicial nature, in matters other than criminal matters, by any person or body of persons duly authorised by law to exercise such functions and powers, notwithstanding that such person or such body of persons is not a judge or a court appointed or established as such under the Constitution.

While this has been generally seen as reflecting the anxiety of the framers of the constitution that the extensive powers of compulsory land acquisition vested in the Land Commission should not be successfully challenged, there is no reason why it should be given so restricted a scope. It is true that the validity of these powers under the Irish Free State constitution, which contained no similar provision, had been the subject of elaborate discussion in the celebrated case of *Lynham v. Butler (No. 2)*[27] and that, at the time of the enactment of the present constitution, the Land Commission's activities were at their height. The fact remained that even without the provision contained in the new constitution, those powers had been held by the supreme court to have been administrative rather than judicial in their nature. Even in the days when the number of administrative tribunals was significantly less, there seemed no reason why this provision should be given a narrow reading and, since the constitution should be interpreted as a living document, that seemed an even more pressing consideration in the period following the end of the Second World War as the number of such bodies increased and the courts developed the judicial review jurisdiction to ensure that they stayed within constitutional confines.

It is in that context that the decision in the case I want to examine, *In re the Solicitors Act*, 1954,[28] should be seen. It resulted from the change in the law brought about by the 1954 act in the regulation of the solicitors' profession. Until then the power to strike solicitors off the roll was exclusively vested in the chief justice. Under the new legislation, while the chief justice still enjoyed such a power, it was also vested in a disciplinary committee with a right of appeal to the chief justice. A challenge to the constitutionality of this provision was rejected at first instance by the chief justice but succeeded on appeal in the supreme court. The judge presiding

27 [1933] IR 74.   28 [1960] IR 239.

in the supreme court was Lavery J, the chief justice being obviously unable to sit. The judgment of the court was, however, delivered by Kingsmill Moore J. It would be unwise to infer from that fact alone that the court was divided in its views.

Two possible issues arose: whether the striking off of a solicitor constituted the administration of justice and, if so, whether that was a 'limited' function or power within the meaning of article 37.1. After a detailed discussion of many common law authorities dealing with the question of what constitutes the administration of justice as distinct from an administrative function, Kingsmill Moore J came to this crucial passage in his judgment:

> Historically the act of striking solicitors off the roll has always been reserved to judges. It is necessary for the proper administration of justice that the Courts should be served by legal practitioners of high integrity and professional competence and that the judges should have the power not only of removing those who in their opinion fail to meet the requirements of the office but of retaining those who do. The Act does indeed preserve the power of judges to strike off but in as much as similar power is given to the Committee it affects adversely the Court's power to retain.
>
> It seems to the Court that the power to strike a solicitor off the roll is, when exercised, an administration of justice, both because the infliction of such a severe penalty on a citizen is a matter which calls for the exercise of the judicial power of the State and because to entrust such a power to persons other than judges is to interfere with the necessities of the proper administration of justice.[29]

The judgment went on to find that, as the power so conferred could not be described as 'limited', it could not constitutionally be vested in the committee.

The first part of the passage from the judgment would suggest that the all-important feature which rendered the striking off power judicial rather than administrative in nature was that the courts had a special interest in ensuring the integrity and competence of solicitors and that, accordingly, no body other than judges could discharge that function. The second part of the passage, however, indicates that another factor played a part, namely, the relative severity of the sanction which the committee could impose, depriving a citizen of his livelihood.

If the importance the courts had always attached to the role of judges in maintaining standards of integrity and competence had been the sole determining factor in the court's judgment, it would have followed logically that the court's decision had no implications for other professions which

29 Ibid., p. 275.

played no role in the administration of justice. If, however, as the second part of the passage suggests, the severity of the sanction available was of itself a determining factor, then the same consequences would be inevitable in the case of at least some other professions. At an earlier part of the judgment, Kingsmill Moore J had emphasised that different considerations applied to those professions and occupations which were regulated solely on the basis of contracts between the individual members and the relevant body, and where the disciplinary structure of the profession had no statutory basis. But what was the position of other professions, such as medicine, where professional regulation had a statutory basis but the profession itself played no part in the administration of justice? On one view, the judgment left unresolved the question whether the essential role played by solicitors in the courts process and the control exercised traditionally by judges over their admission and expulsion was a necessary factor in the court's conclusion that the powers granted to the Law Society were constitutionally invalid, or only one of two factors the presence of either of which would have been sufficient to bring about the same result. It is of interest in this context that the submissions advanced on behalf of the plaintiffs not only laid emphasis on the traditional role of the courts but, in the high court at least, took that role as the starting point of the argument that the grant of the power to a body other than the courts was unconstitutional.

That these considerations as to the precise nature of the *ratio* of the decision were far from academic was graphically demonstrated when the legislature enacted a new statutory framework for the medical profession in 1979. While the Medical Practitioners Act of that year empowered the Medical Council to recommend the striking off of a doctor who had been found guilty of professional misconduct by a 'fitness to practice committee', the power to make the order was reserved to the high court. In *M. v. Medical Council*,[30] Finlay P, as he then was, concluded that this clearly reflected the finding of the court in *Re the Solicitors Act, 1954*. The learned president was also of the view that an inevitable consequence of that legal position was that where there were disputed issues of fact in such a case, they had to be resolved by the high court, if necessary on oral evidence.[31] It is understandable that, when the Oireachtas came to enact this legislation and broadly similar legislation regulating the nursing profession, it should have taken the view that, in the absence of an unequivocal indication in the judgment of Kingsmill Moore J that the *ratio* of the decision in the solicitors' case was the unique relationship of the solicitors' profession to the administration of justice, the safer course was to confine the power of striking off doctors to the courts.

---

30 [1984] IR 485.
31 A conclusion subsequently upheld by the supreme court in *K. v. An Bord Altranais* [1990] 2 IR 396.

It may be, of course, that if more than one judgment had been possible in the supreme court in *Re the Solicitors Act, 1954*, the result would have been the same, but it is also a plausible conjecture that the form the judgment ultimately took may have been dictated by the necessity to accommodate different views in the court as to what the critical factor was. It is also worth noting that the second issue in the case – as to whether the powers in question, even if judicial in nature, could properly be regarded as 'limited' within the meaning of article 37.1 – is disposed of at the end of the judgment in a surprisingly perfunctory manner.

The one judgment rule has been considered on a number of occasions by various bodies: the Committee on Court Practice and Procedure, the Constitution Review Group, and the All Party Oireachtas Committee on the Constitution. With only one qualification, they were all in favour of the abolition of the rule: the Constitition Review Group was divided on the question as to whether abolition should extend to the reference procedure under article 26, some of the members being of the view that the unique nature of that procedure, involving as it did no element of conventional litigation, justified the presence of the rule.[32]

The principal argument in favour of the rule – that it enhances the authority of the decision and leads to greater certainty – is not particularly convincing. There have, as I have indicated, been many constitutional decisions of the first importance where more than one judgment has been possible and the recording of minority opinions has simply been a valuable stimulus to discussion as to whether the law is in a satisfactory condition. That should not be a source of discomfort in a mature democracy such as ours. The negative consequences of the rule – the suppression of dissenting views and the unfortunate consequences that flow from seeking to accommodate diverse opinions in a single judgment – are obvious. With all respect to those who took a different view in the Constitution Review Group, those same considerations would seem to apply to references under article 26. Although it would require the cumbersome machinery of a referendum to remove it, the arguments for so doing seem overwhelming: the anomalous rule introduced by ordinary legislation in a particular context will, I hope, ultimately find its proper role as simply part of our legal history.

32 *Report of the Constitution Review Group* (Dublin, 1996).

List of cases

Index

The Irish Legal History Society

(www.irishlegalhistorysociety.com)

Established in 1988 to encourage the study and advance the knowledge of the history of Irish law, especially by the publication of original documents and of works relating to the history of Irish law, including its institutions, doctrines and personalities, and the reprinting or editing of works of sufficient rarity or importance.

PATRONS

The Hon. Mr Justice Murray
Chief Justice of Ireland

Rt. Hon. Sir Brian Kerr
Lord Chief Justice of Northern Ireland

COUNCIL 2005–6

President

His Honour Judge John Martin QC

Vice-Presidents

James I. McGuire, esq.

Professor Norma M. Dawson

Honorary Secretaries

Dr Patrick Geoghegan

Dr Jack Anderson

Honorary Treasurers

R.D. Marshall

John G. Gordon, esq.

Council Members

The Hon. Mr Justice Geoghegan
Ms Rosemary Carson
Dr Séan Donlan
Daire Hogan, esq.
Eanna Molloy SC

The Hon. Sir Anthony Hart
Kevin Costello, esq.
Professor D. Greer QC (hon.)
Dr Colum Kenny
Professor J.O. Ohlmeyer

Professor W.N. Osborough (*ex officio*)